Ultimate Microsoft XDR for Full Spectrum Cyber Defence

Design, Deploy, and Operate Microsoft XDR for Unified Threat Detection, Hunting, and Automated Response across Identities, Endpoints, and Cloud

Ian David Hanley

www.orangeava.com

First Published: September 2025

Published By: Orange Education Pvt Ltd, AVA®

Address: 9, Daryaganj, Delhi, 110002, India

275 New North Road Islington Suite 1314 London,
N1 7AA, United Kingdom

ISBN (PBK): 978-93-49888-71-5

ISBN (E-BOOK): 978-93-49888-18-0

Scan the QR code to explore our entire catalogue

www.orangeava.com

Dedicated To

My Granddad, Ian “Gandhi” Clarke

And

My Wife, Meagan, Along With My Daughters, Lucy and Penelope.

About the Author

Ian David Hanley is a seasoned Cybersecurity Architect, and the founder of Hanley Cloud Solutions. With a career dedicated to helping organizations – from ambitious startups to established Fortune 500 enterprises – secure their Microsoft cloud environments, Ian brings a pragmatic, results-driven approach to modern security challenges. His expertise spans Zero Trust architecture, SIEM/SOAR implementation, threat-informed defense, and enterprise-scale cloud security strategy. If it involves the Microsoft security stack, Ian has likely architected, automated, or optimized it.

A recognized leader in the Microsoft security ecosystem, Ian has architected MSSP-ready services, streamlined alerting through automation frameworks, and improved visibility across Microsoft Defender, Sentinel, Entra ID, and Azure platforms. His work has not only cut operational overhead and costs, but also helped security teams respond with clarity and confidence.

Ian is also the founder and technical voice behind DevSecOpsDad.com, where he shares actionable insights on cloud defense, detection engineering, and real-world application of MITRE ATT&CK tactics. His writing reflects a passion for mentorship, clarity, and enabling others to thrive in the fast-evolving landscape of cloud security.

Beyond his professional work, Ian is a father of two daughters—an experience that has given him a unique perspective on risk management and resilience, both at home and in the SOC.

This book embodies his commitment to sharing hard-earned lessons, guiding security professionals with practical advice, and making Microsoft's powerful XDR capabilities accessible to all.

About the Technical Reviewer

Nitish Kumar is an infrastructure and cloud specialist with two decades of experience in Microsoft ecosystem, including Active Directory, Microsoft 365 services, and IAM solutions. He has a proven track record in scripting, analytical, and interpersonal skills to deliver strategic IT solutions.

Nitish's key skills include PowerShell Scripting, Microsoft Graph, Microsoft 365/ Microsoft Entra ID, Microsoft Defender solutions, Active Directory/PKI, Windows DNS/DHCP/WSUS, and Hyper-V. He holds numerous Microsoft certifications, including Azure and Microsoft 365 expert and associate level certifications.

Currently, he is Lead Consultant at ATOS, where he worked on Entra ID, Co-Pilot, and Active Directory migration projects. Previously, as an Associate Consultant at Tata Consultancy Services, he managed packaging and automation teams and supported DevOps tool automation. During his tenure as Senior Consultant at Coforge Limited, Nitish gained extensive experience with Microsoft Azure and Microsoft 365 services, including migration and security projects.

Nitish has successfully led various projects, such as Entra ID co-pilot grading, AD rationalization, automation of deployment/configuration changes, AD FS to Entra ID migration, and multifactor authentication rollout. His contributions have earned him multiple awards throughout his career. He is also a published author and a respected technical reviewer.

Acknowledgements

I would like to thank a few individuals for their continued and ongoing support throughout the writing of this book.

First and foremost, I would like to thank my wife for continuously encouraging me to write this book. I could have never completed this without her support – she has cooked, cleaned, and changed far more than her fair share of diapers during the course of this project.

Second, I want to thank my granddad, Ian Clarke, who sparked my interest in technology as a kid with his Radio Ham manuals.

I am also truly grateful to my friends and coworkers at KMicro Tech, inc; particularly John Haifa, who both encouraged and supported me throughout the entire process.

To my friends Eric Mannon, Daniel Morris, and Dusty Paulson, who taught me Defender and Sentinel and facilitated my journey into cyber security.

Lastly, my gratitude also goes to the team at Orange Education Pvt Ltd for being supportive, accommodating, and providing me more than the adequate time required to complete this book with perfection.

Preface

This book explores Microsoft's Extended Detection and Response (XDR) strategy, and the unified ecosystem of security tools that support it. It introduces the Microsoft XDR suite as a practical framework for modern security operations, emphasizing integration, visibility, and automation across identities, endpoints, cloud services, and data platforms. The book emphasizes real-world use cases, practical deployments, and the evolution of threat detection as well as response with Microsoft's native tools.

The main purpose of this book is to demystify how Microsoft Defender, Entra ID, and Microsoft Sentinel work together to provide end-to-end protection. Readers will gain practical insights on using Kusto Query Language (KQL), designing cost-efficient detection strategies, and applying automation through SOAR playbooks. Security engineers, architects, SOC analysts, and IT administrators will benefit from clear explanations and tactical walkthroughs that map directly to enterprise challenges.

This book is divided into 12 chapters. It covers Microsoft Defender for Endpoint, Identity, Office 365, Cloud Apps, Entra ID, Microsoft Sentinel's SIEM and SOAR features, as well as the advanced KQL. Readers will develop the ability to design, deploy, and optimize Microsoft's XDR components for unified protection across the digital estate.

Chapter 1. Understanding Microsoft XDR: This chapter explains what Microsoft XDR is, and how it brings security signals together from across the Microsoft ecosystem. It sets the foundation for understanding the role of each Defender and Sentinel component in unified threat detection and response.

Chapter 2. Defender for Endpoint: This chapter introduces Microsoft Defender for Endpoint, and explains how it delivers prevention, detection, and response capabilities for devices. You will also learn about behavioral sensors, automated investigations, and real-world EDR deployments.

Chapter 3. Defender for Identity: In this chapter, you will discover how Defender for Identity provides visibility into on-premises Active Directory environments. The content explores how attacker techniques such as lateral movement and credential theft can be identified using identity-based analytics.

Chapter 4. Defender for Cloud Apps: This chapter details how Defender for Cloud Apps functions as a CASB solution. Here, you will learn about SaaS application visibility, OAuth token management, and real-time policy enforcement across both sanctioned and unsanctioned apps.

Chapter 5. Defender for Office 365: This chapter focuses on email and collaboration protection with Defender for Office 365. Learn how Microsoft defends against phishing, malicious attachments, spoofing, and business email compromise, using multiple layers of detection and sandboxing.

Chapter 6. Entra ID Security: This chapter explores how Microsoft Entra ID (formerly Azure AD), and Identity Protection safeguard access works. The chapter also explains sign-in risk detection, conditional access, and how Microsoft integrates identity security into XDR response workflows.

Chapter 7. Introduction to Microsoft Sentinel: This chapter introduces Microsoft Sentinel as a cloud-native SIEM and SOAR solution. Here, you will learn about its architecture, deployment options, and its role as the central investigative and automation hub for Microsoft XDR.

Chapter 8. Microsoft Sentinel SIEM Capabilities: Dive deeper into Sentinel's SIEM functionality, including analytics rules, workbooks, data connectors, and threat intelligence. This chapter also explains how to optimize ingestion, reduce alert fatigue, and perform real-time threat correlation.

Chapter 9. Microsoft Sentinel SOAR Capabilities: This chapter explains Sentinel's SOAR features, highlighting automation rules and playbooks built with Azure Logic Apps. Real-world examples show how to use automated workflows to speed up incident triage and response.

Chapter 10. Efficient KQL Query Design and Optimization: This chapter teaches the fundamentals of Kusto Query Language (KQL), and how to build performant, cost-conscious queries. It also shows how to monitor ingestion costs, and create efficient queries for both hunting and reporting.

Chapter 11. Hands-On Lab Setup: This chapter walks you through the practical steps for building a Microsoft Security lab environment, combining Microsoft 365 E5 Developer subscriptions and Visual Studio Azure credits, equipping you to safely experiment, while gaining hands-on experience with Microsoft's XDR stack.

Chapter 12. Building and Operating a Mature Unified XDR Strategy: This is the final chapter, and it focuses on operationalizing Microsoft XDR into a unified, outcome-driven strategy, concluding with long-term guidance on maintaining, optimizing, and evolving your XDR posture in a dynamic threat landscape. Featuring a real-world mid-market case study, you will learn how to overcome alert fatigue, retire redundant tools, and drive measurable improvements in MTTR and visibility.

Get a Free eBook

We hope you are enjoying your recently purchased book! Your feedback is incredibly valuable to us, and to all other readers looking for great books.

If you found this book helpful or enjoyable, we would truly appreciate it, if you could take a moment to leave a short review with a 5 star rating on Amazon. It helps us grow, and lets other readers discover our books.

As a thank you, we would love to send you a free digital copy of this book, and a **30%** discount code on your next cart value on our official websites:

www.orangeava.com

www.orangeava.in (For Indian Subcontinent)

☑ **Here's how:**

Leave a review for the book on Amazon.

Take a screenshot of your review, and send an email to **info@orangeava.com** (it can be just the confirmation screen).

Once, we receive your screenshot, we will send you the digital file, within 24 hours.

Thank you so much for your support – it means a lot to us!

Downloading the code bundles and colored images

Please follow the links or scan the QR codes to download the **_Code Bundles and Images_** of the book:

https://github.com/ava-orange-education/Ultimate-Microsoft-XDR-for-Full-Spectrum-Cyber-Defence

The code bundles and images of the book are also hosted on ***https://rebrand.ly/c8e0e0***

In case there's an update to the code, it will be updated on the existing GitHub repository.

Errata

We take immense pride in our work at **Orange Education Pvt Ltd**, and follow best practices to ensure the accuracy of our content to provide an indulging reading experience to our subscribers. Our readers are our mirrors, and we use their inputs to reflect and improve upon human errors, if any, that may have occurred during the publishing processes involved. To let us maintain the quality and help us reach out to any readers who might be having difficulties due to any unforeseen errors, please write to us at :

errata@orangeava.com

Your support, suggestions, and feedback are highly appreciated.

DID YOU KNOW

Did you know that Orange Education Pvt Ltd offers eBook versions of every book published, with PDF and ePub files available? You can upgrade to the eBook version at **www.orangeava.com** and as a print book customer, you are entitled to a discount on the eBook copy. Get in touch with us at: **info@orangeava.com** for more details.

At **www.orangeava.com**, you can also read a collection of free technical articles, sign up for a range of free newsletters, and receive exclusive discounts and offers on Print Books and eBooks.

PIRACY

If you come across any illegal copies of our works in any form on the internet, we would be grateful if you would provide us with the location address or website name. Please contact us at **info@orangeava.com** with a link to the material.

ARE YOU INTERESTED IN AUTHORING WITH US?

If there is a topic that you have expertise in, and you are interested in either writing or contributing to a book, please write to us at **business@orangeava.com**. We are on a journey to help developers and tech professionals to gain insights on the present technological advancements and innovations happening across the globe and build a community that believes Knowledge is best acquired by sharing and learning with others. Please reach out to us to learn what our audience demands and how you can be part of this educational reform. We also welcome ideas from tech experts and help them build learning and development content for their domains.

REVIEWS

Please leave a review. Once you have read and used this book, why not leave a review on the site that you purchased it from? Potential readers can then see and use your unbiased opinion to make purchase decisions. We at Orange Education would love to know what you think about our products, and our authors can learn from your feedback. Thank you!

For more information about Orange Education, please visit **www.orangeava.com**.

Table of Contents

CHAPTER 1
Understanding Microsoft XDR

Introduction

In today's rapidly evolving threat landscape, cyberattacks have grown more sophisticated, frequent, and damaging. From AI-generated phishing campaigns to multi-stage ransomware and supply chain intrusions, adversaries are scaling their tactics faster than ever. According to Forrester and Gartner, 2024 saw a 45% surge in supply chain attacks, a 15% rise in ransomware incidents, and increasingly effective AI-powered phishing lures—trends that expose serious gaps in legacy security systems. While detection is improving, the average dwell time for threats remains at 21 days, underscoring the need for faster, smarter defenses.

To meet this challenge, organizations must adopt a unified and intelligent security strategy—one that integrates data, people, and tools across the enterprise. Traditional, siloed solutions can no longer keep up. This is where Microsoft Extended Detection and Response (XDR) enters the picture, offering a centralized, cloud-native platform that consolidates threat intelligence, streamlines operations, and enables both proactive defense and automated response.

This chapter introduces Microsoft XDR (MXDR), breaking down its components, capabilities, and architectural advantages. From enhancing visibility to accelerating incident response through automation and AI, MXDR empowers security teams to stay ahead of modern threats and reduce operational burden—all through a unified security experience.

Structure

In this chapter, we will cover the following topics:

- Overview and Importance of XDR
- Deep Dive: Key Features of Microsoft XDR

  - Unified Security Operations
  - Incident-Level Visibility
  - Advanced Threat Detection
  - Automated Response
  - Proactive Threat Hunting
  - Integration with Microsoft Entra ID
  - SOC Productivity Enhancements
  - Multi-tenant Support
  - Self-Healing Capabilities
  - Unified Portal

Overview and Importance of XDR

Microsoft Extended Detection and Response (MXDR) represents a significant evolution in cybersecurity. Unlike traditional security solutions that operate in silos, MXDR integrates multiple security tools into a single platform, offering a holistic view of an organization's security posture. This integration is a game changer for several reasons:

- **Unified Security Operations**: By consolidating various security tools, MXDR streamlines operations, reducing complexity and improving efficiency. Security teams can manage and respond to threats from a single platform, enhancing their ability to protect the organization.
- **Incident-Level Visibility**: MXDR provides comprehensive visibility across endpoints, identities, email, collaboration tools, SaaS applications, and cloud workloads. This broad visibility is essential for identifying and mitigating threats that may span multiple vectors.
- **Advanced Threat Detection**: Utilizing Artificial Intelligence (AI) and machine learning, MXDR can detect and prioritize cyber threats based on an astounding 78 trillion daily signals. This capability ensures that security teams can focus on the most critical threats, reducing the risk of breaches.
- **Automated Response**: One of the standout features of MXDR is its ability to automatically disrupt advanced cyberattacks at machine speed. This includes threats such as ransomware and business email compromise, which require swift and decisive action to prevent significant damage.
- **Proactive Threat Hunting**: MXDR empowers security teams to proactively hunt for threats across all workloads. With guided, step-by-step experiences, teams can identify and neutralize threats before they can cause harm.

- **Integration with Microsoft Entra ID**: Seamlessly integrating with Microsoft Entra ID (formerly Azure Active Directory), MXDR enhances identity security, ensuring that only authorized users can access critical resources.
- **SOC Productivity Enhancements**: MXDR boosts Security Operations Center (SOC) productivity with Microsoft Copilot, providing step-by-step guidance and natural language query capabilities. This feature helps SOC teams work more efficiently and effectively.
- **Multi-tenant Support**: For organizations managing multiple tenants, MXDR offers streamlined incident management and threat hunting with a consolidated view. This capability is particularly valuable for managed service providers and large enterprises.
- **Self-Healing Capabilities**: MXDR automates the remediation of affected assets and recurring alerts using custom detection and Kusto Query Language (KQL) queries. This automation reduces the burden on security teams and ensures swift resolution of issues.
- **Unified Portal**: Finally, MXDR offers a single, unified portal for managing security operations, combining MXDR and Security Information and Event Management (SIEM) capabilities. This unified approach simplifies security management and enhances overall effectiveness.

Now that we have a foundational understanding of Microsoft XDR and its significance in modern cybersecurity, let us delve deeper into each of its key features. By exploring these components in detail, you will gain a comprehensive insight into how MXDR integrates various security tools, enhances threat detection, and automates responses to provide a robust defense against cyber threats.

Deep Dive: Key Features of Microsoft XDR

This section will cover the key features of Microsoft XDR in detail.

Unified Security Operations

Unified Security Operations is a cornerstone of Microsoft XDR (MXDR), designed to address the complexities and inefficiencies that often plague traditional security infrastructures. By consolidating various security tools into a single, cohesive platform, MXDR not only streamlines operations but also significantly enhances the efficiency and effectiveness of security teams. Let's explore how this unification transforms security operations and fortifies an organization's defense against cyber threats.

The Challenge of Fragmented Security Tools

In many organizations, security operations are hampered by a fragmented landscape of disparate tools and systems. Each tool may serve a specific purpose, such as endpoint protection, network monitoring, or identity management, but the lack of integration can lead to several challenges:

- **Operational Silos**: Different security tools often operate in isolation, creating silos that hinder collaboration and information sharing among security teams.
- **Increased Complexity**: Managing multiple tools with different interfaces, configurations, and data formats can be overwhelming and error-prone.
- **Delayed Response**: The time required to correlate data from various sources can delay threat detection and response, increasing the risk of successful cyberattacks.
- **Resource Drain**: Maintaining and operating a multitude of security tools demands significant resources, both in terms of personnel and budget.

MXDR Unifies Security Operations

Microsoft XDR addresses these challenges by integrating multiple security tools into a single platform, providing a unified view of an organization's security posture. This unification offers several key benefits:

- **Streamlined Operations**: With MXDR, security teams can manage and respond to threats from a single interface. This consolidation reduces the complexity of security operations, making it easier to monitor and protect the organization.
- **Enhanced Visibility**: A unified platform provides comprehensive visibility across all security domains, including endpoints, identities, email, collaboration tools, SaaS applications, and cloud workloads. This holistic view is crucial for identifying and mitigating threats that span multiple vectors.
- **Improved Efficiency**: By eliminating the need to switch between different tools and interfaces, MXDR enhances the efficiency of security teams. They can quickly access the information they need and take action without unnecessary delays.
- **Centralized Data Correlation**: MXDR automatically correlates data from various sources, providing a more accurate and timely understanding of potential threats. This capability enables faster and more informed decision-making.
- **Reduced Operational Costs**: Consolidating security tools into a single platform can lead to significant cost savings. Organizations can reduce the expenses associated with licensing, maintaining, and training for multiple tools.

Practical Implications for Security Teams

The unification of security operations through MXDR has several practical implications for security teams:

- **Simplified Incident Management**: Security teams can manage incidents more effectively with a unified platform. They can track the entire lifecycle of an incident, from detection to resolution, within a single system.
- **Coordinated Response**: A unified platform facilitates better coordination among team members. They can collaborate more easily, share insights, and execute coordinated responses to threats.
- **Proactive Threat Hunting**: With comprehensive visibility and centralized data, security teams can proactively hunt for threats across all workloads. This proactive approach helps identify and neutralize threats before they can cause significant harm.
- **Enhanced Reporting and Analytics**: MXDR provides advanced reporting and analytics capabilities, enabling security teams to generate detailed reports and gain deeper insights into their security posture. These insights can inform strategic decisions and continuous improvement efforts.

Key Takeaway

Unified Security Operations is a transformative feature of Microsoft XDR, addressing the challenges of fragmented security tools and enhancing the overall effectiveness of security teams. By consolidating various tools into a single platform, MXDR streamlines operations, improves efficiency, and provides comprehensive visibility across the entire security landscape. This unification not only simplifies the management of security operations but also strengthens an organization's ability to detect, investigate, and respond to cyber threats. As we continue to explore the capabilities of MXDR, the importance of a unified approach to security operations will become increasingly evident.

Incident-Level Visibility

Incident-level visibility is a critical feature of Microsoft XDR (MXDR), providing security teams with a comprehensive view across various components of an organization's IT environment. This broad visibility is essential for identifying and mitigating threats that may span multiple vectors, ensuring a robust defense against sophisticated cyberattacks. Let's explore how MXDR achieves this level of visibility and why it is crucial for effective threat management.

The Importance of Comprehensive Visibility

In the modern threat landscape, cyberattacks are increasingly complex and multifaceted. Attackers often exploit multiple vectors, such as endpoints, identities, email, and cloud services, to infiltrate and compromise an organization. Without comprehensive visibility, security teams may miss critical Indicators of Compromise (IOCs) and fail to detect and respond to threats in a timely manner. Comprehensive visibility enables:

- **Early Detection**: By monitoring all potential attack surfaces, security teams can detect threats early in their lifecycle before they can cause significant damage.
- **Contextual Understanding**: Visibility across multiple vectors provides context, helping security teams understand the full scope and impact of an incident.
- **Efficient Response**: With a complete view of the incident, security teams can respond more effectively, addressing all affected areas and preventing further spread.

MXDR Provides Incident-Level Visibility

MXDR achieves incident-level visibility through the integration of various security tools and data sources, creating a unified view of the organization's security posture. Key components include:

- **Endpoints**: MXDR monitors endpoints such as desktops, laptops, and mobile devices for signs of compromise. This includes detecting malware, suspicious behavior, and unauthorized access attempts.
- **Identities**: Integration with Microsoft Entra ID (formerly Azure Active Directory) allows MXDR to monitor user identities and access patterns. This helps detect identity-based attacks, such as credential theft and privilege escalation.
- **Email**: MXDR scans email traffic for phishing attempts, malware attachments, and other email-based threats. This is crucial for preventing Business Email Compromise (BEC) and other email-related attacks.
- **Collaboration Tools**: Tools such as Microsoft Teams and SharePoint are monitored for suspicious activities, ensuring that collaboration platforms do not become vectors for cyberattacks.
- **SaaS Applications**: MXDR provides visibility into SaaS applications, detecting unauthorized access and data exfiltration attempts. This is vital for protecting sensitive data stored in cloud-based services.
- **Cloud Workloads**: MXDR monitors cloud environments, including virtual machines, containers, and serverless functions, for signs of compromise. This ensures that cloud infrastructure remains secure and resilient against attacks.

Technical Implementation

The technical implementation of incident-level visibility in MXDR involves several key technologies and processes:

- **Data Collection and Aggregation**: MXDR collects data from various sources, including endpoint agents, network sensors, and cloud APIs. This data is aggregated into a central repository for analysis.
- **Advanced Analytics**: MXDR leverages advanced analytics, including machine learning and artificial intelligence, to analyze the collected data. This helps identify patterns and anomalies that may indicate a threat.
- **Correlation and Contextualization**: MXDR correlates data from various sources to provide a contextual understanding of incidents. For example, an alert from an endpoint may be correlated with a suspicious login attempt detected by Microsoft Entra ID.
- **Visualization and Reporting**: The unified portal in MXDR provides visualizations and reports that help security teams understand the incident's scope and impact. Dashboards and alerts ensure that critical information is easily accessible.

Benefits of Incident-Level Visibility

The comprehensive visibility provided by MXDR offers several benefits:

- **Holistic Threat Detection**: By monitoring all potential attack surfaces, MXDR ensures that no threat goes undetected. This holistic approach is crucial for identifying sophisticated, multi-vector attacks.
- **Improved Incident Response**: With a complete view of the incident, security teams can respond more effectively, addressing all affected areas and preventing further spread.
- **Reduced Dwell Time**: Early detection and efficient response reduce the dwell time of threats, minimizing the potential damage to the organization.
- **Enhanced Security Posture**: Continuous monitoring and visibility help organizations maintain a strong security posture, proactively identifying and mitigating risks.

Key Takeaway

Incident-level visibility is a fundamental aspect of Microsoft XDR, providing security teams with the comprehensive view needed to detect, investigate, and respond to threats effectively. By integrating data from endpoints, identities, email, collaboration tools, SaaS applications, and cloud workloads, MXDR ensures that no threat goes unnoticed. This broad visibility is essential for maintaining a robust defense against the ever-evolving cyber threat landscape. As we continue to explore the capabilities of MXDR, the importance of comprehensive visibility in securing an organization's IT environment will become increasingly clear.

Advanced Threat Detection

Advanced Threat Detection is a pivotal feature of Microsoft XDR (MXDR), leveraging Artificial Intelligence (AI) and Machine Learning (ML) to identify and prioritize cyber threats. With the ability to process an astounding 78 trillion daily signals, MXDR ensures that security teams can focus on the most critical threats, significantly reducing the risk of breaches. This section explores the technical intricacies of how MXDR achieves advanced threat detection and the benefits it brings to an organization's security posture.

The Role of AI and Machine Learning in Threat Detection

AI and ML are transformative technologies in the realm of cybersecurity. They enable the analysis of vast amounts of data to identify patterns, anomalies, and potential threats that would be impossible for human analysts to detect manually. Here's how AI and ML contribute to advanced threat detection in MXDR:

- **Data Ingestion and Normalization**: MXDR collects data from a wide array of sources, including endpoints, network traffic, cloud services, and user activities. This data is ingested and normalized to ensure consistency and accuracy, forming the foundation for effective analysis.
- **Pattern Recognition**: AI algorithms analyze the normalized data to identify patterns that may indicate malicious activity. This includes recognizing known attack signatures, as well as detecting novel threats through anomaly detection.
- **Behavioral Analysis**: ML models are trained to understand normal behavior within an organization's environment. By continuously learning from new data, these models can detect deviations from the norm that may signify a threat, such as unusual login times or atypical data access patterns.
- **Threat Intelligence Integration**: MXDR integrates threat intelligence feeds from various sources, enriching the data with context about known threats, such as Indicators of Compromise (IOCs) and Tactics, Techniques, and Procedures (TTPs) used by threat actors. This integration enhances the accuracy of threat detection.
- **Real-Time Analysis**: The sheer volume of data processed by MXDR necessitates real-time analysis. AI and ML enable the system to analyze data as it is ingested, providing immediate insights and alerts for potential threats.

Prioritization of Threats

One of the key challenges in cybersecurity is the sheer volume of alerts generated by security tools. MXDR addresses this challenge by prioritizing threats based on their severity and potential impact. Here's how this prioritization works:

- **Risk Scoring**: Each detected threat is assigned a risk score based on various factors, including the threat's behavior, the assets it targets, and its potential impact on the organization. Higher risk scores indicate more critical threats that require immediate attention.
- **Contextual Analysis**: MXDR provides contextual information about each threat, such as its origin, the affected systems, and the potential consequences of the attack. This context helps security teams understand the threat's significance and prioritize their response efforts.
- **Automated Triage**: AI-driven triage processes automatically categorize and prioritize alerts, reducing the burden on security analysts. This automation ensures that the most critical threats are addressed first, while lower-priority alerts are managed appropriately.

Benefits of Advanced Threat Detection

The advanced threat detection capabilities of MXDR offer several significant benefits:

- **Enhanced Accuracy**: By leveraging AI and ML, MXDR can detect threats with greater accuracy than traditional rule-based systems. This reduces the number of false positives and ensures that security teams can focus on genuine threats.
- **Faster Detection and Response**: Real-time analysis and automated prioritization enable faster detection and response to threats. This reduces the dwell time of attackers within the network, minimizing potential damage.
- **Scalability**: The ability to process 78 trillion daily signals means that MXDR can scale to meet the needs of large and complex environments. This scalability ensures that even the most extensive organizations can benefit from advanced threat detection.
- **Proactive Security Posture**: With continuous learning and adaptation, MXDR helps organizations maintain a proactive security posture. By identifying and mitigating threats early, security teams can prevent incidents before they escalate.

Key Takeaway

Advanced Threat Detection is a cornerstone of Microsoft XDR, providing organizations with the tools they need to identify and prioritize cyber threats effectively. By leveraging AI and ML, MXDR can process vast amounts of data, recognize patterns, and detect anomalies that indicate potential threats. This capability ensures that security teams can focus on the most critical threats, reducing the risk of breaches and enhancing the overall security posture of the organization. As we continue to explore the features of MXDR, the importance of advanced threat detection in safeguarding digital assets will become increasingly clear.

Automated Response

Automated response is a critical feature of Microsoft XDR (MXDR), enabling organizations to swiftly and effectively counter advanced cyberattacks. By leveraging automation, MXDR can disrupt threats such as ransomware and business email compromise (BEC) at machine speed, minimizing potential damage and ensuring the security of the organization's assets. This section delves into the technical aspects of automated response in MXDR and its significance in modern cybersecurity.

The Need for Automated Response

In the current threat landscape, cyberattacks are becoming more sophisticated and faster. Traditional manual response methods are often too slow to effectively counter these threats, leading to significant damage and data loss. Automated response addresses this challenge by:

- **Speed**: Automated systems can respond to threats in real-time, significantly reducing the time between detection and mitigation.
- **Consistency**: Automation ensures that responses are consistent and follow predefined protocols, reducing the risk of human error.
- **Scalability**: Automated response can handle a large volume of incidents simultaneously, making it suitable for organizations of all sizes.

MXDR Implements Automated Response

MXDR employs several technologies and methodologies to achieve automated response:

- **Real-Time Threat Detection**: MXDR continuously monitors the environment for signs of malicious activity. When a threat is detected, it triggers an automated response workflow.
- **Predefined Playbooks**: Automated response in MXDR is guided by predefined playbooks. These playbooks outline the steps to be taken when specific types of threats are detected. For example, a playbook for ransomware might include isolating the affected endpoint, terminating malicious processes, and initiating a system restore.
- **Integration with Security Tools**: MXDR integrates with various security tools and systems, such as firewalls, endpoint protection platforms, and email security solutions. This integration allows MXDR to execute automated responses across different layers of the IT environment.

- **Machine Learning and AI**: AI and machine learning algorithms play a crucial role in automated response. They help in accurately identifying threats, determining the appropriate response actions, and continuously improving the response strategies based on new data and threat intelligence.
- **Orchestration and Automation Platforms**: MXDR utilizes orchestration and automation platforms to coordinate and execute response actions. These platforms enable the seamless execution of complex response workflows, involving multiple systems and tools.

Key Automated Response Scenarios

Microsoft XDR automates tailored response actions for high-impact threats such as ransomware, phishing, malware, and business email compromise—rapidly containing infections, restoring systems, and preventing recurrence. These playbook-driven responses reduce manual effort and minimize damage during active attacks.

- **Ransomware**: When MXDR detects ransomware activity, it can automatically isolate the affected endpoint to prevent the spread of the malware. It can also terminate malicious processes, delete malicious files, and initiate a system restore to a known good state.
- **Business Email Compromise (BEC)**: In the case of BEC, MXDR can automatically block the compromised email account, reset the account credentials, and notify the affected users and administrators. It can also scan for and remove any malicious emails sent from the compromised account.
- **Phishing Attacks**: Upon detecting a phishing attempt, MXDR can automatically block the malicious email, quarantine the email for further analysis, and update email filters to prevent similar attacks in the future.
- **Malware**: For malware infections, MXDR can automatically isolate the infected system, remove the malware, and perform a thorough scan to ensure no remnants of the malware remain.

Benefits of Automated Response

The automated response capabilities of MXDR offer several significant benefits:

- **Reduced Response Time**: Automated response actions are executed in real-time, significantly reducing the time it takes to mitigate threats. This rapid response is crucial for minimizing the impact of cyberattacks.
- **Enhanced Accuracy**: Automation ensures that response actions are executed accurately and consistently, following predefined protocols. This reduces the risk of human error and ensures that threats are effectively neutralized.
- **Resource Efficiency**: By automating routine response tasks, MXDR frees up security teams to focus on more complex and strategic activities. This

improves the overall efficiency and effectiveness of the Security Operations Center (SOC).

- **Scalability**: Automated response can handle a large volume of incidents simultaneously, making it suitable for organizations with extensive and complex IT environments.

Key Takeaway

Automated response is a standout feature of Microsoft XDR, providing organizations with the ability to swiftly and effectively counter advanced cyberattacks. By leveraging real-time detection, predefined playbooks, and integration with various security tools, MXDR can disrupt threats such as ransomware and business email compromise at machine speed. This capability not only reduces the risk of significant damage but also enhances the overall efficiency and effectiveness of the organization's security operations. As we continue to explore the features of MXDR, the importance of automated response in maintaining a robust cybersecurity posture will become increasingly evident.

Proactive Threat Hunting

Proactive threat hunting is a vital component of MXDR, enabling security teams to actively search for threats across all workloads before they can cause harm. Unlike traditional reactive approaches that rely on alerts and Indicators of Compromise (IOCs), proactive threat hunting involves actively seeking out potential threats using advanced tools and techniques. This section explores the technical aspects of proactive threat hunting in MXDR and its significance in enhancing an organization's security posture.

The Need for Proactive Threat Hunting

In the evolving threat landscape, attackers often employ sophisticated techniques to evade detection. Relying solely on automated alerts and reactive measures can leave organizations vulnerable to Advanced Persistent Threats (APTs) and other stealthy attacks. Proactive threat hunting addresses this challenge by:

- **Identifying Hidden Threats**: Proactive hunting can uncover threats that automated systems may miss, such as zero-day exploits and advanced malware.
- **Reducing Dwell Time**: By actively searching for threats, security teams can detect and mitigate attacks earlier, reducing the time attackers spend in the network.
- **Enhancing Threat Intelligence**: Threat hunting provides valuable insights into emerging threats and attacker Tactics, Techniques, and Procedures (TTPs), enriching the organization's threat intelligence.

MXDR Facilitates Proactive Threat Hunting

MXDR empowers security teams with the tools and capabilities needed for effective proactive threat hunting:

- **Comprehensive Data Collection**: MXDR collects and aggregates data from a wide range of sources, including endpoints, network traffic, cloud services, and user activities. This comprehensive data collection provides the foundation for thorough threat hunting.
- **Advanced Analytics and Machine Learning**: MXDR leverages advanced analytics and machine learning to identify patterns and anomalies that may indicate malicious activity. These technologies help hunters focus on the most promising leads.
- **Guided, Step-by-Step Experiences**: MXDR provides guided threat hunting experiences, offering step-by-step instructions and best practices. This guidance helps both novice and experienced hunters conduct effective hunts.
- **Custom Queries and Scripts**: Threat hunters can use custom queries and scripts to search for specific IOCs and behaviors. MXDR supports powerful query languages such as Kusto Query Language (KQL) for detailed and flexible searches.
- **Integration with Threat Intelligence**: MXDR integrates with various threat intelligence feeds, providing hunters with up-to-date information on known threats and emerging trends. This integration enhances the effectiveness of threat hunting efforts.

Key Techniques in Proactive Threat Hunting

Proactive threat hunting in MXDR involves several key techniques:

- **Hypothesis-Driven Hunting**: Hunters start with a hypothesis about potential threats based on threat intelligence, recent incidents, or known vulnerabilities. They then use MXDR's tools to test and refine their hypothesis.
- **Behavioral Analysis**: By analyzing user and system behaviors, hunters can identify deviations from the norm that may indicate malicious activity. This includes unusual login patterns, data access anomalies, and abnormal network traffic.
- **Anomaly Detection**: MXDR's machine learning models help identify anomalies that could signify a threat. Hunters investigate these anomalies to determine if they are benign or malicious.
- **IOC Searches**: Hunters search for specific indicators of compromise, such as known malware hashes, suspicious IP addresses, and malicious domain names. MXDR's query capabilities make it easy to conduct these searches across all data sources.

- **TTP Analysis**: By studying the tactics, techniques, and procedures used by attackers, hunters can identify signs of these activities within their environment. This proactive approach helps uncover sophisticated attacks.

Benefits of Proactive Threat Hunting

The proactive threat hunting capabilities of MXDR offer several significant benefits:

- **Early Detection**: Proactive hunting helps detect threats earlier in their lifecycle, before they can cause significant damage. This early detection is crucial for minimizing the impact of attacks.
- **Improved Incident Response**: By identifying threats proactively, security teams can respond more effectively and efficiently. This reduces the time and resources needed to contain and remediate incidents.
- **Enhanced Security Posture**: Continuous threat hunting helps organizations stay ahead of attackers, maintaining a strong security posture. It also provides valuable insights that can inform security strategies and defenses.
- **Increased Threat Intelligence**: Proactive hunting generates valuable threat intelligence, enriching the organization's understanding of the threat landscape and improving overall security awareness.

Key Takeaway

Proactive threat hunting is a critical feature of Microsoft XDR, empowering security teams to actively search for and neutralize threats before they can cause harm. By leveraging comprehensive data collection, advanced analytics, guided experiences, and integration with threat intelligence, MXDR enables effective and efficient threat hunting. This proactive approach not only enhances early detection and incident response but also strengthens the organization's overall security posture. As we continue to explore the capabilities of MXDR, the importance of proactive threat hunting in safeguarding digital assets will become increasingly clear.

Integration with Microsoft Entra ID

The integration of Microsoft XDR with Microsoft Entra ID (formerly Azure Active Directory) is a powerful feature that significantly enhances identity security. This seamless integration ensures that only authorized users can access critical resources, providing a robust defense against identity-based attacks. In this section, we will explore the technical aspects of this integration and its importance in modern cybersecurity.

The Role of Identity Security

Identity security is a cornerstone of any comprehensive cybersecurity strategy. As organizations increasingly adopt cloud services and remote work, ensuring that only authorized users can access sensitive resources becomes paramount. Identity-based attacks, such as credential theft and privilege escalation, are among the most common and damaging types of cyber threats. Effective identity security involves:

- **Authentication**: Verifying the identity of users before granting access to resources.
- **Authorization**: Ensuring that authenticated users have the appropriate permissions to access specific resources.
- **Monitoring**: Continuously monitoring user activities to detect and respond to suspicious behavior.

MXDR Integrates with Microsoft Entra ID

Microsoft Entra ID is a comprehensive Identity and Access Management (IAM) solution that provides robust authentication, authorization, and monitoring capabilities. MXDR leverages these capabilities to enhance identity security through seamless integration. Here's how this integration works:

- **Single Sign-On (SSO)**: MXDR supports Single Sign-On (SSO) through Microsoft Entra ID, allowing users to authenticate once and gain access to multiple applications and services. This reduces the risk of credential theft by minimizing the number of times users need to enter their credentials.
- **Multi-Factor Authentication (MFA)**: MXDR enforces Multi-Factor Authentication (MFA) for accessing critical resources. MFA adds an extra layer of security by requiring users to provide additional verification, such as a code sent to their mobile device, in addition to their password.
- **Conditional Access Policies**: MXDR integrates with Microsoft Entra ID's conditional access policies to enforce access controls based on specific conditions, such as user location, device compliance, and risk level. This ensures that access is granted only under secure conditions.
- **Identity Protection**: MXDR utilizes Microsoft Entra ID's Identity Protection features to detect and respond to identity-based threats. This includes monitoring for compromised credentials, risky sign-ins, and suspicious user behavior.
- **Role-Based Access Control (RBAC)**: MXDR leverages Role-Based Access Control (RBAC) to manage permissions and ensure that users have access only to the resources they need for their role. This principle of least privilege reduces the risk of unauthorized access.
- **Audit Logs and Reporting**: MXDR integrates with Microsoft Entra ID's audit logs and reporting capabilities to provide comprehensive visibility into user activities. This helps security teams monitor access patterns, detect anomalies, and investigate incidents.

Technical Implementation

The technical implementation of MXDR's integration with Microsoft Entra ID involves several key components:

- **Directory Synchronization**: MXDR synchronizes with Microsoft Entra ID to ensure that user identities and access permissions are up-to-date. This synchronization is typically achieved through Azure AD Connect or similar tools.
- **API Integration**: MXDR uses APIs provided by Microsoft Entra ID to access identity-related data and enforce security policies. This API integration enables real-time monitoring and response to identity-based threats.
- **Security Information and Event Management (SIEM)**: MXDR integrates with SIEM systems to correlate identity-related events with other security data. This correlation provides a holistic view of security incidents and enhances threat detection and response.
- **Custom Policies and Rules**: Security teams can define custom policies and rules within MXDR to enforce specific identity security requirements. These policies can be tailored to the organization's unique needs and risk profile.

Benefits of Integration with Microsoft Entra ID

The integration of MXDR with Microsoft Entra ID offers several significant benefits:

- **Enhanced Security**: By leveraging the robust authentication, authorization, and monitoring capabilities of Microsoft Entra ID, MXDR enhances overall identity security. This reduces the risk of identity-based attacks and unauthorized access.
- **Improved User Experience**: Features such as SSO and MFA improve the user experience by simplifying the authentication process and reducing the need for multiple passwords. This also enhances security by reducing the risk of credential theft.
- **Comprehensive Visibility**: The integration provides comprehensive visibility into user activities, enabling security teams to monitor access patterns, detect anomalies, and respond to incidents effectively.
- **Streamlined Management**: The integration simplifies the management of user identities and access permissions, reducing administrative overhead and ensuring that security policies are consistently enforced.
- **Proactive Threat Detection**: By continuously monitoring user activities and enforcing conditional access policies, MXDR can proactively detect and respond to identity-based threats before they can cause significant harm.

Key Takeaway

The seamless integration of Microsoft XDR with Microsoft Entra ID significantly enhances identity security, ensuring that only authorized users can access critical resources. By leveraging advanced authentication, authorization, and monitoring capabilities, this integration provides a robust defense against identity-based attacks. As we continue to explore the features of MXDR, the importance of strong identity security in protecting an organization's digital assets will become increasingly evident.

SOC Productivity Enhancements

Security Operations Centers (SOCs) are the nerve centers of an organization's cybersecurity efforts, responsible for monitoring, detecting, and responding to security incidents. However, SOC teams often face challenges such as alert fatigue, complex workflows, and the need for rapid decision-making. Microsoft XDR (MXDR) addresses these challenges by boosting SOC productivity with Microsoft Copilot, which provides step-by-step guidance and natural language query capabilities. This section explores the technical aspects of these enhancements and their impact on SOC efficiency and effectiveness.

The Challenges Faced by SOC Teams

SOC teams are tasked with managing a high volume of security alerts and incidents, often under significant time pressure. Key challenges include:

- **Alert Fatigue**: SOC analysts are inundated with alerts, many of which are false positives. This can lead to alert fatigue, where critical alerts may be overlooked.
- **Complex Workflows**: Investigating and responding to incidents involves complex workflows that require coordination across multiple tools and systems.
- **Skill Gaps**: SOC teams may have varying levels of expertise, making it difficult to ensure consistent and effective responses to incidents.
- **Time Constraints**: Rapid detection and response are crucial to minimizing the impact of security incidents, but manual processes can be time-consuming.

MXDR Enhances SOC Productivity

MXDR enhances SOC productivity through the integration of Microsoft Copilot, which provides several key capabilities:

- **Step-by-Step Guidance**: Microsoft Copilot offers guided workflows that help SOC analysts navigate complex incident response processes. This guidance ensures that even less experienced analysts can follow best practices and respond effectively to incidents.

- **Natural Language Query Capabilities**: Copilot allows SOC analysts to interact with MXDR using natural language queries. This simplifies the process of retrieving information, running queries, and generating reports, making it more accessible and efficient.
- **Automated Playbooks**: MXDR includes automated playbooks that standardize and streamline incident response actions. These playbooks can be triggered automatically based on specific alerts or manually by SOC analysts.
- **Contextual Insights**: Copilot provides contextual insights and recommendations based on the current incident, helping analysts make informed decisions quickly. This includes suggesting relevant queries, highlighting critical data points, and offering remediation steps.
- **Collaboration Tools**: MXDR integrates with collaboration tools such as Microsoft Teams, enabling SOC teams to communicate and coordinate more effectively. Analysts can share insights, discuss incidents, and collaborate on response actions in real-time.

Technical Implementation

The technical implementation of SOC productivity enhancements in MXDR involves several components:

- **Integration with Microsoft Copilot**: Copilot is integrated into the MXDR platform, providing a user-friendly interface for interacting with the system. This integration leverages Natural Language Processing (NLP) and machine learning to understand and respond to analyst queries.
- **Guided Workflows**: Guided workflows are built into MXDR, offering step-by-step instructions for common incident response tasks. These workflows are designed to be intuitive and easy to follow, reducing the learning curve for new analysts.
- **Automated Playbooks**: Playbooks are predefined sets of actions that can be executed automatically or manually. They are created using a combination of scripting and automation tools, ensuring that response actions are consistent and repeatable.
- **Contextual Analysis**: Copilot uses contextual analysis to provide relevant insights and recommendations. This involves analyzing the current incident, correlating data from various sources, and presenting actionable information to the analyst.
- **Collaboration Integration**: MXDR integrates with collaboration platforms such as Microsoft Teams, enabling seamless communication and coordination among SOC team members. This integration supports real-time chat, file sharing, and collaborative incident management.

Benefits of SOC Productivity Enhancements

The productivity enhancements provided by MXDR offer several significant benefits:

- **Reduced Alert Fatigue**: By providing guided workflows and contextual insights, MXDR helps analysts prioritize and focus on the most critical alerts, reducing the risk of alert fatigue.
- **Improved Efficiency**: Natural language query capabilities and automated playbooks streamline incident response processes, allowing analysts to work more efficiently and effectively.
- **Consistent Responses**: Guided workflows and automated playbooks ensure that incident response actions are consistent and follow best practices, regardless of the analyst's experience level.
- **Enhanced Collaboration**: Integration with collaboration tools facilitates better communication and coordination among SOC team members, improving overall incident response.
- **Faster Decision-Making**: Contextual insights and recommendations help analysts make informed decisions quickly, reducing the time it takes to detect, investigate, and respond to incidents.

Key Takeaway

SOC productivity enhancements provided by Microsoft XDR, through the integration of Microsoft Copilot, significantly improve the efficiency and effectiveness of security operations. By offering step-by-step guidance, natural language query capabilities, automated playbooks, and contextual insights, MXDR empowers SOC teams to manage and respond to incidents more effectively. These enhancements not only reduce alert fatigue and improve efficiency but also ensure consistent and informed responses to security threats. As we continue to explore the capabilities of MXDR, the importance of boosting SOC productivity in maintaining a robust cybersecurity posture will become increasingly evident.

Multi-tenant Support

Multi-tenant support is a crucial feature of MXDR, designed to meet the needs of organizations managing multiple tenants, such as Managed Service Providers (MSPs) and large enterprises. This capability allows for streamlined incident management and threat hunting across multiple environments, providing a consolidated view that enhances efficiency and effectiveness. In this section, we will explore the technical aspects of multi-tenant support in MXDR and its significance for organizations with complex security requirements.

The Need for multi-tenant Support

Organizations managing multiple tenants face unique challenges in maintaining security across diverse environments. Key challenges include:

- **Complexity**: Managing security for multiple tenants involves dealing with different configurations, policies, and data sources, which can be complex and time-consuming.
- **Visibility**: Ensuring comprehensive visibility across all tenants is essential for effective threat detection and response, but it can be difficult to achieve with siloed systems.
- **Scalability**: As the number of tenants grows, the ability to scale security operations without compromising performance or effectiveness becomes critical.
- **Consistency**: Applying consistent security policies and practices across all tenants is necessary to maintain a robust security posture.

MXDR Provides Multi-tenant Support

MXDR addresses these challenges by offering robust multi-tenant support, enabling organizations to manage security across multiple tenants from a single, unified platform. Key features include:

- **Consolidated View**: MXDR provides a consolidated view of security incidents and alerts across all tenants. This unified dashboard allows security teams to monitor and manage incidents from a central location, improving situational awareness and response times.
- **Tenant Isolation**: While providing a consolidated view, MXDR ensures that data and operations for each tenant remain isolated. This isolation is crucial for maintaining data privacy and compliance with regulatory requirements.
- **Customizable Policies**: MXDR allows organizations to define and apply customizable security policies for each tenant. This flexibility ensures that the specific security needs and compliance requirements of each tenant are met.
- **Centralized Threat Hunting**: Security teams can conduct threat hunting activities across all tenants from a single interface. This centralized approach streamlines the process of identifying and mitigating threats, reducing the time and effort required.
- **Role-Based Access Control (RBAC)**: MXDR supports RBAC, enabling organizations to assign specific roles and permissions to users based on their responsibilities. This ensures that only authorized personnel can access and manage security operations for each tenant.
- **Automated Workflows**: MXDR includes automated workflows that can be applied across multiple tenants. These workflows standardize incident

response actions, ensuring consistency and efficiency in handling security incidents.

Technical Implementation

The technical implementation of multi-tenant support in MXDR involves several key components:

- **Data Aggregation and Segregation**: MXDR aggregates data from multiple tenants while ensuring that each tenant's data is segregated. This segregation is achieved through logical partitioning and access controls, maintaining data privacy and security.
- **Unified Dashboard**: The unified dashboard in MXDR provides a comprehensive view of security incidents and alerts across all tenants. This dashboard is designed to be intuitive and customizable, allowing security teams to focus on the most critical information.
- **Policy Management**: MXDR includes a policy management framework that allows organizations to define and apply security policies for each tenant. Policies can be customized based on the specific needs and compliance requirements of each tenant.
- **Threat Hunting Tools**: MXDR provides advanced threat hunting tools that can be used across multiple tenants. These tools include custom queries, machine learning models, and behavioral analysis capabilities, enabling effective threat detection and mitigation.
- **Access Controls**: RBAC is implemented to ensure that only authorized users can access and manage security operations for each tenant. Access controls are enforced through authentication and authorization mechanisms integrated with Microsoft Entra ID.

Benefits of Multi-tenant Support

The multi-tenant support capabilities of MXDR offer several significant benefits:

- **Enhanced Efficiency**: By providing a consolidated view and centralized management, MXDR reduces the complexity and time required to manage security across multiple tenants. This enhances the efficiency of security operations.
- **Improved Visibility**: A unified dashboard and centralized threat hunting tools provide comprehensive visibility across all tenants, enabling security teams to detect and respond to threats more effectively.
- **Scalability**: MXDR's multi-tenant support is designed to scale with the organization, allowing security operations to grow without compromising performance or effectiveness.
- **Consistency**: Automated workflows and customizable policies ensure that

consistent security practices are applied across all tenants, maintaining a robust security posture.

- **Data Privacy and Compliance**: Tenant isolation and RBAC ensure that data privacy and compliance requirements are met, protecting sensitive information and adhering to regulatory standards.

Key Takeaway

Multi-tenant support is a critical feature of Microsoft XDR, providing organizations with the tools and capabilities needed to manage security across multiple tenants effectively. By offering a consolidated view, customizable policies, centralized threat hunting, and robust access controls, MXDR enhances the efficiency, visibility, and scalability of security operations. As we continue to explore the capabilities of MXDR, the importance of multi-tenant support in maintaining a secure and compliant environment for organizations with complex security requirements will become increasingly evident.

Self-Healing Capabilities

Self-healing capabilities are a standout feature of Microsoft XDR (MXDR), designed to automate the remediation of affected assets and recurring alerts. By leveraging custom detection and Kusto Query Language (KQL) queries, MXDR reduces the burden on security teams and ensures swift resolution of issues. This section explores the technical aspects of self-healing capabilities in MXDR and their significance in enhancing an organization's security posture.

The Need for Self-Healing Capabilities

In the dynamic threat landscape, security teams are often overwhelmed by the volume of alerts and incidents they need to manage. Manual remediation processes can be time-consuming and prone to human error, leading to delays in resolving issues and increasing the risk of further damage. Self-healing capabilities address these challenges by:

- **Automating Remediation**: Automatically resolving issues without human intervention, reducing the workload on security teams.
- **Ensuring Consistency**: Applying standardized remediation actions consistently across all incidents, minimizing the risk of errors.
- **Speeding Up Resolution**: Quickly addressing threats and vulnerabilities, reducing the time attackers have to exploit them.

How MXDR Implements Self-Healing Capabilities

MXDR implements self-healing capabilities through a combination of custom detection mechanisms and KQL queries. Here's how it works:

- **Custom Detection**: MXDR allows security teams to define custom detection rules that identify specific threats and vulnerabilities. These rules can be tailored to the organization's unique environment and risk profile.
- **Kusto Query Language (KQL)**: KQL is a powerful query language used to search and analyze large datasets. In MXDR, KQL queries are used to detect anomalies, correlate events, and trigger automated remediation actions.
- **Automated Playbooks**: When a custom detection rule or KQL query identifies an issue, MXDR can trigger an automated playbook. These playbooks define the steps to be taken to remediate the issue, ensuring a swift and consistent response.
- **Integration with Security Tools**: MXDR integrates with various security tools and systems, such as endpoint protection platforms, firewalls, and identity management solutions. This integration allows MXDR to execute remediation actions across different layers of the IT environment.
- **Continuous Monitoring and Learning**: MXDR continuously monitors the environment and learns from new data and incidents. This continuous learning helps improve the accuracy of detection rules and the effectiveness of remediation actions over time.

Key Components of Self-Healing Capabilities

Self-healing in Microsoft XDR relies on a combination of custom detection rules, real-time KQL queries, automated playbooks, and seamless orchestration with other security tools to quickly identify and remediate threats without human intervention. This integrated approach ensures consistent, rapid, and scalable responses across the entire environment.

- **Detection Rules**: Custom detection rules are the foundation of self-healing capabilities. These rules define the conditions under which an issue is identified and a remediation action is triggered. Detection rules can be based on various criteria, such as specific IOCs, behavioral patterns, and threshold values.
- **KQL Queries**: KQL queries are used to search for and analyze data in real-time. These queries can be highly specific, targeting particular events or behaviors, or broad, looking for patterns across large datasets. KQL's flexibility and power make it an essential tool for detecting and responding to threats.
- **Automated Playbooks**: Playbooks are predefined sets of actions that are executed automatically when a detection rule or KQL query identifies an issue. Playbooks can include actions such as isolating affected endpoints, terminating malicious processes, and applying patches or updates.

- **Integration and Orchestration**: MXDR's integration with other security tools and systems enables it to orchestrate complex remediation actions across the entire IT environment. This orchestration ensures that all necessary steps are taken to resolve the issue and prevent further damage.

Benefits of Self-Healing Capabilities

The self-healing capabilities of MXDR offer several significant benefits:

- **Reduced Workload**: By automating remediation actions, MXDR reduces the workload on security teams, allowing them to focus on more strategic tasks and complex incidents.
- **Faster Resolution**: Automated remediation actions are executed in real-time, significantly reducing the time it takes to resolve issues. This rapid response minimizes the window of opportunity for attackers.
- **Consistency and Accuracy**: Automated playbooks ensure that remediation actions are applied consistently and accurately, reducing the risk of human error and ensuring that issues are resolved effectively.
- **Improved Security Posture**: Continuous monitoring and automated remediation help maintain a strong security posture by quickly addressing threats and vulnerabilities. This proactive approach reduces the risk of successful attacks and minimizes potential damage.
- **Scalability**: Self-healing capabilities enable organizations to scale their security operations without a corresponding increase in manual effort. This scalability is particularly valuable for large enterprises and organizations with complex IT environments.

Key Takeaway

Self-healing capabilities are a critical feature of Microsoft XDR, providing organizations with the tools to automate the remediation of affected assets and recurring alerts. By leveraging custom detection rules and KQL queries, MXDR ensures swift and consistent resolution of issues, reducing the burden on security teams and enhancing overall security posture. As we continue to explore the capabilities of MXDR, the importance of self-healing capabilities in maintaining a resilient and secure IT environment will become increasingly evident.

Unified Portal

The unified portal in Microsoft XDR (MXDR) is a pivotal feature that combines Extended Detection and Response (XDR) and Security Information and Event Management (SIEM) capabilities into a single, cohesive platform. This unified approach simplifies security management, enhances overall effectiveness, and provides a comprehensive view of an organization's security posture. In this section, we will explore the technical aspects of the unified portal and its significance in modern cybersecurity operations.

The Need for a Unified Portal

In many organizations, security operations are fragmented across multiple tools and platforms, each with its own interface, data formats, and workflows. This fragmentation can lead to several challenges:

- **Complexity**: Managing multiple security tools increases operational complexity, making it difficult for security teams to maintain a cohesive security strategy.
- **Inefficiency**: Switching between different tools and interfaces can be time-consuming and inefficient, slowing down threat detection and response.
- **Data Silos**: Disparate tools often result in data silos, where critical security information is isolated and not easily accessible, hindering comprehensive threat analysis.
- **Inconsistent Policies**: Applying consistent security policies across multiple tools can be challenging, leading to gaps in security coverage.

MXDR's Unified Portal Addresses These Challenges

The unified portal in MXDR addresses these challenges by integrating XDR and SIEM capabilities into a single platform. This integration offers several key benefits:

- **Centralized Management**: The unified portal provides a centralized interface for managing all security operations. Security teams can monitor, detect, investigate, and respond to threats from a single location, reducing complexity and improving efficiency.
- **Comprehensive Visibility**: By consolidating data from various sources, the unified portal offers comprehensive visibility into the organization's security posture. This holistic view is crucial for identifying and mitigating threats that span multiple vectors.
- **Streamlined Workflows**: The unified portal streamlines security workflows by providing integrated tools and features. Analysts can perform tasks such as threat hunting, incident response, and reporting without switching between different platforms.
- **Consistent Policies**: The unified portal allows for the application of consistent security policies across the entire organization. This ensures that security measures are uniformly enforced, reducing the risk of gaps in coverage.
- **Enhanced Collaboration**: The unified portal facilitates better collaboration among security team members. Integrated communication tools and shared dashboards enable teams to work together more effectively.

Technical Implementation

The technical implementation of the unified portal in MXDR involves several key components:

- **Data Aggregation and Normalization**: MXDR aggregates data from various sources, including endpoints, network traffic, cloud services, and user activities. This data is normalized to ensure consistency and accuracy, forming the foundation for effective analysis and response.
- **Integrated Dashboards**: The unified portal features integrated dashboards that provide real-time visibility into security metrics, alerts, and incidents. These dashboards are customizable, allowing security teams to focus on the most relevant information.
- **Advanced Analytics and Correlation**: MXDR leverages advanced analytics and correlation engines to analyze aggregated data. This analysis helps identify patterns, anomalies, and potential threats, providing actionable insights for security teams.
- **Automated Playbooks and Response**: The unified portal includes automated playbooks that standardize and streamline incident response actions. These playbooks can be triggered automatically based on specific alerts or manually by analysts.
- **Role-Based Access Control (RBAC)**: RBAC is implemented to ensure that only authorized users can access and manage security operations. This access control is enforced through authentication and authorization mechanisms integrated with Microsoft Entra ID.
- **Integration with Third-Party Tools**: The unified portal supports integration with third-party security tools and platforms. This interoperability ensures that organizations can leverage their existing security investments while benefiting from the unified approach of MXDR.

Benefits of the Unified Portal

The unified portal in MXDR offers several significant benefits:

- **Simplified Security Management**: By consolidating XDR and SIEM capabilities into a single platform, the unified portal simplifies security management, reducing the operational burden on security teams.
- **Improved Efficiency**: Integrated tools and streamlined workflows enhance the efficiency of security operations, enabling faster detection, investigation, and response to threats.
- **Comprehensive Threat Analysis**: The unified portal provides a holistic view of security data, enabling comprehensive threat analysis and more informed decision-making.

- **Consistent Security Policies**: The ability to apply consistent security policies across the entire organization ensures uniform protection and reduces the risk of security gaps.
- **Enhanced Collaboration and Communication**: Integrated communication tools and shared dashboards facilitate better collaboration among security team members, improving overall effectiveness.
- **Scalability and Flexibility**: The unified portal is designed to scale with the organization, accommodating growth and evolving security needs. Its flexibility allows for integration with existing security tools and platforms.

Key Takeaway

The unified portal in Microsoft XDR is a transformative feature that combines XDR and SIEM capabilities into a single, cohesive platform. By providing centralized management, comprehensive visibility, streamlined workflows, and consistent security policies, the unified portal simplifies security management and enhances overall effectiveness. As we continue to explore the capabilities of MXDR, the importance of a unified approach to security operations in maintaining a robust cybersecurity posture will become increasingly evident.

Conclusion

As cyber threats grow in scale and complexity, modern security operations require tools that move beyond fragmented defenses. Microsoft XDR delivers a unified, intelligent solution that empowers organizations to detect, investigate, and respond to threats with speed and precision. By consolidating signals across domains, leveraging AI-driven insights, and automating response actions, Microsoft XDR transforms reactive operations into proactive defense. From identity protection with Entra ID to advanced analytics and guided threat hunting through Copilot, the capabilities covered in this chapter illustrate how Microsoft XDR equips security teams to stay ahead of adversaries while optimizing efficiency.

Building on this foundation, the next chapter explores Microsoft Defender for Endpoint—a critical pillar of the XDR ecosystem. As the first line of defense against endpoint threats, Defender for Endpoint delivers comprehensive protection, telemetry-rich visibility, and integrated investigation and response capabilities. Whether deployed in cloud, on-premises, or hybrid environments, it plays a central role in securing modern enterprises at the device level.

References

- Forrester. (2024, January). Top Cybersecurity Threats in 2024. Forrester Research. https://www.forrester.com/report/top-cybersecurity-threats-in-2024/RES177239
- Gartner. (2024, February). Gartner Unveils Top Eight Cybersecurity Predictions for 2024. Gartner, Inc. https://www.gartner.com/en/newsroom/press-releases/2024-02-05-gartner-unveils-top-eight-cybersecurity-predictions-for-2024
- Microsoft. (2024). Microsoft Security: Signals and Intelligence. Microsoft. https://www.microsoft.com/en-us/security/business/security-intelligence
- Microsoft. (2024, March 13). Microsoft Copilot for Security: General Availability Announcement. Microsoft Security Blog. https://www.microsoft.com/en-us/security/blog/2024/03/13/microsoft-copilot-for-security-now-generally-available/
- Microsoft. (2023). What is Microsoft Entra ID? Microsoft Learn. https://learn.microsoft.com/en-us/entra/fundamentals/whatis
- Microsoft. (2024). Kusto Query Language Overview. Microsoft Learn. https://learn.microsoft.com/en-us/azure/data-explorer/kusto/query/
- Microsoft. (2024). What is Microsoft Defender XDR? Microsoft Learn. https://learn.microsoft.com/en-us/security/defender-xdr/overview

CHAPTER 2

Defender for Endpoint

Introduction

In today's evolving threat landscape, securing enterprise endpoints is more critical than ever. Microsoft Defender for Endpoint is a comprehensive solution designed to help organizations prevent, detect, investigate, and respond to advanced cyber threats across their devices. Seamlessly integrated within the broader Microsoft 365 security ecosystem, it combines robust protection, real-time telemetry, and world-class threat intelligence to deliver a unified and proactive defense strategy for modern enterprises.

Structure

In this chapter, we will cover the following topics:

- Overview
- Importance as an EDR and AV Solution
- How EDR Works
- Deployment Deep Dives:
    - Cloud
    - On-Prem
    - Hybrid
- Troubleshooting

Overview

Defender for Endpoint combines several key capabilities:

- **Endpoint Detection and Response (EDR):** This feature continuously monitors and collects data from endpoints, providing real-time detection and response to threats. It uses behavioral sensors, cloud security analytics, and threat intelligence to identify and mitigate sophisticated attacks.

  - **Continuous Monitoring**: EDR continuously monitors endpoint activities, collecting telemetry data such as process information, network activities, and file changes. This data is analyzed to detect suspicious behaviors and potential threats.
  - **Behavioral Sensors**: These sensors are built into Windows 10 and later versions, capturing detailed information about system activities. They help identify anomalies and malicious behaviors that traditional signature-based detection might miss.
  - **Cloud Security Analytics**: The collected data is sent to the Microsoft cloud, where advanced analytics and machine learning models analyze it. This helps in identifying patterns and correlations that indicate sophisticated attacks.
  - **Threat Intelligence**: EDR leverages Microsoft's extensive threat intelligence to stay updated on the latest threats. This intelligence is used to enhance detection capabilities and provide context for alerts.
  - **Response Actions**: When a threat is detected, EDR can automatically or manually initiate response actions such as isolating the device, terminating malicious processes, and removing malicious files.
- **Antivirus (AV):** Defender for Endpoint includes a powerful antivirus engine that protects against a wide range of malware, including viruses, ransomware, and spyware. It leverages machine learning and AI to detect and block new and emerging threats.
  - **Machine Learning and AI**: The antivirus engine uses machine learning and artificial intelligence to detect and block new and emerging threats. This proactive approach helps in identifying malware based on behavior rather than relying solely on known signatures.
  - **Cloud-Delivered Protection**: Defender Antivirus leverages cloud-based threat intelligence to provide real-time protection. This ensures that endpoints are protected against the latest threats as soon as they are identified.
  - **Behavioral Blocking and Containment**: The antivirus engine can block threats based on their behavior, even if they have started executing. This is particularly effective against fileless malware and other advanced threats.
  - **Offline Protection**: Defender Antivirus also provides protection when the device is offline; the solution includes a local threat intelligence database that is regularly updated when the device is online. This database helps identify and block known threats based on the latest information available, even while the device is offline.

- **Threat and Vulnerability Management:** This proactive approach helps identify, assess, and remediate vulnerabilities and misconfigurations across endpoints, reducing the attack surface.
  - **Continuous Asset Discovery and Monitoring**: TVM continuously discovers and monitors assets within the organization, providing a real-time view of software, hardware, and network configurations.
  - **Vulnerability Assessment**: It assesses vulnerabilities and misconfigurations across endpoints, identifying weaknesses that could be exploited by attackers to create an **Exposure Score** (just like golf, a low score is better than a high score here). Score Levels: The exposure score ranges from 0 to 100, with lower scores indicating lower vulnerability. It's typically categorized into three levels:
    - 0-29: Low exposure
    - 30-69: Medium exposure
    - 70-100: High exposure
  - **Risk-Based Prioritization**: TVM uses risk-based prioritization to focus on the most critical vulnerabilities. It considers factors such as the likelihood of exploitation and the potential impact on the organization.
  - **Remediation and Tracking**: TVM provides actionable security recommendations and tracks remediation efforts. It integrates with tools such as Microsoft Intune to streamline the remediation process.
- **Automated Investigation and Remediation**: By automating routine tasks and providing actionable insights, Defender for Endpoint helps security teams respond more quickly and efficiently to incidents.
  - **Automated Investigations**: When an alert is triggered, AIR automatically starts an investigation. It uses various inspection algorithms to analyze the threat and determine its scope.
  - **Dynamic Scope**: If the same threat is detected on other devices, the investigation scope expands to include those devices. This ensures a comprehensive response to widespread threats.
  - **Remediation Actions**: Based on the investigation findings, AIR can take remediation actions such as quarantining files, stopping malicious processes, and removing scheduled tasks.
  - **Action Center**: All remediation actions are tracked in the Action Center, where security teams can review, approve, or undo actions as needed.

Importance as an EDR and AV Solution

As an EDR and AV solution, Defender for Endpoint plays a critical role in the Microsoft Extended Detection and Response (XDR) platform. Here's why:

- **Comprehensive Threat Protection:** Defender for Endpoint provides a multi-layered defense strategy, combining EDR and AV capabilities to protect against a wide range of threats, from common malware to sophisticated, targeted attacks.
- **Integration with Microsoft XDR:** As part of the Microsoft XDR platform, Defender for Endpoint integrates with other security solutions such as Microsoft Defender for Identity, Microsoft Defender for Office 365, and Microsoft Sentinel. This integration enables a unified approach to threat detection and response across the entire digital estate.
- **Enhanced Visibility and Control:** With its advanced analytics and threat intelligence, Defender for Endpoint offers deep visibility into endpoint activities and potential threats. This visibility is crucial for identifying and mitigating risks before they can cause significant damage.
- **Efficiency and Automation:** The platform's automated investigation and remediation capabilities reduce the burden on security teams, allowing them to focus on more strategic tasks. This efficiency is vital for maintaining a strong security posture in the face of evolving threats.

In summary, Microsoft Defender for Endpoint is a vital component of the Microsoft XDR platform, providing robust EDR and AV capabilities that enhance an organization's ability to protect, detect, and respond to threats effectively.

Behind the Scenes of Endpoint Detection and Response

Endpoint Detection and Response (EDR) solutions such as Microsoft Defender for Endpoint operate by continuously monitoring endpoint activities and collecting telemetry data to detect and respond to threats in real-time. Here's a deeper look at how EDR functions, including its use of function and DLL hooks:

Core Components and Mechanisms

- **Behavioral Monitoring**: EDR solutions monitor the behavior of applications and processes on endpoints. This involves tracking system calls, file modifications, network connections, and other activities to identify suspicious patterns.

- **Telemetry Collection**: Data is collected from endpoints, including process creation, file access, registry changes, and network activity. This telemetry is analyzed to detect anomalies and potential threats.
- **Function and DLL Hooks**: EDR solutions often use hooks to intercept and monitor function calls and DLL (Dynamic Link Library) operations. This allows the EDR to observe and control the behavior of applications at a granular level.
    - **Function Hooks**: By hooking into specific functions, the EDR can monitor and modify the behavior of these functions. For example, it can intercept calls to functions that handle file operations, network communications, or process creation.
    - **DLL Injection**: EDR can inject its own DLLs into running processes to gain visibility and control. This technique allows the EDR to monitor API calls and detect malicious activities such as code injection or unauthorized access.

Common Examples

- **Process Creation Monitoring**: When a new process is created, the EDR hooks into the process creation functions to log details such as the parent process, command line arguments, and the executable path. This helps in identifying suspicious processes that may be part of an attack chain.

  Example of a Callback Routine in Process Creation

  In Windows, callback routines can be registered to monitor and respond to process creation events. One common method is using the **`PsSetCreateProcessNotifyRoutineEx`** function, which allows a driver to register a callback routine that the system calls whenever a process is created or deleted.

  Here's an example of a callback routine for process creation:

```
#include <ntddk.h>

VOID CreateProcessNotifyRoutineEx(
    _Inout_ PEPROCESS Process,
    _In_ HANDLE ProcessId,
    _In_opt_ PPS_CREATE_NOTIFY_INFO CreateInfo
)
{
    if (CreateInfo) {
        // Process is being created
        DbgPrint("Process created: %wZ (PID: %d)\n", CreateIn-
fo->ImageFileName, ProcessId);
    } else {
        // Process is being deleted
```

```
        DbgPrint("Process terminated: (PID: %d)\n", ProcessId);
    }
}

NTSTATUS DriverEntry(
    _In_ PDRIVER_OBJECT DriverObject,
    _In_ PUNICODE_STRING RegistryPath
)
{
    NTSTATUS status;

    // Register the process creation callback
    status = PsSetCreateProcessNotifyRoutineEx(CreateProcessNoti-
fyRoutineEx, FALSE);
    if (!NT_SUCCESS(status)) {
        DbgPrint("Failed to register process creation callback:
0x%X\n", status);
        return status;
    }

    DbgPrint("Driver loaded successfully\n");
    return STATUS_SUCCESS;
}
```

Explanation

Callback Routine Definition:

- The **`CreateProcessNotifyRoutineEx`** function is defined to handle process creation and termination events. It takes three parameters:
  - **Process:** A pointer to the process object.
  - **ProcessId**: The ID of the process being created or deleted.
  - **CreateInfo:** A pointer to a **`PS_CREATE_NOTIFY_INFO`** structure that contains information about the process being created. If **`CreateInfo`** is NULL, the process is being deleted.

Callback Routine Registration:

- In the **`DriverEntry`** function, the **`PsSetCreateProcessNotifyRoutineEx`** function is called to register the **`CreateProcessNotifyRoutineEx`** callback routine. The second parameter is **`FALSE`**, indicating that the callback is being registered (not removed).

Callback Routine Invocation:

- The callback routine is invoked by the system whenever a process is created or deleted. If a process is being created, **`CreateInfo`** is not **`NULL`**, and the routine prints the process name and ID. If a process is being deleted, **CreateInfo** is **NULL**, and the routine prints the process ID.

This example demonstrates how an EDR solution can use callback routines to monitor process creation events, providing visibility into process activities on the system. By analyzing these events, the EDR can detect and respond to suspicious behavior in real-time.

- **File System Monitoring**: EDR solutions hook into file system functions to track file operations like creation, deletion, and modification. This involves intercepting calls to file system functions and redirecting them to custom routines that log and analyze these operations. This is crucial for detecting ransomware activities, where files are encrypted or deleted. The following is an example of how this can be implemented using a file system filter driver.

  File System Filter Driver Example

  A file system filter driver can be used to hook into file system operations. The following is a simplified example in C that demonstrates how to hook into file creation, deletion, and modification operations:

```
#include <ntddk.h>

NTSTATUS DriverEntry(
    _In_ PDRIVER_OBJECT DriverObject,
    _In_ PUNICODE_STRING RegistryPath
);

VOID UnloadDriver(
    _In_ PDRIVER_OBJECT DriverObject
);

NTSTATUS CreateFileCallback(
    _In_ PDEVICE_OBJECT DeviceObject,
    _In_ PIRP Irp
);

NTSTATUS DeleteFileCallback(
    _In_ PDEVICE_OBJECT DeviceObject,
    _In_ PIRP Irp
);

NTSTATUS ModifyFileCallback(
    _In_ PDEVICE_OBJECT DeviceObject,
    _In_ PIRP Irp
);
```

```
NTSTATUS DriverEntry(
    _In_ PDRIVER_OBJECT DriverObject,
    _In_ PUNICODE_STRING RegistryPath
)
{
    UNREFERENCED_PARAMETER(RegistryPath);

    DriverObject->DriverUnload = UnloadDriver;

    // Hook into file system operations
    DriverObject->MajorFunction[IRP_MJ_CREATE] = CreateFileCall-
back;
    DriverObject->MajorFunction[IRP_MJ_SET_INFORMATION] = Modify-
FileCallback;

    DbgPrint("File system filter driver loaded\n");

    return STATUS_SUCCESS;
}

VOID UnloadDriver(
    _In_ PDRIVER_OBJECT DriverObject
)
{
    UNREFERENCED_PARAMETER(DriverObject);
    DbgPrint("File system filter driver unloaded\n");
}

NTSTATUS CreateFileCallback(
    _In_ PDEVICE_OBJECT DeviceObject,
    _In_ PIRP Irp
)
{
    PIO_STACK_LOCATION stack = IoGetCurrentIrpStackLocation(Irp);
    DbgPrint("File created: %wZ\n", &stack->FileObject->File-
Name);

    // Pass the IRP down the driver stack
    IoSkipCurrentIrpStackLocation(Irp);
    return IoCallDriver(DeviceObject, Irp);
}

NTSTATUS DeleteFileCallback(
    _In_ PDEVICE_OBJECT DeviceObject,
    _In_ PIRP Irp
)
{
```

```
    PIO_STACK_LOCATION stack = IoGetCurrentIrpStackLocation(Irp);
    DbgPrint("File deleted: %wZ\n", &stack->FileObject->File-
Name);

    // Pass the IRP down the driver stack
    IoSkipCurrentIrpStackLocation(Irp);
    return IoCallDriver(DeviceObject, Irp);
}

NTSTATUS ModifyFileCallback(
    _In_ PDEVICE_OBJECT DeviceObject,
    _In_ PIRP Irp
)
{
    PIO_STACK_LOCATION stack = IoGetCurrentIrpStackLocation(Irp);
    DbgPrint("File modified: %wZ\n", &stack->FileObject->File-
Name);

    // Pass the IRP down the driver stack
    IoSkipCurrentIrpStackLocation(Irp);
    return IoCallDriver(DeviceObject, Irp);
}
```

Explanation

Driver Entry and Unload:

- The **DriverEntry** function initializes the driver and sets up the callback functions for file system operations. The **UnloadDriver** function is called when the driver is unloaded.

Hooking File System Operations:

- The **DriverObject->MajorFunction** array is used to hook into specific file system operations. In this example, **IRP_MJ_CREATE** is hooked to monitor file creation, **IRP_MJ_SET_INFORMATION** for file modifications or deletions.

Callback Functions:

- **CreateFileCallback**: This function is called whenever a file is created. It logs the file name and passes the IRP (I/O Request Packet) down the driver stack.
- **DeleteFileCallback**: This function is called whenever a file is deleted. It logs the file name and passes the IRP down the driver stack.
- **ModifyFileCallback**: This function is called whenever a file is modified. It logs the file name and passes the IRP down the driver stack.

By using these hooks, an EDR solution can monitor and log file system activities, providing visibility into potentially malicious operations such as unauthorized file creation, modification, or deletion. This information is crucial for detecting and responding to threats in real-time.

- **Registry Monitoring**: By hooking into registry functions, the EDR can monitor changes to critical registry keys and values. This helps in detecting persistence mechanisms used by malware to survive reboots.

  Registry Callback Routine Example

  Windows provides a mechanism to register callback routines for registry operations using the CmRegisterCallback function. Here's a simplified example in C:

```
#include <ntddk.h>

NTSTATUS RegistryCallback(
    _In_ PVOID CallbackContext,
    _In_ PVOID Argument1,
    _In_ PVOID Argument2
);

VOID UnloadDriver(
    _In_ PDRIVER_OBJECT DriverObject
);

NTSTATUS DriverEntry(
    _In_ PDRIVER_OBJECT DriverObject,
    _In_ PUNICODE_STRING RegistryPath
)
{
    UNREFERENCED_PARAMETER(RegistryPath);
    NTSTATUS status;
    LARGE_INTEGER cookie;

    // Register the registry callback
    status = CmRegisterCallback(RegistryCallback, NULL, &cookie);
    if (!NT_SUCCESS(status)) {
        DbgPrint("Failed to register registry callback: 0x%X\n",
status);
        return status;
    }

    DriverObject->DriverUnload = UnloadDriver;
    DbgPrint("Registry monitoring driver loaded\n");
    return STATUS_SUCCESS;
}
VOID UnloadDriver(
    _In_ PDRIVER_OBJECT DriverObject
```

```
)
{
    UNREFERENCED_PARAMETER(DriverObject);
    DbgPrint("Registry monitoring driver unloaded\n");
}

NTSTATUS RegistryCallback(
    _In_ PVOID CallbackContext,
    _In_ PVOID Argument1,
    _In_ PVOID Argument2
)
{
    UNREFERENCED_PARAMETER(CallbackContext);

    REG_NOTIFY_CLASS regNotifyClass = (REG_NOTIFY_CLASS)
(ULONG_PTR)Argument1;

    if (regNotifyClass == RegNtPreSetValueKey) {
        PREG_SET_VALUE_KEY_INFORMATION preSetValueInfo
= (PREG_SET_VALUE_KEY_INFORMATION)Argument2;
        DbgPrint("Registry key set: %wZ\n", preSetValueInfo->
Object);
    }

    return STATUS_SUCCESS;
}
```

Explanation

Driver Entry and Unload:

- The **DriverEntry** function initializes the driver and registers the **RegistryCallback** function using **CmRegisterCallback**. The **UnloadDriver** function is called when the driver is unloaded.

Registry Callback Registration:

- **CmRegisterCallback** is used to register the **RegistryCallback** function, which will be called for various registry operations. The cookie parameter is used to identify the callback registration.

Callback Function:

- The **RegistryCallback** function is called whenever a registry operation occurs. The **Argument1** parameter indicates the type of registry operation (for example, **RegNtPreSetValueKey** for setting a registry value), and **Argument2** provides additional information about the operation.

- In this example, the callback function checks if the operation is **RegNtPreSetValueKey** (setting a registry value) and logs the registry key being set.

By using these hooks, an EDR solution can monitor and log changes to critical registry keys and values, providing visibility into potentially malicious activities such as unauthorized modifications to the registry. This information is crucial for detecting and responding to threats in real-time.

- **Network Activity Monitoring**: EDR hooks into network-related functions to capture details about network connections, such as IP addresses, ports, and protocols. This is essential for identifying command-and-control (C2) communications used by attackers.

Network Hooking Example

A kernel-mode driver can be used to hook into network-related functions such as NtDeviceIoControlFile, which is used for various network operations. Here's a simplified example in C:

```
#include <ntddk.h>

NTSTATUS DriverEntry(
    _In_ PDRIVER_OBJECT DriverObject,
    _In_ PUNICODE_STRING RegistryPath
);

VOID UnloadDriver(
    _In_ PDRIVER_OBJECT DriverObject
);

NTSTATUS NetworkIoControlCallback(
    _In_ PDEVICE_OBJECT DeviceObject,
    _In_ PIRP Irp
);

NTSTATUS DriverEntry(
    _In_ PDRIVER_OBJECT DriverObject,
    _In_ PUNICODE_STRING RegistryPath
)
{
    UNREFERENCED_PARAMETER(RegistryPath);

    DriverObject->DriverUnload = UnloadDriver;

    // Hook into network-related functions
    DriverObject->MajorFunction[IRP_MJ_DEVICE_CONTROL]
= NetworkIoControlCallback;
```

```
    DbgPrint("Network monitoring driver loaded\n");

    return STATUS_SUCCESS;
}

VOID UnloadDriver(
    _In_ PDRIVER_OBJECT DriverObject
)
{
    UNREFERENCED_PARAMETER(DriverObject);
    DbgPrint("Network monitoring driver unloaded\n");
}

NTSTATUS NetworkIoControlCallback(
    _In_ PDEVICE_OBJECT DeviceObject,
    _In_ PIRP Irp
)
{
    PIO_STACK_LOCATION stack = IoGetCurrentIrpStackLocation(Irp);

    if (stack->Parameters.DeviceIoControl.IoControlCode == IOCTL_
TCP_QUERY_INFORMATION_EX) {
        DbgPrint("Network connection detected\n");
        // Log network connection details here
    }

    // Pass the IRP down the driver stack
    IoSkipCurrentIrpStackLocation(Irp);
    return IoCallDriver(DeviceObject, Irp);
}
```

Explanation

Driver Entry and Unload:

- The **DriverEntry** function initializes the driver and sets up the callback function for network-related operations. The **UnloadDriver** function is called when the driver is unloaded.

Hooking Network Functions:

- The **DriverObject->MajorFunction[IRP_MJ_DEVICE_CONTROL]** is used to hook into device control operations, which include network-related functions. The **NetworkIoControlCallback** function is registered to handle these operations.

Callback Function:

- The `NetworkIoControlCallback` function is called whenever a device control operation occurs. It checks if the operation is related to network connections (for example, `IOCTL_TCP_QUERY_INFORMATION_EX`) and logs the network connection details.
- The callback function then passes the IRP (I/O Request Packet) down the driver stack to ensure normal operation.

By using these hooks, an EDR solution can monitor and log network activities, providing visibility into network connections and communications. This information is crucial for detecting and responding to network-based threats in real-time.

Advanced Techniques

- **Exploit Protection**: Defender for Endpoint includes exploit protection features that apply various mitigations to prevent exploitation of vulnerabilities. These mitigations can include techniques such as:
  - **Data Execution Prevention (DEP)**
    - **Data Execution Prevention (DEP)** is a security feature that helps prevent code execution from non-executable memory regions. It leverages the No eXecute (NX) bit on modern CPUs to mark certain areas of memory as non-executable. This means that even if an attacker manages to inject malicious code into these regions, the code cannot be executed.
    - **How It Works:** DEP monitors programs to ensure they do not execute code from data pages such as the default heap, stacks, and memory pools. If a program tries to execute code from a non-executable region, DEP raises an exception, preventing the execution of potentially harmful code.
    - **Protection Scope:** DEP is particularly effective against buffer overflow attacks, where attackers attempt to execute arbitrary code by overflowing a buffer and overwriting the return address.
  - **Address Space Layout Randomization (ASLR)**
    - **Address Space Layout Randomization (ASLR)** is a security technique that randomizes the memory addresses used by system and application processes. By randomizing the location of key data areas, ASLR makes it difficult for attackers to predict the memory addresses where their malicious code will be executed.
    - **How It Works:** ASLR randomizes the base address of executable and library files, stack, heap, and other memory regions each time

a program is run. This randomness forces attackers to guess the location of critical memory areas, significantly reducing the likelihood of successful exploitation.

- **Protection Scope:** ASLR is effective against attacks that rely on knowing the exact location of executable code, such as Return-Oriented Programming (ROP) attacks.

- **Control Flow Guard (CFG) to protect against memory corruption attacks**
  - **Control Flow Guard (CFG)** is a security feature designed to prevent control flow integrity violations. It ensures that indirect calls in a program only go to valid, intended locations, thereby preventing attackers from redirecting the flow of execution to malicious code.
  - **How It Works**: CFG creates a map of all valid indirect call targets at compile time. During runtime, it checks each indirect call against this map to ensure it is valid. If an invalid call is detected, CFG blocks the execution, preventing the attack.
  - **Protection Scope**: CFG is particularly effective against control flow hijacking attacks, such as those that exploit vulnerabilities to redirect execution to malicious code.

- **Automated Response**: When a threat is detected, the EDR can automatically take actions such as isolating the affected endpoint, terminating malicious processes, or removing malicious files. This helps in containing the threat and preventing further damage.

  Triggering Automated Investigations:

  - Automated investigations can be initiated in two primary ways:
    - **Alert-Triggered**: When an alert is generated due to a detected threat, an automated investigation is automatically started. For example, if a malicious file is detected on a device, an alert is triggered, and the investigation begins.
    - **Manual Initiation**: Security operators can manually start an automated investigation if they notice suspicious activity or high-risk indicators on a device.

  Investigation Process:

  - During an automated investigation, Defender for Endpoint uses various inspection algorithms to analyze the threat. It examines the context and behavior of the detected threat, correlates it with other alerts, and expands the investigation scope if similar threats are found on other devices.

- The investigation process includes collecting and analyzing evidence, such as file hashes, process details, and network connections, to determine the threat's nature and impact.

Remediation Actions:

- Based on the investigation findings, Defender for Endpoint can take several remediation actions to neutralize the threat. These actions include:
    - **Quarantining Malicious Files**: Isolating and removing malicious files from the system to prevent further damage.
    - **Stopping Malicious Processes**: Terminating processes that are identified as malicious.
    - **Removing Scheduled Tasks**: Deleting scheduled tasks that are set up by malware to persist on the system.
    - **Isolating Devices**: Temporarily isolating compromised devices from the network to prevent the spread of the threat.

Action Center:

- All remediation actions, whether pending or completed, are tracked in the Action Center. Security teams can review, approve, or reject pending actions and undo completed actions if necessary.

Benefits of Automated Response

- **Reduced Alert Volume**: Automated response significantly reduces the volume of alerts that security teams need to handle manually. By automating routine investigations and remediations, it allows security analysts to focus on more complex and high-value tasks.
- **Faster Remediation**: Automated response accelerates the remediation process, ensuring that threats are neutralized quickly and efficiently. This rapid response helps minimize the potential impact of security incidents.
- **Consistency and Accuracy**: Automated investigations follow predefined algorithms and playbooks, ensuring consistent and accurate responses to threats. This reduces the risk of human error and ensures that best practices are applied uniformly.
- **Scalability**: Automated response capabilities enable organizations to scale their security operations without a proportional increase in staffing. This is particularly important for large enterprises with extensive and diverse IT environments.

In summary, EDR solutions such as Microsoft Defender for Endpoint leverage a combination of behavioral monitoring, telemetry collection, and advanced techniques such as function and DLL hooks to provide comprehensive protection against advanced threats. These capabilities enable security teams to detect, investigate, and respond to threats effectively, ensuring the security of enterprise environments.

Deployment Deep Dive

Deployment Types for Microsoft Defender for Endpoint

There are three types of deployment methods:

- Cloud-Based
- On-Premises
- Hybrid Deployment

Let's take a closer look at each. All of the following deployment types require a license and system requirements are listed as follows:

Licensing: Verify that you have the appropriate licenses for Microsoft Defender for Endpoint and Microsoft Endpoint Manager (Intune). This can be done through the Microsoft 365 admin center or the Azure portal.

- Defender for Endpoint Plan 1 and Plan 2 (standalone or as part of other Microsoft 365 plans - https://learn.microsoft.com/en-us/defender-endpoint/microsoft-defender-endpoint)
- Microsoft Defender for Business (for small and medium-sized businesses - https://learn.microsoft.com/en-us/defender-business/mdb-overview)
- To onboard servers to the standalone versions of Defender for Endpoint, server licenses are required. You can choose from:
    - Microsoft Defender for Servers Plan 1 or Plan 2 (as part of the Defender for Cloud - https://learn.microsoft.com/en-us/azure/defender-for-cloud/defender-for-cloud-introduction).
    - Microsoft Defender for Endpoint for Servers
    - Microsoft Defender for Business servers (for small and medium-sized businesses only)

For more detailed information about licensing requirements for Microsoft Defender for Endpoint, see Microsoft Defender for Endpoint licensing information (https://learn.microsoft.com/en-us/office365/servicedescriptions/microsoft-365-service-descriptions/microsoft-365-tenantlevel-services-licensing-guidance/microsoft-365-security-compliance-licensing-guidance#microsoft-defender-for-endpoint).

System Requirements: Ensure that all devices meet the system requirements (https://learn.microsoft.com/en-us/defender-endpoint/minimum-requirements#hardware-and-software-requirements) for Microsoft Defender for Endpoint. This includes having the necessary operating system versions and hardware specifications. Defender for Endpoint supports macOS, Linux, Windows Subsystem for Linux (WSL), Android, iOS, and most Windows OS after Windows 10.

Hardware Requirements (Windows)

For Windows devices:

- **CPU:** Minimum 2 cores (4 cores preferred).
- **Memory:** Minimum 1 GB RAM (4 GB preferred).
- **Storage:** Follows Windows OS requirement—no extra allocation beyond OS need (https://learn.microsoft.com/en-us/defender-endpoint/minimum-requirements).

Note: Hardware must be sufficient to run the supported OS (Windows 10/11 or Server) .

Network, Storage and OS Configuration

- Choose your **data storage region** (EU, UK, or US)—this selection is irreversible learn.microsoft.com.
- **IPv4** must be enabled; IPv6-only setups need transitional support such as DNS64/NAT64 learn.microsoft.com.
- Devices need internet access (direct or via proxy) for cloud connectivity.

Windows OS: Supported Editions

- **Client:** Windows 10/11 (Pro, Enterprise, Education, Pro Education, IoT, LTSC, ARM).
- **Server:** Windows Server 2012 R2, 2016, ≥ 1803, 2019, 2022, 2025 (including core editions), plus virtual instances (Azure Virtual Desktop, Windows 365).
- **Legacy** (with MMA agent): Windows 7 SP1, Windows 8.1, Windows Server 2008 R2 SP1 – supported only via Log Analytics agent.

Other Platforms

- **macOS, Linux, Android, iOS, Windows Subsystem for Linux** are supported (specific versions required; check full compatibility charts).

Linux Requirements

For Linux endpoints:

- **CPU:** ≥ 1 core (more recommended for heavy use).
- **Memory:** ≥ 1 GB RAM.
- **Disk:** ≥ 2 GB free, more recommended.

- **Networking:** Access to *.endpoint.security.microsoft.com.
- Requires **systemd** and admin privileges.
- Supports mainstream distros (RHEL 7.2+, CentOS, Ubuntu 16.04+, Debian 9–12, SUSE, Oracle, Amazon Linux, Fedora, ARM64-based distros, etc.).

Microsoft Defender Antivirus Requirements

- Defender Antivirus must be **installed** and either active or **passive**, with **signature updates enabled.**
- On servers using third-party AV, run Defender in **passive mode** or uninstall to avoid conflicts.

For more details about minimum system requirements for Defender for Endpoint, please refer to the following official documentation from Microsoft: https://learn.microsoft.com/en-us/defender-endpoint/minimum-requirements#hardware-and-software-requirements

Cloud-Based Deployment for Microsoft Defender for Endpoint

Overview of Cloud-Based Deployment

Cloud-based deployment of Microsoft Defender for Endpoint leverages the scalability and flexibility of the cloud to provide comprehensive endpoint security. This method simplifies the deployment process by reducing the need for on-premises infrastructure and ensuring that endpoints are always protected with the latest security updates and threat intelligence. Cloud-based deployment is particularly beneficial for organizations with a distributed workforce, as it allows for centralized management and rapid scaling of security measures.

Steps for Deploying via Microsoft Endpoint Manager (Intune)

1. **Prepare Your Environment**:

   a. **System Requirements**: Ensure that all devices meet the system requirements (https://learn.microsoft.com/en-us/defender-endpoint/minimum-requirements#hardware-and-software-requirements) for Microsoft Defender for Endpoint. This includes having the necessary operating system versions and hardware specifications. Defender for Endpoint supports macOS, Linux, Windows Subsystem for Linux (WSL), Android, iOS, and most Windows OS versions after Windows 10.

   b. **Enable Intune Connection**

      i. Navigate to https://intune.microsoft.com and select **`Endpoint`**

Security blade, then expand the **Setup** dropdown and select **Microsoft Defender for Endpoint**.

ii. Scroll down to **Compliance policy evaluation** and turn on **Connect Windows devices version x.x.x. and above to Microsoft Defender for Endpoint**, illustrated as follows:

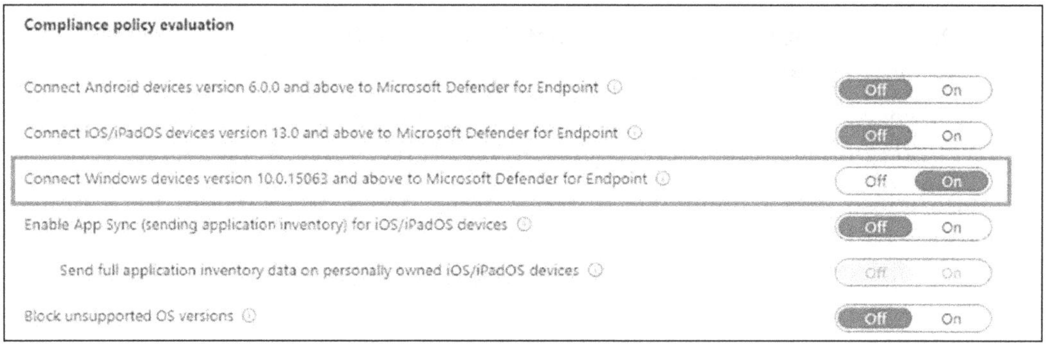

***Figure 2.1**: Connect Devices to Intune*

iii. Refresh the page and confirm the **Connection status**:

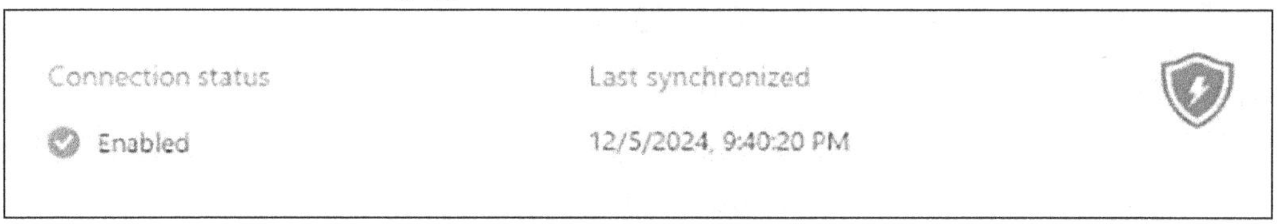

***Figure 2.2**: Connection Status*

c. **Enable Defender Connection**

i. Navigate to https://security.microsoft.com and open up the **settings** blade at the very bottom of the left menu, then select **Endpoints**.

ii. Select **Advanced features** and enable the **Microsoft Intune Connection**, then select **Save**.

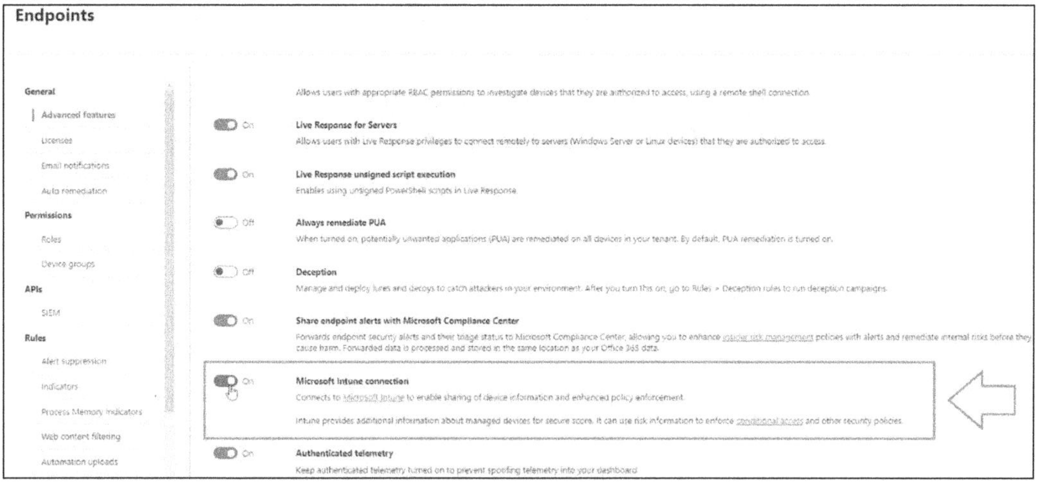

Figure 2.3: *Integration with Defender for Endpoint*

2. **Onboard Devices**:

   a. **Create a Device Configuration Profile**: Back in Intune, navigate to **`Endpoint Security`** > **`Endpoint Detection and Response`** > **`Create policy`**.

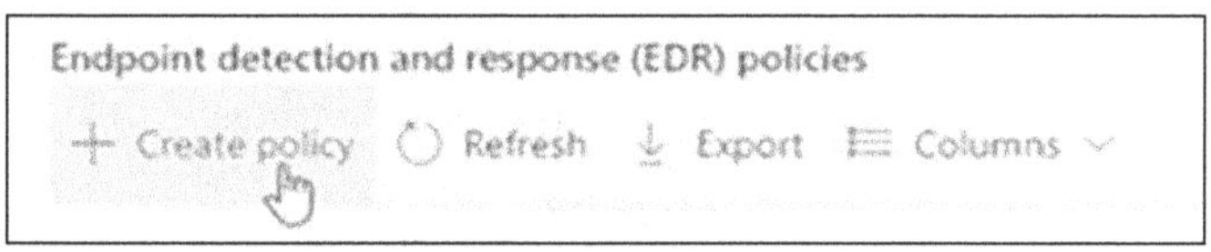

Figure 2.4: *Create Onboarding Policy*

Select **`Windows`** as the platform and **`Endpoint protection`** as the profile type, and click **`Create`**:

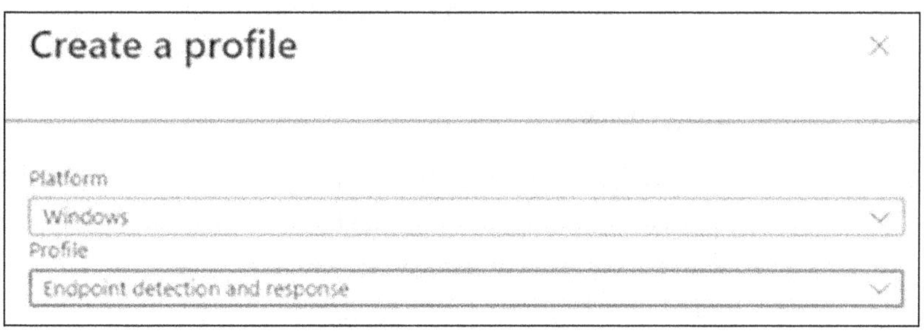

Figure 2.5: *Configure Onboarding Profile*

   b. Give it a **`Name`** and **`Description`**.

   c. Select **`Auto from connector`** in the **`Package type`** drop-down. If the connection between Defender and Intune is not configured, then `the` **`Auto from connector`** option will not be available. This setting automatically populates the onboarding blob storage information devices pull from during onboarding.

d. **Configure Endpoint Protection Settings**: Within the profile, configure settings such as enabling real-time protection, cloud-delivered protection, and automatic sample submission. These settings ensure that devices are protected against the latest threats.

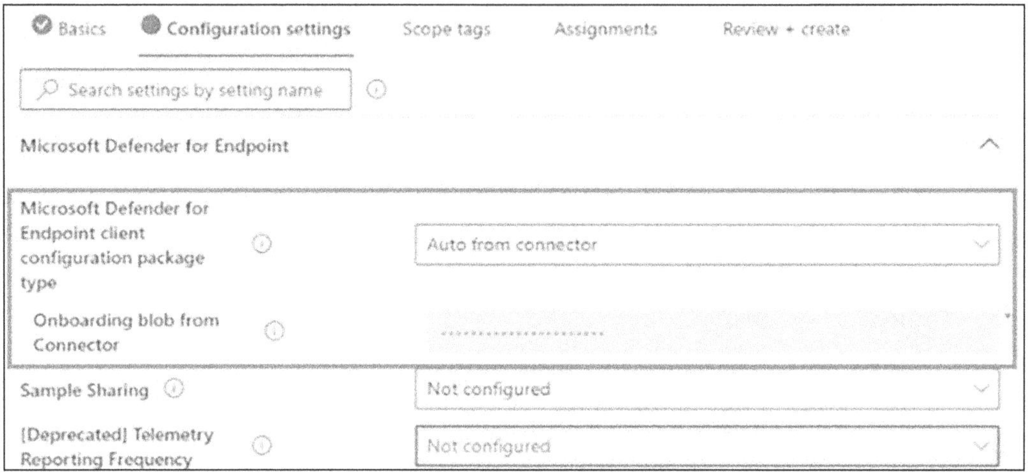

***Figure 2.6**: Endpoint Protection Settings*

e. **Assign the Profile to Devices**: Assign the configuration profile to the appropriate device groups. This step ensures that all targeted devices are onboarded to Defender for Endpoint and receive the necessary security configurations. *Do not mix and match user and device groups.* If you do not use dynamic device groups, it's easier to manage using user groups because users can change devices, in which case you must manually update their devices.

3. **Monitor Onboarding Status**:

a. **Admin Center Monitoring**: Use the Intune portal to monitor the status of device onboarding. Ensure that all devices are successfully enrolled and that Defender for Endpoint is active on each device.

b. **Troubleshooting**: The most typical issue is with the underlying **`MSSense.exe service`**. Open up the **`services.msc`** menu and verify that the service is switched from **`manual`** to **`automatic`**. If that isn't your issue, the troubleshooting tool is actually a great resource to figure out where the gaps are in your deployment:

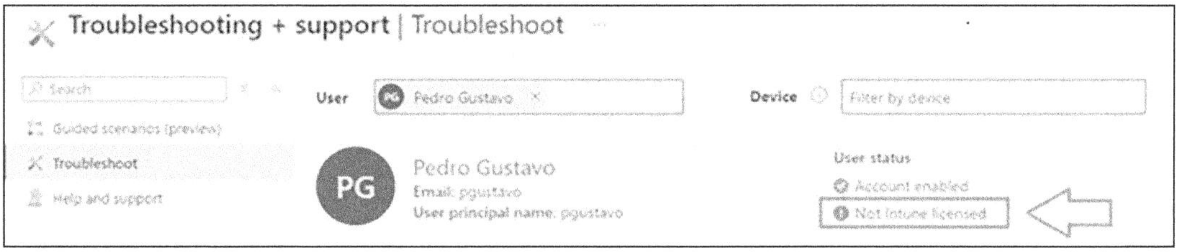

Figure 2.7: *Troubleshooting*

Configuring Policies and Settings in the Cloud

Security Baselines:

Apply Security Baselines: Microsoft provides predefined security baselines that include recommended settings for Defender for Endpoint. These baselines help ensure that your devices are configured according to best practices. However, they're not a long-term solution; it's best practice to deploy Endpoint Protection, AV, Attack Surface Reduction (ASR) and other policies for a more granular and fine-tuned approach rather than relying on the out-of-the-box baselines. If you think about it, threat actors have access to the same out-of-the-box baselines and so are more prepared to evade and exploit them.

Endpoint Protection Policies:

- **Create and Deploy Policies**: In the Microsoft Endpoint Manager admin center, navigate to **`Endpoint security`** > **`Antivirus`** to create and deploy antivirus policies. Configure settings such as scan schedules, exclusion lists, and remediation actions.
- **Monitor Policy Compliance**: Use the compliance reports in Microsoft Endpoint Manager to monitor the status of your endpoint protection policies. Ensure that all devices comply with the configured policies and take corrective actions if necessary.

By following these steps and configuring the appropriate policies and settings, organizations can effectively deploy and manage Microsoft Defender for Endpoint in a cloud-based environment, ensuring robust protection for their endpoints.

Deep Dive into On-Premises Deployment for Microsoft Defender for Endpoint

Overview of On-Premises Deployment

On-premises deployment of Microsoft Defender for Endpoint involves installing and managing the security solution within an organization's local infrastructure. This method is suitable for environments with strict regulatory requirements, limited internet connectivity, or specific security policies that necessitate on-premises management. The deployment process typically involves using tools such as Group Policy or Microsoft Endpoint Configuration Manager (MECM) to onboard devices, configure security settings, and ensure continuous protection.

Steps for Deploying via Group Policy

1. **Download Installation and Onboarding Packages**:

    a. **Access the Microsoft Defender Portal**: Navigate to https://security.microsoft.com to download the necessary installation and onboarding packages. Scroll all the way to the bottom of the left menu to **`Settings`**, select **`Endpoints`**, then go down to the bottom of that menu to **`Device management`** and select the **`Onboarding`** blade.

    b. **Download Packages**: Select the appropriate packages for your server versions (for example, Windows Server 2016, Windows Server 2012 R2). The installation package typically includes an MSI file, while the onboarding package contains scripts for onboarding devices.

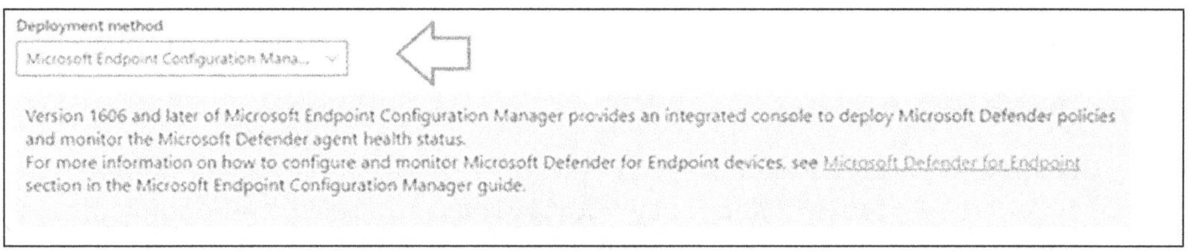

Figure 2.8: *Select Deployment Method*

2. **Apply Installation Packages**:

    a. **Install the MSI Package**: Use Group Policy to distribute and install the Microsoft Defender for Endpoint agent on target devices. This involves creating a Group Policy Object (GPO) that runs the MSI package on the specified endpoints.

    b. **Configure Microsoft Defender Antivirus**: Ensure that Microsoft Defender Antivirus is enabled and up to date on all endpoints. This may involve re-enabling the feature if it was previously disabled.

    c. **Verify Onboarding**: Check the Microsoft Defender portal to ensure that all devices are successfully onboarded and reporting to the service.

Configuring Policies and Settings On-Premises

1. **Group Policy Management**:

    a. **Create and Deploy GPOs**: Use Group Policy Management Console (GPMC) to create and deploy GPOs that configure security settings for Defender for

Endpoint. This includes settings for real-time protection, cloud-delivered protection, and automatic sample submission.

b. **Configure Security Settings**: Within the GPOs, configure specific security settings such as scan schedules, exclusion lists, and remediation actions. These settings ensure that endpoints are protected according to organizational policies.

2. **Endpoint Configuration Manager (MECM)**:

   a. **Deploy and Manage Defender for Endpoint**: Use MECM to deploy and manage Defender for Endpoint across the organization. MECM provides advanced capabilities for managing large-scale deployments, including software updates, compliance settings, and detailed reporting.

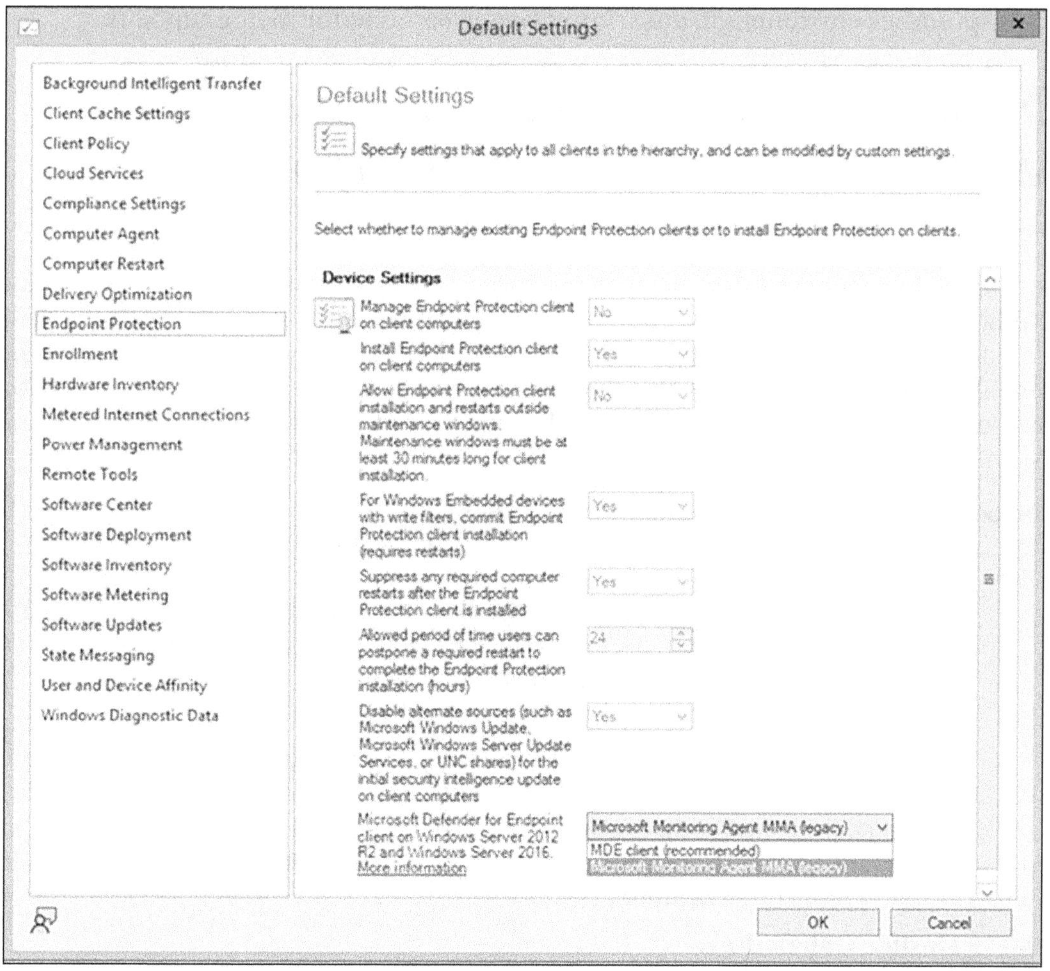

Figure 2.9: MECM Configuration

b. **Monitor and Remediate**: Use MECM to monitor the status of Defender for Endpoint deployments and take remediation actions as needed. This includes ensuring that all endpoints are compliant with security policies and addressing any issues that arise.

Note: *Up-level devices, such as Windows Server version 1803, need the onboarding configuration file. Starting Current Branch 2207, for down-level server operating system devices, you can choose between Microsoft Defender for Endpoint (MDE) Client (recommended) or Microsoft Monitoring Agent (MMA) (legacy) in the Client Settings. For Windows 8.1 devices, you need to use Microsoft Monitoring Agent (MMA) (legacy) in the Client Settings.*

By following these steps and configuring the appropriate policies and settings, organizations can effectively deploy and manage Microsoft Defender for Endpoint in an on-premises environment, ensuring robust protection for their endpoints.

Deep Dive into Hybrid Deployment for Microsoft Defender for Endpoint

Overview of Hybrid Deployment

Hybrid deployment combines both cloud-based and on-premises methods to provide a flexible and comprehensive security solution. This approach is ideal for organizations with a mix of cloud and on-premises infrastructure, allowing them to leverage the benefits of both deployment types. Hybrid deployment ensures seamless integration and consistent security policies across all environments, providing robust protection for endpoints regardless of their location.

Combining Cloud and On-Premises Deployment

- **Unified Management:**
  - **Centralized Console**: Use Microsoft Endpoint Manager to manage both cloud-based and on-premises devices from a single console. This unified management approach simplifies administration and ensures that security policies are consistently applied across all devices.
  - **Integration with Microsoft Defender for Cloud**: Integrate Defender for Endpoint with Microsoft Defender for Cloud to extend protection to servers and other critical infrastructure. This integration provides advanced threat detection and response capabilities for both cloud and on-premises environments.
- **Flexible Onboarding:**
  - **Cloud-Based Onboarding**: For devices that are primarily cloud-managed, use Microsoft Endpoint Manager (Intune) to onboard and configure

Defender for Endpoint. This involves creating and assigning device configuration profiles, enabling real-time protection, and setting up cloud-delivered protection.

  - **On-Premises Onboarding**: For on-premises devices, use tools like Group Policy or Microsoft Endpoint Configuration Manager (MECM) to deploy and manage Defender for Endpoint. This includes downloading installation packages, applying onboarding scripts, and configuring security settings locally.

- **Consistent Policies:**
  - **Security Baselines**: Apply and customize security baselines to ensure that all devices, whether cloud-based or on-premises, adhere to best practices. These baselines include recommended settings for antivirus protection, firewall rules, and attack surface reduction.
  - **Endpoint Protection Policies**: Create and deploy endpoint protection policies that cover both cloud and on-premises devices. Configure settings such as scan schedules, exclusion lists, and remediation actions to maintain a consistent security posture.

Best Practices for Hybrid Environments

- **Centralized Monitoring:**
  - **Microsoft Defender Security Center**: Use the Microsoft Defender Security Center to monitor and manage security incidents across all environments. This centralized platform provides visibility into threats and allows for coordinated response actions.
  - **Advanced Threat Analytics**: Leverage advanced threat analytics to detect and respond to sophisticated attacks. This includes using machine learning and AI to identify patterns and anomalies that indicate potential threats.
- **Regular Updates:**
  - **Patch Management**: Ensure that both cloud-based and on-premises devices receive regular security updates and patches. Use tools such as Windows Update for Business and MECM to automate the update process and maintain compliance.
  - **Threat Intelligence**: Keep all devices updated with the latest threat intelligence from Microsoft. This ensures that endpoints are protected against the latest threats and vulnerabilities.
- **Integration with Other Security Solutions:**
  - **Microsoft Defender for Identity**: Integrate Defender for Endpoint with Microsoft Defender for Identity to enhance threat detection and response

capabilities. This integration helps identify and mitigate identity-based attacks.

- **Microsoft Defender for Office 365**: Extend protection to email and collaboration tools by integrating Defender for Endpoint with Microsoft Defender for Office 365. This provides comprehensive security coverage across all communication channels.

By following these steps and best practices, organizations can effectively deploy and manage Microsoft Defender for Endpoint in a hybrid environment, ensuring robust protection for their endpoints.

Troubleshooting

Common Issues

- **Service Settings Not Correctly Enabled**:
  - **Issue**: Some features of Defender for Endpoint may not be fully enabled, leading to reduced protection.
  - **Troubleshooting**: Ensure that all advanced features are enabled in the Microsoft Defender Security Center > Endpoints > Advanced Features. This includes real-time protection, cloud-delivered protection, and automatic sample submission.
- **Policy Conflicts:**
  - **Issue**: Conflicts between Group Policy, Intune, and other configuration management tools can cause inconsistent settings.
  - **Troubleshooting**: Review and document all existing policies. Use the Microsoft Endpoint Manager admin center to prioritize MDM policies over Group Policies where necessary.
- **Onboarding Failures:**
  - **Issue**: Devices fail to onboard to Defender for Endpoint, often due to connectivity issues or misconfigurations.
  - **Troubleshooting**: Verify that devices meet the minimum requirements and have the necessary network connectivity. Use the onboarding troubleshooting guide provided by Microsoft to resolve specific errors.
- **Integration Problems:**
  - **Issue**: Integration with other Microsoft security solutions or third-party tools may not work as expected.
  - **Troubleshooting**: Ensure that all integration prerequisites are met. Check for updates and compatibility issues with other security solutions. Follow the integration guides for detailed steps.

- **Performance Impacts:**
  - **Issue**: Security scans and other operations may impact device performance.
  - **Troubleshooting**: Schedule scans during off-peak hours and configure performance settings to balance security and usability. Monitor device performance and adjust settings as needed.

Troubleshooting Steps for Specific Scenarios

1. **Troubleshooting Onboarding Issues**:
   - **Scenario**: Devices are not appearing in the Microsoft Defender Security Center after onboarding.
   - **Steps**:
     a. **Check Connectivity**: Ensure that the device can connect to the required Microsoft Defender for Endpoint URLs and IP addresses.
     b. **Verify Configuration**: Confirm that the onboarding script or configuration profile has been correctly applied.
     c. **Review Logs**: Check the device logs for any errors related to the onboarding process. Use the Microsoft Defender for Endpoint troubleshooting guide for detailed steps.
2. **Resolving Policy Conflicts**:
   - **Scenario**: Conflicting policies from Group Policy and Intune are causing inconsistent security settings.
   - **Steps**:
     a. **Document Policies**: List all existing policies applied to the devices.
     b. **Prioritize MDM Policies**: In the Microsoft Endpoint Manager admin center, configure the MDM policy to take precedence over Group Policy.
     c. **Test and Validate**: Apply the changes to a test group of devices and validate that the correct policies are enforced.
3. **Addressing Performance Issues**:
   - **Scenario**: Devices experience slow performance during security scans.
   - **Steps**:
     a. **Adjust Scan Schedules**: Schedule scans during times when device usage is low.
     b. **Configure Performance Settings**: In the Microsoft Defender Security Center, adjust performance settings to optimize scan impact.

c. **Monitor and Adjust**: Continuously monitor device performance and make adjustments as needed to balance security and usability.

By understanding these common issues and following the troubleshooting steps, organizations can ensure a smooth and effective deployment of Microsoft Defender for Endpoint in a cloud-based environment.

Troubleshooting Steps for Specific Scenarios

1. **Troubleshooting Onboarding Issues**:
    - **Scenario**: Devices are not appearing in the Microsoft Defender Security Center after onboarding.
    - **Steps**:
        a. **Check Connectivity**: Ensure that the device can connect to the required Microsoft Defender for Endpoint URLs and IP addresses.

        b. **Verify Configuration**: Confirm that the onboarding script or configuration profile has been correctly applied.

        c. **Review Logs**: Check the device logs for any errors related to the onboarding process. Use the Microsoft Defender for Endpoint troubleshooting guide for detailed steps.
2. **Resolving Policy Conflicts**:
    - **Scenario**: Conflicting policies from Group Policy and MECM are causing inconsistent security settings.
    - **Steps**:
        a. **Document Policies**: List all existing policies applied to the devices.

        b. **Prioritize MDM Policies**: In the Microsoft Endpoint Manager admin center, configure the MDM policy to take precedence over Group Policy.

        c. **Test and Validate**: Apply the changes to a test group of devices and validate that the correct policies are enforced.
3. **Addressing Performance Issues**:
    - **Scenario**: Devices experience slow performance during security scans.
    - **Steps**:
        a. **Adjust Scan Schedules**: Schedule scans during times when device usage is low.

        b. **Configure Performance Settings**: In the Microsoft Defender Security Center, adjust performance settings to optimize scan impact.

c. **Monitor and Adjust**: Continuously monitor device performance and make adjustments as needed to balance security and usability.

By understanding these common issues and following the troubleshooting steps, organizations can ensure a smooth and effective deployment of Microsoft Defender for Endpoint in an on-premises environment.

Conclusion

Microsoft Defender for Endpoint stands as a cornerstone of the Microsoft XDR ecosystem, delivering robust protection across an organization's diverse endpoint landscape. By unifying endpoint detection and response, antivirus, vulnerability management, and automated investigation capabilities, it empowers security teams to detect, respond, and recover from threats with precision and speed. Whether deployed in the cloud, on-premises, or through a hybrid approach, Defender for Endpoint offers the scalability, visibility, and integration needed to meet the demands of modern cyber defense. Its deep hooks into the operating system, paired with intelligent automation and continuous telemetry analysis, provide not just protection—but resilience. As organizations strive for proactive and scalable security, Defender for Endpoint proves itself not only as a defense mechanism but also as an enabler of operational efficiency and strategic risk reduction.

Building upon the endpoint foundation, the next chapter shifts focus to identity security—another vital pillar of enterprise defense. Microsoft Defender for Identity extends the XDR strategy into the identity plane, offering deep insights and protection for both on-premises Active Directory and cloud-based identities. By bridging hybrid environments with continuous monitoring and threat detection, it equips organizations to detect lateral movement, credential abuse, and other identity-based threats with speed and clarity.

Helpful Links and References

- Microsoft. (n.d.). *Enable Defender for Endpoint in Microsoft Defender for Cloud.* Microsoft Learn. https://learn.microsoft.com/en-us/azure/defender-for-cloud/enable-defender-for-endpoint
- Microsoft. (n.d.). *Troubleshoot onboarding for Microsoft Defender for Endpoint.* Microsoft Learn. https://learn.microsoft.com/en-us/defender-endpoint/troubleshoot-onboarding
- Microsoft. (n.d.). *Configure server endpoints for Microsoft Defender for Endpoint.* Microsoft Learn. https://learn.microsoft.com/en-us/defender-endpoint/configure-server-endpoints
- Microsoft. (n.d.). *Deployment guide for Microsoft Defender for Endpoint.*

Microsoft Learn. https://learn.microsoft.com/en-us/defender-endpoint/production-deployment

- Microsoft. (n.d.). *Automated investigations overview*. Microsoft Learn. https://learn.microsoft.com/en-us/defender-endpoint/automated-investigations
- Microsoft. (n.d.). *Threat and Vulnerability Management in Microsoft Defender*. Microsoft Learn. https://learn.microsoft.com/en-us/defender-vulnerability-management/defender-vulnerability-management
- Microsoft. (n.d.). *Microsoft Defender Antivirus on Windows*. Microsoft Learn. https://learn.microsoft.com/en-us/defender-endpoint/microsoft-defender-antivirus-windows
- Microsoft. (n.d.). *Overview of Endpoint Detection and Response capabilities*. Microsoft Learn. https://learn.microsoft.com/en-us/defender-endpoint/overview-endpoint-detection-response
- Microsoft. (n.d.). *Respond to machine alerts in Defender for Endpoint*. Microsoft Learn. https://learn.microsoft.com/en-us/defender-endpoint/respond-machine-alerts
- Microsoft. (n.d.). *Customize exploit protection settings*. Microsoft Learn. https://learn.microsoft.com/en-us/defender-endpoint/customize-exploit-protection
- Microsoft. (n.d.). *Exploit protection reference*. Microsoft Learn. https://learn.microsoft.com/en-us/defender-endpoint/exploit-protection-reference
- Microsoft. (n.d.). *Exposure score in Threat and Vulnerability Management*. Microsoft Learn. https://learn.microsoft.com/en-us/defender-vulnerability-management/tvm-exposure-score
- Microsoft Tech Community. (2020, January 27). *Turn on Mandatory ASLR in Windows Security*. Microsoft Tech Community. https://techcommunity.microsoft.com/discussions/windows-security/turn-on-mandatory-aslr-in-windows-security/1186989
- Microsoft. (n.d.). *Microsoft Defender for Endpoint documentation overview*. Microsoft Learn. https://learn.microsoft.com/en-us/defender-endpoint/
- Microsoft. (n.d.). *Enable the Microsoft Intune connection in Microsoft Defender for Endpoint*. Microsoft Learn. https://learn.microsoft.com/en-us/mem/intune/protect/advanced-threat-protection
- Microsoft. (n.d.). *Microsoft Defender Antivirus compatibility*. Microsoft Learn. https://learn.microsoft.com/en-us/microsoft-365/security/defender-endpoint/microsoft-defender-antivirus-compatibility
- Microsoft. (n.d.). *Registering callbacks with PsSetCreateProcessNotifyRoutineEx*. Microsoft Learn. https://learn.microsoft.com/en-us/windows-hardware/drivers/ddi/ntddk/nf-ntddk-pssetcreateprocessnotifyroutineex

CHAPTER 3
Defender for Identity

Introduction

Microsoft Defender for Identity is a comprehensive, cloud-based security solution designed to protect your organization's identities from advanced cyber threats. Leveraging signals from both on-premises Active Directory and cloud identities, it provides robust monitoring and protection across hybrid environments, extending powerful cloud-based protection to your on-premises environment.

Structure

In this chapter, we will cover the following topics:

- Overview
- Importance as an MDI
- How MDI Enhancements to IAM
- Behind the Scenes of MDI
- Deployment Deep Dive
    - gMSA Accounts (DSA and Action)
    - Configure DC's
    - Advanced Auditing
    - ADFS Configuration
    - CA Configuration
- Troubleshooting

Overview

Defender for Identity uses advanced behavioral analytics to establish a baseline of normal activities for users, devices, and resources, continuously monitoring for deviations that could indicate suspicious or malicious behavior. It detects threats in real-time by analyzing data from various sources, such as domain controllers and Active Directory Federation Services (AD FS), identifying patterns that match known attack techniques like pass-the-hash and pass-the-ticket. When a potential threat is detected, Defender for Identity provides detailed, actionable alerts and can automatically respond by isolating compromised accounts or blocking suspicious activities. Its integration with Extended Detection and Response (XDR) solutions enhances threat detection and response capabilities by correlating identity signals with other security data

Key Features and Capabilities

1. **Proactive Identity Security**:
   - **Identity Security Posture Assessments**: Continuously evaluate and improve your identity security posture with insights and recommendations.
   - **Lateral Movement Paths**: Identify and mitigate potential lateral movement paths that attackers could exploit.
2. **Threat Detection and Response**:
   - **Real-Time Analytics**: Detect threats using advanced analytics and data intelligence.
   - **Suspicious Activity Investigation**: Investigate alerts and user activities with clear, actionable incident information.
   - **Automatic Response**: Respond to attacks with automated actions to contain and mitigate threats.
3. **Comprehensive Monitoring**:
   - **Hybrid Environment Coverage**: Monitor and extend cloud-based security to complex, on-premises based identity environments, including domain controllers and Active Directory Federation Services.
   - **Entity Behavior Monitoring**: Track and analyze behavior of all entities, including user and computer accounts.

Importance of Defender for Identity

In today's digital landscape, protecting identities is crucial for maintaining the security and integrity of your organization. Defender for Identity plays a vital role by:

- **Reducing Attack Surface**: By providing insights into identity configurations and security best practices, it helps minimize vulnerabilities and makes it harder for attackers to compromise credentials.
- **Enhancing Threat Detection**: With its ability to detect and respond to advanced threats in real-time, it ensures that potential attacks are identified and mitigated swiftly.

- **Supporting Hybrid Environments**: As organizations increasingly operate in hybrid environments, Defender for Identity offers seamless protection across both on-premises and cloud infrastructures.

By integrating **Defender for Identity** into your security strategy, you can significantly enhance your organization's ability to protect its identities and respond to emerging threats effectively.

Behind the Scenes of Defender for Identity

Here's a detailed look at how **Microsoft Defender for Identity** operates:

1. **Data Collection**

   Defender for Identity collects data from various sources in your IT environment, including:

   - **Domain Controllers (DCs)**: These servers in your Active Directory (AD) domain hold user accounts, group memberships, and access permissions. This involves two group managed service accounts or gMSAs; one with read privileges to ingest data, and the other with write privileges used to disable a user in on-premises AD.
   - **Active Directory Federation Services (AD FS)**: If AD FS is in use for single sign-on (SSO) across cloud and on-premises applications in your environment, Defender for Identity collects and monitors these login attempts.
   - **Windows Security Events**: Logs generated by Windows devices offer valuable insights into user activities and potential security incidents.
   - **Deep Packet Inspection**: MDI leverages NPCAP drivers on DCs to identify where requests are coming from to help identify lateral movement, as just one example.

2. **Behavioral Analytics**

   Defender for Identity leverages sophisticated behavioral analytics to create a standard of typical activities for users, devices, and resources. It consistently observes for any deviations from this standard, which may signal suspicious or harmful actions. For example: If a user account suddenly starts accessing resources that it typically does not, MDI will flag this as suspicious activity. Security teams can then investigate and take appropriate action.

3. **Threat Detection**

   The solution detects threats in real-time by analyzing the collected data and identifying patterns that match known attack techniques. This includes detecting:

- **Suspicious Activities**: Such as unusual login attempts, privilege escalations, and lateral movement within the network.
- **Known Malicious Attacks**: Including pass-the-hash, pass-the-ticket, and other credential theft techniques.

Here's an example: If MDI detects a pass-the-hash attack, it will generate an alert and provide detailed information about the compromised account and the systems it accessed. This allows security teams to quickly isolate the affected systems and prevent the attacker from moving laterally.

4. **Incident Investigation**

   When a potential threat is detected, Defender for Identity provides detailed, actionable alerts. Security teams can investigate these alerts using the provided incident information, which includes the context and timeline of the suspicious activities. For example: when MDI detects that a non-sensitive user account has access to a sensitive system, it will highlight this path. You can then take steps to restrict access or enhance monitoring of that account to prevent potential lateral movement.

5. **Automated Response**

   Defender for Identity can automatically respond to detected threats by taking actions such as isolating compromised accounts or blocking suspicious activities. This rapid response helps contain and mitigate threats before they can cause significant damage. For example: If MDI detects that a compromised account is attempting to access multiple systems, it can automatically disable the account and notify the security team. This prevents the attacker from using the account to move laterally within the network.

6. **Integration with the XDR Stack**

   Microsoft Defender for Identity is fully integrated with Extended Detection and Response (XDR) solutions, providing a unified view of security across all environments. Here's how it ties into the XDR stack:

   - **Unified Threat Detection and Response**:
     - Defender for Identity integrates with Microsoft Defender XDR to provide a comprehensive security solution that covers endpoints, identities, email, applications, and more. This integration enhances the ability to detect and respond to identity-based threats by correlating identity signals with other security data.

- **Enhanced Visibility and Context**:
    - XDR provides comprehensive visibility into security events, and when combined with Defender for Identity, it offers deeper insights into identity-related activities. This helps in understanding the full scope of an attack and taking appropriate actions.
- **Automated and Coordinated Response**:
    - By integrating with XDR, Defender for Identity can automate responses to detected threats across different security domains. For example, if an identity is compromised, XDR can coordinate actions such as isolating affected endpoints, blocking malicious emails, and revoking access to sensitive applications.
- **Holistic Security Posture**:
    - Integration ensures that security teams have a holistic view of the organization's security posture, enabling them to identify and address vulnerabilities more effectively. This unified approach helps in maintaining a robust defense against sophisticated cyber threats.

Using gMSA Accounts for Microsoft Defender for Identity (MDI)

Microsoft Defender for Identity (MDI) requires two types of Group Managed Service Accounts (gMSA) to read signals from your on-premises AD and to write changes: the Directory Service Account (DSA) and the Action Account, respectively.

A Group Managed Service Account (gMSA) is considered more secure than a regular service account for several reasons including, but not limited to:

- **Automated Password Management**: The passwords for gMSAs are automatically generated and rotated by Windows. This eliminates the need for manual password management, which can often lead to security vulnerabilities if not handled properly.
- **Strong Passwords**: The passwords for gMSAs are 240-byte, randomly generated passwords. The complexity and length of these passwords minimize the likelihood of compromise by brute force or dictionary attacks.
- **Limited Access**: Only specific servers that are allowed to use the gMSA can retrieve the account's password from Active Directory. This limits the potential for misuse and compromise.

In the context of Microsoft Defender for Identity, using a gMSA for the Directory Service Account adds an extra layer of security. The gMSA DSA is used by MDI to connect to the domain controller and query data on entities seen in network traffic, monitored events, and monitored Event Tracing for Windows (ETW) activities.

By using a gMSA, the DSA benefits from the automated password management and strong password policies of the gMSA, reducing the risk of the DSA being compromised.

This is particularly important in multi-forest, multi-domain environments, where a unique gMSA DSA is recommended for each forest or domain.

The following is a breakdown of both gMSA accounts required to fully leverage Microsoft Defender for Identity in your environment:

1. **Directory Service Account (DSA)**

   The DSA is primarily used for read-only operations within Active Directory. It is responsible for collecting data from domain controllers and other identity-related components. This account needs to have the necessary permissions to read various attributes and logs from Active Directory to monitor and analyze user activities and detect potential threats.

   Key Characteristics:

   - **Read-Only Permissions**: The DSA requires read-only access to Active Directory.
   - **Data Collection**: It collects data from domain controllers, including security logs and user activities.
   - **Monitoring**: It helps in establishing a baseline of normal activities and detecting anomalies.

2. **Action Account**

   The Action Account is used for taking remediation actions in response to detected threats. This account needs to have write permissions to perform actions such as resetting passwords, disabling accounts, and other necessary interventions to mitigate threats.

   Key Characteristics:

   - **Write Permissions**: The Action Account requires write permissions to perform actions such as password resets and account disabling.
   - **Remediation**: It is used to take corrective actions when a threat is detected.
   - **Optional Configuration**: While using a dedicated gMSA for the Action Account is optional, it is recommended to avoid using the same account for both DSA and Action purposes to minimize security risks. This is a great example of the Principle of Least Privilege in action!

By using these two gMSA accounts, MDI ensures comprehensive coverage for both monitoring and responding to identity-related threats, enhancing the overall security posture of your organization.

Deployment Deep Dive

The first step is downloading the MDI sensor deployment package from the Security portal.

Download the MDI Sensor

1. In Microsoft 365 Defender (https://security.microsoft.com/), go to **`Settings`** and then **`Identities`**.

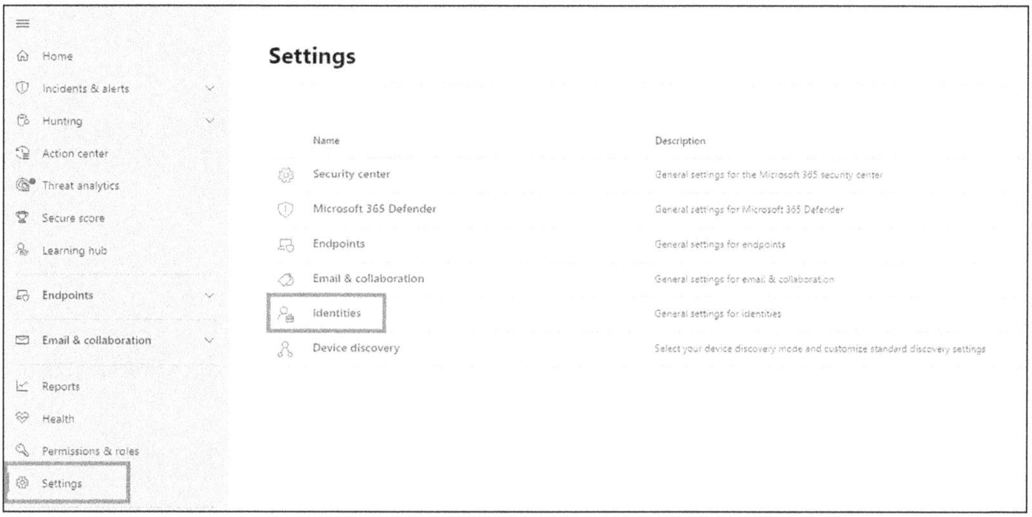

***Figure 3.1**: Defender for Identities Portal Access*

2. Select the **`Sensors`** page, which displays all of your Defender for Identity sensors.

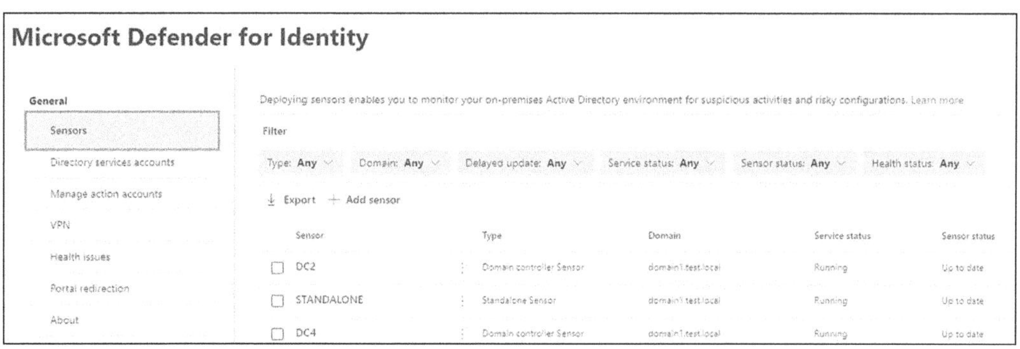

***Figure 3.2**: Sensors Blade*

3. Select **`Add sensor`**.

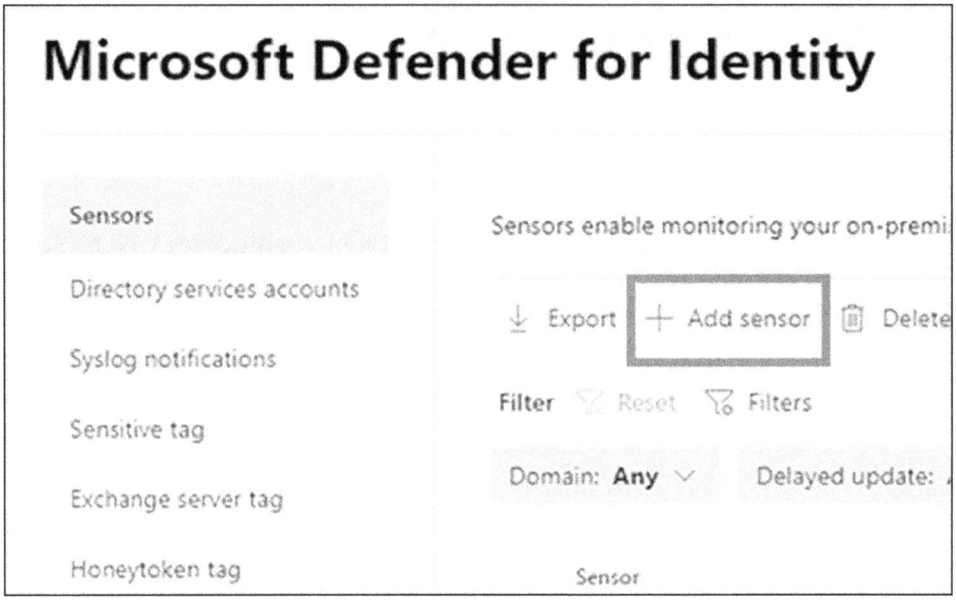

Figure 3.3: Add Sensor

4. A pane will open, providing you with a button to download the sensor installer and a generated access key.

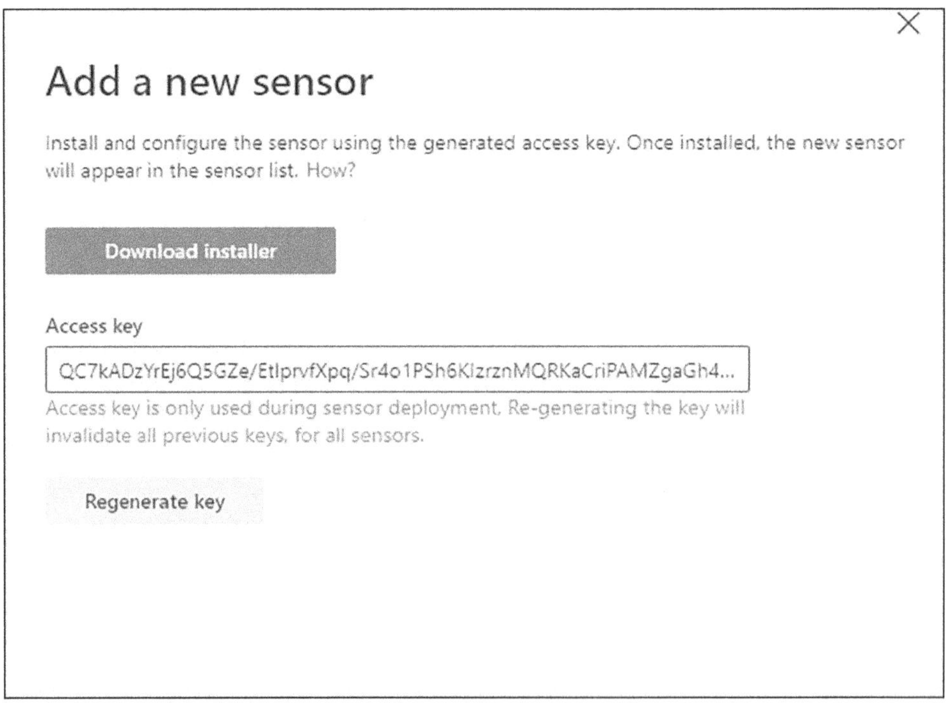

Figure 3.4: Access Key

5. Select **`Download installer`** to save the package locally. The zip file includes the following files:
    a. The Defender for Identity sensor installer
    b. The configuration setting file with the required information to connect to the Defender for Identity cloud service
    c. NPCAP drivers
6. Copy the **`Access key`**. The access key is required for the Defender for Identity sensor to connect to your Defender for Identity workspace. The access key is a one-time-password for sensor deployment, after which all communication is performed using certificates for authentication and TLS encryption. Use the **`Regenerate key`** button if you ever need to regenerate the new access key. It won't affect any previously deployed sensors, because it's only used for initial registration of the sensor during installation. This is so it knows which tenant to associate itself with when it "phones home" for the first time.
7. Copy the package to the dedicated server or domain controller onto which you're installing the Defender for Identity sensor.

Install the MDI Sensor

Pre-Requisites & Important Notes

Make sure Microsoft .NET Framework 4.7 or later is installed on the machine. If Microsoft .NET Framework 4.7 or later isn't installed, the Defender for Identity sensor setup package will install it, which may **reboot** the server.

Perform the following steps on the domain controller:

1. Verify the machine has connectivity to the relevant Defender for Identity cloud service endpoint(s).
2. Extract the installation files from the zip file. Installing directly from the zip file will fail.
3. Install NPCAP drivers (uninstall if previously deployed by another tool such as Nmap or Wireshark on the DC) first. You can reinstall them again after the MDI sensor.
4. Next, run Azure ATP sensor **`setup.exe`** with elevated privileges (Run as administrator) and follow the setup wizard.
5. On the **`Welcome`** page, select your language and select **`Next.`**

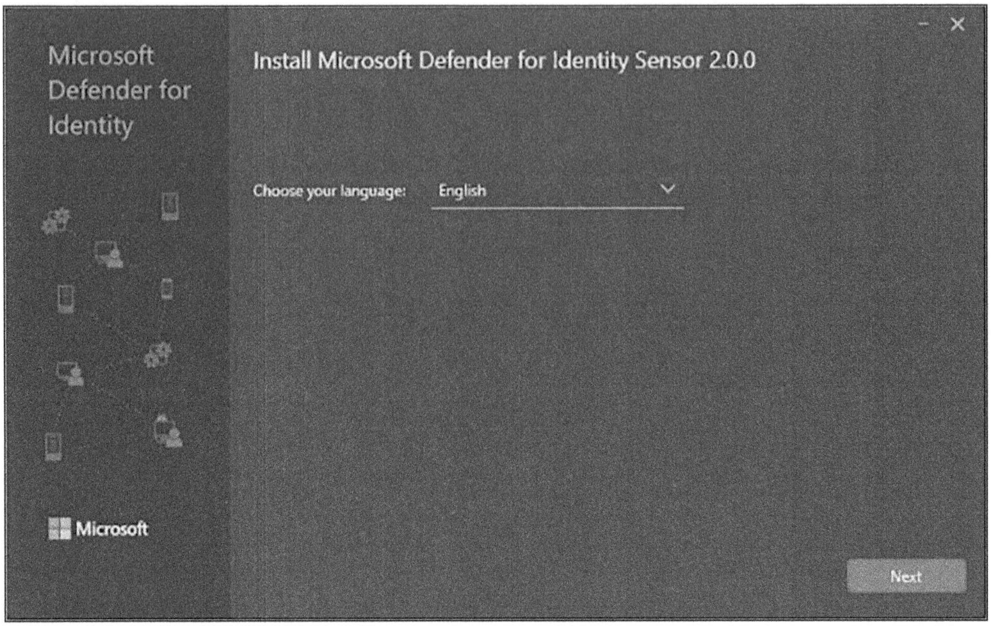

Figure 3.5: *Install Defender for Identity Sensor Wizard*

6. The installation wizard automatically checks if the server is a domain controller/ AD FS server or a dedicated server. If it's a domain controller / AD FS / CA server, the Defender for Identity sensor is installed. If it's a dedicated server, the Defender for Identity standalone sensor is installed. Select **`Next`**.

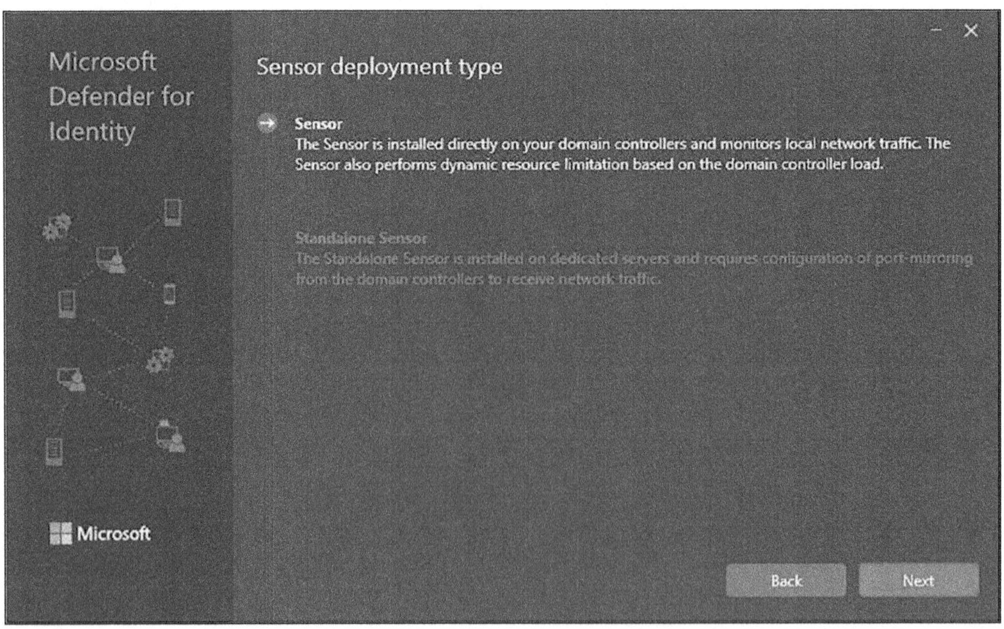

Figure 3.6: *Sensor Deployment Type is Auto-Completed*

7. Under **Configure the sensor**, enter the installation path and the access key that you copied from the previous step, based on your environment:

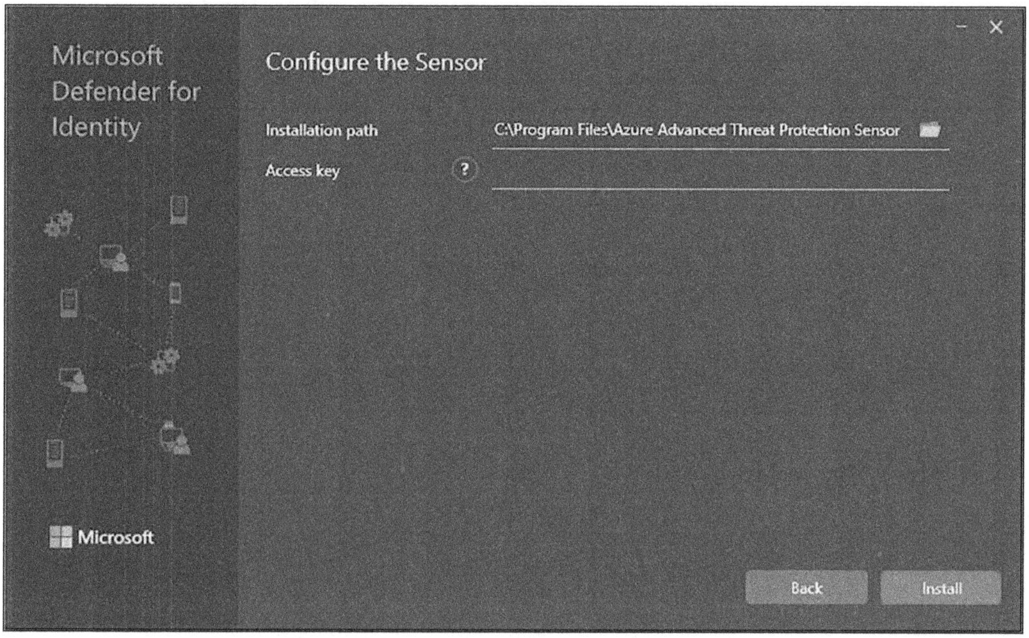

Figure 3.7: *Installation Path and Access Key*

   - **Installation path**: The location where the Defender for Identity sensor is installed. By default, the path is %programfiles%\Azure Advanced Threat Protection sensor. Leave the default value.
   - **Access key**: Retrieved from the Microsoft 365 Defender portal in the previous step.

8. Select **Install** to deploy the following components:
   - KB 3047154 (for Windows Server 2012 R2 only)
   - Defender for Identity sensor service and Defender for Identity sensor updater service
   - Microsoft Visual C++ 2013 Redistributable

Note(s):

- Don't install KB 3047154 on a virtualization host (the host that is running the virtualization - it's fine to run it on a virtual machine). This may cause port mirroring to stop working properly and decrease your coverage.
- If Wireshark is installed on the Defender for Identity sensor machine, after you run Wireshark, you need to restart the Defender for Identity sensor, because it uses the same NPCAP drivers.

- Beginning with version 2.176, when installing the sensor from a new package, the sensor's version under **Add/Remove Programs** will appear with the full version number (for example, 2.176.x.y), as opposed to the static 2.0.0.0 that was previously shown. It will continue to show that version (the one installed through the package) even though the version will be updated through the automatic updates from the Defender for Identity cloud services. The real version can be seen in the sensor settings page in the portal, in the executable path or in the file version.

Group Managed Service Account (gMSA) Requirements

You can create a gMSA only if the forest schema has been updated to Windows Server 2012, the master root key for Active Directory has been deployed, and there is at least one Windows Server 2012 DC in the domain in which the gMSA will be created.

Membership in **Domain Admins** or the ability to create msDS-GroupManagedServiceAccount objects, is the minimum required to complete the following procedures.

KDS Root Key

The KDS Root Key is used to securely retrieve the account password for the gMSA.

To check if you already have a KDS root key, follow these steps:

1. Launch **Active Directory Sites and Services.**
2. In the toolbar, select **View** and enable **Show Services Node**.
3. Expand **Services**, then **Group Key Distribution Service**, then **Master Root Keys**.
4. If you have a KDS root key listed here, you can skip to the next section.

Note(s):

- You can verify that the key has been created by going back to Active Directory Sites and Services and refreshing the Master Root Keys window.
- This key, even though you specified the **effectiveimmediately** parameter, cannot actually be used for 10 hours. This is a built-in safeguard to make sure that the key is replicated to all domain controllers before use.
- If you need a KDS Root Key immediately, use:

```
Add-kdsRootKey -EffectiveTime ((get-date).AddHours(-10))
```

Creating a DSA for use with Defender for Identity – 2 Approaches

There are couple of different ways to peel this potato, depending on your domain infrastructure. There are essentially 3 parts to creating a gMSA to use as the DSA for MDI:

1. **Create gMSA**
2. **Grant Permissions**
3. **Define Principals**

The following PowerShell script is designed to facilitate simple deployments (a handful of DCs on a single domain) by creating a Group Managed Service Account **(gMSA)** and granting it the necessary read privileges for use as a **Directory Service Account (DSA)** in Microsoft Defender for Identity. This script applies to the **default domain controllers OU** and is particularly useful for automating the setup of a gMSA for use as a DSA for smaller MDI deployments:

```
# Description: This script is helpful for simple deployments on a
single domain. It creates a gMSA and grants it the required read
privileges for use as a DSA in Defender for Identity

# Step 1: Prompt the user for the domain and a name for the DSA
that will be created in step 3.

# Validate that the domain and gMSA account name are provided and
meet the naming conventions.
$domain = Read-Host -Prompt "Please enter the domain"
$gmsaAccountName = Read-Host -Prompt "Please enter the gMSA ac-
count name"

# Step 2: Set HostsGroup to Default Domain Controllers OU (this
way, this automatically applies to newly added DCs and reduces
overhead)
$gMSA_HostsGroup = Get-ADGroup -Identity 'Domain Controllers'

# Step 3: Create new gMSA using Read-Host input from above
statements:
New-ADServiceAccount -Name "$gmsaAccountName" -DNSHostName
"$gmsaAccountName.$domain" -PrincipalsAllowedToRetrieveManaged-
Password $gMSA_HostsGroup

# Step 4: Grab distinguished name for Deleted Objects
$distinguishedName = ([adsi]'').distinguishedName.Value
$deletedObjectsDN = "CN=Deleted Objects,$distinguishedName"

# Step 5: Make current user the Owner of Deleted Objects
(required for next step)
dsacls.exe "$deletedObjectsDN" /takeOwnership
```

```
# Step 6: Assign read permissions for Deleted Objects to DSA
account
# This requires current user account to have ownership
(see previous command)
dsacls "$deletedObjectsDN" /G "$domain\$(gmsaAccountName):LCRP"

# Note: dsacls.exe can be finicky, if it fails to pass the
DSA_AccountName as a variable, re-run the last step with
your details hardcoded, for example:
dsacls 'CN=Deleted Objects,DC=contoso,DC=net' /g 'contoso.
net\svc-MDI$:

Source: https://github.com/EEN421/Defender-for-Identity/blob/
Main/Create%20DSA%20-%20Simple.ps1
```

The next script is designed to facilitate custom MDI setups for advanced, multi-domain environments.

- It allows the user to specify a HostGroup and the domain controllers with the MDI sensor installed.
- Prompts the user for the domain, a name for the group of domain controllers, and a name for the Group Managed Service Account (gMSA).
- Prompts the user for the principals (these should be the domain controllers with the MDI sensor installed) allowed to retrieve the password/use the gMSA on behalf of MDI.
- After importing the required Active Directory module, the script creates a new group, adds the specified members to it, and then creates a new gMSA associated with it.

This is particularly useful for automating the setup of Directory Service Accounts (DSAs) in MDI deployments across multiple domains:

```
# Description: This script facilitates a custom setup for more
advanced, multi-domain environments by allowing the user specify
a HostGroup and DC's with the MDI sensor installed.

# Note: In a multi-domain environment, it's best practice to
leverage separate gMSA's per domain to act as DSA's for MDI.

# Step 1: Prompt the user for the domain and a name for the DSA
that will be created in step 4:
$domain = Read-Host -Prompt "Please enter the domain"
$DSA_HostsGroupName = Read-Host -Prompt "Please enter a name for
your group of DC's"
$DSA_AccountName = Read-Host -Prompt "Please enter a name for
your gMSA account"
```

```
# Step 2: Prompt the user for the principals allowed to retrieve
the password (principals will be your domain controllers with the
MDI sensor installed):
$principals = Read-Host -Prompt "Please enter the principals
(separated by a comma)"
$principalsArray = $principals -split ',' | ForEach-Object {
$_.Trim() }

# Step 3: Import the required PowerShell module:
Import-Module ActiveDirectory

# Step 4: Create the group and add the members
$DSA_HostsGroup = New-ADGroup -Name $DSA_HostsGroupName
-GroupScope Global -PassThru
$principalsArray | ForEach-Object { Get-ADComputer -Identity $_ }
|
    ForEach-Object { Add-ADGroupMember -Identity $DSA_HostsGroup-
Name -Members $_ }

# Step 5: Create the gMSA and associate it with the group:
New-ADServiceAccount -Name $DSA_AccountName -DNSHostName "$DSA_
AccountName.$domain" -PrincipalsAllowedToRetrieveManagedPassword
$DSA_HostsGroup

# Step 6: Grab distinguished name for Deleted Objects
$distinguishedName = ([adsi]'').distinguishedName.Value
$deletedObjectsDN = "CN=Deleted Objects,$distinguishedName"
# Step 7: Make current user the Owner of Deleted Objects
(required for next step)
dsacls.exe "$deletedObjectsDN" /takeOwnership

# Step 8: Assign read permissions for Deleted Objects to DSA
account
# This requires current user account to have ownership
(see previous command)
dsacls "$deletedObjectsDN" /G "$domain\$(DSA_AccountName):LCRP"

# Note: dsacls.exe can be finicky, if it fails to pass the
DSA_AccountName as a variable, re-run the last step with
your details hardcoded, for example:
dsacls 'CN=Deleted Objects,DC=contoso,DC=net' /g 'contoso.
net\svc-MDI$:LCRP'

source: https://github.com/EEN421/Defender-for-Identity/blob/
Main/New%20DSA%20(Advanced).ps1
```

The second script is more scalable than the first one because it allows the user to specify a HostGroup as well as the domain controllers with the Microsoft Defender for Identity (MDI) sensor installed that go into it. *This flexibility makes it more adaptable to larger, more complex network, and multi-domain environments.*

In contrast, the first script is designed for simple deployments on a single domain. It sets the HostGroup to the default Domain Controllers Organizational Unit (OU), which automatically applies to newly added domain controllers for less maintenance/overhead. While this is efficient for a single domain, it may not scale well for multi-domain environments.

Logon As a Service

Automating this part and appending it to either of the above scripts to create a DSA proved problematic, so one can typically just go the old-fashioned way and configure this next part with a group policy object that applies to one's domain controllers *after* running one of the previous DSA creation scripts:

1. Open the Group Policy Management Editor and go to the **`Computer Configuration`** -> **`Policies -> Windows Settings`** -> **`Security Settings`** -> **`Local Policies`** -> **`User Rights Assignment`** -> **`Log on as a service policy`**, and add your DSA account, illustrated in the following screenshot:

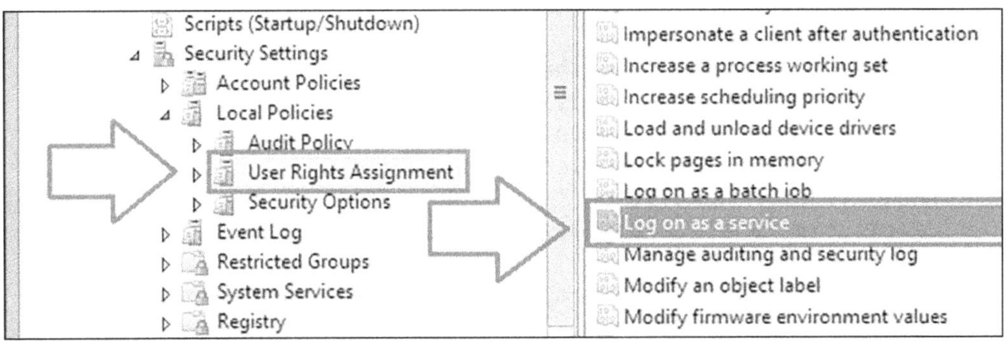

Figure 3.8: *Logon As a Service Permission*

When granting your gMSA account **Logon As a Service** permissions, you won't always be able to find your gMSA from the search box without taking the steps illustrated in the next two screenshots:

2. Select **`Object Types`**.

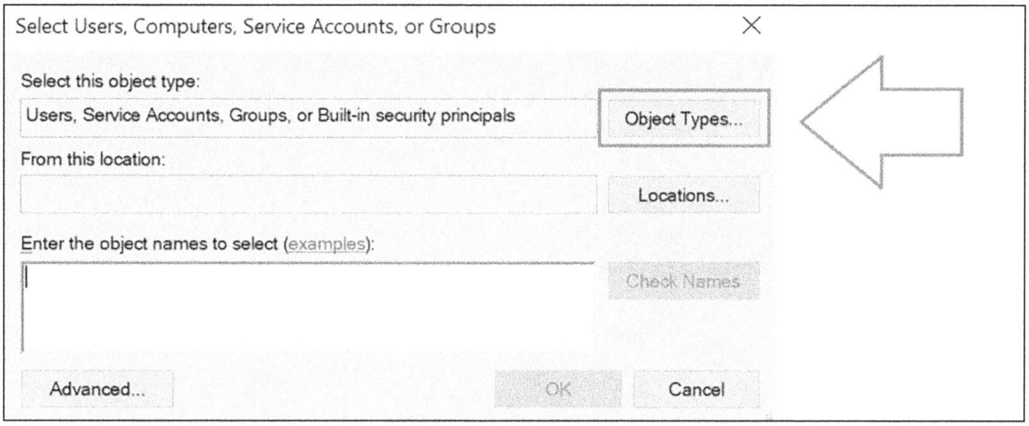

Figure 3.9: *Object Types*

3. Make sure the **`Service Accounts`** box is checked:

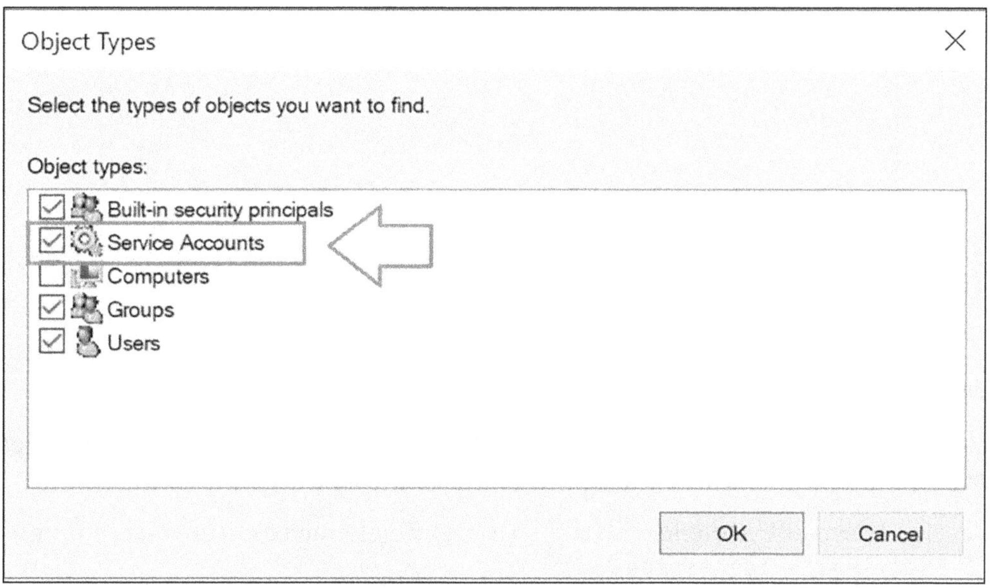

Figure 3.10: *Service Accounts*

4. Now your gMSA will show up in the search box, and you can grant **`Logon As a Service`**:

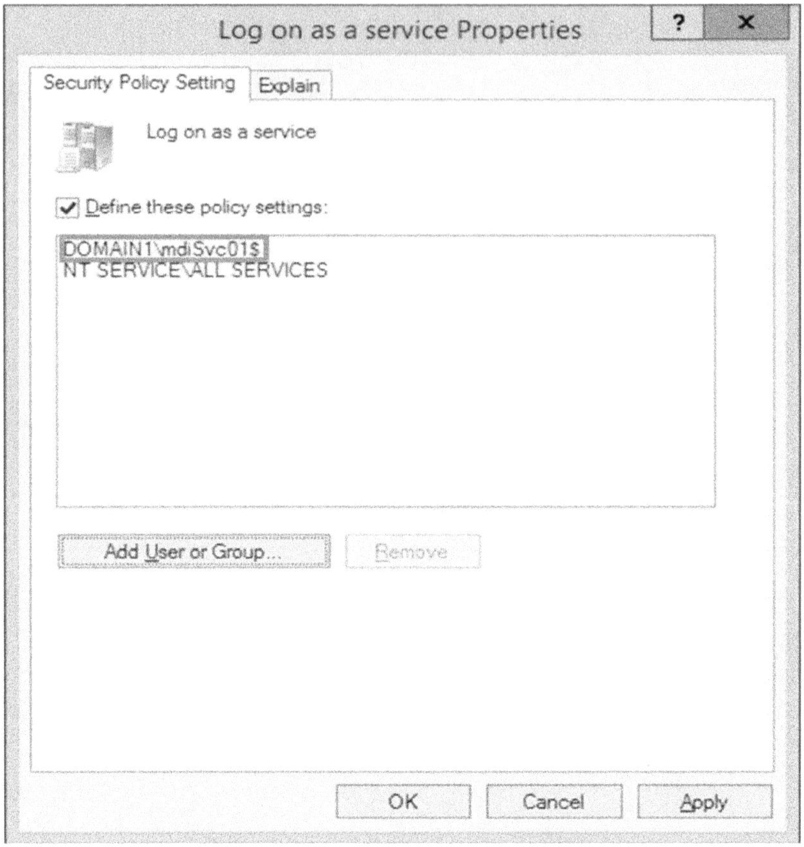

***Figure 3.11**: Apply Logon as a Service to gMSA*

Register your DSA in MDI Portal (Now part of the Defender XDR Portal)

To connect your sensors with your Active Directory domains, you'll **need to configure Directory Service accounts in Microsoft Defender XDR.**

1. In Microsoft Defender XDR (https://login.microsoftonline.com), go to **`Settings > Identities`**
2. Select **`Directory Service accounts`**
3. Select **`+Add credentials`** and enter the **`Account name`** and **`Domain`**, then check the **`Group Managed Service Account`** box, illustrated as follows:

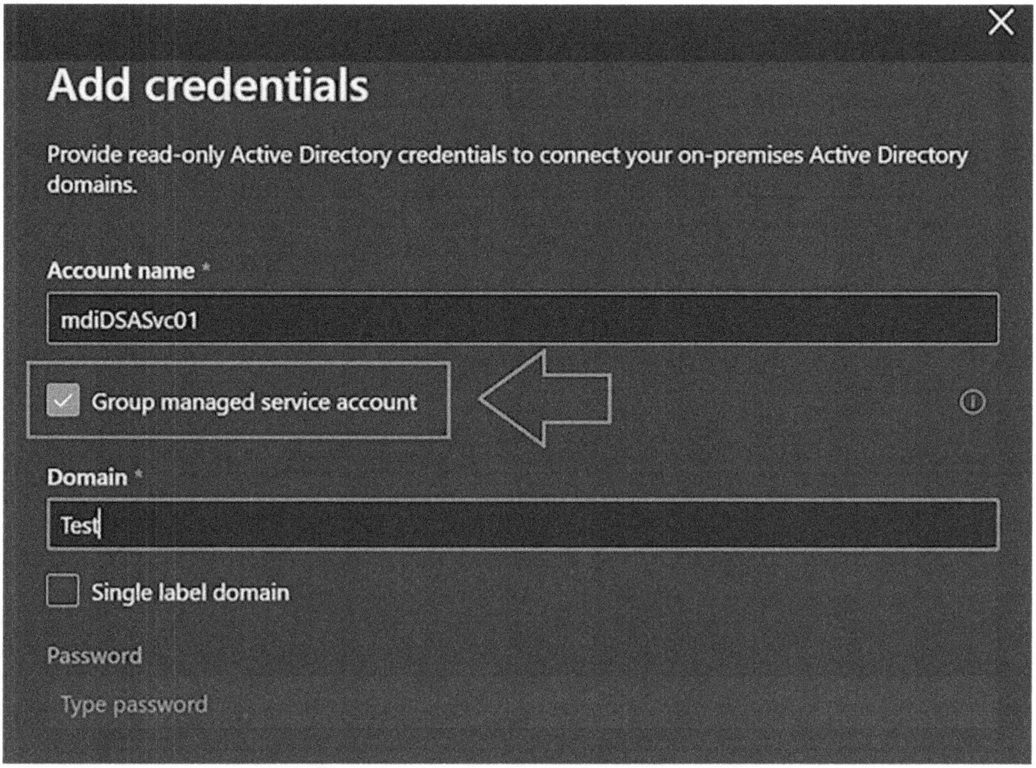

Figure 3.12: *Add Credentials in MDI Portal*

Creating an Action Account for use with Defender for Identity

Creating a Group Managed Service Account (gMSA) for use as an Action Account in Microsoft Defender for Identity involves several steps. Here is a detailed guide:

1. **Prerequisites**

   Ensure you have the necessary permissions to create and manage gMSA accounts. You will need administrative privileges on the domain controller.

2. **Create the gMSA Account**

   Use PowerShell to create the gMSA account. Follow these steps:

   a. **Open PowerShell as an Administrator**: Right-click the PowerShell icon and select `Run as Administrator`.

   b. **Generate a Root Key for immediate use (if not already done)**: This is important to know: even though you specified the effectiveimmediately parameter, it cannot actually be used for 10 hours. This is a built-in safeguard to make sure that the key is replicated to all domain controllers before use. If you need a KDS Root Key immediately, use the following

Powershell command (note that this does not need to be done twice, so if you have already taken this step previously while creating the DSA account using the above instructions, then you can skip this step and move to step 3):

```
Add-kdsRootKey -EffectiveTime ((get-date).AddHours(-10))
```

c. **Create a Security Group for the gMSA**: This group will have permissions to retrieve the gMSA password. This can be your default Domain Controllers group so that new DC's will automatically inherit this privilege, reducing overhead, or specific OU's depending on the complexity of the environment (number of forests, and more):

```
New-ADGroup -Name "gMSA_Password_Retrievers" -SamAccountName
"gMSA_Password_Retrievers" -GroupScope Global -GroupCategory
Security
```

d. **Create the gMSA Account**: Replace gMSA_ActionAccount with your desired account name.

```
New-ADServiceAccount -Name "gMSA_ActionAccount" -DNSHostName
"yourdomain.com" -PrincipalsAllowedToRetrieveManagedPassword
"gMSA_Password_Retrievers"
```

e. **Install the gMSA on the Domain Controller**: This step ensures the domain controller can use the gMSA.

```
Install-ADServiceAccount -Identity "gMSA_ActionAccount"
```

Alternatively, you can automate this and apply directly to the DC's with the following script:

```
# Step 1: Prompt the user for the domain and a name for the DSA
that will be created in step 3.
# Validate that the domain and gMSA account name are provided and
meet the naming conventions.
$domain = Read-Host -Prompt "Please enter the domain"
$gmsaAccountName = Read-Host -Prompt "Please enter the gMSA
account name"

# Step 2: Set HostsGroup to Default Domain Controllers OU (this
way, this automatically applies to newly added DCs and reduces
overhead)
$gMSA_HostsGroup = Get-ADGroup -Identity 'Domain Controllers'

# Step 3: Create new gMSA using Read-Host input from above
statements:
New-ADServiceAccount -Name "$gmsaAccountName" -DNSHostName
"$gmsaAccountName.$domain" -PrincipalsAllowedToRetrieveManaged-
Password $gMSA_HostsGroup
```

`source: https://github.com/EEN421/Defender-for-Identity/blob/Main/Create%20gMSA%20Action%20Account.ps1`

3. **Assign Permissions to the gMSA Account**

   Grant the necessary permissions to the gMSA account to perform actions such as resetting passwords and disabling accounts.

   1. **Open Active Directory Users and Computers**: Navigate to the relevant domain or Organizational Unit (OU).
   2. **Set Permissions**:
      a. Right-click the domain or OU and select **`Properties`**.
      b. Go to the **`Security`** tab and click **`Advanced`**.
      c. Click **`Add`** and then **`Select a principal`**.
      d. Ensure **`Service accounts`** is checked in **`Object types`**.
      e. Enter the name of the gMSA account (for example, gMSA_ActionAccount) and click **`OK`**.
      f. In the **`Applies to`** field, select **`Descendant User objects`**.
      g. Add the following permissions to allow the account to take action:
         i. **Reset password**: Allow
         ii. **Read pwdLastSet**: Allow
         iii. **Write pwdLastSet**: Allow
         iv. **Read userAccountControl**: Allow
         v. **Write userAccountControl**: Allow
      h. While it would be much easier to simply assign the equivalent of **`Write.ALL`**, this would be considered an unnecessary attack surface should the account become compromised. To adhere to the principles of Least Privilege and Zero Trust Network Architecture (ZTNA), we must "assume breach" and configure our accounts as such to limit the blast-radius if the worst were to happen. With these privileges, the Action account can only reset passwords and disable user accounts. Conversely, the DSA only has read privileges.

4. **Assign Log on as a Service Right**

   This is just like what we did for the DSA account earlier. Ensure the gMSA account has the **Log on as a service** right on each domain controller running the Defender for Identity sensor. This setting should replicate to other DC's depending on your DC Sync/Replication config.

   a. **Open Local Security Policy**: Navigate to `Security Settings` > `Local Policies` > `User Rights Assignment`.

   b. **Add the gMSA Account**: Find `Log on as a service` and add the gMSA account.

5. **Configure Defender for Identity to Use the gMSA**

   Add the gMSA account in the Microsoft Defender portal.

   a. **Go to the Microsoft Defender Portal**: Navigate to `Settings` > `Identities` > `Microsoft Defender for Identity` > `Manage action accounts`.

   b. **Create New Account**:

      i. Click `+Create new account`.

      ii. Enter the account name and domain, then select `Save`.

Important Insights to Note

- **Separation of Accounts**: Avoid using the same gMSA for both the Directory Service Account (DSA) and the Action Account to minimize security risks.
- **Security Best Practices**: Ensure the gMSA account is not used on servers other than domain controllers to prevent potential password retrieval by attackers.
- **Multi-Forest Environments**: If you have multiple forests, ensure the gMSA account is trusted in all forests or create separate accounts for each forest.

By following these steps, you can create and configure both Directory Service Accounts (DSA) and Action Accounts for MDI via Group Managed Service Accounts for added security in Microsoft Defender for Identity, ensuring robust security and effective threat mitigation.

Advanced Auditing Policy Configuration

Not all DC's are configured for advanced auditing out of the box. For MDI to provide full coverage, we need to modify the Advanced Audit Policies of your domain controller using the following instructions:

1. Log in to the server as Domain Administrator.
2. Open the Group Policy Management Editor from `Server Manager > Tools > Group Policy Management.`
3. Expand the `Domain Controllers Organizational Units`, right-click `Default Domain Controllers Policy`, and then select `Edit`.

Note(s):

Use the Default Domain Controllers Policy or a dedicated Group Policy Object (GPO) to set these policies.

Using the Default Domain Controllers Policy reduces overhead when onboarding new DC's down the road, they are automatically joined to this group so you don't have to retrace these steps. You could also do this with a separate add-on policy in parallel with your Default Domain Controllers policy.

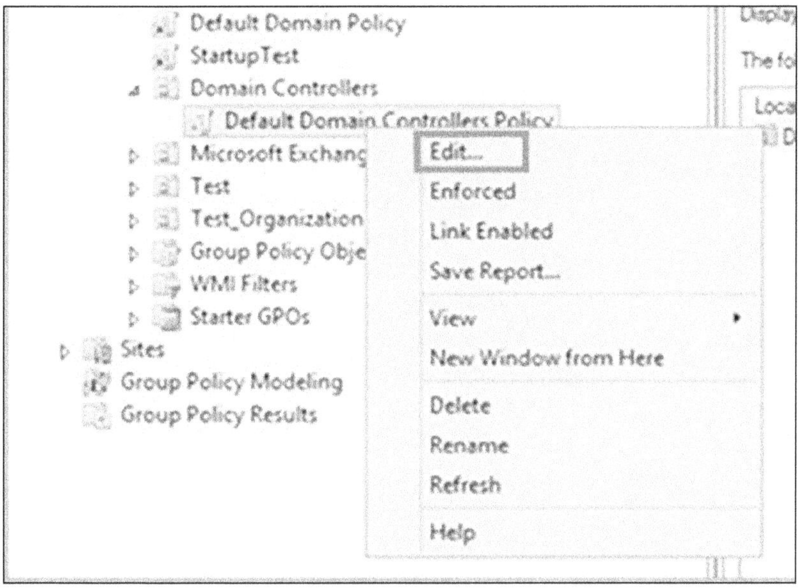

Figure 3.13: *Edit Default Domain Controllers Policy*

4. From the window that opens, **`Computer Configuration`** > **`Policies`** > **`Windows Settings`** > **`Security Settings`** and depending on the policy you want to enable, do the following:

   i. Go to **`Advanced Audit Policy Configuration`** > **`Audit Policies`**.

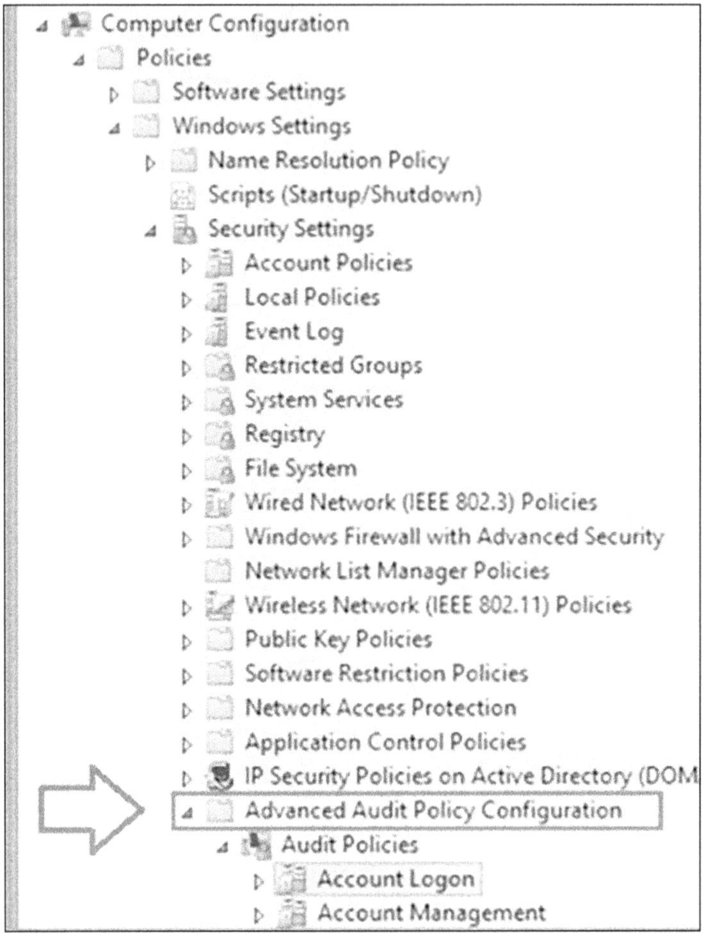

***Figure 3.14:** Advanced Audit Policy Configuration*

ii. Under **Audit Policies**, edit each of the following policies and select **Configure the following audit events for both Success and Failure events**. Audit Policies, Subcategories, and EventID Triggers are listed in the following table:

Audit policy	Subcategory	Triggers event IDs
Account Logon	Audit Credential Validation	4776
Account Management	Audit Computer Account Management	4741, 4743
Account Management	Audit Distribution Group Management	4753, 4763
Account Management	Audit Security Group Management	4728, 4729, 4730, 4732, 4733, 4756, 4757, 4758

Account Management	Audit User Account Management	4726
DS Access	Audit Directory Service Access	4662 - For this event, it is also necessary to Configure object auditing, discussed on the next page
DS Access	Audit Directory Service Changes	5136
System	Audit Security System Extension	7045

Table 3.1: *Audit Policies, Subcategories, and corresponding EventIDs*

All of the above should have both "Success" and "Failure" boxes checked, illustrated as follows:

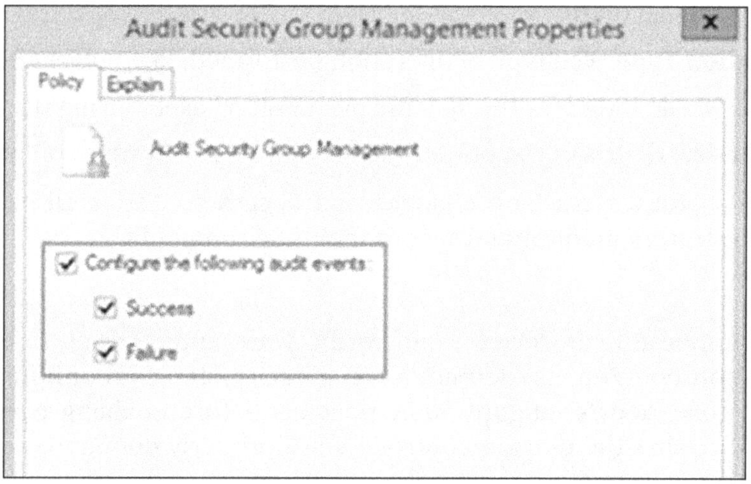

Figure 3.15: *Audit Success and Failure Events*

5. From an elevated command prompt, type **`gpupdate`**, then press *enter*. This forces the DC to update its Group Policies.

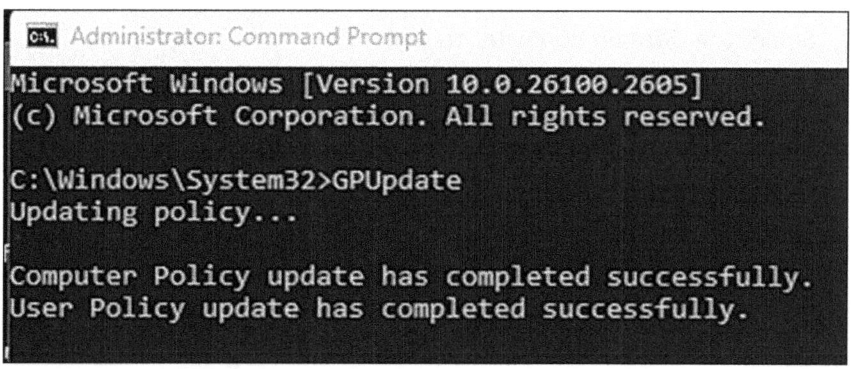

Figure 3.16: *GPUpdate from CMD Prompt*

6. After applying via GPO, the new events will be visible in the Event Viewer, under **`Windows Logs`** -> **`Security`**.

Configure Object Auditing

To collect 4662 events, it is necessary to configure object auditing on the user, group, and computer objects. This is not typically configured by default. Event ID 4662 is logged every time an operation is performed on an object within Active Directory. This event is part of the "Audit Directory Service Access" category and is generated when a user creates, modifies, or deletes objects in Active Directory.

Here are some key details about Event ID 4662:

- **Object Server**: Always "DS" (Directory Service).
- **Object Type**: The type of object being accessed, such as user, group, or organizational unit.
- **Operation Type**: The type of operation performed, like "Object Access".
- **Access Mask**: Indicates the specific permissions used during the operation.
- **Properties**: GUIDs of the properties on which each permission was exercised.

This event is useful for tracking changes and access to Active Directory objects, helping administrators monitor and secure their environments.

Note(s):

- It is important to review and verify your audit policies (https://learn.microsoft.com/en-us/defender-for-identity/deploy/configure-windows-event-collection#configure-audit-policies) before enabling event collection to ensure that the domain controllers are properly configured to record the necessary events.
- If configured properly, this auditing should have minimal effect on server performance.

    1. Go to the **`Active Directory Users and Computers`** console.
    2. Select the domain you want to audit.
    3. Select the **`View`** menu and select **`Advanced Features`**.
    4. Right-click the domain and select **`Properties.`**

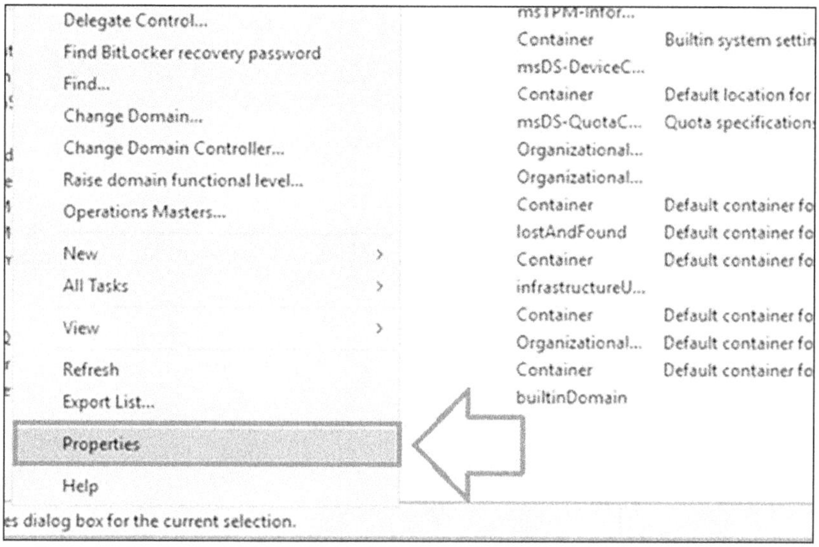

Figure 3.17: *Active Directory Users and Computers Domain*

5. Go to the **`Security`** tab, select **`Advanced`**.

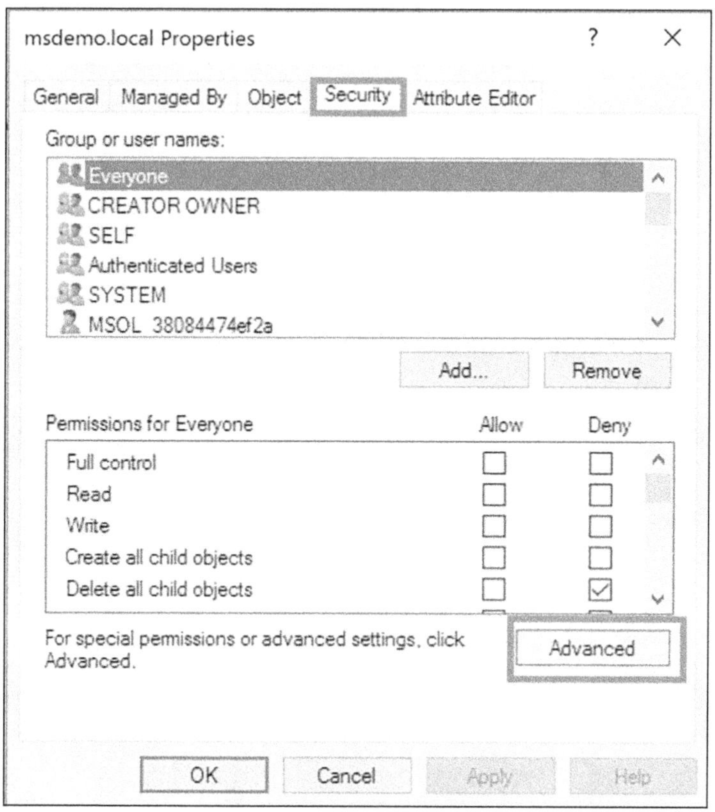

Figure 3.18: *Advanced Button Under Security Tab*

6. In **`Advanced Security Settings`**, choose the **`Auditing`** tab and select **`Add`**:

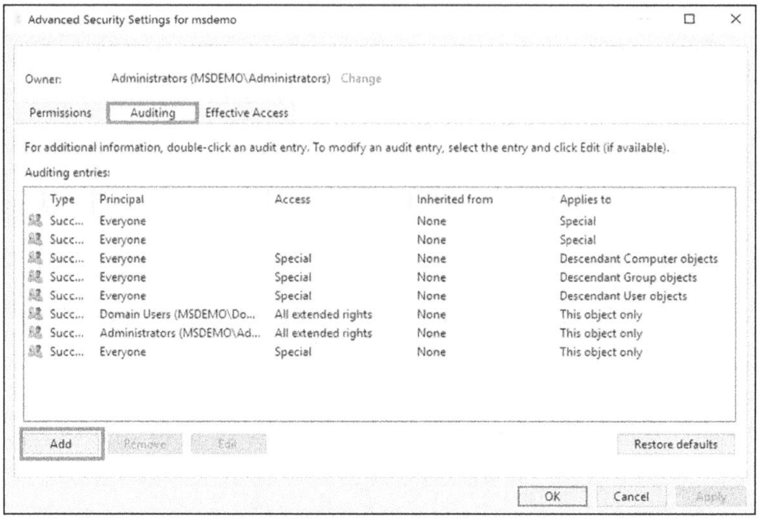

Figure 3.19: *Add Auditing Permissions*

7. Select a principal:

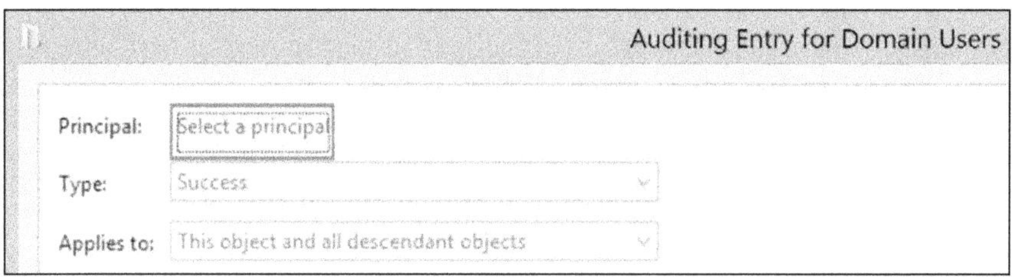

Figure 3.20: *Select a Principal*

8. Under **`Enter the object name to select`**, type **`Everyone.`** Then select Check Names, followed by **`OK`**.

Figure 3.21: *Select Check Names*

9. Make the following selections in Auditing Entry:

    a. For **`Type`**, select **`Success`**.

    b. For **`Applies to`** select **`Descendant User`** objects.

    c. Under **`Permissions`**, scroll down and select the **`Clear all button`** (illustrated in the next screenshot).

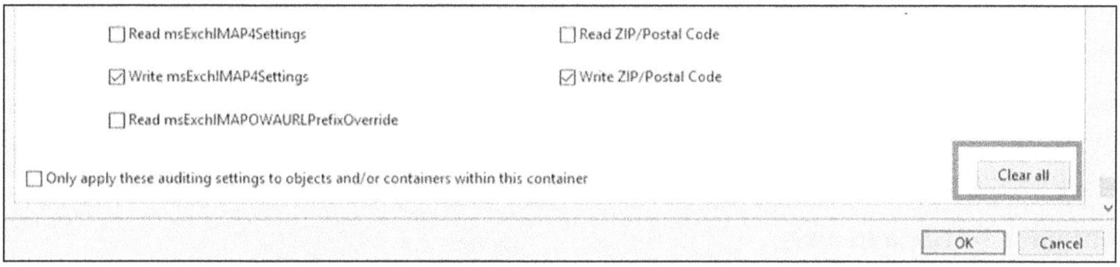

Figure 3.22: *Clear All Permissions*

    d. Then scroll back up and select **`Full Control`**. All the permissions will be selected. Then uncheck the **`List contents`**, **`Read all properties`**, and **`Read permissions`**. Select **`OK`**. This will set all the Properties settings to Write. Now when triggered, all relevant changes to directory services will appear as 4662 events.

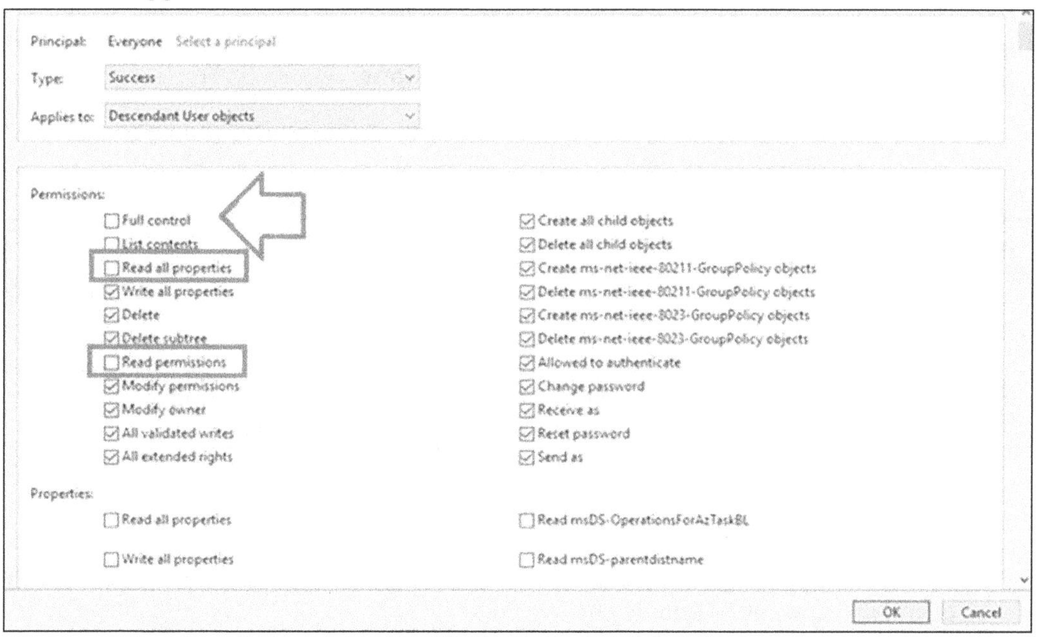

Figure 3.23: *Permissions Template*

10. Then repeat the steps above, but for **`Applies to`**, select the following object types:
    - Descendant Group Objects
    - Descendant Computer Objects
    - Descendant msDS-GroupManagedServiceAccount Objects
    - Descendant msDS-ManagedServiceAccount Objects

Note(s):

Assigning the auditing permissions on the 'All descendant objects' would work as well, but we only require the object types as detailed above to adhere to the principle of least privilege and ZTNA.

Configure NTLM auditing

This section describes the extra configuration steps needed to audit Event ID 8004.

- Domain group policies to collect Windows Event 8004 should **only** be applied to domain controllers.
- When Windows Event 8004 is parsed by Defender for Identity Sensor, Defender for Identity NTLM authentication activities are enriched with the server-accessed data.

1. Open **`Group Policy Management`** and go to the **`Default Domain Controllers Policy`** > **`Local Policies`** > **`Security Options`**.
2. Under **`Security Options`**, configure the specified security policies as follows:

Security policy setting	Value
Network security: Restrict NTLM: Outgoing NTLM traffic to remote servers	Audit all
Network security: Restrict NTLM: Audit NTLM authentication in this domain	Enable all
Network security: Restrict NTLM: Audit Incoming NTLM Traffic	Enable auditing for all accounts

***Table 3.2**: Security Policy Configuration Values*

Active Directory Federation Services (ADFS) Auditing

1. Go to the **`Active Directory Users`** and **`Computers console`**, and select the domain you want to enable the logs on.
2. Go to **`Program Data`** > **Microsoft** > **`ADFS`**:

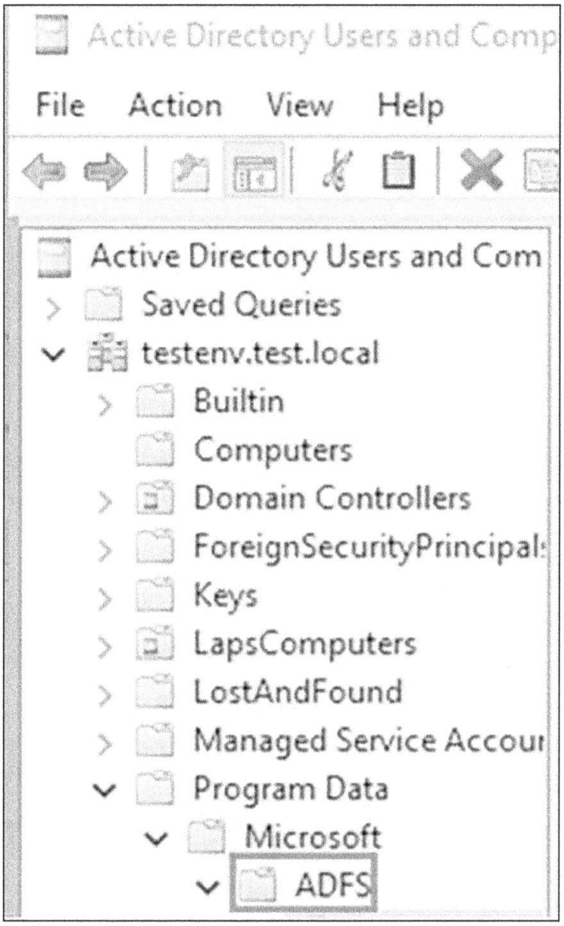

Figure 3.24: ADFS

3. Right-click **AD FS** and select **Properties**.
4. Go to the **Security** tab and select **Advanced** > **Advanced Security Settings** > **Auditing** tab > **Add** > **Select a principal**.
5. Under **Enter the object name to select**, enter **Everyone**.
6. Select **Check Names** > **OK**.
7. You'll then return to **Auditing Entry**. Make the following selections:
   - For **Type** select **All**.
   - For **Applies to** select **This object and all descendant objects**.
   - Under **Permissions**, scroll down and select **Clear all**. Scroll up and select **Read all properties and Write all properties**.

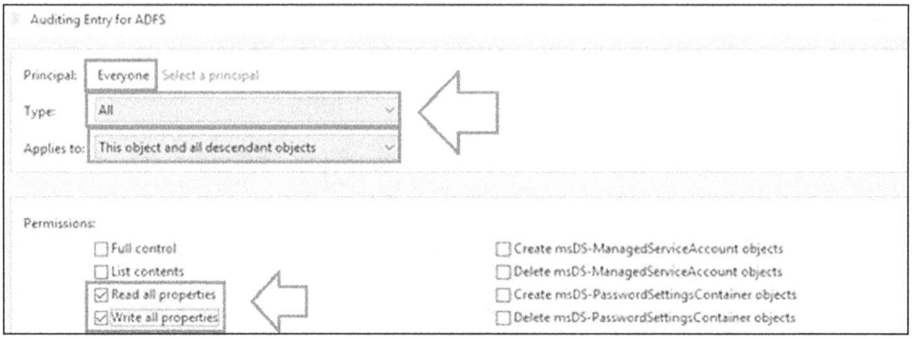

***Figure 3.25**: Auditing Permissions for ADFS*

Configure auditing on the certificate authority (CA)

If you're working with a dedicated server with Active Directory Certificate Services (AD CS) configured, make sure to configure auditing as follows to view dedicated alerts and Secure Score reports:

1. Create a group policy to apply to your AD CS server. Edit it and configure the following auditing settings:
    a. Go to and select:

       Computer Configuration\Policies\Windows Settings\Security Settings\Advanced Audit Policy Configuration\Audit Policies\Object Access\Audit Certification Services.

    b. Select to configure audit events for **Success** and **Failure**.

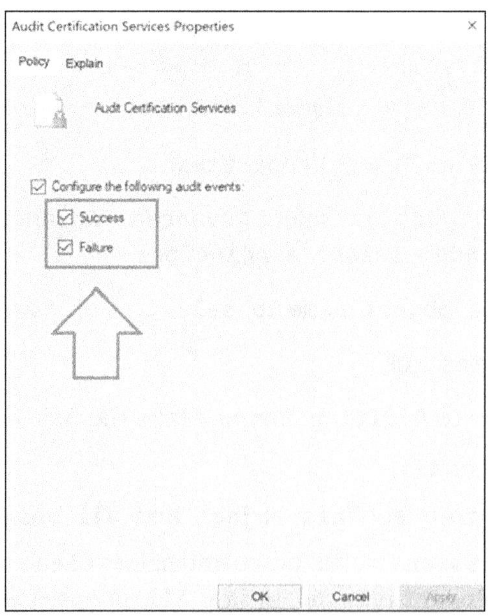

***Figure 3.26**: Audit Success and Failure*

To Configure CA auditing using the GUI:

1. Select **Start** -> **`Certification Authority`** (MMC Desktop application). Right-click your CA's name and select **`Properties`**.

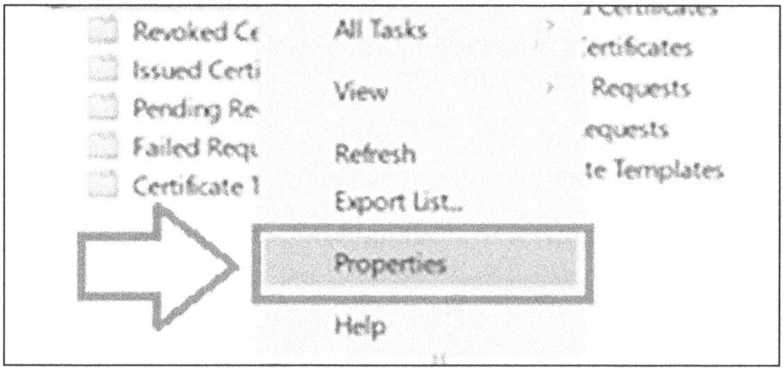

Figure 3.27: *CA Domain Properties*

2. Select the **Auditing** tab, select all the events you want to audit, and then select **`Apply`**.

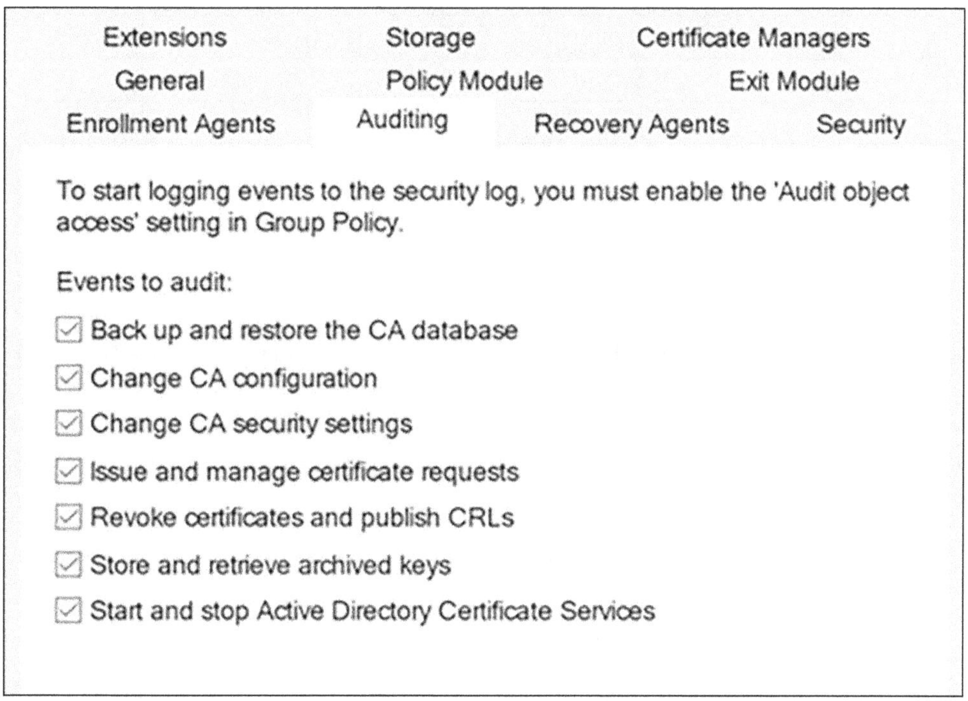

Figure 3.28: *CA Auditing Properties*

Configure Auditing on Configuration Container

1. Open ADSI Edit by selecting **Start** > **Run**. Enter **ADSIEdit.msc** and select **OK**.
2. On the **Action** menu, select **Connect to**.
3. In the **Connection Settings** dialog box, under **Select a well-known Naming Context**, select **Configuration** > **OK**.
4. Expand the Configuration container to show the Configuration node, beginning with **CN=Configuration,DC=...**
5. Right-click the Configuration node and select **Properties**.

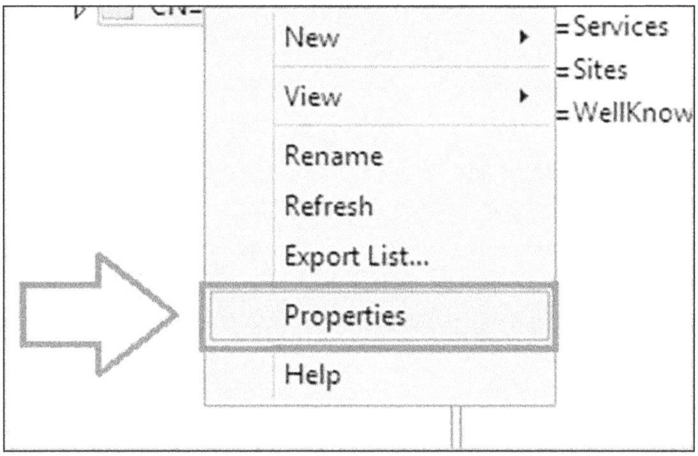

***Figure 3.29**: Configuration Container Properties*

a. Select the **Security** tab > **Advanced**.

b. In the **Advanced Security Settings**, select the **Auditing** tab > **Add**.

c. Click **Select a principal**.

d. Under **Enter the object name to select**, enter **Everyone** and select **Check Names** > **OK**.

e. You'll then return to **Auditing Entry**. Make the following selections:

- For **Type**, select **All**.
- For **Applies to**, select **This object and all descendant objects**.
- Under **Permissions**, scroll down and select **Clear all**. Scroll up and select **Write all properties**.

f. Select **Ok**.

Troubleshooting

If you have a Defender for Identity sensor on VMware virtual machines, you might receive the health alert Some network traffic is not being analyzed. This can happen because of a configuration mismatch in VMware. If you're getting this alert, take the following steps to resolve it:

1. On the Guest OS, set the following to **Disabled** in the virtual machine›s NIC configuration: **`IPv4 TSO Offload`**.

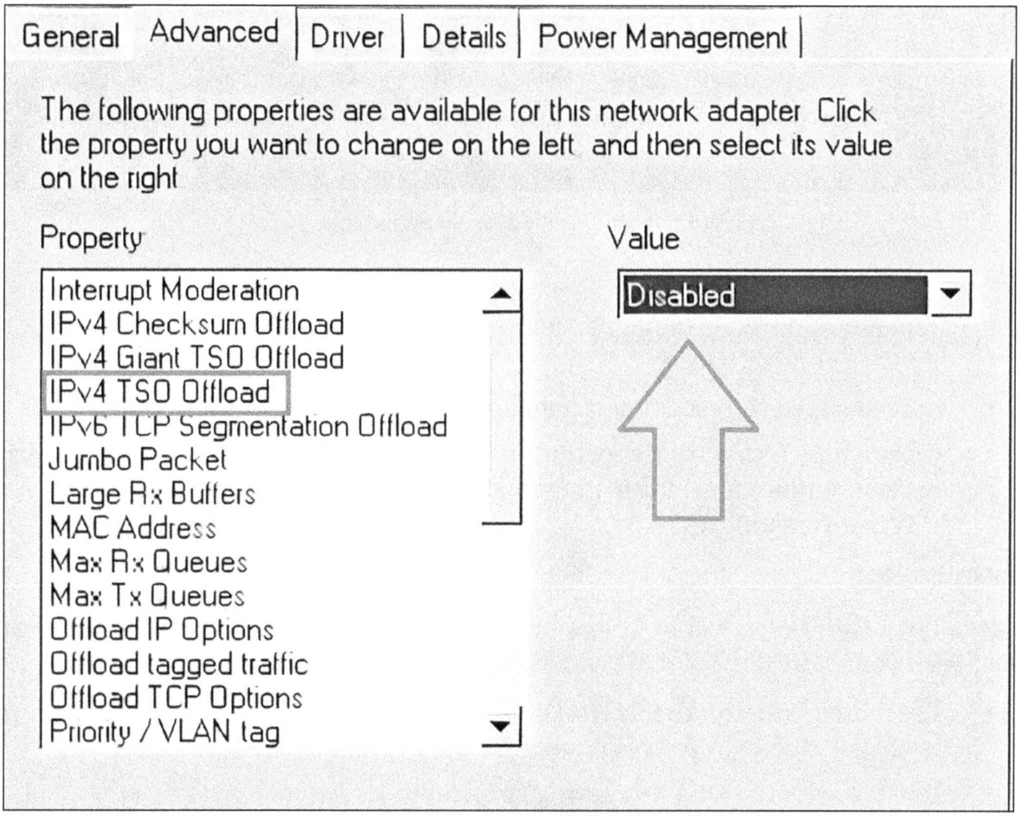

Figure 3.30: *IPv4 TSO Offload*

2. Use the following **`PowerShell cmdlet`** to determine whether Large Send Offload (LSO) is enabled:

```
Get-NetAdapterAdvancedProperty | Where-Object DisplayName -Match
"^Large*"
```

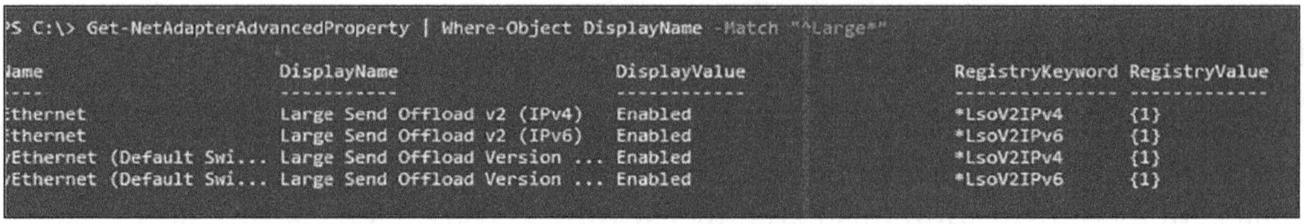

Figure 3.31: *Get-NetAdapterAdvancedProperty*

3. If LSO is enabled, use the following powershell command to disable it:

   `Disable-NetAdapterLso -Name {name of adapter}`

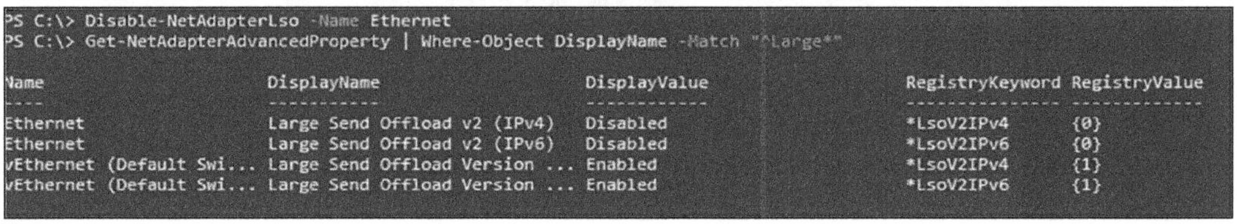

Figure 3.32: *Disabled Large Send Offload*

Note(s):

- Depending on your configuration, these actions might cause a brief loss of network connectivity.
- You may need to restart your machine for these changes to take effect.
- These steps may vary depending on your VMWare version. Check VMWare documentation for information about how to disable LSO/TSO for your VMWare version.

Known Issues:

9 times out of 10, there will be a helpful Sensor Health Alert corresponding to any issues with your MDI setup and it is an easy fix:

- A resource issue on the DC (MDI shuts itself down on the DC when resource usage gets too high to avoid tanking a DC in production)
- An issue with the **DSA** not having sufficient privileges to read what it needs
- Some DC's were not correctly added as Principals Allowed to Retrieve the DSA's gMSA Password.

Other known issues and how to fix them are listed in the official Microsoft Documentation.

Pro-Tip: *Something I often forget about, is the time it takes for the next Kerberos ticket to be issued after creating a new gMSA or adding a DC to the Hostgroup of* ***Principals Allowed to Retrieve the gMSA Password****. The issue is that the gMSA won't immediately* *work because the DC's are waiting on the next ticket which could be hours away. You can fix and request a new ticket with this with the following command:*

```
klist -li 0x3e7 purge
```

Lesser-Known Issues:

If something's wrong (sensor won't start, for example) and there are no helpful Sensor Health Alerts in the MDI/XDR portal, then the *next place to look is in the MDI logs on the DCs themselves*. The Defender for Identity logs are located in a subfolder called Logs where Defender for Identity is installed; the default location is: C:*Program Files**Azure Advanced Threat Protection Sensor**version number*\\Logs

You will want to examine all of the log files, not just the ones with "error" in the title for the bigger picture to make sense. Here is an example:

Sensor Won't Start, no Active Health Alerts; a recently deployed MDI with a gMSA as the DSA was acting like it was stuck in a boot loop before eventually timing out; it kept bouncing between starting and stopped.

Because there were no Sensor Health Alerts, the MDI logs on one of the DCs revealed the following clues from the log files:

Microsoft.Tri.Sensor.Errors.log:

```
2024-04-15 21:28:12.4525 Error DirectoryServicesClient+<Create
LdapConnectionAsync>d__47 Microsoft.Tri.Infrastructure.Extended
Exception: CreateLdapConnectionAsync failed [DomainController
DnsName=DC.domain.local]

2024-04-15 21:28:12.4837 Error DirectoryServicesClient Microsoft.
Tri.Infrastructure.ExtendedException: Failed to communicate with
configured domain controllers [ _domainControllerConnectionDatas
=DC.domain.local]
```

The preceding log entries indicate an issue with the DSA gMSA account permissions, keeping it from creating the LDAP connection. It means the gMSA used as a DSA does not have **Logon As a Service** permissions required for Remote Impersonation, or the DC is not able to retrieve the gMSA password (normally there would be a health alert for that). We ruled these out with our DSA validator script. Nothing from the official Microsoft Documentation applied here, so we move on to the next log:

Microsoft.Tri.Sensor.log:

```
2024-04-16 11:05:36.3069 Info  RemoteImpersonationManager Get-
GroupManagedServiceAccountTokenAsync finished [UserName=mdiDSAS
vc01 Domain=Domain.local IsSuccess=True]

2024-04-16 11:05:36.3382 Info  DirectoryServicesClient Create
LdapConnectionAsync failed to connect [DomainControllerDnsName
```

```
=DC.Domain.local Domain=domain.local UserName=mdiDSASvc01 Result-
Code=82]
```

The preceding log entries confirm that the gMSA DSA actually does have Logon As a Service privileges and the DC was able to successfully complete Remote Impersonation so what could it be? Google told me ResultCode 82 was an issue with the gMSA account but that's all (Bing wasn't much better).

Solution: Adding the gMSA to Domain Users allowed the DSA to make the LDAP connection and start the sensor service on the DCs.

Confirming your DSA - Making sure the script worked

To test the functionality of a Group Managed Service Account (gMSA) to be used as a Directory Service Account (DSA) in Microsoft Defender for Identity (MDI), you can run the following script which installs and imports the **DefenderForIdentity module**, then prompts the user for the gMSA to test.

It checks whether the gMSA works on the current domain controller, returns a list of other principals or domain controllers that can use this gMSA, and tests the DSA identity with a ***-Detailed*** *switch.* **This script is particularly useful for troubleshooting and validating the setup of DSAs in MDI deployments:**

```
# Description: This script prompts for the gMSA used as the
Directory Service Account (DSA) for your domain in Defender for
Identity (MDI)

# Install & import DFI module:
Install-Module DefenderForIdentity
Import-Module DefenderForIdentity

# Print new line to console:
Write-Host "`n"

# Prompt for gMSA to test:
$identity = Read-Host -Prompt 'Please specify gMSA to test
against'

# Test on this DC:
Write-Host "`nDoes this gMSA work on this DC (true/false)?"
Test-ADServiceAccount -Identity $identity

# Return a list of other principals/DC's that can use this gMSA:
Write-Host "`nPrincipals allowed to retrieve the PW for this
gMSA?"
(Get-ADServiceAccount -Identity $identity -Properties *).Principals
AllowedToRetrieveManagedPassword
```

```
# Test DSA Identity with -Detailed switch:
Write-Host "`nThe following is applicable only to Directory
Service Accounts (DSA):"
Test-MDIDSA -Identity $identity -Detailed
```

Source: https://github.com/EEN421/Defender-for-Identity/blob/Main/DSA%20 Validator.ps1

Here is what a successful run looks like against a gMSA that is ready to rock and roll with all the required permissions to function as a DSA for MDI.

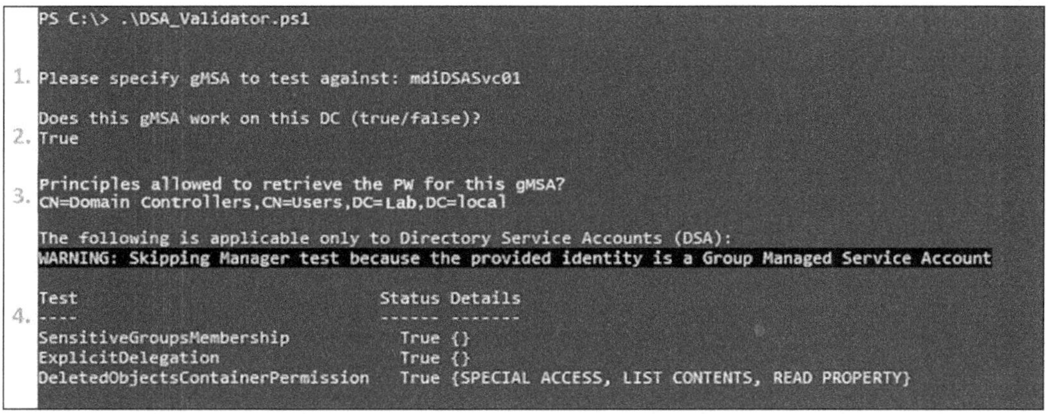

Figure 3.33: *DSA_Validator.ps1 Script Output*

1. First, the script prompts for the gMSA to validate.
2. Here you can see that, after prompting for the gMSA to verify, the DC we ran the script from is allowed to use the gMSA.
3. Next you can see which principals are allowed to use the gMSA. Note that this DC is a member of the default domain controller group listed as a principal allowed to use the gMSA.
4. Finally, it checks whether the gMSA has sufficient permissions to the objects it needs in your domain, such as Deleted Objects for example.

Note: If you see False for any of these or your hostgroup containing your DCs is not listed as a **`PrincipalAllowedToRetrieveManagedPassword`** as illustrated, then this gMSA is not ready to be used as a Directory Service Account (DSA) in the Defender for Identity portal.

Conclusion

Microsoft Defender for Identity (MDI) delivers critical visibility and response capabilities across hybrid identity infrastructures by correlating domain controller activity, behavioral analytics, and real-time threat detection. With its seamless integration into the Microsoft XDR ecosystem, MDI empowers security teams to proactively detect credential-based attacks and automate remediation actions with precision. By leveraging hardened deployment practices, advanced auditing, and gMSA-based service accounts, organizations can build a resilient identity defense posture aligned with Zero Trust principles. While identity remains a foundational pillar of security, the growing adoption of SaaS and third-party cloud applications introduces new risks beyond traditional boundaries. In the next chapter, we'll explore how Microsoft Defender for Cloud Apps extends your protection surface as a Cloud Access Security Broker (CASB), offering visibility into Shadow IT, governing cloud application usage, and enforcing policy-driven controls across your cloud footprint.

Helpful Links and References

- Hanley, I. (2024, April 18). *gMSA Based DSA Accounts for Defender for Identity*. Hanley.Cloud. https://www.hanley.cloud/2024-04-18-gMSA-based-DSA-Accounts-for-Defender-for-Identity/
- Hanley, I. (2024). *Create DSA - Simple.ps1*. GitHub. https://github.com/EEN421/Defender-for-Identity/blob/Main/Create%20DSA%20-%20Simple.ps1
- Hanley, I. (2024). *New DSA (Advanced).ps1*. GitHub. https://github.com/EEN421/Defender-for-Identity/blob/Main/New%20DSA%20(Advanced).ps1
- Hanley, I. (2024). *DSA Validator.ps1*. GitHub. https://github.com/EEN421/Defender-for-Identity/blob/Main/DSA%20Validator.ps1
- Microsoft. (n.d.). *What is Microsoft Defender for Identity?* Microsoft Learn. https://learn.microsoft.com/en-us/defender-for-identity/what-is
- Microsoft. (n.d.). *Deploy Microsoft Defender for Identity sensor*. Microsoft Learn. https://learn.microsoft.com/en-us/defender-for-identity/install-sensor
- Microsoft. (n.d.). *Manage action accounts*. Microsoft Learn. https://learn.microsoft.com/en-us/defender-for-identity/manage-action-accounts
- Microsoft. (n.d.). *Configure NTLM auditing for Defender for Identity*. Microsoft Learn. https://learn.microsoft.com/en-us/defender-for-identity/configure-windows-event-collection#configure-auditing
- Microsoft. (n.d.). *Defender for Identity health alerts*. Microsoft Learn. https://learn.microsoft.com/en-us/defender-for-identity/health-alerts
- Microsoft. (n.d.). *Troubleshooting known issues*. Microsoft Learn. https://learn.microsoft.com/en-us/defender-for-identity/troubleshooting-known-issues#sensor-failed-to-retrieve-group-managed-service-account-gmsa-credentials
- Microsoft. (n.d.). *Event ID 4662: An operation was performed on an object*. Microsoft Learn. https://learn.microsoft.com/en-us/previous-versions/

windows/it-pro/windows-10/security/threat-protection/auditing/event-4662

- Microsoft. (n.d.). *Configure object auditing using* ADSI *Edit*. Microsoft Learn. https://learn.microsoft.com/en-us/windows-server/security/audit/configure-object-auditing
- Microsoft. (n.d.). *Configure auditing for* AD CS. Microsoft Learn. https://learn.microsoft.com/en-us/windows-server/networking/technologies/ad-cs/ad-cs-auditing
- Microsoft. (n.d.). *Advanced security audit policy settings*. Microsoft Learn. https://learn.microsoft.com/en-us/windows/security/threat-protection/auditing/advanced-security-audit-policy-settings
- Windows Active Directory. (2024, February 3). *Microsoft Defender for Identity: A Comprehensive Overview*. https://www.windows-active-directory.com/microsoft-defender-for-identity-a-comprehensive-overview.html

CHAPTER 4
Defender for Cloud Apps

Introduction

Microsoft Defender for Cloud Apps (MDCA) is a security solution that helps organizations protect and manage their use of cloud applications. Acting as a Cloud Access Security Broker (CASB), MDCA provides visibility into cloud app usage, detects Shadow IT, and safeguards against app-based threats. It integrates with Microsoft's Extended Detection and Response (XDR) capabilities to offer advanced threat protection and continuous monitoring, ensuring that organizations can securely leverage cloud applications while maintaining compliance.

Structure

In this chapter, we will cover the following topics:

- Overview
- Importance of CASB
- Behind the Scenes of MDCA
- Deployment Deep Dive
  - Configure Endpoint Integration
  - Sanctioning Applications
  - Activity Policies
  - File Policies
  - Cloud Discovery Policies
  - Threat Protection Policies
  - Information Protection Policies
- Troubleshooting

Overview

Microsoft Defender for Cloud Apps (MDCA) is a cloud-native security solution designed to provide robust protection for cloud applications. It enables organizations to gain deep visibility, secure data, and control app access while addressing cloud-specific threats. By functioning as a Cloud Access Security Broker (CASB), MDCA offers visibility into cloud app usage, helps detect Shadow IT, and provides protection against app-based threats. The solution integrates with Microsoft's XDR capabilities, enabling the correlation of signals from across multiple attack vectors, which enhances overall security.

Key Features and Capabilities

- **Cloud Security Posture Management (CSPM)** Defender for Cloud Apps ensures continuous monitoring of cloud app configurations. It identifies misconfigurations, suggests remediation steps, and helps ensure cloud apps meet compliance standards. The solution enables organizations to assess security configurations, monitor permissions, and configure security settings based on best practices.
- **Shadow IT Discovery** Defender for Cloud Apps leverages network traffic analysis, firewalls, proxies, and Defender for Endpoint to detect and identify cloud apps used by employees, even those outside the organization's formal IT policies (Shadow IT). This capability identifies both sanctioned and unsanctioned apps, enabling security teams to assess risks and take appropriate action, such as blocking high-risk apps or monitoring behaviors.
- **Advanced Threat Protection** MDCA integrates machine learning and behavioral analytics to detect abnormal behaviors that could indicate compromised accounts or malicious activities. It correlates this data across endpoints, identities, and cloud applications to detect threats. This integration with Microsoft's XDR enhances its capabilities, providing deeper insight into cloud app vulnerabilities.
- **Information Protection** The platform's Data Loss Prevention (DLP) capabilities protect sensitive data across cloud apps by classifying and tagging data such as Personally Identifiable Information (PII), intellectual property, and financial records. MDCA uses predefined and custom classification labels to ensure critical information is safeguarded.
- **OAuth App Management** MDCA secures OAuth-enabled apps by managing permissions and privileges. It monitors the use of OAuth tokens, identifies apps requesting excessive permissions, and enables administrators to approve or revoke access to ensure that only trusted applications access critical data.

Importance of Modern CASB Solutions

Modern Cloud App Security Brokers (CASBs) are crucial for securing cloud environments by providing visibility, control, and protection over cloud app usage. As organizations increasingly adopt cloud services, CASBs help mitigate the risks of shadow IT, unauthorized data access, and compliance violations. They enforce policies for Data Loss Prevention (DLP), manage user access, and detect malicious activities through advanced threat analytics. Microsoft Defender for Cloud Apps stands out as a leading CASB solution, integrating seamlessly with Microsoft's broader security ecosystem, including Microsoft Defender for Endpoint and Defender XDR, to offer real-time monitoring, advanced threat protection, and automated response capabilities. This comprehensive approach helps organizations balance security with productivity, ensuring their cloud applications remain secure and compliant.

Behind the Scenes of Defender for Cloud Apps

Defender for Cloud Apps functions through a combination of data collection, advanced analytics, and seamless integrations with other Microsoft Defender solutions. It enables organizations to proactively protect their cloud environments while improving visibility and compliance.

Data Collection and Analysis

- **API Integrations with Cloud Providers:** Defender for Cloud Apps integrates with cloud platforms such as Microsoft 365, Salesforce, AWS, and Google Cloud, pulling telemetry data to monitor cloud app activities. This data helps detect unusual behaviors, configurations, or user actions, triggering alerts and enabling appropriate responses.
- **Network Traffic Analysis:** The solution also analyzes network traffic using Cloud Discovery to detect unsanctioned cloud apps accessed by employees, even those that may bypass traditional security controls. By monitoring this traffic, Defender for Cloud Apps identifies apps that are not formally sanctioned but may still pose a risk.
- **Behavioral Analytics:** MDCA uses machine learning and UEBA to analyze user behavior across cloud applications. It tracks actions such as login patterns, access to sensitive files, and changes in cloud settings. If abnormal patterns are detected, MDCA raises alerts to trigger automated investigations or manual responses by security teams.

Blocking and Controlling Unsanctioned Apps

- **Risk Assessment and Blocking:** MDCA evaluates each cloud app for risk based on over 90 indicators, such as compliance certifications, encryption, and privacy policies. Once an app is identified as risky or unsanctioned, administrators can create policies to block it or require Multi-Factor Authentication (MFA) for access. These policies can be enforced in real time through integration with Microsoft Entra Conditional Access.

- **DNS Blocking:** If an app is deemed unsanctioned, Defender for Cloud Apps can block access to the app at the DNS level. When a user attempts to access an unsanctioned app, the DNS request is intercepted and blocked, effectively preventing access. This policy can apply organization-wide or be customized for specific user groups.

Integration with Microsoft Defender XDR

MDCA integrates tightly with Microsoft Defender XDR, which enhances its threat detection and response capabilities. By correlating signals from multiple sources, including Defender for Endpoint, Defender for Identity, and Microsoft Sentinel, MDCA enables a unified security strategy.

- **Unified Threat Detection:** The integration allows MDCA to correlate data from cloud apps with endpoint, identity, and network information, giving security teams a comprehensive view of potential threats across the organization.
- **Automated Playbooks:** Defender for Cloud Apps integrates with Sentinel to enable automated incident response through pre-defined playbooks. These playbooks can automate actions such as blocking malicious cloud apps, isolating affected devices, or notifying security teams, significantly reducing response times.
- **Holistic Security Posture:** The combined capabilities of MDCA and Defender XDR provide a comprehensive security posture that spans endpoints, identities, and cloud applications, ensuring that all potential attack vectors are secured and monitored.

Real-Time Session Control and Enforcement

- **Conditional Access and Session Controls:** Defender for Cloud Apps leverages Microsoft Entra's Conditional Access to enforce real-time session controls. For example, if a risky session is detected, the solution can restrict certain actions like downloading sensitive files, while allowing the user to continue accessing the app for read-only purposes.
- **App-to-App Protection:** OAuth app management in Defender for Cloud Apps secures apps that interact with other applications. This is particularly critical for applications with extensive access to sensitive data, allowing administrators to revoke permissions and monitor token usage.

Sanctioning and Unsanctioning Apps

- **Unsanctioning an Application:** When an organization decides to unsanction an application, MDCA blocks access to it using DNS blocking. The policy can be created to apply to the entire organization or targeted user groups. MDCA notifies users who attempt to access the blocked app and provides a path for them to contact IT support if necessary.
- **Sanctioning an Application:** Conversely, when an organization decides to sanction an app, MDCA allows access by enabling DNS whitelisting. The solution ensures that only secure and compliant apps are accessible, with real-time monitoring to maintain visibility and control over sanctioned apps.

Conclusion

Microsoft Defender for Cloud Apps is an essential tool for managing and securing cloud environments. By providing visibility into cloud app usage, detecting unsanctioned applications, enforcing DLP policies, and integrating with Microsoft Defender XDR, it offers a comprehensive security solution for modern enterprises. With advanced capabilities such as behavioral analytics, session control, and OAuth app protection, MDCA ensures that organizations can securely embrace the cloud without sacrificing control or compliance.

Deployment Deep Dive

Step 1: Integrating MDCA with Microsoft Defender for Endpoint (MDE)

Start by ensuring you have **administrator** privileges to configure MDCA. The deployment process starts in the **Microsoft Security Portal**, where you will configure your cloud app environment.

1. In the **`Microsoft Security Portal`**, go to settings and locate **`Endpoints`**:

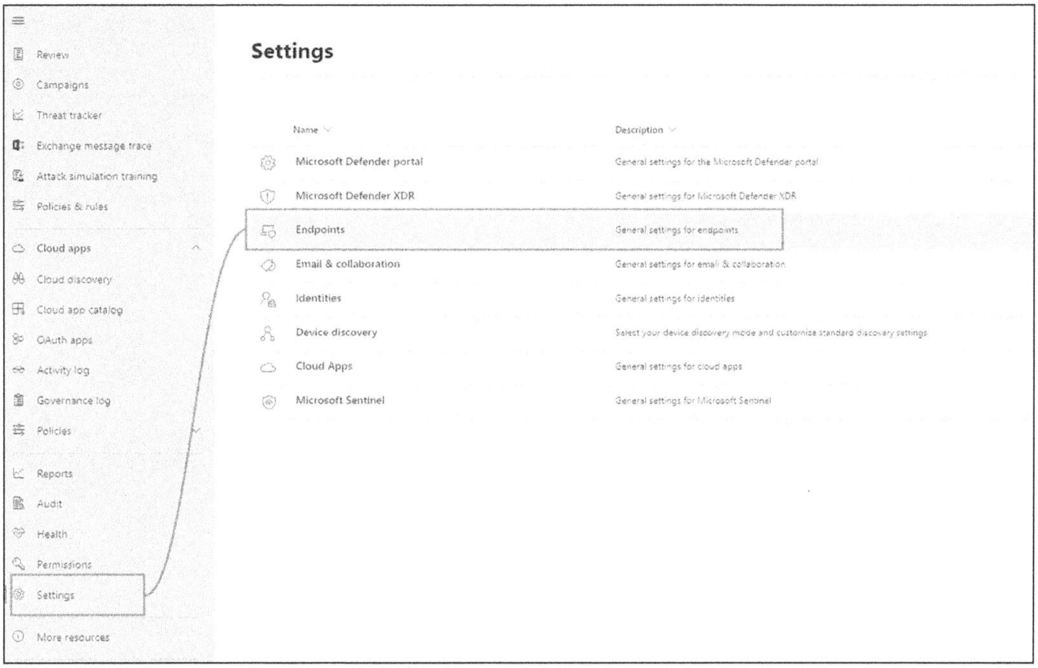

Figure 4.1: *Defender for Endpoint Settings*

2. Go to **General > Advanced Features**, then turn **On** the toggle for **Microsoft Defender for Cloud Apps**.

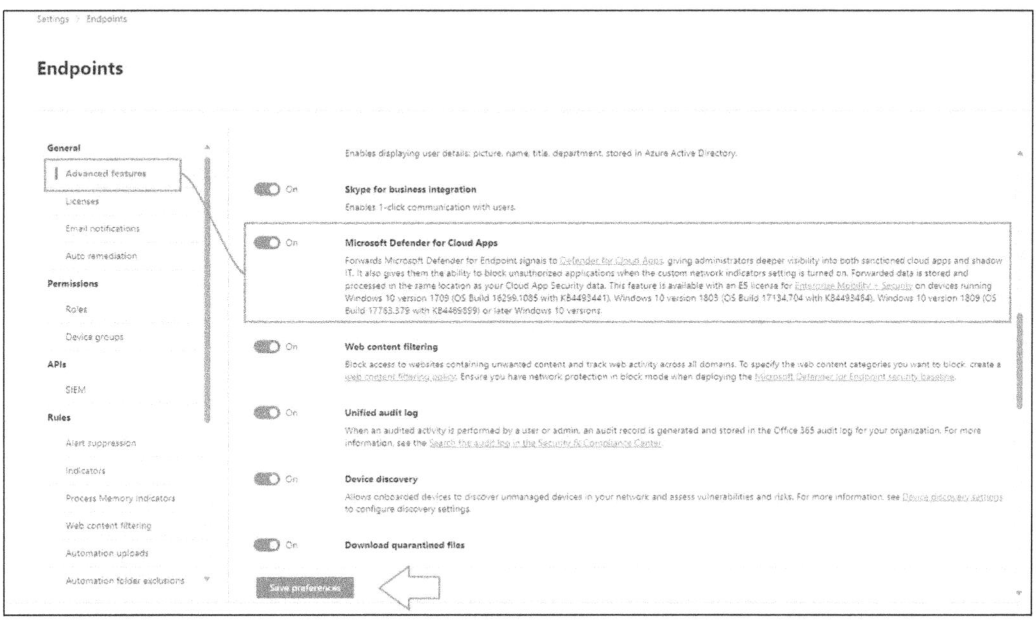

Figure 4.2: *Defender for Endpoint Advanced Settings*

3. Also located in **General > Advanced Features** is **Custom Network Indicators.** Toggle this to **On** as well.

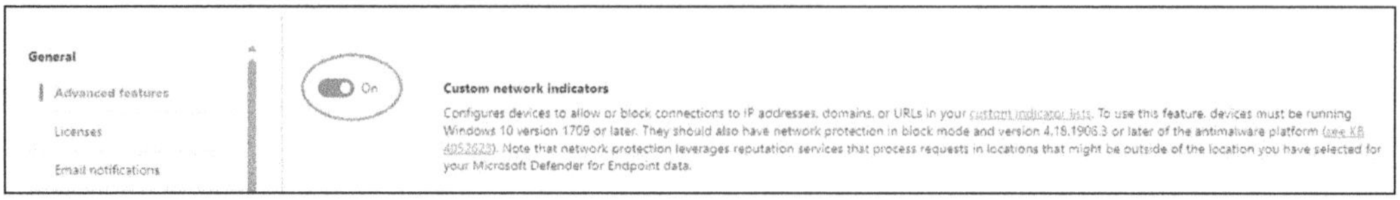

Figure 4.3: *Custom Network Indicators Toggle*

Step 2: Deploying Defender for Cloud Apps (MDCA)

1. Navigate to **`Cloud Apps`** under Microsoft Defender **`settings:`**

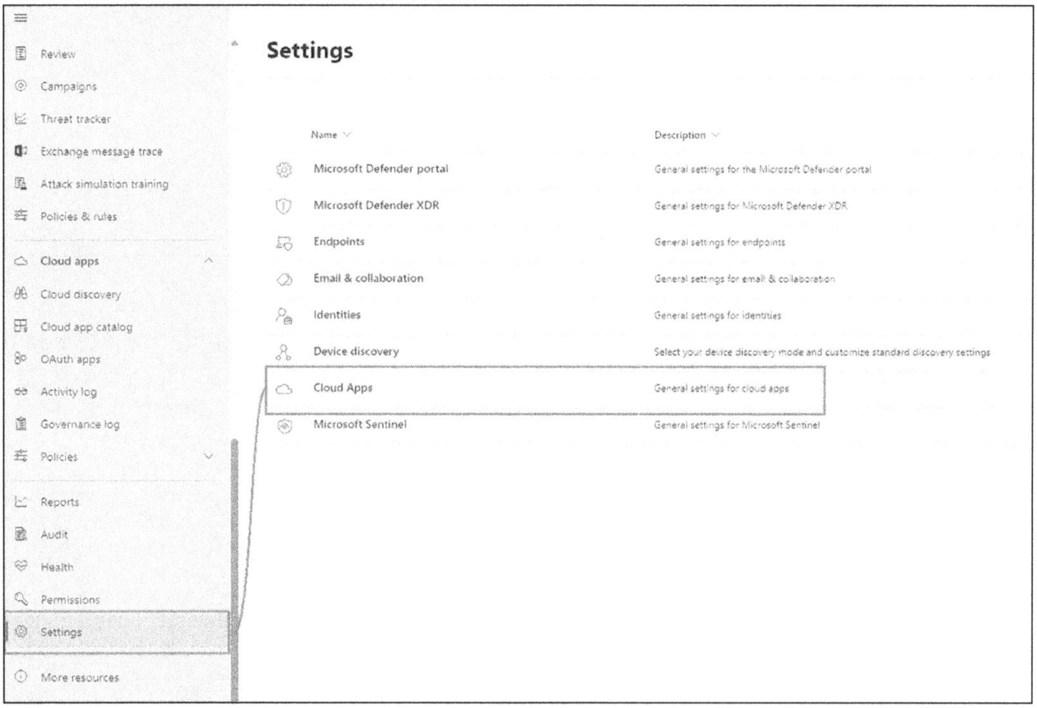

Figure 4.4: *Defender for Cloud Apps Settings*

2. Locate **`Microsoft Defender for Endpoint`** and enable it:

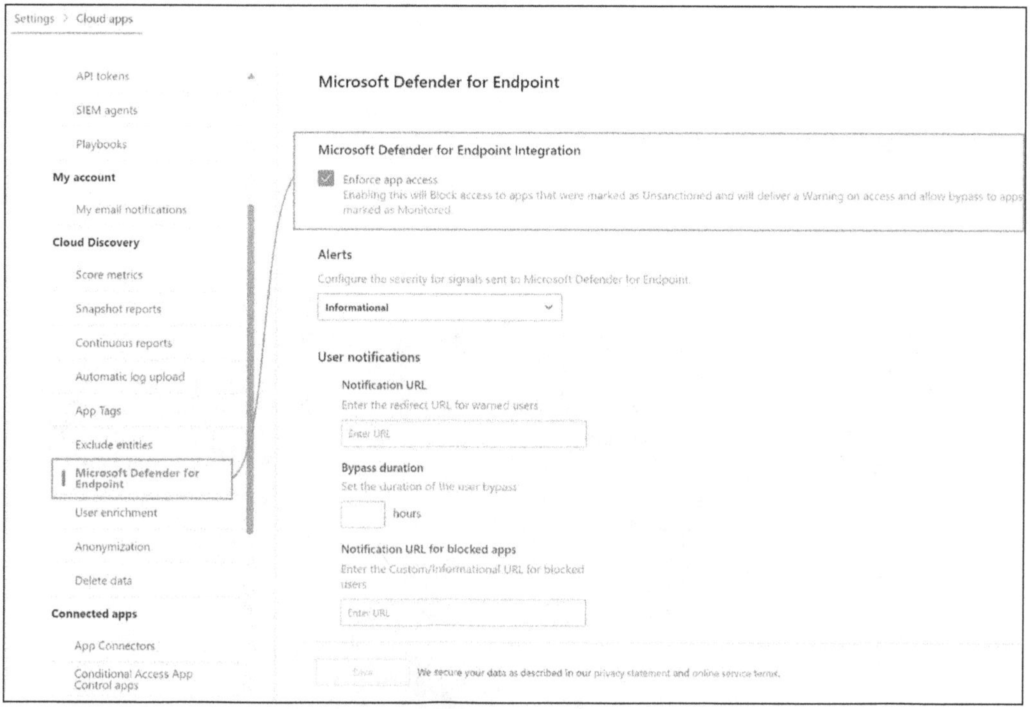

Figure 4.5: *Defender for Endpoint Integration*

Enabling this feature sends telemetry collected by Defender for Endpoint over to Defender for Cloud Apps. You can confirm by going back to **`the unified security portal > Settings> Cloud Apps >Automatic Log Upload`** and verifying the following entry populates (it can take a few hours for data to populate):

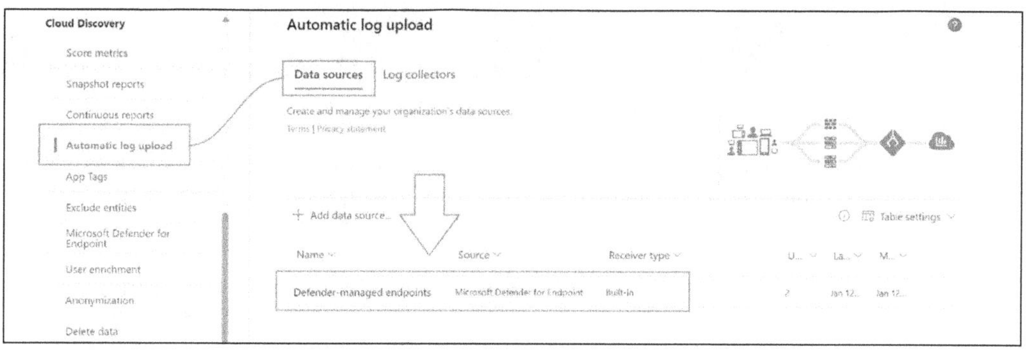

Figure 4.6: *Automatic Log Upload*

With the integration established, MDCA will now have the full visibility needed to track, monitor, and manage cloud application usage on endpoints.

Step 3: Investigating Cloud App Usage

With MDCA and MDE now fully integrated, you can start investigating which cloud applications are being accessed, how often, and how much bandwidth they consume.

1. In the **`Microsoft Defender for Cloud Apps`** dashboard, go to the **`Cloud Discovery blade.`**
2. Here, you can view app activity, including the amount of traffic each application is consuming:

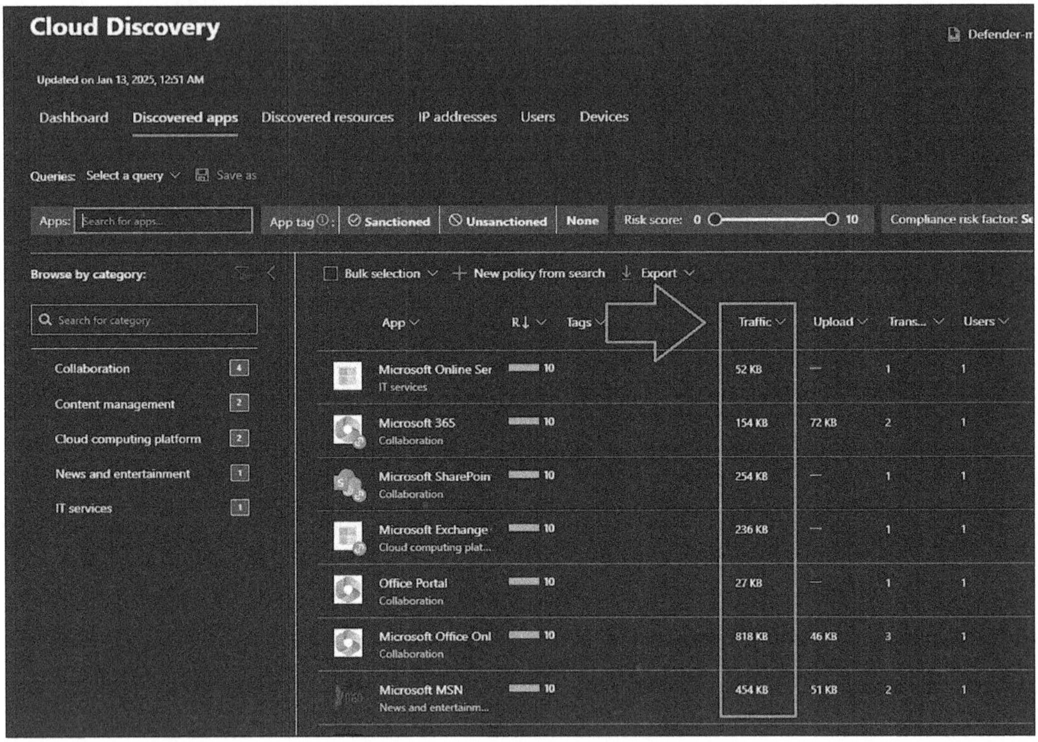

***Figure 4.7**: Cloud App Traffic*

3. Sort the apps by traffic usage, compliance, or other parameters relevant to your investigation. This will help identify any applications consuming excessive bandwidth or posing potential security risks.
4. Drill down into each application to view detailed usage reports and determine if they comply with your company's standards:

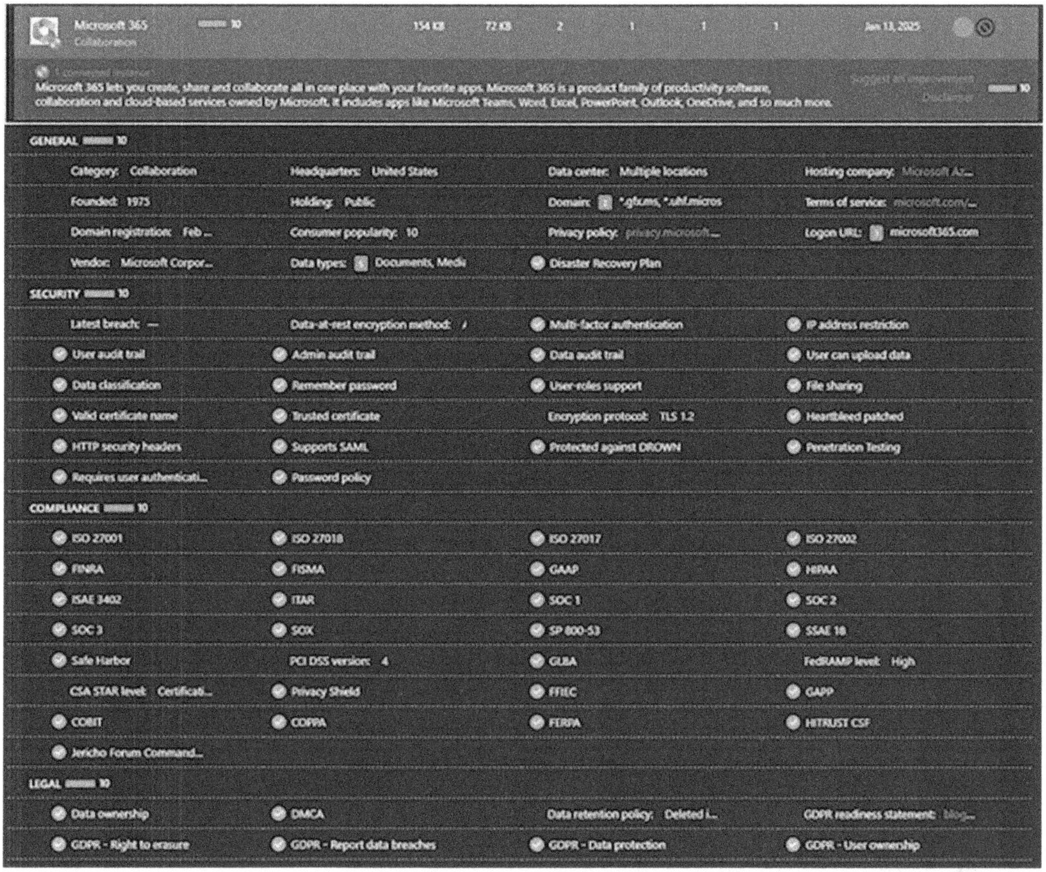

Figure 4.8: *Cloud App Details*

5. Click into the application for a more detailed, graphical display.

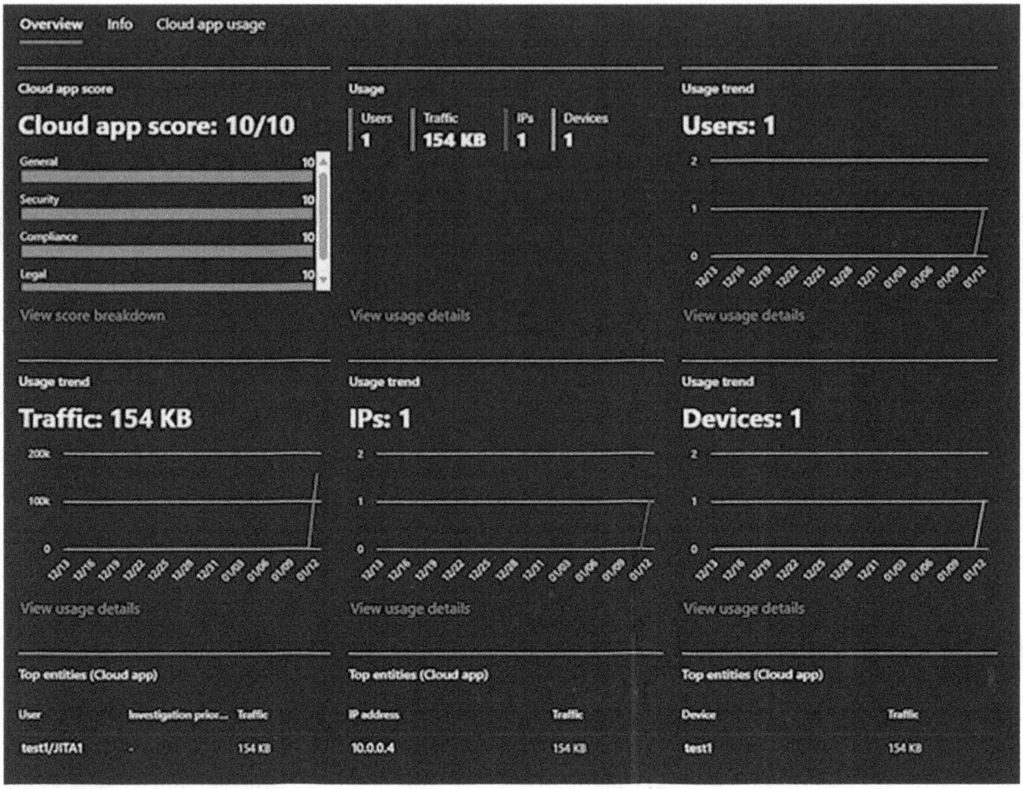

Figure 4.9: *App Details Overview*

Step 4: Blocking Unwanted Applications

Now that you have visibility into your cloud app usage, it's time to block the unwanted applications that are consuming unnecessary bandwidth or are non-compliant with company policy. MDCA allows you to block apps directly from the portal.

1. In the **`Cloud Discovery`** section, browse through the **`Cloud App Catalogue.`**
2. Find the applications you want to block and select them. You can block access to the app entirely and categorize it as "unsanctioned,' illustrated here:

Figure 4.10: *Unsanctioned Applications*

3. Mark the app as "unsanctioned" to prevent its usage across your network.
4. After blocking an app, perform a test by attempting to access the blocked app on a device that is monitored by MDCA. You should see the app's access automatically restricted:

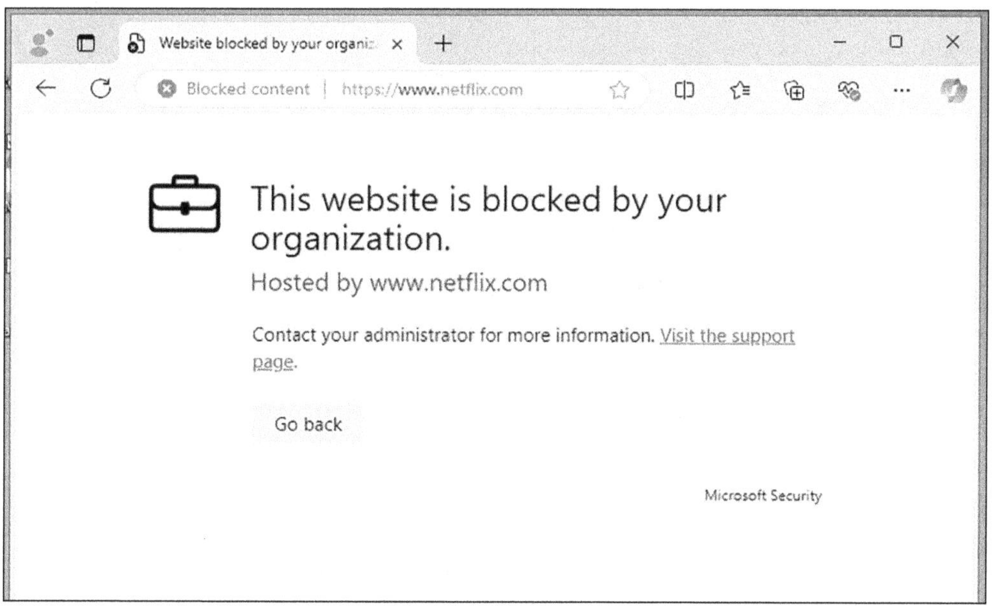

Figure 4.11: *End User Experience for Unsanctioned Apps*

Un-sanction an unwanted Application on your Firewall (for devices that don't support the MDE agent).

So what about those weird Linux distros that don't support MDE (yet)... they need protection too right? If they're behind a firewall appliance, check out this awesome MDCA feature that becomes available once you've un-sanctioned a few unwanted applications...

- From the `Cloud Discovery Dashboard` go to the `Actions` drop down, located in the top-right hand corner of the screen, and click `Generate Block Script...`:

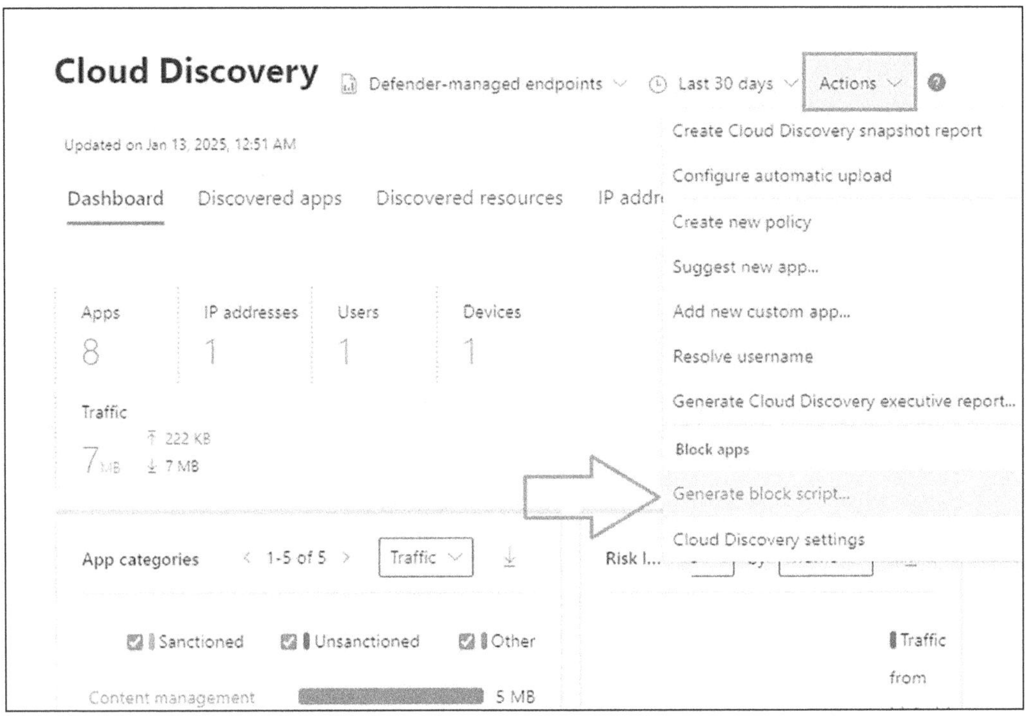

Figure 4.12: *Generate Block Script*

- Select your Firewall vendor:

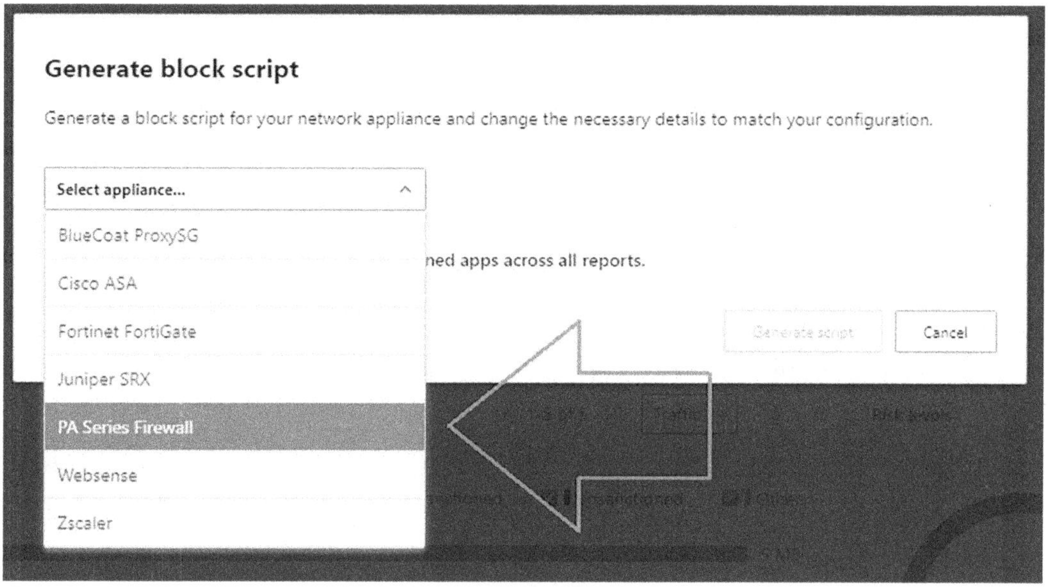

Figure 4.13: *Select Appliance*

- Copy and paste the output from a privileged exec state in your firewall to block the unwanted applications at the DNS level
- Here is an example excerpt from an output for a Palo Alto firewall that blocks Netflix, Steam Games, Epic Games, and more:

```
set application $serviceName1 category $pancategory subcategory
$pansubcategory technology browser-based risk $panrisk signature
s1 and-condition a1 or-condition o1 operator pattern-match
context http-req-host-header pattern epicgames.com

Set rulebase security rule rule$serviceName1 application $service
Name1 from any to any action deny set application $serviceName
 category $pancategory subcategory $pansubcategory technology
browser-baes risk $panrisk signature s1 and-condition a1
or-condition o1 operator pattern-match context http-req-host-
header pattern epicgames.com

Set rulebase security rule rule$serviceName1 application $service
Name1 from any to any action deny set application $serviceName
 category $pancategory subcategory $pansubcategory technology
browser-baes risk $panrisk signature s1 and-condition a1
or-condition o1 operator pattern-match context http-req-host-
header pattern api.epicgames.dev

Set rulebase security rule rule$serviceName1 application $service
Name1 from any to any action deny
```

```
set application $serviceName2 category $pancategory subcategory
$pansubcategory technology browser-based risk $panrisk signature
s1 and-condition a1 or-condition o1 operator pattern-match
context http-req-host-header pattern netflix.com

Set rulebase security rule rule$serviceName1 application $service
Name2 from any to any action deny set application $serviceName
 category $pancategory subcategory $pansubcategory technology
browser-baes risk $panrisk signature s1 and-condition a1
or-condition o1 operator pattern-match context http-req-host-
header pattern netflix.com

Set rulebase security rule rule$serviceName1 application $service
Name2 from any to any action deny set application $serviceName
 category $pancategory subcategory $pansubcategory technology
browser-baes risk $panrisk signature s1 and-condition a1
or-condition o1 operator pattern-match context http-req-host-
header pattern nflxvideo.net

Set rulebase security rule rule$serviceName2 application $servi-
ceName2 from any to any action deny
```

What happens if someone has already downloaded the Steam Games app and signed in before you've unsanctioned the application? Because they've signed in, the app has already 'phoned home' and retrieved a new token for authentication. The application will continue to work until the token expires and the app is forced to try and phone home for a new key and gets intercepted when it tries to resolve to the address block associated with Steam Games, at which point it will fail. This means that a user could potentially continue to use an un-sanctioned application temporarily until it's token expires.

File Policies in Microsoft Defender for Cloud Apps

File Policies in Microsoft Defender for Cloud Apps (MDCA) allow organizations to automate a variety of tasks, such as compliance scanning, legal eDiscovery, Data Loss Prevention (DLP) for sensitive content, and more. These policies leverage cloud provider APIs and can monitor files based on over 20 metadata filters, such as file type and access level.

Supported File Types

MDCA can perform content inspection on over 100 file types, including popular formats such as Microsoft Office, Open Office, and XML, as well as compressed and rich text formats. The system extracts text from these files to assess content and apply policies.

Policy Components

Each file policy combines three key components:

- **Content Scan:** Utilizes preset templates or custom expressions to inspect file content.
- **Context Filters:** These include user roles, file metadata (like sharing level), organizational group integration, and collaboration context.
- **Automated Actions:** These actions are automatically applied based on the policy's results, ensuring governance and remediation.

Note: *Only the first triggered policy's governance action will be applied. For example, if one policy applies a sensitivity label to a file, another policy cannot apply a different label to the same file.*

Once a policy is enabled, it continuously scans files in the cloud environment to detect violations, whether for at-rest data or newly created content. Violations are flagged, and alerts are generated in real-time. Policies can be reviewed through the console or detailed reports.

Example Use Cases for File Policies

- **Publicly Shared Files:** Receive alerts for any files that are publicly shared, based on the file's sharing level.
- **Files with the Organization's Name in the Filename:** Get alerted when files containing your organization's name are publicly shared.
- **External Domain Sharing:** Set up alerts for files shared with specific external domains, such as competitors.
- **Quarantining Unmodified Shared Files:** Automatically quarantine shared files that haven't been modified recently to ensure they are properly secured.
- **Sharing with Unauthorized Users:** Receive alerts when files are shared with unauthorized users.
- **Sensitive File Extensions:** Set alerts for files with specific extensions that may be at a higher risk, such as certificate files.

Note: *You can configure up to 50 file policies in Defender for Cloud Apps.*

Creating a New File Policy

Follow these steps to create a new file policy in Microsoft Defender for Cloud Apps:

1. **Access the Policy Management Page:**

   a. In the Microsoft Defender Portal, navigate to **`Cloud Apps`** > **`Policies`** > **`Policy Management`** and select the **`Information Protection`** tab.

2. **Create the Policy:**
   a. Click **`Create policy`** and select **`File policy`**.
   b. Name the policy, provide a description, and optionally, base it on a template (for more information, see **Control Cloud Apps with Policies**).

3. **Define Policy Severity:**
   a. Choose the severity level for the policy, which determines whether a notification will be triggered when the policy matches.

4. **Link to Risk Type:**
   a. Select a risk type for the policy to help with searching and filtering. By default, file policies are categorized under **DLP**.

5. **Set Filters for File Selection:**
   a. Narrow down the policy's scope by applying filters based on file metadata, sharing level, and other criteria. Be as specific as possible to reduce false positives.

Note: *When using the filter, "Contains" only matches full words. For instance, searching "malware" will match files with "virus_malware" but not "malwarevirusfile.exe". Use the "Equals" filter for exact matches.*

6. **Apply Filters:**
   a. Choose specific folders and user groups for which the policy will apply. This ensures the policy covers relevant files and users.

7. **Content Inspection Method:**
   a. Select between **`Built-in DLP`** or **`Data Classification Services`** (recommended). You can also define custom expressions or use preset ones to inspect file content.
   b. For advanced use, specify a regular expression to exclude files, and set the minimum number of violations required before the policy is triggered.

8. **Select Governance Actions:**
   a. Choose the appropriate governance actions (for example, quarantine, block, label) that should be applied when a file violates the policy.

9. Finalize and Monitor the Policy:
    a. After creating the policy, you can monitor the matches and violations through real-time reports. The policy will be automatically enabled and begin scanning files.

Best Practices for File Policies

- **Avoid Resetting Policies:** Only reset policies in production environments when absolutely necessary, as this triggers a full scan, potentially affecting performance.
- **Use Specific Folder Filters:** When applying policies to a folder and its subfolders, select the "**`Apply to > Selected folders`**" option.
- **Narrow Filtering Criteria:** Use narrow filters for faster performance and more accurate results.
- **Consolidate Policies:** If multiple policies apply to the same service (for example, SharePoint, OneDrive), consider consolidating them into a single policy for efficiency.
- **Enable File Monitoring:** Ensure file monitoring is enabled in settings and that at least one policy is active to avoid automatic disabling after seven days of inactivity.

File Policy Reference

File policies in MDCA are API-driven and based on over 20 metadata filters (for example, file owner, sharing level). These filters, combined with content inspection, allow for precise policy enforcement. Actions can be automated to govern collaboration, security, and investigation.

Key Policy Components:

- **Filters:** Set conditions based on file metadata.
- **Content Inspection:** Narrow down results using DLP engines, custom or preset expressions.
- **Actions:** Automatically enforce collaboration, security, and investigation actions.
- **Extensions:** Use third-party engines to enhance DLP or anti-malware capabilities.

File Policy Queries

To make investigations easier, custom queries can be saved for later use:

1. Use the file filters to refine your search.
2. Save the query for future use by clicking **`Save as`**.

3. Access saved queries from the **Queries** section to reuse them.

Viewing File Policy Results

1. In the Microsoft Defender Portal, navigate to **Cloud Apps** > **Policies** > **Policy Management** and select the **Information Protection** tab.
2. Filter the results by **File policy type** to review policy matches.
3. For detailed information, select the policy to view violations, including file collaborators and specific violations, such as Social Security numbers.

Cloud Discovery Policies in Microsoft Defender for Cloud Apps

Microsoft Defender for Cloud Apps provides deep visibility into cloud application usage, allowing organizations to uncover high-risk behaviors and potential security gaps. It enables proactive detection of abnormal user actions and potential threats within sanctioned applications. Through policy-driven alerts and automation, security teams can quickly respond to suspicious activities. Backed by Microsoft's robust threat intelligence and research capabilities, Defender for Cloud Apps supports compliance efforts and strengthens control over approved cloud environments.

Note: *Microsoft Defender for Cloud Apps is now part of Microsoft Defender XDR, which enhances its capabilities by correlating signals across the Microsoft Defender suite, providing incident-level detection, investigation, and response capabilities. For more information, see* ***Microsoft Defender for Cloud Apps in Microsoft Defender XDR***.

The Cloud Discovery dashboard provides a comprehensive view of all the cloud apps in your environment, categorizing them by function and enterprise readiness. It identifies associated users, IP addresses, devices, and transactions, and conducts risk assessments without requiring agent installation on endpoint devices.

Prerequisites

To ensure continuous Cloud Discovery reports, configure automatic log uploads or enable integration with **Defender for Endpoint** for enhanced monitoring and reporting.

Detecting High-Volume or Widespread App Usage

Defender for Cloud Apps can detect new apps with high user activity or significant traffic volume within your organization.

Steps:

1. In the Microsoft Defender Portal, go to **`Cloud Apps`** > **`Policies`** > **`Policy Management`**, and create a new **`App Discovery`** policy.
2. Choose the **`New high volume app`** or **`New popular app`** template.
3. Customize policy filters according to your organization's needs.
4. Configure actions to trigger when an alert is generated.

   Note: *An alert is generated once for each new app that has not been discovered in the last 90 days.*

Detecting Risky or Non-Compliant App Usage

Identify cloud apps that may not meet your organization's security standards and pose potential risks.

Steps:

1. Go to **`Cloud Apps`** > **Policies** > **`Policy Management`** and create a new **`App Discovery`** policy.
2. Select the **`New risky app`** template.
3. Adjust the **`Risk Score`** and **`Compliance risk factor`** to define the level of risk that triggers an alert.
4. Optionally, set traffic thresholds for triggering alerts.
5. Enable **`Trigger a policy match if all the following occur on the same day`** and configure additional filters.
6. Set governance actions, such as tagging the app as unsanctioned, which will automatically block access to the app when the policy is matched.
7. Optionally, integrate with Secure Web Gateways to block app access directly.

Detecting Use of Unsanctioned Business Apps

Detect when employees are using unsanctioned apps instead of approved, business-ready apps.

Steps:

1. In the **Cloud App Catalog**, search for your business-ready apps and tag them with a custom app tag.
2. Follow the steps for detecting **high volume or widespread app usage**.
3. Apply an **App tag filter** for the business-ready apps you created.

4. Configure governance actions, such as tagging the app as unsanctioned, which will automatically block access when the policy is matched.
5. Optionally, use **Secure Web Gateways** to block access.

Detecting Unusual Usage Patterns on Your Network

Monitor for anomalous traffic patterns (uploads/downloads) originating from internal users or IP addresses.

Steps:

1. In the Microsoft Defender Portal, go to **`Cloud Apps`** > **`Policies`** > **`Policy Management`** and create a **`Cloud Discovery Anomaly Detection`** policy.
2. Select the **`Anomalous behavior in discovered users`** or **`Anomalous behavior in discovered IP addresses`** template.
3. Customize the filters to meet your organization's requirements.
4. Use **`Risk score filters`** to focus on anomalies involving risky apps.
5. Set **`anomaly detection sensitivity`** using the slider.

Note: *The anomaly detection engine requires a few days of data to establish a baseline of normal traffic behavior, after which alerts are generated for deviations.*

Detecting Anomalous Behavior in Non-Sanctioned Storage Apps

Identify anomalous behavior in cloud storage apps that are not sanctioned for use within your organization.

Steps:

1. In the Microsoft Defender Portal, go to **`Cloud Apps`** > **`Policies`** > **`Policy Management`** and create a **`Cloud Discovery Anomaly Detection`** policy.
2. Filter by **`App category equals Cloud storage`**.
3. Set the filter **`App tag does not equal Sanctioned`**.
4. Enable the **`Create an alert`** option and select the policy's severity level.
5. Configure actions to take when an alert is triggered.

Detecting Risky OAuth Apps

Get visibility and control over OAuth apps used within services such as Google Workspace, Microsoft 365, and Salesforce. Risky OAuth apps often request high permissions and have limited community use.

Prerequisites:

Ensure that **Google Workspace**, **Microsoft 365**, or **Salesforce** is connected using app connectors.

Steps:

1. In the Microsoft Defender Portal, go to **`Cloud Apps`** > **`Policies`** > **`Policy Management`** and create a new **`OAuth App Policy`**.
2. Select the appropriate **`App`** (Google Workspace, Microsoft 365, or Salesforce).
3. Set the **`Permission level filter`** to **`High`** (available for Google Workspace and Microsoft 365).
4. Apply the filter **`Community use equals Rare`**.
5. Configure actions, such as revoking OAuth app access for apps that meet the policy criteria.

Note: *Supported for **Google Workspace**, **Microsoft 365**, and **Salesforce** app stores.*

Threat Protection Policies in Microsoft Defender for Cloud Apps

Microsoft Defender for Cloud Apps empowers organizations to monitor and respond to risky user behavior, security threats, and misuse across cloud services. It provides detailed insights into both user and administrator actions, enabling the creation of automated policies that trigger alerts when unusual or unsafe activities occur. By tapping into Microsoft's expansive threat intelligence network, this solution reinforces the security of approved applications and helps maintain oversight and governance across your cloud infrastructure.

Note:

- *Microsoft Defender for Cloud Apps is now integrated with Microsoft Defender XDR, which correlates signals across the Microsoft Defender suite for advanced detection, investigation, and response.*
- *When integrating Defender for Cloud Apps with Microsoft Defender for Identity, Defender for Identity policies also appear in the policy management section. For a list of Defender for Identity policies, refer to **Security Alerts**.*

Detecting User Activity from Unfamiliar Locations

Automatically detect user access or activities from locations that have not been visited by any other users within your organization.

Prerequisites:

Ensure at least one app is connected via app connectors or onboarded using Conditional Access with session controls.

Steps:

This detection is enabled by default, and no additional configuration is required. Alerts will trigger automatically when user activity from unfamiliar locations is detected. For more information, see **Anomaly Detection Policies**.

Detecting Compromised Accounts via Impossible Travel

Detect user access or activities from two different locations within a timeframe shorter than the time it would take to travel between the two.

Prerequisites:

Ensure at least one app is connected via app connectors or onboarded using Conditional Access with session controls.

Steps:

1. This alert is preconfigured by default to notify you whenever activity indicating impossible travel is identified.
2. Optional: Customize anomaly detection settings to:
    a. Specify users and groups to include.
    b. Define the types of sign-ins to monitor.
    c. Adjust the sensitivity of alerts.

Detect Suspicious Activity from Employees on Unpaid Leave

Detect when an employee on unpaid leave accesses your organization's cloud resources, which should not happen during their leave period.

Prerequisites:

- Ensure at least one app is connected via app connectors.
- Set up a security group in Microsoft Entra ID specifically for users on unpaid leave, and assign the appropriate users to this group.

Steps:

1. Create the user group in **Microsoft Entra ID** for users on unpaid leave.
2. In the Microsoft Defender Portal, go to **`Cloud Apps`** > **`Policies`** > **`Policy Management`**, and create a new **`Activity Policy`**.

3. Filter for the unpaid leave user group.
4. Optional: Set governance actions, such as **`Suspend user`**.
5. Create the file policy.

Detect Outdated Browser or OS Usage

Detect when a user is using an outdated browser or operating system, which could present compliance or security risks.

Prerequisites:

Ensure at least one app is connected via app connectors or onboarded using Conditional Access with session controls.

Steps:

1. In the Microsoft Defender Portal, create a new **`Activity Policy`**.
2. Set the filter to **`User agent tag equals "Outdated browser" and "Outdated operating system`**."
3. Set governance actions, such as **Notify user**, to prompt the user to update their browser/OS.
4. Create the Activity policy.

Detect Admin Activity from Risky IP Addresses

Detect admin activity originating from IP addresses deemed risky and notify the system admin for investigation.

Prerequisites:

- Ensure at least one app is connected via app connectors.
- Configure **IP address ranges** in the **Settings** page, marking internal subnets and egress IP addresses.

Steps:

1. In the Microsoft Defender Portal, create a new **`Activity Policy`**.
2. Set the filter to detect risky IP addresses and administrative activity.
3. Configure the governance actions to notify users or take other appropriate actions.
4. Create the policy.

Detect Service Account Activity from External IP Addresses

Monitor service account activity originating from external IP addresses, as this could signal unusual behavior or a potential account compromise.

Prerequisites:

- Ensure at least one app is connected via app connectors.
- Define a naming convention for service accounts, for example, accounts starting with "svc."

Steps:

1. In the Microsoft Defender Portal, create a new **`Activity Policy`**.
2. Set filters for **User name** to match your service account naming convention and **IP address** to exclude internal IP addresses.
3. Configure governance actions based on detected violations.
4. Create the policy.

Detect Mass Downloads (Data Exfiltration)

Detect when a user downloads a large number of files in a short period, which may indicate data exfiltration.

Prerequisites:

Ensure at least one app is connected via app connectors or onboarded using Conditional Access with session controls.

Steps:

1. In the Microsoft Defender Portal, create a new **`Activity Policy`**.
2. Set filters to exclude non-interactive activities, such as those from Microsoft Azure.
3. Select relevant download activity types.
4. Set governance actions and create the policy.

Detect Potential Ransomware Activity

Automatically detect potential ransomware activity based on user and app behavior patterns.

Prerequisites:

Ensure at least one app is connected via app connectors.

Steps:

1. This detection is automatically enabled out-of-the-box. No additional configuration is required.
2. You can customize the scope of the detection and set governance actions to be applied when an alert is triggered.

Note: *This applies to* ***Microsoft 365***, ***Google Workspace***, ***Box***, *and* ***Dropbox***.

Detect Malware in Cloud Apps

Leverage Microsoft's threat intelligence capabilities to identify malware-infected files within your cloud applications.

Prerequisites:

- For **Microsoft 365** malware detection, ensure you have the appropriate **Defender for Microsoft 365** license.
- Ensure at least one app is connected via app connectors.

Steps:

This detection comes pre-enabled by default and requires no further configuration.

Detect Rogue Admin Takeover

Identify repeated administrative activity that may indicate a rogue admin or malicious intentions.

Prerequisites:

Ensure at least one app is connected via app connectors.

Steps:

1. In the Microsoft Defender Portal, create a new **`Activity Policy.`**
2. Customize filters for repeated activity and set a timeframe for violations.
3. Set filters to detect password updates, changes, and resets.
4. Configure governance actions, such as notifications or suspension.
5. Create the policy.

Detect Suspicious Inbox Manipulation Rules

Identify instances where unusual inbox rules are created on a user's email account, which may suggest the account has been compromised.

Requirements:

Microsoft Exchange must be in use for email services.

Steps:

This detection is enabled by default and will automatically generate alerts when suspicious inbox rule activity is observed—no manual configuration is necessary.

Detect Leaked Credentials

Detect when compromised credentials are being used inside your organization, matching them against public data such as dark web leaks.

Prerequisites:

Ensure at least one app is connected via app connectors.

Steps:

This detection is enabled by default to alert you when leaked credentials are identified.

Detect Anomalous File Downloads

Flag instances where users download an abnormally large volume of files during a single session, as this may point to potential data exfiltration or malicious activity.

Prerequisites:

Ensure at least one app is connected via app connectors or onboarded using Conditional Access with session controls.

Steps:

This detection is configured by default to alert you when an anomalous file download occurs. You can customize the scope of the detection and specify the actions to take when a violation is detected.

Detect Anomalous File Shares

Monitor for sessions where users engage in excessive file-sharing activity, as this behavior may indicate a security incident or attempted data leak.

Prerequisites:

Ensure at least one app is connected via app connectors or onboarded using Conditional Access with session controls.

Steps:

This detection is configured to alert you when multiple file-sharing activities occur. Customize the scope and actions as needed.

Detect Anomalous Activities from Infrequent Regions

Detect activities originating from countries or regions that are infrequent for the user or organization.

Prerequisites:

Ensure at least one app is connected via app connectors or onboarded using Conditional Access with session controls.

Steps:

This detection is automatically configured to alert you when anomalous activities occur from infrequent regions. You can further customize the scope and alert actions.

Detect Activity by Terminated Users

Detect when a user who has been terminated from your organization attempts to access cloud resources.

Prerequisites:

Ensure at least one app is connected via app connectors.

Steps:

This detection is automatically enabled to alert you when terminated users attempt to access sanctioned apps. Customization options are available for the scope of detection and actions.

Information Protection Policies in Microsoft Defender for Cloud Apps

Defender for Cloud Apps provides automated enforcement of various file protection processes, including continuous compliance scans, legal eDiscovery tasks, and Data Loss Prevention (DLP) for sensitive content shared externally. With the ability to monitor over 20 metadata filters (such as access level and file type), Defender for Cloud Apps ensures that your cloud environment is secured and compliant with organizational policies.

Detect and Prevent External Sharing of Sensitive Data

Detect when files containing Personally Identifiable Information (PII) or other sensitive data are shared externally, violating your company's security policies.

Prerequisites:

Ensure at least one app is connected via app connectors.

Steps:

1. In the Microsoft Defender Portal, go to **`Cloud Apps`** > **`Policies`** > **`Policy Management`** and create a new **`File policy`**.
2. Set the filter **`Access Level`** to **`Public (Internet)`**, **`Public`**, or **`External`**.
3. Under the **`Inspection method`**, select **`Data Classification Service (DCS)`** and choose the type of sensitive data to inspect.
4. Configure **`Governance actions`** to take when violations are detected, such as **`Remove external users`** and **`Remove public access`** for files in Google Workspace.
5. Create the file policy.

Detect Externally Shared Confidential Data

Detect when confidential files, labeled using **Microsoft Purview Information Protection**, are shared externally, violating company policies.

Prerequisites:

- Ensure at least one app is connected via app connectors.
- Enable **Microsoft Purview Information Protection** integration.

Steps:

1. In the Microsoft Defender Portal, go to **`Cloud Apps`** > **`Policies`** > **`Policy Management`** and create a new **`File policy`**.
2. Set the **`Sensitivity label`** filter to **`Confidential`** (or your organization's equivalent).
3. Set the **`Access Level`** filter to **`Public (Internet)`**, **`Public`**, or **`External`**.
4. Optionally, set **Governance actions** for when violations are detected.
5. Create the file policy.

Detect and Encrypt Sensitive Data at Rest

Detect sensitive data, such as PII, stored in cloud apps, and apply sensitivity labels to restrict access to company employees only.

Prerequisites:

- Ensure at least one app is connected via app connectors.
- Enable **Microsoft Purview Information Protection** integration.

Steps:

1. In the Microsoft Defender Portal, go to **`Cloud Apps`** > **`Policies`** > **`Policy Management`** and create a new **`File policy`**.
2. Under **`Inspection method`**, select **`Data Classification Service (DCS)`** and choose the type of sensitive information to inspect.
3. Under **`Governance actions`**, select **`Apply sensitivity label`** and choose the appropriate label to restrict access.
4. Create the file policy.

Note: *At present, sensitivity labels can be applied directly only within* Box, Google Workspace, *SharePoint Online, and OneDrive for Business.*

Detect Stale Externally Shared Data

Detect files that haven't been modified recently but are still shared externally or publicly.

Prerequisites:

Ensure at least one app is connected via app connectors.

Steps:

1. In the Microsoft Defender Portal, go to **`Cloud Apps`** > **`Policies`** > **`Policy Management`** and create a new **`File policy`**.
2. Select the **`Stale externally shared files`** template.
3. Customize the **`Last modified`** filter to align with your organization's policy.
4. Optionally, set **`Governance actions`** such as making files private or notifying the last editor.
5. Create the file policy.

Detect Data Access from Unauthorized Locations

Detect when files are accessed from locations not typically associated with your organization, indicating a potential data leak or malicious access.

Prerequisites:

Ensure at least one app is connected via app connectors.

Steps:

1. In the Microsoft Defender Portal, go to **`Cloud Apps`** > **`Policies`** > **`Policy Management`** and create a new **`Activity policy`**.

2. Set the filter for **`Activity type`** to file-related actions such as **`View`**, **`Download`**, **`Access`**, or **`Modify`**.
3. Set the **`Location`** filter to exclude your organization's expected locations.
4. Optionally, create **`Governance actions`** such as **`Suspend user`**.
5. Create the Activity policy.

Detect and Protect Confidential Data in Non-Compliant SharePoint Sites

Detect and protect confidential files stored in SharePoint sites that do not comply with your company's security policies.

Prerequisites:

Sensitivity labels must be configured within your organization.

Steps:

1. In the Microsoft Defender Portal, go to **`Cloud Apps`** > **`Policies`** > **`Policy Management`** and create a new **`File policy`**.
2. Set the **`Sensitivity label`** filter to **`Confidential`** (or your organization's equivalent).
3. Set the **`Parent folder`** filter to exclude compliant folders.
4. Under **`Alerts`**, select **`Create an alert for each matching file`**.
5. Optionally, configure **`Governance actions`**, such as quarantining the file or notifying the file owner.
6. Create the file policy.

Detect Externally Shared Source Code

Detect when files containing potential source code are shared externally, which could lead to intellectual property exposure.

Prerequisites:

Ensure at least one app is connected via app connectors.

Steps:

1. In the Microsoft Defender Portal, go to **`Cloud Apps`** > **`Policies`** **`> Policy Management`** and create a new **`File policy`**.
2. Apply the **`Externally shared source code`** template.
3. You can optionally tailor the list of file extensions to align with the specific source code formats used within your organization.

4. Optionally, set **`Governance actions`** for detected violations.
5. Create the file policy.

Detect Unauthorized Access to Group Data

Detect when files belonging to specific user groups are accessed by users who do not belong to those groups, which could signal an insider threat.

Prerequisites:

Ensure at least one app is connected via app connectors.

Steps:

1. In the Microsoft Defender Portal, go to **Cloud Apps** > **Policies** > **Policy Management** and create a new **Activity policy**.
2. Set the filter for **Repeated activity** and specify the **Minimum repeated activities** and **Timeframe**.
3. Set the **Activity type** filter to include file actions such as **View**, **Download**, **Access**, or **Modify**.
4. Set the **User group** filter to select the relevant user group.
5. Set **`Governance actions`** such as **`Suspend user`**.
6. Create the file policy.

Detect Publicly Accessible S3 Buckets

Protect against potential data leaks by detecting publicly accessible AWS S3 buckets.

Prerequisites:

Ensure your AWS instance is connected via app connectors.

Steps:

1. In the Microsoft Defender Portal, go to **`Cloud Apps`** > **`Policies`** > **`Policy Management`** and create a new **`File policy`**.
2. Apply the **`Publicly accessible S3 buckets (AWS)`** template.
3. Set the **`Governance actions`** to make the S3 buckets private.
4. Create the file policy.

Detect and Protect GDPR-Related Data

Detect files containing personal data subject to GDPR compliance, and apply sensitivity labels to ensure only authorized personnel have access.

Prerequisites:

- Ensure at least one app is connected via app connectors.
- Enable **Microsoft Purview Information Protection** integration and configure GDPR labels.

Steps:

1. In the Microsoft Defender Portal, go to **`Cloud Apps`** > **`Policies`** > **`Policy Management`** and create a new **`File policy`**.
2. Under **`Inspection method`**, select **`Data Classification Service (DCS)`** and choose information types related to GDPR (for example, EU debit card number, EU passport number).
3. Set **`Governance actions`** to apply sensitivity labels.
4. Create the file policy.

Note: *The ability to apply sensitivity labels is currently limited to* Box, *Google Workspace, SharePoint Online, and OneDrive for Business.*

Block Downloads for External Users in Real-Time

Prevent external users from downloading company data in real-time to avoid potential data exfiltration.

Prerequisites:

- Deploy **Conditional Access App Control** for Microsoft Entra apps.
- Ensure the app is SAML-based and utilizes **Microsoft Entra ID** for SSO.

Steps:

1. In the Microsoft Defender Portal, go to **`Cloud Apps`** > **`Policies`** > **`Policy Management`** and create a new **`Session policy.`**
2. Under **`Session control type`**, select **`Control file download (with inspection)`**.
3. Set **`User`** to **`External users`**.
4. Optionally, set **`File filters`** for more granular control.
5. Under **`Actions`**, select **`Block`** and customize the message users receive.
6. Create the policy.

Enforce Read-Only Mode for External Users

Prevent external users from printing or copying company data by enforcing read-only mode in real-time.

Prerequisites:

- Deploy **Conditional Access App Control** for Microsoft Entra apps.
- Ensure the app is SAML-based and utilizes **Microsoft Entra ID** for SSO.

Steps:

1. In the Microsoft Defender Portal, go to **`Cloud Apps`** > **`Policies`** > **`Policy Management`** and create a new **`Session policy`**.
2. Under **`Session control type`**, select **`Block activities`**.
3. Set **`Activity type`** to include **`Print`** and **`Cut/Copy`**.
4. Optionally, set **`Inspection method`** to apply DLP scans.
5. Under **`Actions`**, select **`Block`** and customize the block message.
7. Create the policy.

Block Upload of Unclassified Documents in Real-Time

Prevent the upload of unclassified documents by external users to your cloud environment.

Prerequisites:

- Deploy **Conditional Access App Control** for Microsoft Entra apps.
- Ensure the app is SAML-based and uses **Microsoft Entra ID** for SSO.
- Ensure **Microsoft Purview Information Protection** sensitivity labels are configured.

Steps:

1. In the Microsoft Defender Portal, go to **`Cloud Apps`** > **`Policies`** > **`Policy Management`** and create a new **`Session policy`**.
2. Under **`Session control type`**, select **`Control file upload (with inspection)`**.
3. Set the **`Sensitivity label`** filter to exclude unclassified files.
4. Optionally, set **`Inspection method`** for DLP scans.
5. Under **`Actions`**, select **`Block`** and customize the block message.
6. Create the policy.

Note: *For a list of supported file types, see the* ***Microsoft Purview Information Protection integration prerequisites****.*

Troubleshooting Microsoft Defender for Cloud Apps (MDCA)

1. **Access and Session Control Issues**

Issue: Users are unable to access certain cloud applications or face session control problems.

Solution:

- **Verify Requirements:** Confirm that your environment meets the necessary prerequisites, such as valid licensing, supported Single Sign-On (SSO) configurations, and compatible browsers.
- **User Monitoring Page:** Ensure the "Notify users that their activity is being monitored" setting is enabled in MDCA. Customize the message if needed.
- **Downtime Behavior:** Configure the default access behavior during system downtime to either allow or block access to sensitive content when policy enforcement is unavailable.

2. **Data Loss Prevention (DLP) Policy Misconfigurations**

Issue: DLP policies are not functioning as expected, leading to data exposure or unauthorized access.

Solution:

- **Review Policies:** Check that your DLP policies are accurately configured to protect sensitive data. Ensure they are applied to the appropriate apps and data types.
- **Test Policies:** Test DLP policies in a controlled environment to verify they trigger the expected actions, like blocking or encrypting data transfers.
- **Policy Updates:** Regularly update your policies to account for new threats and changes in compliance requirements.

3. **Anomaly Detection and Behavioral Analytics**

Issue: Anomalies are not being detected, or false positives generate unnecessary alerts.

Solution:

- **Behavioral Baselines:** Make sure MDCA has accurate baselines for user activity to differentiate normal behavior from anomalies.
- **Refine Policies:** Adjust anomaly detection sensitivity to minimize false positives. Tailor criteria based on specific organizational needs.

- **XDR Integration:** Integrate MDCA with Microsoft XDR to enhance threat detection by correlating data across endpoints, identities, and cloud apps.

4. **OAuth App Management**

Issue: OAuth apps are requesting excessive permissions, creating potential security risks.

Solution:

- **Review Permissions:** Regularly audit OAuth apps and their permissions. Identify apps requesting excessive or unnecessary permissions.
- **Approve/Revocation:** Approve or revoke access to apps based on their risk assessments. Limit access to only trusted apps.
- **User Education:** Train users to recognize the risks of granting unnecessary permissions and report suspicious apps.

5. **Clipboard and File Control Issues**

Issue: Clipboard actions (cut, copy, paste) or file controls (download, upload, print) are not being blocked as expected.

Solution:

- **Verify Session Proxying:** If the session is being proxied, check the Microsoft Defender Portal under the Cloud Apps section. Use the "Applied action" filter to confirm that file activities are marked as blocked.
- **Review Policies:** Expand activity logs to confirm that the correct policies are being enforced. If the policies aren't applied, ensure they are properly configured.
- **Default Behavior During Downtime:** If "Access blocked/allowed due to Default Behavior" appears, it indicates that downtime occurred. Adjust default behavior in the portal under Conditional Access App Control and check system downtime notifications via Microsoft 365.

6. **File Download Protection Issues**

Issue: Downloads of sensitive data are not being protected, particularly on unmanaged devices.

Solution:

- **Activity Log Review:** Use the activity log to verify that file download activities are protected. Check for any blocked activity and verify policy enforcement.
- **Check File Types:** Ensure that files being protected are of supported types, such as .docx, .xlsx, .pptx, or PDF if Unified Labeling is enabled. Adjust session

policies to block downloads of unsupported files or where protection is unsuccessful.

- **Downtime Verification:** Review the Microsoft 365 Service Health Dashboard for downtime notifications.

Conclusion

In an era defined by widespread cloud adoption and increasingly sophisticated threats, Microsoft Defender for Cloud Apps emerges as a cornerstone of enterprise cloud security. By offering granular visibility, real-time control, and seamless integration with the broader Microsoft Defender XDR suite, MDCA enables organizations to detect, respond to, and prevent risks across sanctioned and unsanctioned cloud applications. Its powerful policy engine, data protection features, and automated enforcement capabilities empower security teams to maintain compliance without sacrificing agility. Whether managing OAuth permissions, uncovering Shadow IT, or safeguarding sensitive data in motion and at rest, Defender for Cloud Apps equips organizations with the intelligence and control needed to secure their modern cloud environments confidently and comprehensively.

As we continue our exploration of Microsoft's XDR capabilities, we now shift focus to a critical pillar of modern threat protection: email security. In the following chapter, we will examine Defender for Office 365—its architecture, policy configuration, and integrated threat protection strategies—demonstrating how it fortifies Microsoft 365 environments against phishing, malware, and business email compromise.

Helpful Links and Resources

- Gartner. (2023). *What is a Cloud Access Security Broker* (CASB)? Gartner. https://www.gartner.com/en/information-technology/glossary/cloud-access-security-broker-casb
- Hanley, I. (2025, January 13). *Deploy Defender for Cloud Apps (MDCA) & Block Unwanted Applications.* Hanley.Cloud. https://www.hanley.cloud/2025-01-13-Deploy-Defender-for-Cloud-Apps-MDCA-&-Block-Unwanted-Applications/
- Microsoft. (2024). *Cloud Discovery and app governance in Defender for Cloud Apps.* Microsoft Learn. https://learn.microsoft.com/en-us/defender-cloud-apps/governance-discovery
- Microsoft. (2024). *Deploy Conditional Access App Control.* Microsoft Learn. https://learn.microsoft.com/en-us/defender-cloud-apps/proxy-deployment-aad
- Microsoft. (2024). *Integrate Defender for Endpoint with Defender for Cloud Apps.* Microsoft Learn. https://learn.microsoft.com/en-us/defender-cloud-apps/mde-govern

- Microsoft. (2024). *Manage OAuth apps in Microsoft Defender for Cloud Apps.* Microsoft Learn. https://learn.microsoft.com/en-us/defender-cloud-apps/oauth-apps
- Microsoft. (2024). *Microsoft 365 Defender.* Microsoft Learn. https://learn.microsoft.com/en-us/defender-xdr/microsoft-365-defender
- Microsoft. (2024). *Microsoft Defender for Cloud Apps documentation.* Microsoft Learn. https://learn.microsoft.com/en-us/microsoft-defender/cloud-apps
- Microsoft. (2024). *Pilot and deploy Microsoft Defender for Cloud Apps.* Microsoft Learn. https://learn.microsoft.com/en-us/defender-xdr/pilot-deploy-defender-cloud-apps
- Microsoft. (2024). *Policies in Microsoft Defender for Cloud Apps.* Microsoft Learn. https://learn.microsoft.com/en-us/defender-cloud-apps/policy-cloud-apps
- Microsoft. (2024). *Security portal.* Microsoft. https://security.microsoft.com
- Microsoft. (2024). *Sensitivity labels in Microsoft Purview Information Protection.* Microsoft Learn. https://learn.microsoft.com/en-us/microsoft-365/compliance/sensitivity-labels
- Microsoft. (2024). *Troubleshooting Conditional Access App Control for end users.* Microsoft Learn. https://learn.microsoft.com/en-us/defender-cloud-apps/troubleshooting-proxy-end-users
- Microsoft. (2024). *What is Conditional Access?* Microsoft Learn. https://learn.microsoft.com/en-us/entra/identity/conditional-access/overview

CHAPTER 5
Defender for Office 365

Introduction

Email remains a central pillar of modern communication, allowing individuals and organizations across the globe to share ideas, conduct business, and collaborate on critical projects in real time. However, the very ease and ubiquity of email communication have also made it a prime target for cybercriminals seeking to infiltrate networks, steal sensitive data, and exploit both human and technical vulnerabilities. In an ever-evolving threat landscape—marked by sophisticated phishing attacks, zero-day malware, ransomware campaigns, and social engineering—robust email security is no longer a luxury; it is a business imperative.

Microsoft Defender for Office 365 (often referred to simply as MDO) answers this imperative by offering a multifaceted security solution purpose-built to protect organizations that rely on Microsoft 365 for email, collaboration, and productivity. MDO combines advanced threat intelligence, real-time monitoring, policy-based controls, and tight integration with the broader Microsoft security ecosystem to defend mailboxes, shared files, and collaboration tools from a wide array of cyberattacks. Through features such as Safe Attachments, Safe Links, and advanced machine learning (ML) detection, MDO provides continuous and adaptive coverage.

In the sections that follow, we will explore the capabilities, configuration, and operational processes that enable Microsoft Defender for Office 365 to be a cornerstone of your organization's security architecture. We will detail how to deploy the solution effectively, integrate it with Microsoft Defender for Endpoint (part of Microsoft's extended detection and response suite), and apply best practices that help you align it with both organizational policies and specific threat scenarios.

By the end of this chapter, you should have a solid grasp of how to install, configure, and maintain Microsoft Defender for Office 365 so that it operates in harmony with your broader security infrastructure. In doing so, your organization will be better equipped to mitigate the risks posed by malicious actors who target users' inboxes and collaboration platforms.

Structure

In this chapter, we will cover the following topics:

- Overview
- Importance of Modern Email Security
- Behind the Scenes with Defender for Office 365
- Deployment Deep Dive
- Configure Endpoint Integration
- Policy Types and Configuration
    - Anti-Phishing Policies
    - Anti-Spam Policies
    - Safe Attachments Policies
    - Safe Links Policies
    - Threat Protection Policies
    - Information Protection Policies
    - Email Authentication: DMARC, DKIM, and SPF
    - Quarantine Policies
- Troubleshooting

Overview

Defender for Office 365 provides layered protection for email, files, and collaboration channels across Microsoft 365. At a high level, it leverages capabilities such as Safe Attachments to detonate suspicious files, Safe Links to dynamically scan URLs at click time, and advanced machine learning models to detect and block phishing. Integration with other Microsoft security services streamlines monitoring and remediation, enabling a unified defense against a wide range of threats.

Administrators can configure policies, investigate incidents, and automate response processes, ensuring a proactive and comprehensive security posture for their Office 365 environment. The following are some of the key features and capabilities that make Defender for Office 365 a critical component of Microsoft's broader security offering:

Safe Attachments

- **Sandboxing for email attachments**: Suspicious attachments are opened and tested in a virtual sandbox environment before reaching the recipient. This helps detect unknown (zero-day) malware and viruses.

- **Real-time protection**: Attachments deemed safe are then released to the user's inbox, and any malicious attachments are blocked or quarantined for review.

Safe Links

- **Time-of-click protection**: Malicious links in emails or Office documents are dynamically analyzed at the moment the user clicks them. If the destination is deemed unsafe, the user is prevented from accessing it.

Figure 5.1: *Time-of-Click Protection*

- **Rewriting URLs**: Links are redirected through Microsoft's secure routing service, enabling continuous scanning in case a URL becomes malicious after it is delivered.

Figure 5.2: *URL Rewrite*

Anti-Phishing Policies

- **Machine learning-based detection**: Defender for Office 365 uses advanced algorithms to identify and block phishing emails by examining sender reputation, email content, and user impersonation attempts.
- **Impersonation protection**: Specific checks against user and domain impersonation tactics, preventing targeted spear-phishing attacks.
- **User and domain impersonation safeguards**: Administrators can configure custom policies to protect high-value targets (for example, executives) and critical domains.

Real-Time Detection and Alerts

- **Threat intelligence**: Integration with the Microsoft Intelligent Security Graph provides up-to-date information on emerging threats.

- **Immediate notification**: Security teams can receive alerts and detailed incident information as soon as threats are detected, speeding up response time.

Automated Investigation & Response (AIR)

- **Automated playbooks**: Defender for Office 365 can automatically investigate alerts, gather additional data, and perform remediation actions (for example, quarantining messages) with minimal manual intervention.
- **Incident correlation**: Related alerts and events are grouped into a single incident, giving security teams a consolidated view of the threat campaign.

Threat Explorer and Real-Time Reports

- **Threat Explorer (or Explorer)**: Provides deep visibility into email traffic and threats across the organization. Analysts can search for threats by sender, recipient, subject, or malware type.
- **Real-time dashboards**: Interactive reports allow security administrators to spot trends, identify common threat vectors, and drill down into specific incidents.

Attack Simulation Training

- **Phishing simulations**: Organizations can run simulated phishing campaigns to train employees on how to identify and report suspicious emails.
- **Automated training modules**: After a simulated (or real) phishing attempt, targeted users can receive just-in-time learning content to reinforce best practices.

Collaboration Tool Protection

- **SharePoint, OneDrive, Teams integration**: Defender for Office 365 helps protect files stored in or shared via these services by scanning for malicious content and blocking files if threats are detected.
- **Consistent security policies**: Ensures uniform enforcement of safe links and safe attachments across Microsoft 365 collaboration platforms.

Multi-Platform Email Protection

- **Cross-email client compatibility**: Whether users access email via Outlook, Outlook on the web, or mobile devices, Defender for Office 365 provides a consistent layer of security.
- **Support for hybrid scenarios**: Organizations in hybrid environments (combining on-premises and cloud mailboxes) can configure policies to extend protection across both.

Integration with Microsoft 365 Defender

- **Unified security portal**: Administrators can manage Defender for Office 365 and other Microsoft 365 Defender solutions from a single dashboard.
- **Advanced hunting (Plan 2)**: Allows security teams to run custom queries across email, endpoints, and identity data to proactively hunt for threats and indicators of compromise.

Plan 1 vs. Plan 2 Highlights

- **Plan 1** includes core features such as Safe Attachments, Safe Links, anti-phishing policies, basic reporting, and quarantine.
- **Plan 2** adds advanced threat intelligence, automation, hunting, and investigation capabilities, including Threat Explorer, automated investigation and response, and Attack Simulation Training.

Benefits of Defender for Office 365

Advanced Threat Protection

- Leverages capabilities such as **Safe Attachments** and **Safe Links** to detect and block zero-day exploits, targeted phishing, and ransomware before they reach end users.
- Backed by Microsoft's global threat intelligence network, which continually updates protection mechanisms in real-time.

Automated and Streamlined Security Operations

- **Automated Investigation and Remediation** (AIR) features reduce analyst workload by investigating suspicious emails or attachments and taking predefined mitigation steps automatically.
- Enables security teams to focus on complex threats rather than time-consuming manual tasks.

Security Awareness and Training

- Integrated **attack simulations** and tailored phishing tests help employees recognize and avoid social engineering attempts.
- According to the Ponemon Institute, organizations with regular employee training reduce phishing susceptibility significantly, lowering breach costs.

Comprehensive Visibility and Analytics

- Real-time dashboards and **advanced threat analytics** offer immediate insights into threats targeting the organization, allowing teams to respond swiftly.
- Facilitates proactive threat hunting by correlating signals from email traffic with other Microsoft 365 services.

Scalable Cloud-Based Solution

- Continuously updated with the latest threat intelligence, ensuring organizations always have the most current defenses.
- Easily scales as businesses grow, requiring minimal overhead compared to on-premises security solutions.
- Assists with meeting compliance requirements such as **HIPAA**, **GDPR**, and **FINRA** by enforcing DLP and secure email policies automatically.

Importance of Modern Email Security

Modern threats often arrive in the form of socially engineered attacks or malicious links/files delivered via email. As organizations continue to rely heavily on email and collaboration platforms, safeguarding these avenues becomes paramount. Key reasons why advanced email security (such as MDO) is crucial include:

Escalating Phishing Threats

- According to the Verizon 2021 Data Breach Investigations Report, 36% of data breaches involve phishing, underscoring the growing sophistication of socially engineered attacks.
- Organizations must prioritize advanced email security to protect employees who regularly rely on email and collaboration platforms.

Business Email Compromise (BEC)

- The FBI's Internet Crime Complaint Center (IC3) 2020 Internet Crime Report indicates that BEC resulted in over $1.8 billion in reported losses in 2020.
- Cybercriminals often impersonate vendors, executives, or partners to trick employees into revealing credentials or initiating fraudulent payments.

Malware and Ransomware Infection Vectors

- The IBM Security X-Force Threat Intelligence Index highlights email attachments as a primary avenue for delivering malware or ransomware.
- Such malicious files can exfiltrate sensitive data, compromise devices, and even encrypt critical information for ransom.

Brand Protection and Reputation

- When compromised accounts send harmful emails, the resulting damage goes beyond internal security–organizations risk tarnishing their public image and damaging brand trust.

Data Loss Prevention (DLP)

- The IBM-Ponemon Cost of a Data Breach Report estimates that the average cost of a data breach exceeded $4 million in 2021.
- Advanced DLP policies help identify, classify, and safeguard sensitive data, preventing accidental or malicious leaks via email.

Compliance Obligations

- Regulations such as HIPAA (45 CFR Part 164), GDPR (Regulation (EU) 2016/679), and FINRA Rule 3110 demand robust email security protocols.
- Non-compliance can lead to significant financial penalties and legal repercussions.

Comprehensive Protection with Microsoft Defender for Office 365

- Delivers end-to-end threat detection, automated incident response, and deep insights for security teams.
- Aligns with best practices such as the NIST Cybersecurity Framework (https://www.nist.gov/cyberframework) to enhance overall organizational resilience against email-based threats.
- Learn more about Microsoft Defender for Office 365 (https://www.microsoft.com/en-us/security/business/threat-protection/microsoft-defender-office-365).

Microsoft Defender for Office 365 addresses these challenges head-on by delivering comprehensive threat detection, automated response, and in-depth insights to security teams.

How Defender for Office Works Under the Hood

Defender for Office 365 operates as a **multilayered** security solution integrated into your Microsoft 365 environment. It leverages **global threat intelligence**, advanced analytics, and continuous scanning of mail flow to proactively neutralize threats. According to the Verizon 2021 Data Breach Investigations Report (https://www.verizon.com/business/resources/reports/dbir/), email remains one of the top vectors for data breaches, reinforcing the importance of comprehensive solutions such as Defender for Office 365.

Defender for Office 365 employs a combination of proactive and reactive defense mechanisms designed around layered security concepts. This approach ensures that if one layer misses a threat, subsequent layers can still detect and neutralize it.

Email Flow Analysis

- **Inbound and Outbound Inspection**: All messages, whether inbound (from external senders) or outbound (from internal mailboxes), are scanned in transit. MDO checks headers, sender reputation, embedded links, and attachments for signs of malicious or suspicious content.
- **Sandbox Detonation (Safe Attachments)**: Attachments flagged as suspicious are opened within a secure, virtual machine environment where any malicious behavior can be observed. Should the file exhibit malware-like actions, it can be quarantined before reaching the recipient.
- **Behavioral and Heuristic Analysis:** Beyond signature matching, MDO uses heuristic and behavioral checks to identify any anomaly that might indicate an emerging or zero-day threat.

Safe Links (Time-of-Click Protection)

- **URL Rewriting**: When emails contain hyperlinks, MDO rewrites each URL with a protective prefix. This allows Defender for Office 365 to evaluate the safety of the link at the moment a user clicks, rather than solely relying on checks performed at delivery time.
- **Real-Time Blocks:** If a site previously deemed safe is found to be malicious at a later point (for example, the domain was compromised post-delivery), MDO can still block user access by redirecting the user to a warning or block page.

Advanced Threat Intelligence and Machine Learning

- **Global Signal Integration**: Microsoft collects billions of signals daily from sources such as Office 365, Windows endpoints, Azure Active Directory, and the broader web. Threat intelligence gleaned from these sources feeds into MDO.
- **ML Models and Pattern Recognition**: Defender for Office 365 trains machine learning algorithms to identify anomalies, suspicious domains, and user impersonation attempts. Over time, these models become more accurate by learning from both false positives and actual threats.

Automated Investigation & Response (AIR)

- **Playbook-Driven Actions**: For higher-tier Defender for Office 365 plans (Plan 2), administrators can configure automated playbooks. For instance, if MDO detects a phishing campaign targeting multiple recipients, it can automatically quarantine the messages across all mailboxes, block the sender, and escalate to security admins.
- **Incident Correlation**: Alerts involving the same malicious email campaign or threat actor are grouped into a single incident, simplifying investigation and

providing context. This grouping is especially useful for large organizations that receive significant volumes of alerts.

Integration with the Microsoft 365 Defender Suite

- **Defender for Endpoint**: Shares signals about compromised devices that might be sending malicious emails internally.
- **Defender for Cloud Apps**: Monitors suspicious activity in cloud applications.
- **Defender for Identity**: Correlates identity-based attacks with email threats, especially in lateral movement scenarios.

Through these integrations, a single malicious action in one domain of the network can trigger an automated analysis or response across other parts of the environment—leading to quicker mitigation and more effective containment.

Automated Investigation & Response (AIR)

- **Auto-Remediation**
  - When Defender for Office 365 identifies malicious content, it can **automatically remove** harmful emails from user mailboxes and quarantine suspicious items.
  - It also proactively **blocks repeated threats**, preventing threat actors from exploiting the same method across multiple emails or user accounts.
- **Playbooks & Alerts**
  - Security teams can create **automated playbooks** that trigger specific remediation actions when certain conditions are met (for example, multiple user reports of a phishing email).
  - **Real-time alerts** ensure analysts are notified of high-risk incidents, such as **mass phishing campaigns** or zero-day exploits.

Why It Matters: By automating repetitive tasks, security analysts can focus on more complex threats—a key advantage, given the strain on many SOC teams as reported by the Ponemon Institute (https://www.ibm.com/security/data-breach).

Integration with Defender XDR

- **Holistic Ecosystem of Defender Solutions**
  - Defender for Office 365 shares signals with **Microsoft Defender for Endpoint**, **Microsoft Defender for Cloud Apps**, and **Microsoft Defender for Identity**.
  - This allows for **holistic attack detection** and **cross-product incident correlation**, giving security teams a single pane of glass for threat visibility.

Why It Matters: Today's threats often span multiple vectors (email, endpoints, cloud services). Integrating email security with a broader XDR platform aligns with best practices recommended by the NIST Cybersecurity Framework (https://www.nist.gov/cyberframework) to enhance prevention, detection, and response capabilities.

Deployment Deep Dive

Deployment Deep Dive

Proper deployment of Defender for Office 365 is critical to ensuring full coverage and minimal disruption to business operations. This section outlines a structured approach to rolling out MDO, from verifying licenses to executing pilot tests.

Licensing and Plan Confirmation

1. **Access the Microsoft 365 Admin Center**: Ensure your organization has the correct licensing (Plan 1 or Plan 2) assigned to each mailbox or user that needs protection.
2. **Review Trial or Hybrid Licensing**: If you are in a hybrid scenario (some mailboxes on-premises, some in the cloud), confirm that necessary connectors are established and that licenses match your intended coverage.

Enabling and Verifying the Service

1. **Log In as an Administrator**: Use a Global Administrator or Security Administrator account to sign into the Microsoft 365 Defender portal.
2. **Navigate to Threat Policies:** Under **Email & collaboration** > **Policies & rules**, locate **Threat policies** to confirm that Microsoft Defender for Office 365 is enabled.
3. **Review Default Policies**: Microsoft sets up baseline policies for anti-spam, anti-phishing, and anti-malware. Verify these are active and set to recommended levels for a starting point.

Configuring Mail Flow

1. **Mail Flow Rules (Transport Rules)**: You can create custom rules to append disclaimers, detect specific attachments, or automatically quarantine messages based on particular conditions.
2. **Enhanced Filtering for Connectors**: In hybrid environments, ensure Enhanced Filtering is enabled so that MDO can accurately detect the true sender origin and apply the correct protection measures.

Policy Customization

1. **Define Anti-Phishing Settings**

    a. **Impersonation Protection**: Add high-value targets (CEO, CFO) for extra screening.

   b. **Domain Spoofing**: Configure thresholds to flag domains that closely resemble legitimate ones.

2. **Adjust Safe Attachments & Safe Links**

   a. **Dynamic Delivery**: Determine if you want users to see the email body before attachments are fully scanned.

   b. **URL Tracking**: Decide on user-level click tracking for auditing and behavioral analysis.

3. **Quarantine Configuration**

   a. **Quarantine Duration**: Set how long quarantined emails are stored before automatic deletion.

   b. **Access and Release Controls**: Restrict or allow specific roles to release quarantined messages.

Testing and Validation

1. **Pilot Group**: Select a small set of users or a department (often IT or a subset of your security team) to validate settings.
2. **Attack Simulation**: Use MDO's Attack Simulation Training (Plan 2) to run phishing simulations. Evaluate user responses and gauge detection effectiveness.
3. **Monitor Dashboards**: Regularly check the security portal's dashboards to see if genuine threats are being caught and whether false positives remain minimal.

Following these steps helps ensure a smooth transition to Defender for Office 365, avoiding operational disruptions such as incorrectly quarantined emails or unscanned messages that slip through.

Configure Endpoint Integration

One of the most powerful aspects of Defender for Office 365 is its seamless integration with other solutions in Microsoft's ecosystem, most notably Microsoft Defender for Endpoint (MDE). By unifying email and endpoint signals, security teams can respond holistically to threats.

Unified Threat Visibility

- **Single Pane of Glass**: The Microsoft 365 Defender portal shows incidents that include both mailbox and device signals.

- **Automatic Incident Correlation**: A phishing email leading to endpoint compromise will link the user's mailbox alert with the device infection alert.

Deployment Considerations

- **Endpoint Onboarding**: Ensure all relevant devices (Windows, macOS, Linux, and mobile platforms, where applicable) are onboarded to MDE.
- **License and Policy Overlaps**: If your organization has E5 or other premium plans, verify that you have all the necessary roles to manage cross-solution integrations.
- **Testing Scenarios**: Consider simulating a scenario where a user receives a malicious attachment that, once opened, attempts to run malware on the endpoint. Observe how MDO and MDE coordinate detection and remediation.

Example Use Case

- **Phishing Email with Malicious Macro:**
    - MDO identifies the email as suspicious and quarantines it immediately.
    - If the macro is enabled and runs on a device, MDE detects malicious activity, isolates the endpoint, and marks the related alert in the unified portal.
- **Automated Investigation & Response:**
    - MDO blocks subsequent emails from the same sender.
    - MDE prevents lateral movement from the compromised device until the investigation is complete.
    - Security admin receives a single correlated incident that includes both the email and endpoint details.

Policy Types and Configuration

Within Defender for Office 365, multiple policy types cater to specific threat vectors. Each policy can be fine-tuned to align with organizational requirements and security tolerances.

***Figure* 5.3:** *Policy Types*

Anti-Phishing Policies

The following is a breakdown of each setting in the Anti-Phishing policy and how it helps protect your organization:

Phishing threshold & protection

- **Phishing threshold**
    - This setting determines how aggressively the anti-phishing engine looks for and flags suspicious emails. A scale of 1 (least aggressive) to 4 (most aggressive) is often used; a lower number (like 2) indicates a less *aggressive* detection approach, potentially catching more phishing attempts (but also risking more false positives).
- **User impersonation protection: Off (0 senders specified)**
    - **What it does**: User impersonation protection looks for attempts to impersonate specific high-profile users (for example, executives) within your organization.
    - When it is turned off, and no specific senders are listed, then the anti-phishing engine will *not* specifically look for impersonation of individual users based on the user list.
- **Domain impersonation protection: On for owned domains, Off for 0 domain(s) specified**
    - **What it does**: Domain impersonation checks for email senders spoofing or mimicking your organization's domains.
    - **On,** for your owned domains (that is, the engine is monitoring attempts to pretend to be your actual domain), but there are no additional *external* or *partner* domains specified. This means that if attackers try to impersonate your owned domain, the system will take action; if they impersonate other domains, no special protection is configured.
- **Trusted impersonated senders and domains: On for 0 domain(s) and 2 sender(s)**
    - **What it does**: Sometimes, legitimate emails might appear to impersonate a user or domain (for example, marketing or vendor tools). You can add trusted senders or domains to reduce false positives.
    - **On**, indicating that any addresses or domains in the trusted list (2 senders, 0 domains) will be exempted from impersonation checks.
- **Mailbox intelligence: On**
    - **What it does**: Mailbox intelligence learns user communication patterns over time–who they typically email, what legitimate messages look like, and

so on. It uses this info to detect anomalies, such as sudden impersonation attempts.

  - **On**, providing adaptive protection based on normal mail flow behavior.

- **Mailbox intelligence for impersonations**
  - **What it does**: This specifically uses Mailbox Intelligence to identify potential impersonations of user accounts (based on anomalies in sending patterns, display names, and so on).
  - **On**, so if it sees unusual sending behavior that suggests impersonation of a known contact, it can act.
- **Spoof intelligence**
  - **What it does**: Spoof intelligence focuses on detecting messages that have forged or faked email addresses or sending infrastructure (that is, forging the "From" header).
  - **On**, meaning these spoof checks are active and will potentially quarantine, reject, or junk mail that fails those checks.

Actions

- **If a message is detected as user impersonation: Quarantine the message (`DefaultFullAccessPolicy`)**
  - Messages flagged as impersonating a user are sent to quarantine, where only designated admins or users with appropriate privileges can review or release them.
- **If a message is detected as domain impersonation: Move the message to the recipients' Junk Email folders**
  - Domain impersonation attempts are less severe than user impersonations (according to this policy), so they are not quarantined outright. Instead, they are delivered but placed in Junk Email.
- **If Mailbox Intelligence detects an impersonated user: Move the message to the recipients' Junk Email folders**
  - If Mailbox Intelligence flags the email as suspicious for impersonation, the policy sends it to Junk Email, rather than quarantining.
- **If the message is detected as spoof and DMARC Policy is set as `p=quarantine`: Quarantine the message (`DefaultFullAccessPolicy`)**
  - If DMARC says "quarantine" and the message is detected as spoofed, the policy follows DMARC guidance, sending it to quarantine.
- **If the message is detected as spoof and DMARC Policy is set as `p=reject: Reject the message`**

  - If DMARC says "reject," the message will be outright rejected (bounced) and not delivered.
- **If the message is detected as spoof by spoof intelligence: Move the message to the recipients' Junk Email folders**
  - For spoof detection outside the DMARC scenario, these messages go to Junk Email.

Safety Tips and Indicators

- **First contact safety tip**
  - **What it does**: If enabled, a banner is displayed when a user receives an email from someone they have not communicated with before.
  - **When Off,** no banner will appear for first-time contacts.
- **User impersonation safety tip**
  - **What it does**: Displays a warning tip/badge if an email might be impersonating a user.
  - When **On**, recipients see a warning in suspicious emails.
- **Domain impersonation safety tip**
  - **What it does**: Displays a warning if the domain appears to be impersonated.
  - When **On**, recipients see a warning in suspicious emails.
- **Unusual characters safety tip**
  - **What it does**: If an email has unusual or potentially deceptive characters (for example, homograph attacks with non-Latin characters), this tip warns the user.
  - When **On**, users are notified of suspicious text or characters.
- **Unauthenticated senders symbol (?)**
  - **What it does**: Displays a question mark (?) in the sender photo/avatar location in Outlook or OWA if the message fails certain authentication checks.
  - When **On**, provides a quick visual indicator to end users that the sender is not authenticated.
- **Show "via" tag**
  - **What it does**: If an email is sent via a different domain or on behalf of someone else, a "via" tag appears in the sender line, giving recipients more context about the true sender path.
  - When **On**, increases transparency for users.

- **Honor DMARC record policy when the message is detected as spoof**
    - **What it does**: Respects the DMARC policy (`p=none/quarantine/reject`) set by the sending domain.
    - When **On**, the system will follow the configured DMARC policy for spoofed messages.

Anti-Spam Policy

The following is a list of each setting in the Defender for Office (formerly Office 365 ATP) anti-spam policy (inbound) and a brief explanation of what it means or how it functions:

- **Bulk email threshold**
    - This setting determines how aggressively the filter treats messages classified as bulk mail (often marketing or mass mail). The higher the number, the more lenient the system is toward bulk email. A threshold of 6 is somewhat in the moderate range—so bulk messages that score higher than 6 are more likely to be flagged as spam.
- **URL to .biz or .info websites**
    - Defender for Office can specifically watch for links leading to .biz or .info domains—commonly associated with spam or questionable content. When set to "Off," the filter will *not* take special action solely based on links to these TLDs.
- **Image links to remote sites**
    - This checks if emails contain embedded images hosted on remote servers. Spammers sometimes use remotely hosted images to track opens or to hide malicious content. "Off" means no special filtering based on this criterion.
- **Numeric IP address in URL**
    - Spammers often hide malicious links by using raw IP addresses (for example, http://192.168.1.1/) instead of domain names. When "Off," the filter will not specifically flag URLs containing numeric IPs.
- **URL redirect to other port**
    - Attackers may redirect users to non-standard ports to bypass certain security filters. "Off" means no special filtering or actions are taken for such redirects.
- **Empty messages**
    - This checks for messages that contain no content (completely empty). "Off" means these messages are not treated differently by this particular filter rule.

- **JavaScript or VBScript in HTML**
  - If "On," the filter would scrutinize or block emails containing JavaScript/ VBScript in the HTML body, as these can be used for malicious payloads. Currently, it is disabled.
- **Object tags in HTML**
  - HTML `<object>` tags can be used to embed files or malicious scripts. With "Off," no extra scrutiny is applied to emails containing `<object>` tags.
- **Frame or iframe tags in HTML**
  - `<frame>` or `<iframe>` tags can load external content, sometimes used maliciously. This is "Off," so no special filtering occurs based on frames/ iframes.
- **Embedded tags in HTML**
  - "Embedded" can refer to embedded objects (such as `<embed>` tags), which can hide malicious or tracking content. Currently not enforced.
- **Form tags in HTML**
  - `<form>` tags can be used for phishing (for example, asking for credentials). This option, when "On," would filter or block emails containing suspicious forms. It is disabled here.
- **Web bugs in HTML**
  - Web bugs (tiny, often invisible images) are used to track whether an email was opened. Defender for Office can flag these, but it is currently disabled.
- **Sensitive words**
  - This checks for certain high-risk or flagged words/phrases often associated with spam or offensive content. "Off" means it is not scanning or taking action on these keywords.
- **SPF record: hard fail**
  - Sender Policy Framework (SPF) checks whether the sending server is authorized to send mail for a domain. A "hard fail" indicates the domain's SPF says "This server is NOT authorized," and the email should fail. With "Off," the filter does not automatically reject or quarantine messages on SPF hard fail.
- **Conditional Sender ID filtering: hard fail**
  - Similar to SPF, Sender ID aims to detect email spoofing by verifying the sender's IP against the purported sending domain. "Hard fail" can be enforced if there is a mismatch. "Off" means no special enforcement.

- **Backscatter**
    - Backscatter are bounce messages sent to users because spammers spoofed their address. When "On," the system can detect and filter these unwanted bounce messages. It is "Off," so no special handling is applied.
    - Test mode action
    - Defender for Office can be placed into a test mode to see how changes would impact mail flow without actually blocking or quarantining. This is set to "None," so no test mode is enabled.
- **Bulk email spam action**
    - This indicates that messages identified as "bulk" or marketing are actively subjected to spam action (for example, moved to Junk folder or quarantined). This complements the Bulk email threshold set to 6.
- **International spam - languages**
    - When enabled, emails in specific languages known for higher spam volume can be flagged. This is disabled, so no special filtering by language.
- **International spam - regions**
    - Similar to languages, but for geographic regions. "Off" means the policy does not specifically look at the sending region for spam classification.

Anti-Spam Policies

The following is a breakdown of each setting in your **Defender for Office anti-malware policy** and its role in protecting your organization:

- **Enable the common attachments filter: On**
    - **What it does**: This filter targets potentially dangerous attachment types known to be used for delivering malware (for example, executables, scripts).
    - **Effect**: Any message containing attachments that match these high-risk file types will be flagged for the action specified in the policy (in this case, reject with an NDR).
- **Customize file types**
    - **File types listed**: .ace, .ani, .apk, .app, .appx, .arj, .bat, .cmd, .com, .deb, and 40 other file extensions.
    - **Meaning**: These are specific file types that have been historically associated with malware or are capable of executing code. By listing them here, you are telling Defender to treat these attachments as unsafe and perform the action configured as follows (reject).

- **When these file types are found: Reject the message with a non-delivery receipt (NDR)**
  - **What it does**: If an incoming email (internal or external) has one of the listed file types, the message is outright **rejected**. The sender receives an NDR (non-delivery report), indicating the email was not delivered.
  - **Benefit**: Prevents end users from ever seeing or interacting with potentially malicious attachments.
- **Enable zero-hour auto purge for malware (Recommended): On**
  - **What it does**: Zero-hour Auto Purge (ZAP) for malware continuously monitors messages *after* they have been delivered. If a message is later identified as malicious by updated signatures or threat intelligence, ZAP will retroactively remove it from users' inboxes.
  - **Benefit**: Protects against emerging threats that are discovered shortly after the message arrives. It is a proactive measure to reduce the dwell time of malicious emails.
- **Notify an admin about undelivered messages from internal senders: Send notification to admin tchamtie@kmicro.com**
  - **What it does**: If the policy rejects a message originating from an internal mailbox, it will send a notification to this admin address.
  - **Benefit**: The administrator is immediately aware of potentially malicious or blocked attachments from within the organization, allowing for further investigation.
- **Notify an admin about undelivered messages from external senders: Send notification to admin tchamtie@kmicro.com**
  - **What it does**: Similarly, if an external sender's message is blocked, the same administrator receives a notification.
  - **Benefit**: This ensures visibility into external threats or false positives so the admin can follow up as necessary.
- **Customize notifications: Off**
  - **What it does**: If turned on, you could provide custom text or branding for notification emails.
  - **Current setting**: Since this is off, the default Microsoft-generated notifications are used when a message is blocked or quarantined.
- **Quarantine policy: `AdminOnlyAccessPolicy`**
  - **What it does**: Defines who can access messages that end up in quarantine and what actions they can take (for example, release, preview). "`AdminOnlyAccessPolicy`" means only admins can access or release quarantined messages.

- **Benefit**: Ensures potentially harmful attachments or emails remain restricted until a qualified admin reviews them, preventing users from accidentally releasing threats.

Safe Attachments Policies

Following is a breakdown of each Safe Attachments policy setting and what it does:

- **Safe Attachments detection response: Dynamic Delivery (Preview messages)**
  - **How it works**: When the email is received, the system quickly checks the message body for threats and then delivers the email to the recipient without including the original attachments. Instead, the email may contain placeholders or "preview" versions. In the background, the actual attachments are sent to a sandbox environment for deeper scanning.
  - **Benefit**: This allows users to read or respond to the email almost immediately, while still protecting them from potentially malicious attachments. If the attachments pass the scanning, they are reattached to the email (or a link is provided) after being cleared.
- **Redirect attachments: Enabled**
  - **How it works**: With this option enabled, attachments that need further inspection or those deemed suspicious can be routed to a specific mailbox or person for review.
  - **Benefit**: Ensures that potentially harmful attachments are quarantined or redirected to a safe mailbox for analysis and do not reach the end user directly. This gives administrators or security teams the ability to inspect attachments before end users can access them.
- **Quarantine policy: `AdminOnlyAccessPolicy`**
  - **How it works**: If an attachment or email is determined to be malicious or very high-risk, it is sent to quarantine under the "`AdminOnlyAccessPolicy`."
  - **Benefit**: This means only admins (not end users) can view or release these quarantined items. It prevents users from accidentally releasing potentially harmful attachments and ensures that only authorized security personnel can manage them.

Safe Links Policies

Following is a breakdown of each Safe Links policy setting, explaining how it protects users and how it is configured in this policy:

Protection settings

- **Email**
  - **On**: Safe Links actively checks URLs in emails against a list of known malicious links. When a user clicks a link in an email, the link is validated in real time.
  - **URL Rewriting**: By default, Safe Links rewrites the original URL to a format that goes through the Microsoft filtering service. This allows the system to check the link every time it is clicked.
- **Apply Safe Links to email messages sent within the organization**
  - **On**: Safe Links is not just applied to incoming external messages, but also to internal emails sent from one user to another within the same organization. This helps guard against threats that might originate internally or from compromised internal accounts.
- **Apply real-time URL scanning for suspicious links and links that point to files**
  - **On**: When a user clicks any link—especially those pointing to file downloads or potentially suspicious domains—Safe Links will scan it in real time to determine if it is malicious before allowing the user to proceed.
- **Wait for URL scanning to complete before delivering the message**
  - **On**: With this enabled, the email message will not be fully delivered to the end user (or visible in their mailbox) until Microsoft finishes scanning the links. This ensures that if any link is malicious, it will not reach the user's inbox.
- **Do not rewrite URLs, do checks via Safe Links API only.**
  - **Off**: When this is **off**, Safe Links will rewrite the URLs to a secure format. If it were **on**, Safe Links would *not* rewrite the URLs and would rely solely on a behind-the-scenes API check.
- **Do not rewrite the following URLs in email (0)**
  - **(No URLs listed)**: This option lets admins exclude specific trusted URLs from rewriting. Currently, it is set to zero, meaning no exemptions are set.
- **Teams**
  - **On**: Safe Links is also enabled for Microsoft Teams messages. URLs shared in Teams chats are scanned for malicious content. Notably, Teams Safe Links does *not* rewrite URLs, but checks them in the background at click time.
- **Office 365 Apps**
  - **On**: Safe Links checks URLs within Microsoft 365 Apps (for example, Word,

Excel, PowerPoint, and so on) to protect users if they click embedded links from within those applications. Again, URLs are not rewritten in the apps, but are verified in real time.

- **Track user clicks**
    - **On**: This logs when users click a Safe Links–protected URL. This data can be used in reporting or investigations to track who clicked what link and when.
- **Let users click through to the original URL**
    - **Off**: With this disabled, if a link is deemed malicious, users will be prevented from going to the original URL entirely. If it were **on**, users could choose to bypass the warning page at their own risk.
- **Display the organization branding on notification and warning pages**
    - **Off**: Safe Links can display custom branding or messages on warning pages. If turned on, you might see the company's logo or branding. Currently, it is off, so the default Microsoft warning/notification pages are shown.

Notification settings

- **Use custom notification text**
    - **Off**: When Safe Links detects a malicious link, a default Microsoft warning or notification is displayed. With custom notification text enabled, you could provide a tailored message to users. Currently, no custom text is used.

Threat Protection Policies

Purpose: Offer specialized settings to handle unique or advanced scenarios.

- **Geo-Blocked Emails**
    - Quarantine or reject mail from high-risk regions known for spam or cybercrime.
    - Use caution if your organization legitimately does business worldwide.
- **Attachment File-Type Rules**
    - Automatically quarantine certain file extensions (for example, .exe) or compressed formats.
    - Consider a custom rule for advanced scanning of password-protected archives.
- **High-Risk Sender Thresholds**
    - Implement stricter scanning for newly registered domains or known malicious addresses.

Information Protection Policies

Purpose: Integrate email security with Data Loss Prevention (DLP) and sensitivity labeling to protect sensitive or regulated data.

- **Sensitivity Labels**
    - Configure rules to automatically label emails containing certain sensitive content (for example, personal identifiers, credit card numbers).
    - Decide if labeled emails require encryption or restricted forwarding.
- **DLP Policies**
    - Monitor for content that may violate privacy regulations, such as HIPAA or GDPR.
    - Block or warn users before sending externally if they include unencrypted Personally Identifiable Information (PII).
- **Policy Tips**
    - Provide user-facing tips when they attempt to share sensitive data, guiding them toward secure handling practices.

Email Authentication: DMARC, DKIM, and SPF

Microsoft Defender for Office 365 incorporates key email authentication protocols–**SPF (Sender Policy Framework)**, **DKIM (DomainKeys Identified Mail)**, and **DMARC (Domain-based Message Authentication, Reporting & Conformance)**–to protect users from spoofing, phishing, and domain impersonation.

SPF verifies that messages are sent from authorized servers, that the sender is who he/she claims to be. **DKIM** uses cryptographic signatures to confirm message integrity and sender identity. **DMARC** ties these mechanisms together by specifying a domain's policy on how to handle messages that fail authentication checks.

How Microsoft Defender Applies These:

- **SPF checks** are performed during message receipt. Failing messages are evaluated based on spam policies or DMARC alignment.
- **DKIM** can be enabled per domain. Microsoft 365 automatically signs messages if records are configured, ensuring integrity for outbound mail.
- **DMARC policies** (for example, `p=none`, `p=quarantine`, `p=reject`) are honored when spoofed messages fail both SPF and DKIM.

Configuration Path:

Microsoft 365 Defender Portal → **Email & Collaboration** → **Policies & Rules** → **Threat Policies** → **DKIM**

Monitoring:

Results of SPF/DKIM/DMARC checks are viewable in **Threat Explorer**, **Email Entity** views, and via **Advanced Hunting** (for example, **`EmailEvents`** table using **`AuthenticationDetails`**).

Best Practices:

- Publish DKIM CNAMEs and enable DKIM for all custom domains.
- Implement a DMARC policy with aligned SPF/DKIM to protect brand identity.
- Use spoof intelligence and impersonation protection policies in tandem with authentication protocols.

Quarantine Policies

Quarantine policies define **who can access quarantined messages**, **what actions they can take**, and **how long messages are retained**. These settings directly affect how both users and administrators interact with potentially harmful or suspicious email content.

Key Quarantine Policy Components:

- **Retention Period**: Specify how long a quarantined email remains accessible (default is 15-30 days, depending on policy type).
- **Access Roles**: Restrict release privileges to admins or allow end users to release or report messages.
- **Notification Settings**: Configure daily quarantine summaries to inform users about items held.
- **Message Categories Covered**: Tailor different policies for spam, phishing, malware, or user-reported messages.

Common Policy Configurations:

Threat Type	Action	Quarantine Access
Malware	Reject or Quarantine	Admin-only review (for example, **`AdminOnlyAccessPolicy`**)
Phishing	Quarantine	End-user access with warnings or restricted release
Bulk/Spam	Junk or Quarantine	End-user release allowed (optional)

Table 5.1: *Example Quarantine Policy Configuration*

Advanced Settings:

- Enable **custom user notifications** with branding.
- Allow users to **report false positives** directly from quarantine.
- Use **mail flow rules** to trigger quarantine for specific content types or metadata.

Configuration Path:

Microsoft 365 Defender Portal → **Email & Collaboration** → **Policies & Rules** → **Quarantine Policies**

Why It Matters:

Proper quarantine policy tuning helps strike a balance between **security** and **user experience**, ensuring threats are contained while minimizing disruption from false positives.

Troubleshooting

Even well-implemented solutions can face glitches or require adjustments over time. Following are common issues you may encounter:

Missing or Delayed Emails

- **Symptoms**: Users report non-delivery or extended delays.
- **Causes**: Overly aggressive policy settings, transport rule conflicts, or quarantines going unnoticed.
- **Resolutions**:
  1. **Check Quarantine** regularly to confirm that legitimate messages are not being trapped.
  2. **Refine Policies** by adjusting spam confidence thresholds or adding known good senders to an allow list.
  3. **Mail Flow Rule Audit**: Review any custom rules that might inadvertently move messages to hidden folders.

High False Positives or Negatives

- **Symptoms**: Legitimate emails end up as spam (false positives), or malicious emails slip through (false negatives).
- **Causes**: Inadequate impersonation protection, incomplete domain allow/block lists, or ML models still "learning" your environment.

- **Resolutions:**
    1. **Adjust Impersonation Settings** to protect key executives and commonly spoofed domains.
    2. **Use the Submission Portal** to report false positives/negatives to Microsoft.
    3. **Enable User Reporting**: Make it easy for users to report suspicious emails directly from Outlook.

Safe Links Not Rewriting or Blocking

- **Symptoms**: Users see unaltered URLs, or malicious URLs continue to function when clicked.
- **Causes**: Policy scope is incorrect, the user's mailbox is unlicensed, or a do-not-rewrite domain list is too broad.
- **Resolutions**:
    1. **Check Policy Scopes**: Ensure the policy targets the correct mailboxes, groups, or domains.
    2. **Confirm Licensing** for all affected users.
    3. **Reduce Overly Broad Exceptions**: Re-check the exclude list for any domain that should be covered by Safe Links.

Attachment Scanning Delays

- **Symptoms**: Users complain that they cannot access attachments in a timely manner or that attachments bypass scanning.
- **Causes**: Service congestion, large file volumes, or rare file types.
- **Resolutions**:
    1. **Enable Dynamic Delivery** so users can see email content while attachments are scanned in the background.
    2. **Review Service Health** in the Microsoft 365 Admin Center to rule out platform outages.
    3. **Limit File Size** in certain policies if massive attachments are causing bottlenecks.

Automated Investigation Not Triggering

- **Symptoms**: No evidence of automatic remediation or incident grouping, even though multiple phishing emails are detected.
- **Causes**: Automated investigation disabled, or you only have Plan 1.

- **Resolutions:**
  1. **Upgrade to Plan 2** if you need advanced AIR functionalities.
  2. **Enable Automation** in Threat Policies, ensuring they are set to "Enforce" rather than "Audit."
  3. **Review Roles**: Confirm admin roles can manage or view automated investigation logs.

Licensing or Feature Availability Issues

- **Symptoms**: Missing features such as Threat Explorer, Attack Simulation Training, or advanced dashboards.
- **Causes**: Wrong plan assigned or expired trial license.
- **Resolutions**:
  1. **Check the Microsoft 365 Admin Center** to ensure the correct plan is assigned.
  2. **Renew or Upgrade** if your business requires advanced threat hunting or simulation capabilities.

Reporting and Analytics

Detailed reporting is crucial for both operational awareness and compliance. Defender for Office 365 offers various dashboards and analytics tools:

- **Threat Explorer (Plan 2)**
  - Provides granular insight into detected threats over a specified time period.
  - Allows advanced filtering by sender, recipient, file type, and more.
- **Real-Time Reports**
  - **Email Security Reports**: Show spam, phishing, and malware detection trends.
  - **User Submissions**: Track how often employees report suspicious messages, helpful for gauging security culture.
- **Dashboard Customization**
  - Pin frequent or high-importance widgets (for example, phishing attempts by day, top malicious domains) to your main security dashboard.
  - Schedule regular PDF exports to share with executives or compliance officers.

- **Regulatory and Audit Requirements**
    - Many regulations require that organizations maintain detailed logs of data processing, including email security.
    - Ensure your organization retains logs for the required period (for example, 90 days or longer, depending on regulations).

Conclusion

Microsoft Defender for Office 365 plays a vital role in protecting one of the most frequently targeted vectors in cybersecurity: email and collaboration tools. Its layered defenses—powered by real-time threat intelligence, AI-based phishing detection, and time-of-click URL and attachment scanning—go beyond simple detection to support a proactive and adaptive security posture. When integrated with the broader Microsoft XDR suite, Defender for Office 365 delivers cohesive protection across endpoints, identities, and cloud environments. To fully leverage its potential, organizations should align licensing plans (Plan 1 vs. Plan 2) with their risk tolerance, continuously improve configurations using attack simulations and analytics, and reinforce these technical controls with user education.

Email security is not a one-time setup but an evolving discipline that must keep pace with sophisticated attack methods. Defender for Office 365 benefits from Microsoft's global signal intelligence, enabling it to adapt to new threats through machine learning and telemetry. Human error remains a leading vulnerability, making security awareness training an essential complement to technical defenses. By embedding Defender for Office 365 into a broader security strategy, organizations can turn email from a high-risk vector into a resilient, well-monitored communication layer. In the next chapter, the focus shifts to Microsoft Entra ID—formerly Azure Active Directory—and its role in modern identity security, including conditional access, identity protection, and adaptive trust mechanisms.

Additional Resources

For those seeking a deeper dive into any of the concepts or features mentioned in this chapter, Microsoft offers extensive documentation, learning modules, and community-driven content:

- Microsoft. (n.d.). Microsoft Learn: Defender for Office 365. Microsoft Learn. https://learn.microsoft.com/microsoft-365/security/office-365-security/defender-for-office-365
- Microsoft. (n.d.). Microsoft 365 Defender Portal. Microsoft Security. https://security.microsoft.com

- Microsoft. (n.d.). Safe Links in Microsoft Defender for Office 365. Microsoft Learn. https://learn.microsoft.com/microsoft-365/security/office-365-security/safe-links
- Microsoft. (n.d.). Safe Attachments in Microsoft Defender for Office 365. Microsoft Learn. https://learn.microsoft.com/microsoft-365/security/office-365-security/safe-attachments
- Microsoft. (n.d.). Configure anti-phishing policies in Microsoft Defender for Office 365. Microsoft Learn. https://learn.microsoft.com/microsoft-365/security/office-365-security/set-up-anti-phishing-policies
- Microsoft. (n.d.). Attack Simulation Training in Microsoft Defender for Office 365. Microsoft Learn. https://learn.microsoft.com/microsoft-365/security/office-365-security/attack-simulation-training
- Microsoft. (n.d.). Microsoft Defender for Endpoint. Microsoft Learn. https://learn.microsoft.com/microsoft-365/security/defender-endpoint/microsoft-defender-endpoint
- Microsoft. (n.d.). Microsoft Defender for Office 365 Overview. Microsoft Learn. https://learn.microsoft.com/microsoft-365/security/office-365-security/defender-for-office-365
- National Institute of Standards and Technology. (2018). Framework for Improving Critical Infrastructure Cybersecurity, Version 1.1. NIST. https://nvlpubs.nist.gov/nistpubs/CSWP/NIST.CSWP.04162018.pdf

CHAPTER 6
Entra ID Security

Introduction

Microsoft Entra ID (formerly Azure Active Directory) is a comprehensive cloud-based Identity and Access Management (IAM) platform that helps enterprises secure user identities, manage authentication, and provide conditional access to corporate resources. "Entra ID Security" refers to the breadth of threat detection, monitoring, and response capabilities within Microsoft Entra ID that work together to protect against modern identity-based attacks. This includes risk-based conditional access, Identity Protection, and integration with the broader Microsoft 365 security ecosystem.

Structure

In this chapter, we will cover the following topics:

- Identity is the New Battlefield
- Overview
- Importance of Identity Security
- Integration with Microsoft XDR Ecosystem
- How Entra ID Security Works
- Entra ID Smart Lockout
- Conditional Access Enforcement
- Deployment Deep Dives
- Troubleshooting
- Advanced Detection, Investigation, and Mitigation Strategies

Identity is the New Battlefield

As organizations embrace remote work and cloud-based services, identity security has become a top priority. Cybercriminals increasingly target credentials through **phishing, password spraying, and business email compromise (BEC)**—attacks that have surged in sophistication and scale. Since 2020, reported losses from BEC attacks have risen by nearly **58%. Microsoft Entra ID Security** proactively prevents, detects, and mitigates these threats while ensuring seamless access for employees.

The Evolution of Identity and Access Management (IAM)

IAM has become the **frontline defense** in cybersecurity, driven by several critical factors:

- **Identities Are the Keys to the Kingdom**: User credentials grant access to systems, data, and applications. A compromised identity can provide attackers with **unrestricted access**, making identity protection a top security priority.
- **Managing Complex IT Environments**: Hybrid work, multi-cloud environments, and remote access create challenges in **controlling access**. IAM solutions enforce policies that ensure only authorized users can access sensitive resources.
- **Rise of Sophisticated Cyber Threats**: Attackers use **AI-driven attacks, credential theft, and lateral movement** to infiltrate networks. IAM solutions detect anomalies, enforce least privilege access, and support **Zero Trust Network Architecture (ZTNA)**.
- **Regulatory Compliance**: IAM simplifies compliance with frameworks such as **GDPR, HIPAA, and SOX** by enforcing policies, maintaining audit logs, and enabling rapid incident response.
- **Insider Threat Mitigation**: Insider incidents–malicious or accidental–have increased by **47% since 2022**. IAM solutions **limit access rights and monitor unusual activities**, reducing risk from within.
- **Balancing Security and User Experience**: IAM enhances security while ensuring a frictionless experience. Features such as **Single Sign-On (SSO) and Multi-Factor Authentication (MFA)** streamline access without compromising security.

Securing the Future with Microsoft Entra ID

With identity at the core of modern cybersecurity, **Microsoft Entra ID Security** is essential for organizations seeking **proactive protection, regulatory compliance, and seamless access management**. As threats evolve, **identity security is no longer optional–it is mission-critical**.

Overview

Entra ID Security is built around key pillars that work in unison to protect identities:

- **Identity Protection**: Uses adaptive machine learning to detect risky user sign-ins and risky users. It automatically calculates a user's "risk level" and can enforce remediation actions—such as forcing a password reset or blocking sign-in—based on configurable policies.

- **Conditional Access**: Provides real-time enforcement of policies that govern who can access what, under which conditions. Conditional Access uses signals such as user risk, device compliance, location, and real-time risk detection from multiple sources (for example, Microsoft Defender for Cloud Apps) to allow or block user access.
- **Continuous Monitoring and Telemetry Collection**: Automatically collects identity-related telemetry data from sign-ins, user activities, administrative actions, and third-party integrations. This data is analyzed in the cloud to identify unusual behavior patterns that might indicate suspicious or malicious activity.
- **Behavioral Analysis and Threat Intelligence**: Microsoft's global threat intelligence feeds into Entra ID Security. When Entra sees anomalous sign-in patterns (for example, a user signing in from two far-apart geographic locations within minutes), it flags these events as risk-based sign-ins. Additional signals—such as leaked credentials or repeated sign-in failures—can also elevate user risk.
- **Response Actions**: Entra ID Security can automatically or manually initiate responses to high-risk events, such as requiring Multi-Factor Authentication (MFA), blocking user access, suspending sign-ins, or alerting security teams for further investigation. These response actions contain threats quickly to prevent lateral movement or data exfiltration.

These pillars align closely with Microsoft's Zero Trust principles, where "identity is the new perimeter" and all access requests require verification, regardless of network location.

Importance as an Identity Security Solution

As an enterprise-grade identity solution, Entra ID Security is central to the Microsoft Extended Detection and Response (XDR) ecosystem. Understanding its significance will clarify why it is often considered the foundation of modern cloud security:

- **Comprehensive Identity Protection:** With phishing and credential theft on the rise as just one of countless use-cases, robust identity protection is essential. Entra ID Security monitors sign-in risk, detects compromised credentials, and enforces policies that adapt to the risk level in real time.
- **Integration with Microsoft XDR:** Entra ID Security integrates seamlessly with other Microsoft security services such as Microsoft Defender for Endpoint,

Defender for Cloud Apps, Microsoft Sentinel, and Defender for Office 365. Together, they provide holistic coverage across identities, endpoints, email, and cloud apps. Incidents are correlated across different domains, providing a unified threat picture.

- **Enhanced Visibility and Control:** Centralized dashboards and analytics let security teams review sign-in logs, user risk levels, and policy compliance from one interface. Admins can customize conditional access policies to provide fine-grained control.
- **Efficiency and Automation:** Automated enforcement–such as blocking risky sign-ins or enforcing an MFA prompt–reduces manual intervention. Security analysts can focus on complex incidents, while routine identity threats (such as leaked passwords) are addressed automatically via policy-based actions.

In summary, Entra ID Security is critical for modern organizations by bridging secure access control with real-time threat intelligence, thereby reducing the risk of breaches originating from compromised credentials or unauthorized user access.

Integration with Microsoft XDR Ecosystem

Entra ID Security does not stand alone. It integrates seamlessly with other Microsoft security solutions–such as Defender for Endpoint, Defender for Cloud Apps, Microsoft Sentinel, and now, Microsoft Defender XDR–to create a unified threat response platform. This integration helps correlate identity events with endpoint and network signals, ensuring that suspicious activities are quickly identified and remediated.

A key extension of this integration is the incorporation of Microsoft Entra Privileged Identity Management (PIM). By merging PIM with Defender XDR, organizations gain additional capabilities to protect privileged accounts:

- **Enhanced Threat Detection:** PIM logs all privileged role activations (including suspicious ones such as late-night or foreign IP access) into Entra ID audit logs. Defender XDR then correlates these events with broader security signals (for example, phishing or malware alerts) to detect anomalous activity in real time.
- **Automated Security Response:** Custom detection rules can be created within Defender XDR using Kusto Query Language (KQL) queries that monitor PIM events. For example, unusual activations can trigger high-severity alerts, which in turn activate Microsoft Sentinel playbooks to automatically block access, revoke privileges, or notify security teams.
- **Compliance and Auditing:** The integration logs all privileged identity actions for regulatory compliance and supports audit tracking via Microsoft Purview

Compliance, ensuring that every high-risk event is documented for future analysis.

- **Reduced Attack Surface Area:** Can be configured such that users must submit a justification for their privilege escalation and specify the duration it should be in effect. This way, should an admin user become compromised, the blast radius or damage they can do is significantly reduced.

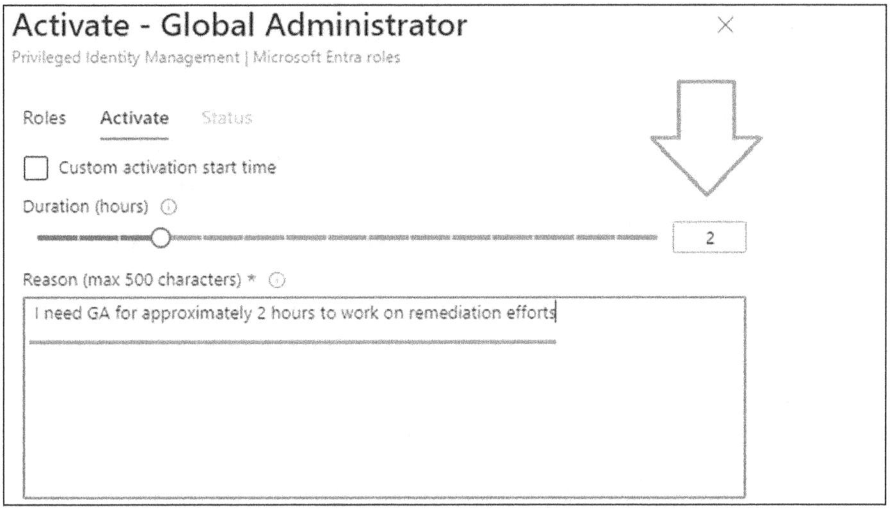

***Figure 6.1**: Activate Privileged Role with PIM*

Best Practices for PIM and Defender XDR Integration

- **Enable Role-Based Access Control (RBAC):** Only allow security teams to manage PIM alerts.
- **Configure Conditional Access Policies:** Block privileged activations from risky locations.
- **Use Microsoft Defender Threat Intelligence:** Cross-correlate privileged activations with known attacker IPs.
- **Regularly Review PIM Activations:** Monitor trends in **Sentinel dashboards**.
- **Implement Just-In-Time (JIT) Access:** Limit **Global Admin & Security Admin activations** to **1-2 hours max**.

How Entra ID Security Works

Entra ID Security uses a blend of signals, machine learning, and automation to protect identities. While endpoint security tools rely on function hooks and DLL injections to monitor operating system behavior, Entra ID's "hooks" occur at the identity and authentication layers. The following provides a deeper look at the mechanisms Entra ID Security uses:

Core Components and Mechanisms

- **Risk Detection and Scoring**
    - **User Risk**: Entra ID assigns risk to users based on factors such as leaked credentials, impossible travel scenarios (sign-ins from geographically distant locations in a short period), or known malicious IP addresses.
    - **Sign-In Risk**: Each sign-in attempt gets assigned a risk score, determined by machine learning models that evaluate anomalies (for example, unfamiliar sign-in properties, atypical device).
- **Telemetry Collection**
    - **Sign-In Logs**: Logs every authentication request, storing fields such as IP address, device ID, location, and authentication method used.
    - **Audit Logs**: Records directory changes, group membership changes, role assignments, and other admin actions.
- **Policy Enforcement**
    - **Conditional Access Policies**: Check sign-in requests against configured conditions–such as device compliance, risk level, and user group membership–and enforce allow/block or prompt for MFA.
    - **Identity Protection Policies**: Automatically respond to risky sign-ins or users, requiring password resets or blocking sign-ins based on threshold rules.
- **Threat Intelligence**
    - **Microsoft Threat Database**: Entra ID leverages a global threat intelligence feed to keep track of known bad IP addresses, leaked credentials, and compromised devices.
    - **Real-Time Signals**: If malicious activity is detected against many organizations, Microsoft adjusts Entra ID's risk algorithms to quickly protect all tenants.
- **Response Actions**
    - **Automated**: Enforce password reset, block a user, or apply MFA if a sign-in meets high-risk criteria.
    - **Manual**: Admins and security analysts can review high-risk users in the portal and take actions such as forcing re-authentication or requiring user sign-out from all sessions.

Entra ID Smart Lockout

Entra ID **Smart Lockout** is a security feature in Microsoft Entra ID (formerly Azure AD) that helps protect user accounts from brute force and password spray attacks. It intelligently locks accounts based on the risk of login attempts, preventing attackers from gaining unauthorized access while minimizing disruptions for legitimate users.

How Smart Lockout Works

Smart Lockout is designed to differentiate between legitimate users who may have mistyped their password and malicious actors attempting to guess credentials.

- **Risk-Based Locking**
  - The system tracks **failed sign-in attempts** for each user.
  - Instead of locking the account based on a fixed number of failed attempts, Smart Lockout **analyzes sign-in patterns** and applies adaptive thresholds based on risk factors.
  - Microsoft's global intelligence (for example, known bad IPs, anomalous sign-in behaviors) helps make more informed decisions.
- **Lockout Duration**
  - If a sign-in attempt fails multiple times, Smart Lockout temporarily prevents further attempts.
  - The **lockout duration increases progressively** for repeated failed attempts.
  - Legitimate users can often regain access sooner, whereas attackers will be blocked longer.
- **IP-Based Differentiation**
  - If Smart Lockout detects multiple failed login attempts from an unfamiliar or known malicious IP address, it **locks the account faster**.
  - If the failed attempts are from a familiar or frequently used IP (such as an office location), it **allows more attempts** before locking out.
- **Self-Recovery for Legitimate Users**
  - If a user enters the correct password from a previously trusted device or location, they can **bypass the lockout** without waiting for the full lockout duration.

Smart Lockout Configurations

Admins can configure Smart Lockout settings in **Microsoft Entra ID (Azure AD) Security** under **Authentication Methods → Password Protection**:

- **Lockout Threshold:** Defines the number of failed sign-in attempts before an account gets locked (for example, 10 failed attempts).
- **Lockout Duration:** Specifies how long the account remains locked before a user can attempt to sign in again (for example, 5 minutes).

- **Reset Counter:** Determines how long failed sign-ins are remembered before resetting the lockout counter.

Default settings:

- Smart Lockout typically locks out after **10 failed attempts**.
- The default **lockout duration is 1 minute**, increasing progressively with repeated failures.

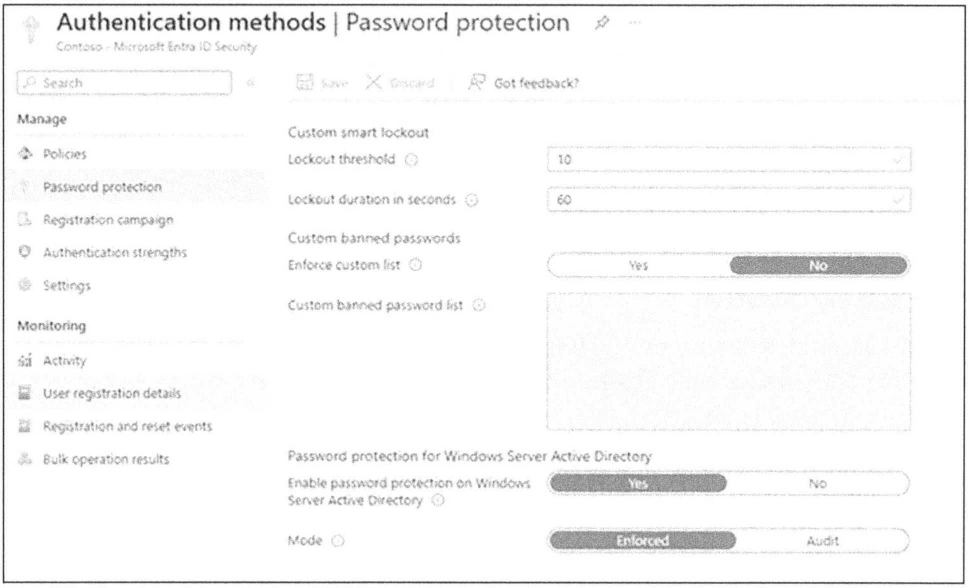

***Figure 6.2**: EntraID Smart Lockout Config.*

This makes it practically insurmountable with today's technology to brute force an account. You can also set a banned password list to prevent your users from using certain keywords from here for further protection.

Benefits of Smart Lockout

- **Reduces False Lockouts:** Helps prevent legitimate users from being locked out due to accidentally mistyped passwords.
- **Protects Against Password Spray Attacks:** Attackers who use common passwords across multiple accounts will be blocked quickly.
- **Uses Microsoft's Threat Intelligence:** Global security signals help prevent attacks before they happen.
- **Minimizes Business Disruptions**: Employees can regain access faster without waiting for manual admin intervention.

Smart Lockout vs. Legacy Account Lockout

Unlike traditional account lockout policies that enforce a **static threshold** (for example, locking accounts after 5 failed attempts for 30 minutes), **Smart Lockout adapts dynamically** to security signals, reducing both **risk** and **user frustration**.

Conditional Access Enforcement

Entra ID relies on policy logic. For instance, you can craft a policy that says:

- *If* user sign-in risk = High
- *Then* require user to reset password or block access.

Those conditions and controls function such as advanced "if/then" statements—whenever sign-in events match high-risk criteria, the user is rerouted to the required control (for example, MFA or block).

Here is a breakdown of an example Conditional Access policy that restricts access to the US and Canada only:

The following illustrates the users to whom this policy applies:

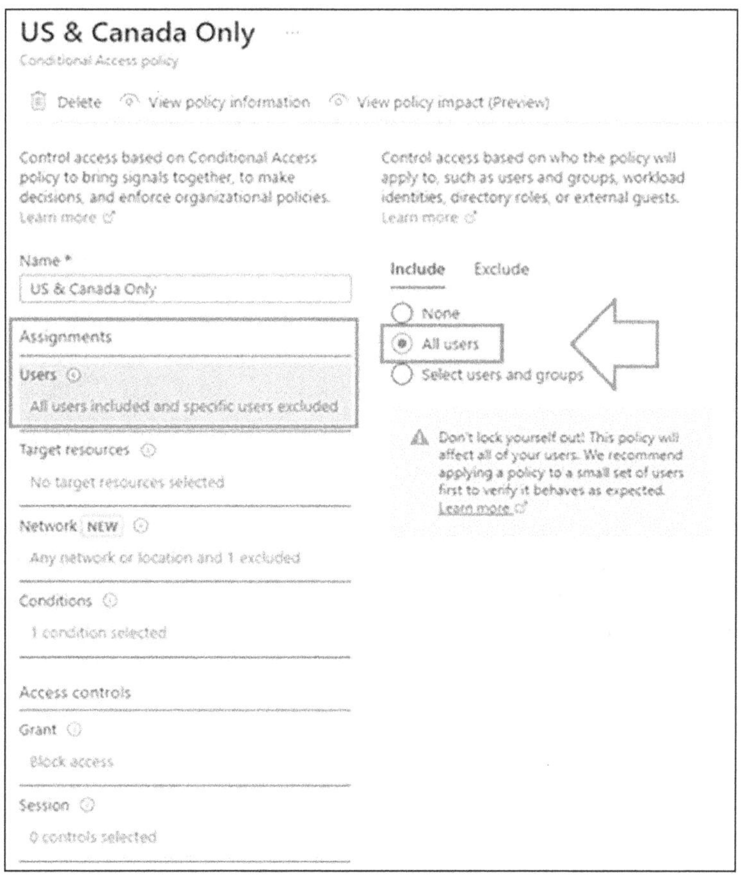

Figure 6.3: *Conditional Access Assignments*

In our example use case, we are protecting our entire organization, so we will apply to all users; however, you can also apply policies to, and exclude, specific individuals or groups to fit your use case.

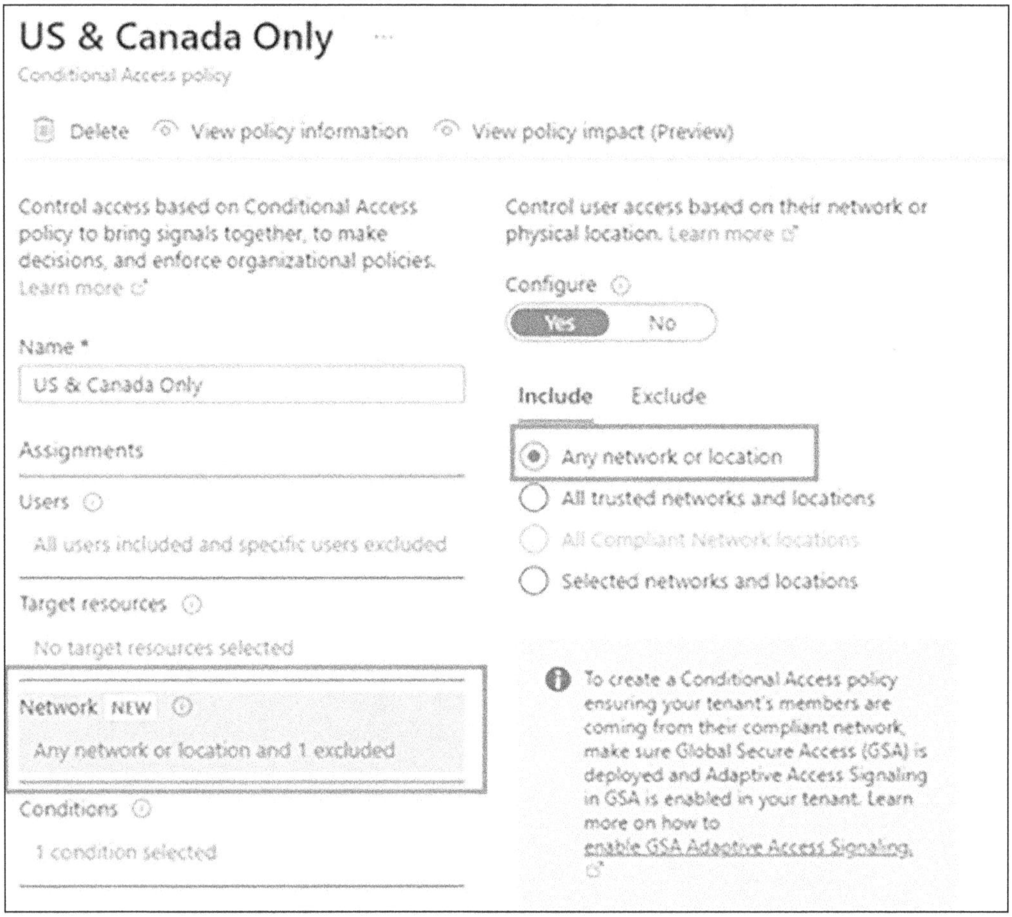

Figure 6.4: *Conditional Access Network Locations*

The preceding screenshot illustrates which networks this policy will apply to. In our example use case, we are taking a black-list approach (opposite of white-list) wherein we black-list/block all access from any network and, in the next image, make an exception for the US and Canada using Named Locations.

Figure 6.5 shows the exception for the US and Canada.

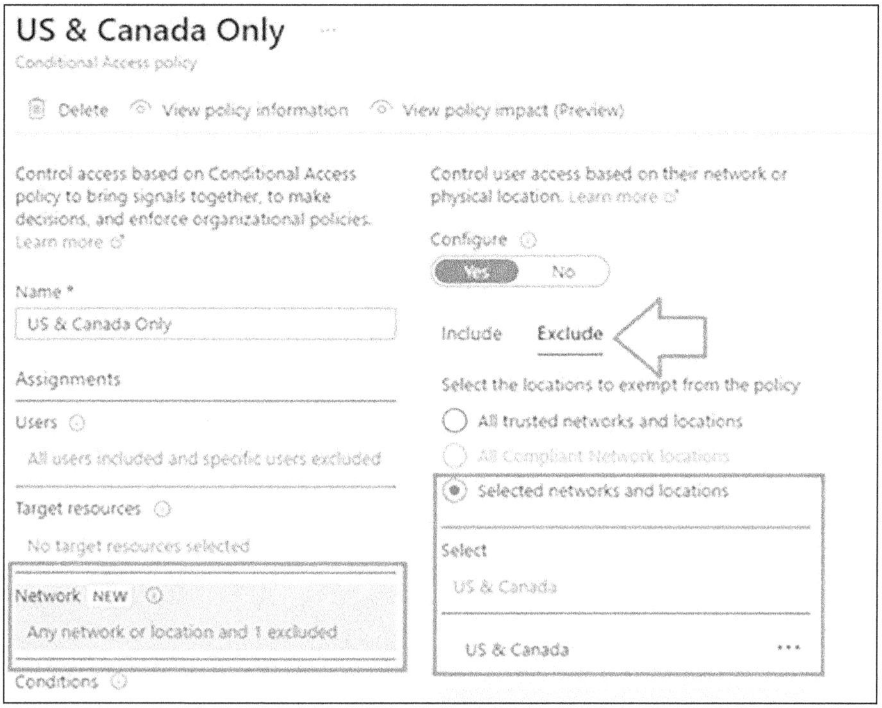

Figure 6.5: *US and Canada Network Location*

This logic relies on previously defined network locations. You can go to **`EntraID Admin Centre >> Protection >> Conditional Access >> Named Locations`** to set them, illustrated as follows:

Figure 6.6: *Named Locations*

The final step in this policy is to set the Access Controls to **Block**, illustrated as follows:

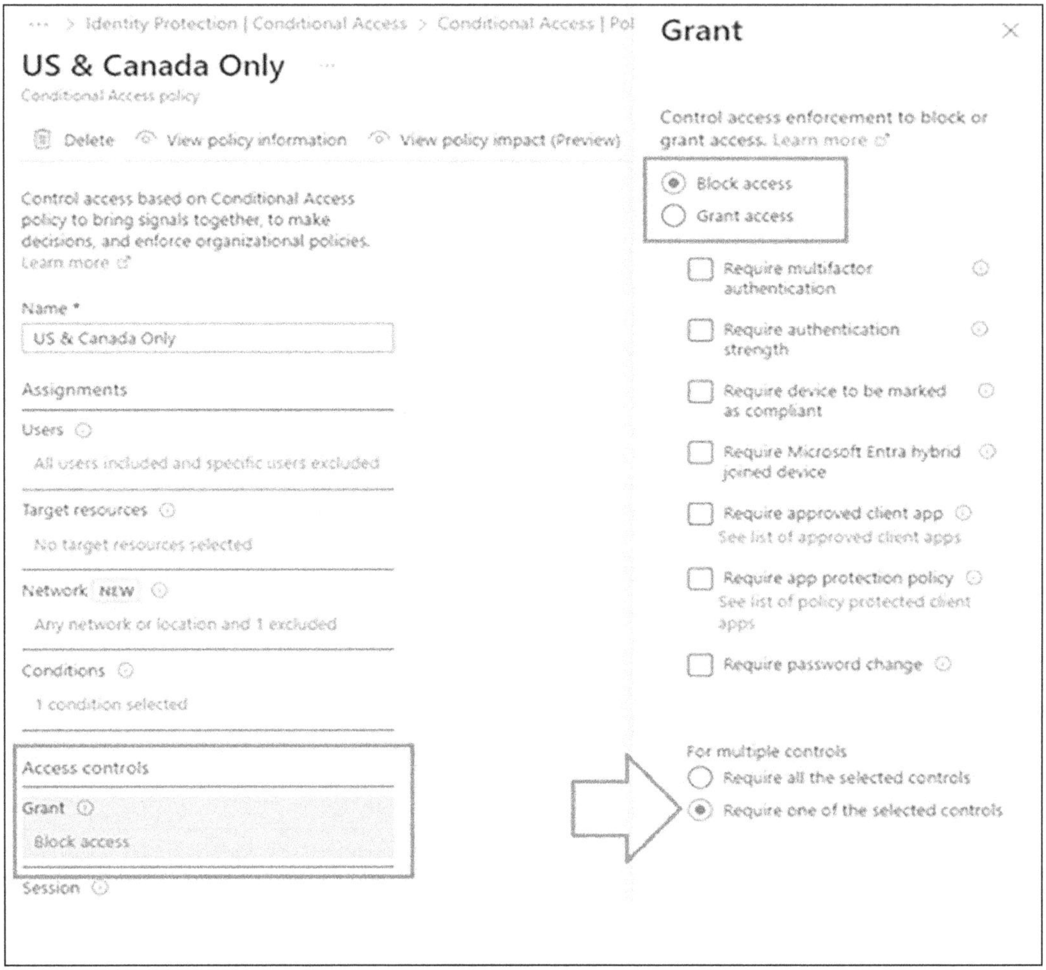

Figure 6.7: *Conditional Access Control*

The end result: A conditional access policy that blocks all sign-ins for all users, from anywhere, except when coming from IP addresses in the US and Canada.

For keeping track of your Conditional Access policies and documenting them in a very clear and visual manner, check out Merril Fernando's idPowerToys Conditional Access Documenter located here: https://r.idpowertoys.merill.net/

Deployment Deep Dives

Entra ID Security can be deployed across various environments and scenarios. While it is inherently cloud-based, many organizations have hybrid or on-premises components–particularly if they maintain an on-premises Active Directory (AD). This chapter will explore core deployment types for Entra ID Security:

- **Cloud-Only**
- **Hybrid** (synchronizing on-prem AD with Entra ID)
- **Federated** (using AD FS or third-party federation services)

Each deployment approach has prerequisite licensing, system requirements, and recommended Microsoft best practices.

Licensing and System Requirements

- **Licensing**
    - **Microsoft Entra ID P1 or P2**: Identity Protection, Conditional Access, and other advanced security features require a Premium P1 or P2 license. P2 includes enhanced risk-based policies and Identity Protection.
    - **Microsoft 365 E3/E5**: These suites may bundle Entra ID Premium licenses.
    - **EMS (Enterprise Mobility + Security)**: EMS E5 includes Entra ID Premium P2, which covers all advanced security features.
- **System Requirements**
    - **Azure Tenant**: An Azure AD/Entra tenant is required to configure policies.
    - **Synchronization Tools** (if hybrid): Azure AD Connect for directory synchronization, or Azure AD Connect Cloud Sync if you prefer a lightweight agent-based model.
    - **Supported Protocols**: Modern authentication protocols such as OAuth2, OpenID Connect, and SAML for Single Sign-On (SSO).

Cloud-Only Deployment for Entra ID Security

Overview of Cloud-Only Deployment:

A cloud-only deployment leverages Microsoft Entra ID without on-premises components. All users and groups reside in the cloud directory, simplifying the environment. This model is often chosen by newer organizations or those that have fully migrated from on-premises infrastructure.

Steps for Deploying in a Cloud-Only Scenario

1. **Create or Verify Your Azure Tenant**
    a. Sign in to the Azure portal (https://login.microsoftonline.com/) to create a new tenant if you do not have one.

b. Configure basic settings, such as custom domain names (for example, contoso.com).

2. **Configure Licensing**

   a. Assign Entra ID Premium licenses to your users.

   b. Make sure users have the necessary licenses for Conditional Access and Identity Protection.

3. **Enable Identity Protection and Conditional Access**

   a. In the Entra admin center, go to **`Protection`** > **`Identity Protection`** to configure user risk and sign-in risk policies.

   b. Enable MFA for all users or, at minimum, for privileged roles. Create a baseline or custom Conditional Access policy that prompts for MFA based on risk or location.

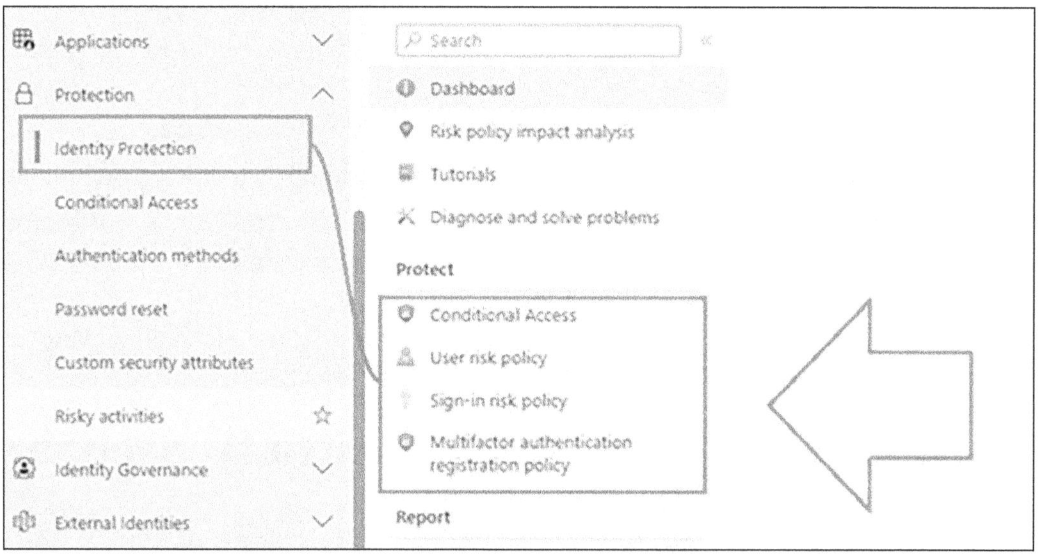

Figure 6.8: *Conditional Access, MFA, and Risk Policies Location*

4. **Configure Self-Service Password Reset (SSPR)**

   a. Allow users to reset their passwords from anywhere, reducing help desk calls.

   b. Integrate with MFA methods (for example, phone, email, authenticator app) to verify identity before password reset.

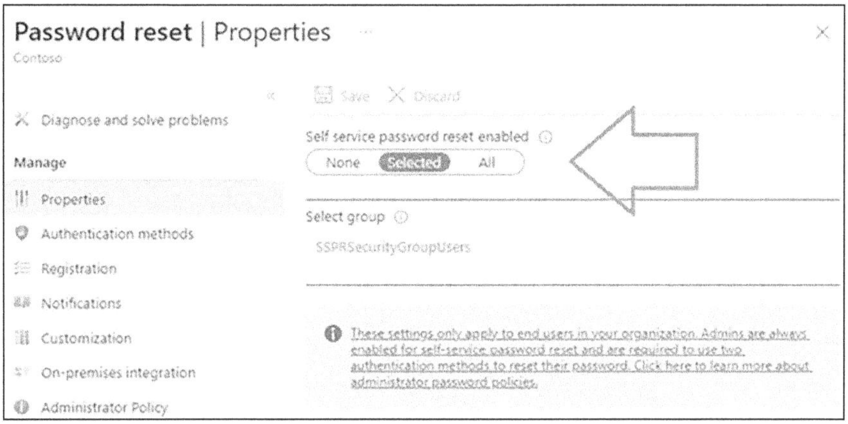

Figure 6.9: *Self Service Password Reset (SSPR)*

5. **Monitor User and Sign-In Risk**
   a. Use the **`Identity Protection Dashboard`** to view risky users and risky sign-ins.
   b. Investigate any high-risk sign-in events or high-risk users, and enforce remediation actions as necessary.

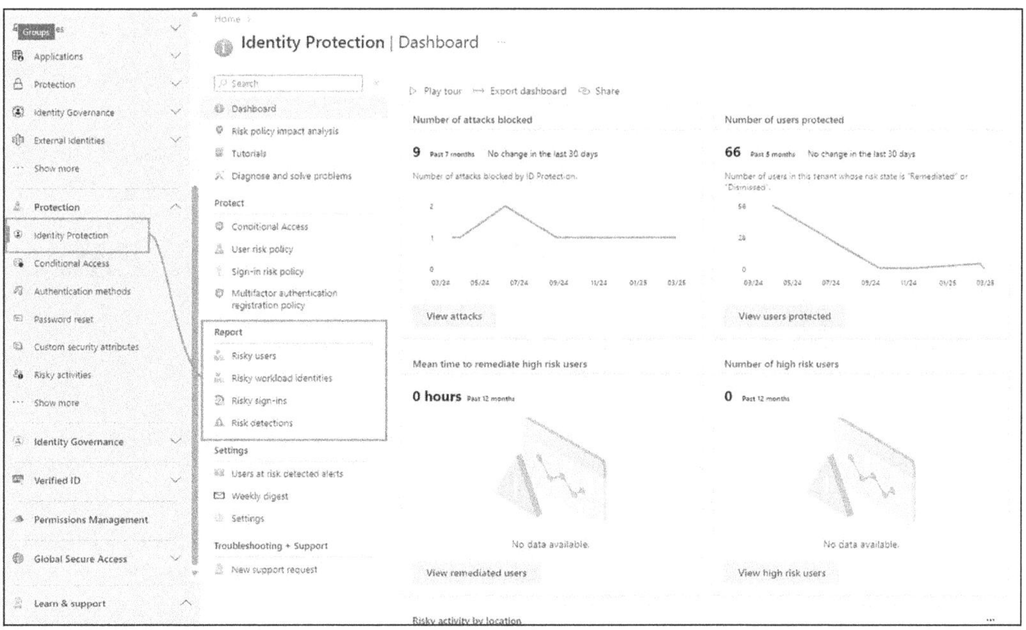

Figure 6.10: *Identity Protection Dashboard*

Configuring Cloud-Only Policies

- **Security Defaults vs. Conditional Access**: Security defaults in Entra ID are a quick way to enforce basic MFA and block legacy authentication. However, Microsoft best practices recommend migrating to full Conditional Access policies for more granular controls. Security Defaults are a great way to get basic protection quickly, but conditional access policies are far more powerful.

- **Application Protection Policies**: If you use Microsoft Intune for device management, enforce device compliance as part of the sign-in condition. This ensures only compliant devices gain access to critical apps.

Troubleshooting Cloud-Only Deployment

- **User Not Prompted for MFA**
    - Ensure the user is correctly assigned a license that includes MFA.
    - Verify that Conditional Access is targeting the correct user or group.
    - Check that Security Defaults (if enabled) are not conflicting with any custom Conditional Access policy.
- **Users Unable to Sign In**
    - Confirm that the user account is not flagged as "risky" and automatically blocked by Identity Protection.
    - Check sign-in logs in Entra ID to see error codes (for example, invalid username/password, conditional access blocks).
- **License Assignment Issues**
    - Verify you have not exceeded your purchased seats.
    - Make sure you have assigned the correct license SKU that includes Identity Protection and Conditional Access.

Deep Dive into Hybrid Deployment for Entra ID Security

Overview of Hybrid Deployment

Hybrid deployment is the most common scenario in large or longstanding enterprises. Here, you have an on-premises Active Directory environment synchronized (or federated) with Microsoft Entra ID. Users and groups may be authored on-premises, then synced to the cloud, enabling consistent credentials across both environments. Entra ID Security sits at the cloud "front door," applying policies to sign-ins that occur from anywhere in the world.

Combining On-Premises and Cloud for Identity Security

- **Azure AD Connect**
    - Synchronizes on-prem AD objects (users, groups, contacts) to Entra ID.

- Can be configured for password hash sync, pass-through authentication, or federation using AD FS.

- **Conditional Access in a Hybrid Context**
  - Even if the user logs on to an on-prem AD-joined device, any attempt to access a cloud app (for example, Exchange Online) still routes through Entra ID.
  - Conditional Access policies trigger based on risk level, sign-in location, or device compliance if you also use Intune.
- **Identity Protection**
  - Risk-based policies remain relevant. If Entra sees suspicious sign-in behavior from a user who typically signs in on-prem, that sign-in can be blocked or require additional verification.
- **Azure AD Connect Health**
  - Provides monitoring for your hybrid identity setup, alerting you if synchronization fails or if an AD FS server has problems. This ensures your hybrid environment stays stable.

Steps for Deploying Hybrid Entra ID Security

1. **Set Up Azure AD Connect**
   a. Install Azure AD Connect on an on-prem Windows Server that can communicate with your domain controllers.
   b. Choose a sign-in method: **Password Hash Sync** (Microsoft's recommended default), **Pass-Through Authentication**, or **Federation**.
2. **Sync Users and Groups**
   a. Perform an initial sync to populate Entra with on-premises identities.
   b. Validate in the **Entra admin center** that your on-prem users appear with matching custom domains.
3. **Configure Conditional Access and MFA**
   a. Even though users are authored on-prem, their authentication to cloud apps (including Microsoft 365) flows through Entra.
   b. Build or import existing Conditional Access policies that require MFA for high-risk sign-ins or block unknown locations.
4. **Enable Identity Protection**
   a. Assign Entra ID Premium P2 to the relevant user population.

   b. Configure risk-based policies to force password resets or block sign-ins if user or sign-in risk is high.

5. **Testing and Validation**

   a. Test sign-ins from both on-prem and external networks.

   b. Check that risk-based policies behave as expected—for example, a sign-in from a known malicious IP address triggers MFA or is blocked.

Best Practices for Hybrid Environments

- **Enforce Modern Authentication**: Disable legacy authentication protocols (IMAP, SMTP, POP) that do not support MFA. This drastically reduces the attack surface.
- **Monitor Sync Errors**: Use Azure AD Connect Health to watch for synchronization or password write-back errors.
- **Consolidate Policies**: Keep your policies well-documented. GPOs might control some on-prem settings, while Conditional Access handles cloud access. Conflict or overlap should be avoided.

Troubleshooting Hybrid Deployment

- **Sync Failures**
    - Check **Event Viewer** on the server hosting Azure AD Connect.
    - Ensure you have not changed service account passwords or blocked required ports (443).
- **User Attributes Not Updating**
    - Verify that attribute filtering in Azure AD Connect is configured properly.
    - Confirm that changes in on-prem AD are not restricted (for example, an OU excluded from sync).
- **Sign-In Risk Warnings**
    - If you see repeated high-risk sign-ins for a user, investigate compromised credentials.
    - Force the user to reset their password on-prem or use the cloud-based SSPR if enabled.

Deep Dive into Federated Deployment for Entra ID Security

Overview of Federated Deployment

Federation refers to using identity providers such as Active Directory Federation

Services (AD FS) or third-party services (Okta, Ping, and more) to handle user authentication, while Entra ID acts as a relying party. Organizations that require advanced or specialized sign-in flows—often for compliance or integration reasons—may choose federation.

- **AD FS**
  - On-premises federation service that validates user credentials locally, then hands a security token to Entra ID.
  - Passwords are never stored or synced to the cloud.
- **Third-Party Identity Providers**
  - Some enterprises maintain a complex identity environment with multiple IDPs.
  - Entra ID still applies conditional access on top of the federated token it receives.

Steps for Deploying Federated Entra ID Security

1. **Set Up Federation (AD FS or Third Party)**
   a. Configure trust between Entra ID and your identity provider.
   b. In AD FS, create a Relying Party Trust for Microsoft 365 or other cloud apps.
2. **Enable Conditional Access**
   a. Even though initial credential validation happens on-prem, Entra ID can still prompt for MFA based on device or location.
   b. This is known as the "claims pipeline": claims pass from AD FS to Entra ID, which in turn applies final policy logic.
3. **Configure Identity Protection**
   a. Risk-based sign-in detection can still occur. If suspicious behavior is detected, Entra ID can prompt for additional authentication—even if AD FS has already issued a token.
4. **Testing and Monitoring**
   a. Federated sign-ins can be trickier to troubleshoot because you have logs in multiple systems: AD FS logs on-prem and Entra sign-in logs in the cloud.
   b. Validate your claims flow by signing in from a test account with different risk scenarios (for example, atypical device or region).

Troubleshooting Federated Deployment

- **Token Issuance Failures**
  - Check AD FS event logs for detailed errors.
  - Verify that the Federation Service Name and endpoints match what is configured in Entra ID.
- **Conditional Access Not Triggering**
  - Make sure the claims from AD FS include the user principal name or other required attributes.
  - Confirm the user or group is targeted by your Conditional Access policy in Entra ID.
- **AD FS Farm Issues**
  - If your AD FS farm is behind a load balancer, ensure SSL certificates and custom domain configurations are valid.
  - Use the **AD FS Rapid Restore Tool** or **Azure AD Connect Health for AD FS** to identify performance or connectivity issues.

How Automated Identity Response Works

While Entra ID does not terminate processes like an endpoint solution, it can quickly contain an identity-based threat:

- **Triggering Automated Investigations**
  - **Alert-Triggered**: High-risk sign-in or detection of leaked credentials can automatically trigger an Identity Protection alert.
  - **Manual Initiation**: Security teams can label a user as compromised in the portal, prompting protective actions.
- **Investigation Process**
  - Entra ID evaluates recent sign-in attempts, changes to authentication methods, and the user's device posture.
  - Checks if suspicious IP ranges or known malicious addresses are involved.
- **Remediation Actions**
  - **Force Password Reset**: Immediately invalidates the user's token and requires a new password at next sign-in.
  - **Block Sign-In**: Suspends the user from authenticating until an admin lifts the block.
  - **Require MFA**: Elevates the user's sign-in process to ensure identity ownership.

- **Action Center (Microsoft 365 Defender Portal)**
    - For organizations integrated with Microsoft 365 Defender, identity-related alerts surface alongside endpoint, email, and cloud app alerts.
    - Security teams can track, approve, or roll back identity-based remediation (such as re-enabling a user after further investigation).

Benefits of Automated Response

- **Reduced Alert Volume**: Automated actions address straightforward credential compromises without manual security team intervention.
- **Faster Containment**: Risks are mitigated in near real-time, limiting threat actor lateral movement.
- **Consistency and Accuracy**: Policies execute the same way every time, avoiding manual errors.

Troubleshooting

Entra ID Security is robust, but misconfigurations or environmental factors can cause issues. This section will address common problems and provide structured steps to resolve them.

Common Issues

- **User Blocked Unintentionally**
    - Overly aggressive risk policies might block legitimate sign-ins from new locations.
    - **Solution**: Adjust user risk policies to better align with your organization's travel/remote work patterns. Add an exclusion group for certain users if necessary.
- **Conflicting Conditional Access Policies**
    - Different administrators or security teams might create overlapping or contradictory policies.
    - **Solution**: Consolidate policy creation under a limited set of admins and regularly audit policies. Use the Policy Simulator to test new rules.
- **Synchronization Errors**
    - In hybrid mode, Azure AD Connect might fail to sync certain attributes or organizational units.
    - **Solution**: Check Azure AD Connect Health. Review filters and ensure the OU or attributes in question are included.

- **Sign-In Latency**
  - Identity-based sign-ins might slow down if your environment or network is experiencing high load.
  - **Solution**: Verify your network throughput, check AD FS or Azure AD Connect server performance, and consider load balancing or additional servers if necessary.
- **Licensing and Feature Availability**
  - If you see certain features "grayed out" or not functioning, you might be missing the necessary license (for example, P2 for Identity Protection).
  - **Solution**: Confirm license assignments in the Microsoft 365 admin center or Entra admin center.

Troubleshooting Steps for Specific Scenarios

Following are detailed steps to help you quickly address common Entra ID Security challenges:

Scenario 1: Users Not Prompted for MFA Despite Conditional Access

- **Policy Scope**: Confirm that the Conditional Access policy targets the correct user or group.
- **Exclusion Check**: Ensure there is not a higher-priority policy or an exclusion group that bypasses MFA.
- **License Assignment**: Make sure the user is licensed for MFA (Entra ID Premium or equivalent).
- **Sign-In Logs**: Review sign-in logs. If the sign-in is marked "MFA Not Required," the user or conditions did not meet the policy triggers.

Scenario 2: High-Risk Sign-Ins Not Being Blocked

- **Risk Policy Configuration**: Check Identity Protection settings. If your user risk policy is set to "Allow Access," then high-risk users will not be blocked.
- **User Exclusions**: Verify that certain VIP or admin accounts have not been excluded.
- **Sign-In Risk vs. User Risk**: Ensure you are configuring the correct policy. You might need to enforce "Block Access" for high sign-in risk or user risk specifically.

Scenario 3: Password Hash Sync Stopped Working

- **Azure AD Connect Health**: Check the Azure portal for alerts related to sync.
- **Event Viewer**: On the server running Azure AD Connect, look for errors (for example, service account password expired).

- **Agent Status**: If you use Cloud Sync, verify the agent's status in the Azure AD Connect Cloud Sync management portal.
- **Network/Firewall**: Confirm port 443 outbound is open to the required Microsoft endpoints.

Scenario 4: Federation Timeout or Failed Logins

- **Federation Service Name**: Ensure it is spelled correctly and matches the SSL certificate for AD FS or the third-party IDP.
- **Token Signing Certificate**: Check if the certificate is nearing expiration or has expired.
- **Relying Party Trust**: Verify that the trust settings in AD FS match the domain in Entra ID.
- **Entra ID Reply URLs**: Make sure the return URL in Entra ID's enterprise application configuration is correct.

Scenario 5: User Prompted for MFA Multiple Times

- **Session Lifetime**: If the "Remember MFA" setting is disabled or short, users may be prompted frequently.
- **Conflicting Policies**: Overlapping rules can cause repeated challenges.
- **Device State**: If the device is not registered or compliant, a new MFA prompt might trigger every time an app or service is accessed.

Advanced Detection, Investigation, and Mitigation Strategies

As threat actors increasingly exploit identity infrastructure to establish persistence and elevate privileges, defenders must adopt proactive strategies to detect, investigate, and mitigate high-impact identity-based attacks. This section provides practical, scenario-driven guidance for responding to advanced threats targeting hybrid identity environments—particularly those involving Azure AD Connect, Password Hash Sync, Active Directory Federation Services (AD FS), and synchronization rule manipulation.

Each scenario is broken down into three actionable components:

- **Detection Strategy**: Key telemetry sources and Microsoft security tools to surface relevant signals.
- **Step-by-Step Investigation**: Procedures for identifying indicators of compromise across Microsoft Entra ID, Defender for Identity, and Sentinel.
- **Mitigation**: Prescriptive controls and architectural recommendations to harden your environment and reduce attack surface.

These blueprints are designed not only to support incident response efforts but also to help security teams build resilient defenses against identity compromise. Whether you are detecting lateral movement on domain controllers, tracing anomalous sync activity, or uncovering token forgery attacks, this section equips you with the tools and techniques to stay ahead of evolving threats.

Azure AD Connect Server Compromise

Detection Strategy:

- **Azure Identity Protection Signals:**
    - Impossible Travel / Atypical travel (from service account usage)
    - Unfamiliar sign-in properties (from on-prem accounts synced)
    - Role elevation or unusual directory changes
- **Azure AD Sign-in logs** (for anomalous activity by sync accounts)
- **Microsoft Defender for Identity** on Domain Controllers to track lateral movement or credential access
- **Sentinel Analytics Rules** detecting sync-related anomalies

Step-by-Step Investigation:

1. **Identify anomalous activity** from the `MSOL_<GUID>` or `AAD_Connect` account:
    a. Go to **Microsoft Entra > Monitoring > Sign-in logs**
    b. Filter by "Service principal sign-in" or "Application"
    c. Look for unexpected sign-in locations, times, or IPs
2. **Check Azure AD Connect Health** for configuration changes:
    a. Go to **Azure AD Connect Health > Sync Errors / Alerts**
    b. Review **Sync Rule Modifications** or recent **admin changes**
3. **Inspect PowerShell Activity**:
    a. Run Get-ADSyncRule and export all custom rules
    b. Compare current config with baselines (if maintained)

Mitigation:

- **Just-In-Time Access** using **PIM** for Entra roles
- **Deploy Microsoft Defender for Identity** on the Azure AD Connect server
- **Use gMSA** (Group Managed Service Account) with limited access for sync
- **Isolate Azure AD Connect** (no outbound internet except to Azure endpoints)

- **Disable unused sync rules and apply scoping filters**

Password Hash Sync Credential Theft

Detection Strategy:

- This is primarily a **defense-in-depth** scenario; detection requires:
  - **Defender for Identity alerts** on LSASS memory access or Mimikatz use
  - **Azure Identity Protection** risk detections on unusual user behavior
  - **Sentinel custom rules** to detect login attempts from multiple tenants/IPs using cracked credentials

Step-by-Step Investigation:

1. **Use Defender for Identity** to detect credential dumping attempts on the sync server.
   a. Alert: Suspected credential theft using LSASS access
2. **Review recent sign-ins** for any cloud accounts synced from AD:
   a. Go to **Microsoft Entra > Sign-in logs**
   b. Search for synced users logging in from unusual IPs or bypassing MFA
3. **Check if PHS was recently re-enabled** (could indicate reconfiguration after compromise):
   a. Azure AD Connect > Sync Services Manager > Synchronization Options

Mitigation:

- **Use only PTA (Pass-through Authentication)** with **MFA** instead of Password Hash Sync when possible
- **Harden Azure AD Connect Server**:
  - Disable RDP
  - Only allow domain-joined accounts with least privilege
- **LSASS Protection**: Enable Credential Guard or run the sync server on Server Core (no LSASS GUI access)
- **Ensure logs from AAD Connect are sent to Microsoft Sentinel**

AD FS Compromise (Golden SAML Attack)

Detection Strategy:

- Azure Identity Protection will not catch Golden SAML directly–it **bypasses Entra ID login flow**.

- You must rely on:
  - **Microsoft Defender for Identity** (on AD FS box) for lateral movement
  - **Azure AD Sign-in logs** to detect **token-based sign-ins without previous interactive login**
  - **Audit logs** for changes to AD FS config

Step-by-Step Investigation:

1. **Review Entra ID sign-in logs** for SAML token-based logins:
   a. Filter by **Client App = Browser** and **Authentication = Federated**
   b. Look for sign-ins **without corresponding token issuance logs** in AD FS
2. **Correlate with AD FS logs** (requires log collection from on-prem)
   a. Look for issuance of tokens outside of expected hours or from anomalous accounts
3. **Verify token signing certificate integrity**:
   a. Check AD FS certificate stores (certlm.msc) for unauthorized or expired certs
   b. Compare against known-good certificate thumbprints

Mitigation:

- **Rotate AD FS Token Signing Certificates** regularly (not just relying on 3–5 year certs)
- **Enable Certificate-Based Alerting** in Sentinel or custom script monitoring
- **Migrate to Entra ID Cloud Authentication** (eliminate AD FS dependency)
- **Implement Conditional Access** policies to detect federated token anomalies (for example, block legacy or token-based sign-ins without MFA)

Manipulation of Synchronization Rules

Detection Strategy:

- **Azure AD Connect Health Alerts** on rule changes
- **Manual review** of sync rule definitions
- Use **Sentinel Watchlist** to compare against baseline rules

Step-by-Step Investigation:

1. **Extract Current Rules**:
   a. `Get-ADSyncRule | Export-Csv "C:\rules.csv"`

2. **Check for anomalous rules**:
   a. Any rules altering group membership or adminRoles attributes
   b. Rules with transformations on **`memberOf`**, **`msDS-PrincipalName`**, **`userPrincipalName`**
3. **Compare timestamps of sync rule changes** with admin activity:
   a. Go to **Microsoft Entra > Audit Logs**
   b. Filter by **Application = Azure AD Connect**

Mitigation:

- **Limit Azure AD Connect Admins** (should not be Domain Admins)
- **Disable unnecessary out-of-box sync rules** (https://learn.microsoft.com/en-us/entra/identity/hybrid/connect/concept-azure-ad-connect-sync-default-configuration)
- **Implement sync scoping filters** to avoid syncing unnecessary objects
- **Log and alert** on sync rule modifications via custom Sentinel alerting
- **Back up sync rules weekly** and store in version-controlled repository (for example, Azure DevOps)

Conclusion

Microsoft Sentinel delivers a robust, cloud-native platform that fuses the analytical depth of SIEM with the operational efficiency of SOAR. Through its deep integration with Log Analytics Workspaces, Microsoft 365 Defender, and Azure Logic Apps, Sentinel enables high-fidelity telemetry ingestion, advanced rule-based detections via KQL, and automated remediation workflows. The extensibility offered by the Content Hub—ranging from data connectors and analytics rules to hunting queries and playbooks—allows for rapid deployment and iterative tuning in dynamic threat environments. Whether provisioned via ARM templates or manually through the portal, Sentinel provides a flexible deployment model that supports both greenfield and mature SOC architectures.

The next chapter will delve into configuring analytics rules, building visual dashboards, and orchestrating response logic to operationalize Sentinel at scale.

Points to Remember

- **Central Role of Identity**: Identities have become the new perimeter; protecting them is paramount.
- **Layered Protection**: Entra ID Security uses Conditional Access, Identity Protection, and real-time threat intelligence to detect and block malicious sign-ins.
- **Flexible Deployment**: Whether you are purely cloud-based, hybrid, or federated, Entra ID Security supports different architectures without sacrificing control or visibility.
- **Automation**: Adaptive policies and automated responses allow security teams to handle routine identity threats quickly, focusing on advanced threats that require human expertise.
- **Integration with Microsoft XDR**: Entra ID Security integrates with tools such as Microsoft Defender for Endpoint, Microsoft Sentinel, and Defender for Office 365, giving you a 360-degree view of enterprise security.

By following Microsoft's best practices—including well-defined Conditional Access policies, careful license assignment, and diligent monitoring—you can build a robust identity security strategy that adapts to evolving threats and secures your organization's most valuable asset: its users' credentials.

Helpful Links, References and Resources

- **A Look at U.S. Business Email Compromise Statistics (2024) - Hashed Out by The SSL Store™** https://www.thesslstore.com/blog/business-email-compromise-statistics/
- **Insider Threats in 2024: 30 Eye-opening Statistics - PrivacySavvy** https://privacysavvy.com/security/business/insider-threats-statistics/
- **Azure Portal:** https://portal.azure.com/
- **Entra Admin Center:** https://entra.microsoft.com/
- **Merril Fernando's idPowerToys Conditional Access Documenter:** https://r.idpowertoys.merill.net/
- **Security Defaults in Microsoft EntraID:** https://learn.microsoft.com/en-us/entra/fundamentals/security-defaults
- **Five Steps to Securing your Identity Infrastructure:** https://learn.microsoft.com/en-us/azure/security/fundamentals/steps-secure-identity
- **What is Microsoft Entra?** https://learn.microsoft.com/en-us/azure/security/fundamentals/steps-secure-identity

- **Microsoft Entra Deployment Plans:** https://learn.microsoft.com/en-us/entra/architecture/deployment-plans
- **Available Authentication and Verification Methods in Entra ID:** https://learn.microsoft.com/en-us/entra/identity/authentication/concept-authentication-methods
- **What is Conditional Access?** https://learn.microsoft.com/en-us/entra/identity/conditional-access/overview

CHAPTER 7
Introduction to Microsoft Sentinel

Introduction

Microsoft Sentinel is a cloud-native Security Information and Event Management (SIEM) and Security Orchestration, Automation, and Response (SOAR) platform that integrates security analytics, threat intelligence, and automated incident response capabilities. By leveraging the scalability and advanced analytics offered by Azure, Sentinel provides organizations with comprehensive threat detection, intelligent investigation, and swift automated response capabilities to modern cybersecurity challenges.

Structure

In this chapter, we will cover the following topics:

- Overview: Defining SIEM and SOAR
- Microsoft Sentinel's Comprehensive SIEM Capabilities
  - Common SIEM Use Cases
  - Real-World SIEM Implementation Example
- Microsoft Sentinel's Comprehensive SOAR Capabilities
  - Common SOAR Use Cases
  - Real-World SOAR Implementation Example
- XDR Integration and Ecosystem
  - Microsoft Native Integrations
  - Third Party Integrations
- Deployment Deep Dive
  - Components

    - Log Analytics Workspace, Microsoft Sentinel, and Microsoft XDR Connector
- Securing Your Sentinel Deployment: Credential, Access, and Network Controls
- Deploying Microsoft Sentinel via ARM Template

Overview: Defining SIEM and SOAR

Security Information and Event Management (SIEM) systems aggregate, analyze, and manage security data across an organization's IT infrastructure. They help detect, analyze, and respond to threats, compliance issues, and anomalies effectively. SIEM solutions typically provide log management, event correlation, real-time monitoring, and forensic analysis capabilities.

Security Orchestration, Automation, and Response (SOAR) solutions enhance operational efficiency by automating repetitive security tasks and orchestrating response actions across multiple platforms. They improve response times, reduce human error, and allow security teams to focus on higher-priority strategic tasks.

Microsoft Sentinel's Comprehensive SIEM Capabilities

Comprehensive security insights are achieved through centralized data collection, intelligent analysis, and clear visualization tools.

- Data aggregation from various sources such as Entra ID, Office 365, third-party security solutions, on-premises systems, and IoT devices.
- Advanced analytics powered by built-in AI and machine learning to detect threats and anomalies in real-time.
- Visual dashboards and reports for clear visibility into security events and trends.
- Compliance and audit capabilities aligned with regulatory standards.

Common SIEM use cases:

- Real-time monitoring and threat detection
- Compliance reporting and management
- Log aggregation and event correlation
- Incident response and forensic analysis

Real-World SIEM Implementation Example:

Scenario

A leading global healthcare provider implemented Microsoft Sentinel to secure sensitive patient data and comply with stringent healthcare regulations such as HIPAA. Prior to Sentinel, the organization struggled with fragmented security solutions, leading to delayed detection and response times.

Implementation

After deploying Sentinel, the organization was able to consolidate logs from multiple hospital locations and remote healthcare facilities into a unified platform. Sentinel's AI-powered analytics rapidly identified unusual access patterns, potential data breaches, and insider threats. For example, Sentinel detected an attempted unauthorized access to electronic health records by a compromised account, triggering an automated alert and isolating the affected user account within minutes.

Outcome

This rapid response prevented sensitive data exposure and ensured compliance with regulatory mandates. Over the first year of deployment, the healthcare provider achieved a 50% reduction in incident response times, significantly reduced risk exposure, and improved regulatory audit outcomes.

Microsoft Sentinel's Comprehensive SOAR Capabilities

Streamlined and automated threat response is enabled through integrated tools, intelligent playbooks, and collaborative workflows.

- Playbooks leveraging Azure Logic Apps to automate incident response and security operations.
- Integration with Microsoft and third-party security tools for streamlined orchestration.
- Intelligent, automated investigation capabilities for rapid threat resolution.
- Collaborative response framework for efficient threat management.

Common SOAR use cases:

- Automated incident response to reduce response time
- Security orchestration across multiple tools
- Threat hunting and proactive security measures
- Workflow automation and efficiency improvement

Real-World SOAR Implementation Example

Scenario

A large retail enterprise faced challenges with manual security operations, including delayed response times, repetitive tasks overwhelming security analysts, and inconsistencies in incident handling across multiple regions.

Implementation

The organization deployed Microsoft Sentinel's SOAR capabilities, utilizing integrated Azure Logic Apps to automate incident responses to phishing threats–one of their most frequent security issues. Sentinel was configured to trigger automated playbooks immediately upon detection of suspicious email activities flagged by Microsoft Defender for Office 365. These playbooks orchestrated responses across multiple systems, performing actions such as quarantining emails, blocking malicious senders, notifying affected users, and opening tickets in their ITSM tool for visibility and tracking.

By leveraging automated workflows, the retail enterprise significantly reduced response times from hours to mere minutes, achieving consistent, standardized threat mitigation across its global operations. Additionally, automation alleviated the manual burden on security analysts, allowing them to refocus efforts toward proactive threat hunting and more complex investigative activities.

Outcome

This implementation resulted in:

- **75% reduction** in the time to contain phishing incidents.
- Improved operational efficiency, allowing analysts to focus on strategic tasks rather than repetitive manual responses.
- Increased consistency and accuracy in incident handling and reporting.

This deployment of Sentinel's SOAR capabilities not only streamlined the enterprise's security operations but also contributed to measurable enhancements in overall cybersecurity posture.

XDR Integration and Ecosystem

Microsoft Sentinel offers robust integration capabilities that enable seamless interoperability with numerous Microsoft solutions and third-party security technologies. These integrations create a unified, cohesive ecosystem, allowing organizations to leverage existing security investments and improve the overall efficacy of threat detection, response, and mitigation efforts.

Microsoft Native Integrations

Deep integrations with Microsoft security platforms provide unified visibility, enriched threat intelligence, and end-to-end protection across identities, endpoints, and cloud environments.

- **Microsoft Defender Suite:** Sentinel integrates directly with Microsoft Defender solutions, including Defender for Endpoint, Defender for Identity, Defender for Office 365, and Defender for Cloud Apps. These integrations enable comprehensive monitoring and unified threat analysis across endpoints, identities, cloud applications, and email.
- **Entra ID:** Sentinel captures identity and access management (IAM) logs and threat signals from Entra ID, enhancing visibility into user authentication, conditional access policies, anomalous login behaviors, and potential identity-based threats.
- **Azure Security Center / Defender for Cloud:** Integration with Defender for Cloud enriches Sentinel with continuous cloud security posture management (CSPM) data, threat protection insights, compliance evaluations, and recommendations for improving security hygiene across Azure, hybrid cloud, and multi-cloud environments.

Third-party Integrations

Extensive third-party integrations transform Microsoft Sentinel into a unified security operations hub, delivering holistic visibility and streamlined threat management across the entire IT ecosystem.

- **Network Security Vendors:** Sentinel integrates with leading network security providers such as Palo Alto Networks, Cisco, Fortinet, and Check Point. Through these integrations, Sentinel ingests firewall logs, VPN access data, intrusion detection/prevention system (IDS/IPS) alerts, and web traffic logs, enabling comprehensive analysis of network-based threats.
- **Endpoint Detection and Response (EDR) Providers:** Sentinel's seamless connectivity with third-party endpoint security solutions such as CrowdStrike Falcon, Carbon Black, and Symantec Endpoint Protection enables security teams to correlate endpoint threat telemetry with broader organizational security insights, thereby improving incident detection and response times.
- **Security Monitoring and Log Management Tools:** Organizations leveraging existing investments in Splunk, IBM QRadar, or Elastic Stack can integrate these solutions with Sentinel, enhancing visibility across diverse log sources. This facilitates centralized analysis, event correlation, and optimized incident response workflows, eliminating security data silos.

- **Threat Intelligence Platforms:** Sentinel integrates with threat intelligence providers such as Anomali, Recorded Future, ThreatConnect, and MISP. By ingesting up-to-date threat intelligence feeds, Sentinel enriches security analytics and facilitates more effective proactive threat hunting and detection.
- **Ticketing and ITSM Solutions:** Integration with IT service management platforms like ServiceNow, Jira Service Management, Zendesk, and BMC Helix ITSM streamlines incident management, enabling automated ticket creation, prioritization, and escalation aligned with organizational incident response procedures.
- **Cloud Infrastructure and SaaS Providers:** Sentinel can also integrate security insights from major cloud platforms such as AWS, Google Cloud Platform (GCP), and SaaS services such as Salesforce and Box. This provides visibility and monitoring capabilities that span multi-cloud and hybrid cloud deployments, facilitating consistent security management across diverse environments.

These integrations collectively enable Microsoft Sentinel to serve as a central security operations hub, empowering security teams with holistic visibility, efficient orchestration, and unified threat management capabilities across an organization's entire IT and cloud infrastructure.

Deployment Deep Dive

Understanding these foundational components is essential, as they define how Microsoft Sentinel collects, organizes, analyzes, and secures data. Mastery of these elements enables teams to design, manage, and scale Sentinel deployments with confidence, efficiency, and cost-effectiveness.

Components

- **Azure Resource Group:** An Azure Resource Group acts as a logical container for organizing and managing Azure resources collectively. It is recommended to name resource groups clearly, typically using a format such as **RG-Descriptor-YourInitials** to make ownership and purpose easily identifiable, especially in shared environments. Clear naming helps prevent accidental deletions during cleanup operations—particularly useful when managers attempt to control costs by identifying and removing unused or unidentified resources. Both Log Analytics Workspaces and Microsoft Sentinel deployments exist within these Azure Resource Groups.
- **Log Analytics Workspace:** A Log Analytics Workspace is a centralized Azure Monitor service designed to collect, store, and analyze logs and telemetry from diverse sources, including on-premises and non-Azure cloud environments. It provides robust querying tools, visualization

capabilities, and alert configuration, seamlessly integrating with numerous Azure services. Beyond IT and security analytics, a Log Analytics Workspace can also serve unique scenarios–for example, setting up alerts from IoT-based solutions, such as environmental sensors for soil conditions, ideal for gardening enthusiasts tracking moisture or temperature conditions. Microsoft Sentinel operates on top of this workspace, harnessing its data-collection and analytical strengths.

- **Microsoft Sentinel:** Microsoft Sentinel is a cloud-native Security Information and Event Management (SIEM) solution built atop Azure Log Analytics Workspaces. Sentinel enhances standard log analytics capabilities by integrating sophisticated security functionalities, including automated threat detection, proactive threat hunting, and incident response powered by advanced AI algorithms and automation.
- **Sentinel Solutions from the Content Hub:** Sentinel Solutions, available via the Microsoft Sentinel Content Hub, offer pre-packaged integrations and configurations, enabling quick deployment of advanced security capabilities. These solutions typically include:
  - **Data Connectors:** Enable streamlined ingestion of logs from multiple external data sources into Sentinel.
  - **Workbooks:** Provide interactive, intuitive dashboards for data analysis and visualization.
  - **Analytics Rules:** Automatically detect threats by analyzing log data patterns and generate timely security alerts.
  - **Hunting Queries:** Empower security analysts to proactively identify hidden threats through targeted searches.
  - **Playbooks:** Automate incident response workflows leveraging Azure Logic Apps, significantly reducing response time.
- **Sentinel Analytics Rules:** Sentinel Analytics Rules are customizable rulesets that automatically identify potential security threats or suspicious behavior by analyzing log data using Kusto Query Language (KQL). These rules run at scheduled intervals, continuously monitoring logs for specific threat indicators. When criteria defined within a rule are met, Sentinel generates alerts and captures critical contextual details, aiding security teams in investigation and response efforts.

  Organizations can create analytics rules using pre-built Microsoft templates or design custom rules tailored to their unique security requirements.
- **Connectors from the Content Hub:** Data Connectors available through the Sentinel Content Hub facilitate the seamless integration and ingestion of log data from diverse technology providers and services into your Sentinel

workspace. These ready-to-use connectors simplify onboarding by reducing setup complexity, providing a central location to discover, manage, and deploy integrations tailored to various vendor-specific data sources.

Log Analytics Workspace, Microsoft Sentinel, and Microsoft XDR Connector

The following steps will explain how to deploy a Log Analytics Workspace to a Resource Group, then adding Microsoft Sentinel and connecting the Microsoft XDR Connector.

Step 1: Create a Log Analytics Workspace

1. Sign in to the Azure Portal (https://portal.azure.com).
2. Navigate to **`Resource Groups`** and select **`Create`** to create a dedicated resource group (for example, RG-Sentinel-XDR).
3. Once your resource group is created, go to **`Azure Monitor`** → **`Log Analytics Workspaces`**.

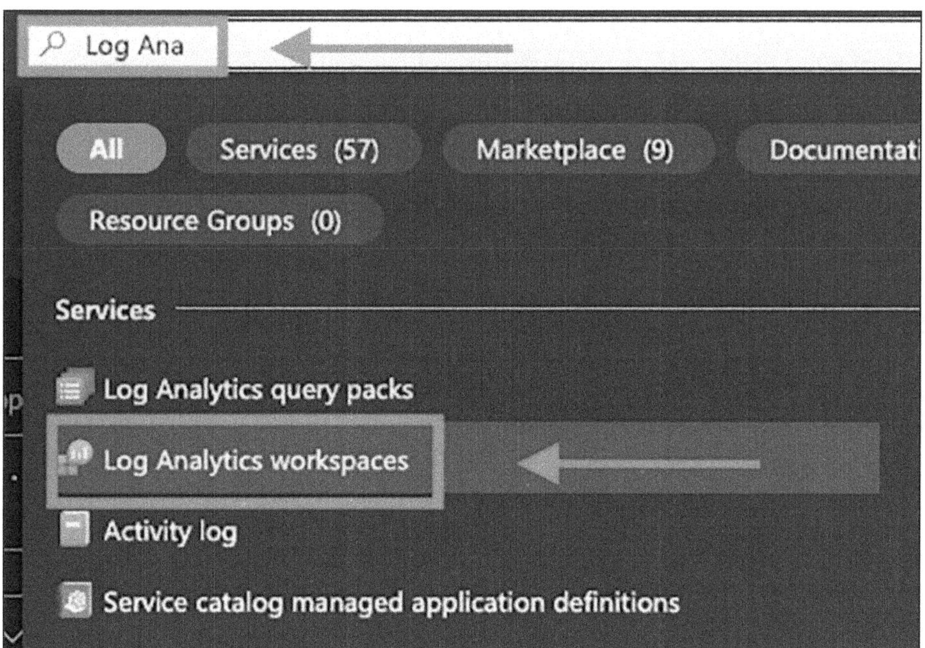

Figure 7.1: *Log Analytics Workspaces*

4. Select **`Create`**.

    a. **`Subscription`**: Choose your subscription.

b. **`Resource Group`**: Select your newly created resource group (my-resource-group in the following illustration).

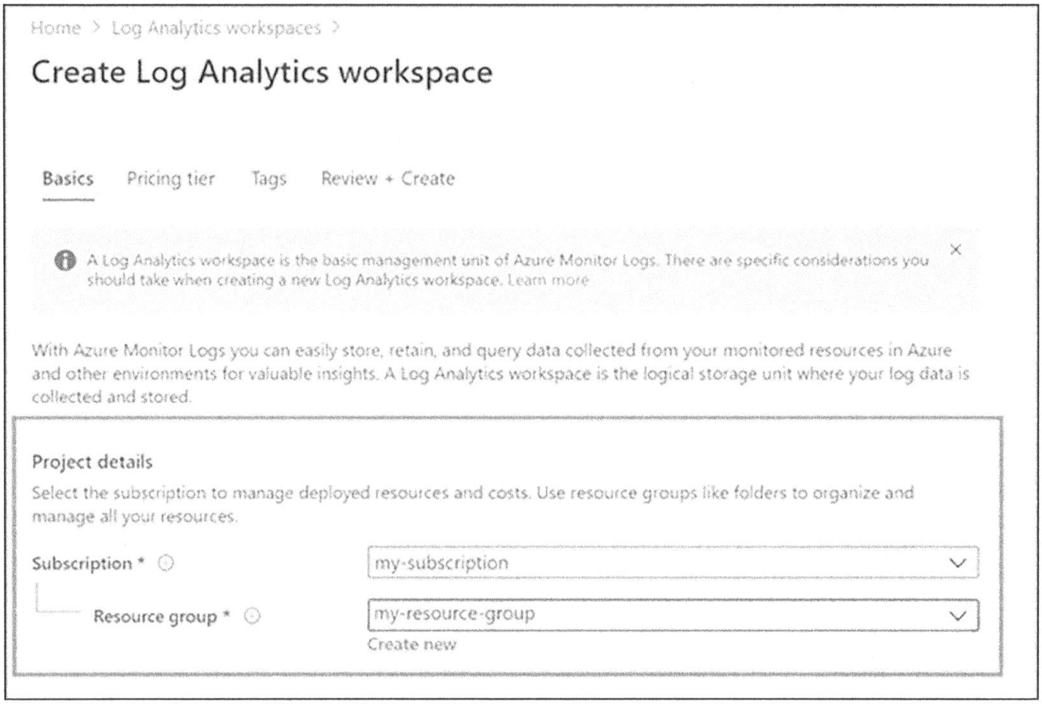

Figure 7.2: *Log Analytics Workspace Details 1*

c. **`Name`**: Provide a descriptive name, for example, my-workspace.

d. **`Region`**: Select a region aligned with compliance and data residency requirements.

Figure 7.3: *Log Analytics Workspace Details 2*

5. Click **`Review + Create`**, then **`Create`** to deploy the workspace.

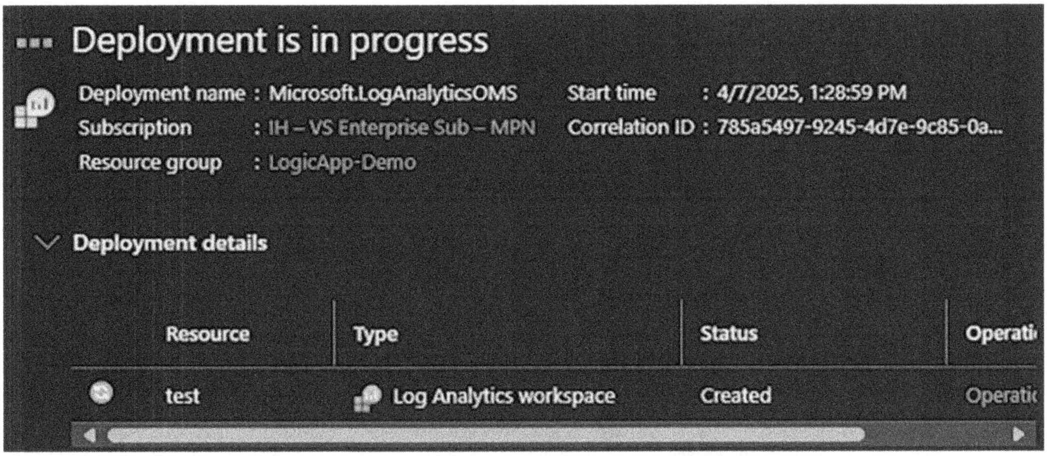

Figure 7.4: *Log Analytics Workspace Deployment in Progress*

You will be notified when your deployment is complete.

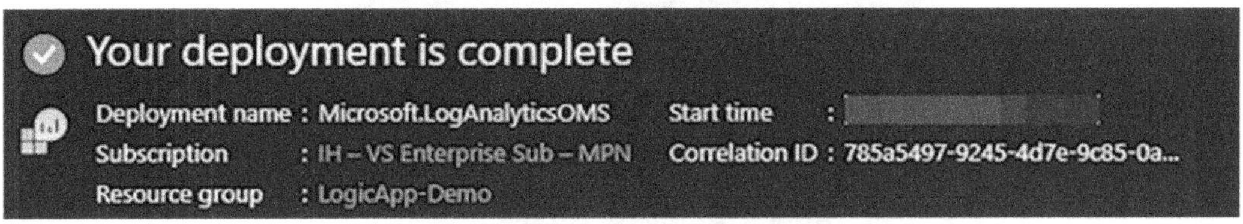

Figure 7.5: *Log Analytics Workspace Deployment Complete*

Step 2: Deploy Microsoft Sentinel

1. After deployment, navigate to the newly created **`Log Analytics Workspace`**.
2. Search for and click on **`Microsoft Sentinel`** from the Azure search bar.
3. Select **`Create`**.
4. Select your **`Log Analytics Workspace`** and click on **`Add`**.

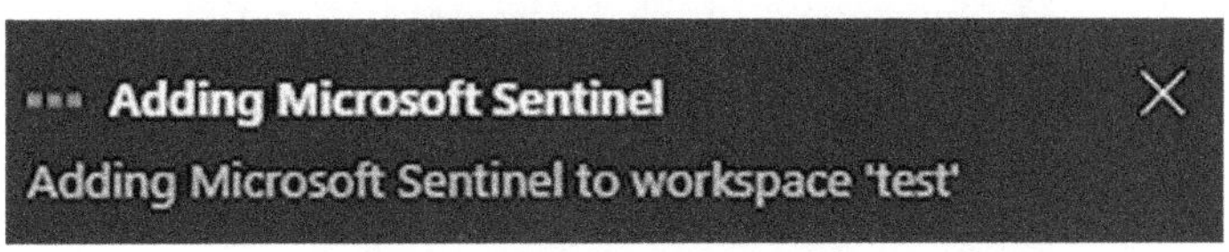

Figure 7.6: *Adding Microsoft Sentinel*

5. **Microsoft Sentinel** is now active and ready for configuration.

Step 3: Configure Microsoft 365 Defender (XDR) Connector

1. Within the Microsoft Sentinel workspace, navigate to **`Content Hub`**.
2. Search for **`Microsoft Defender XDR`** and select it.

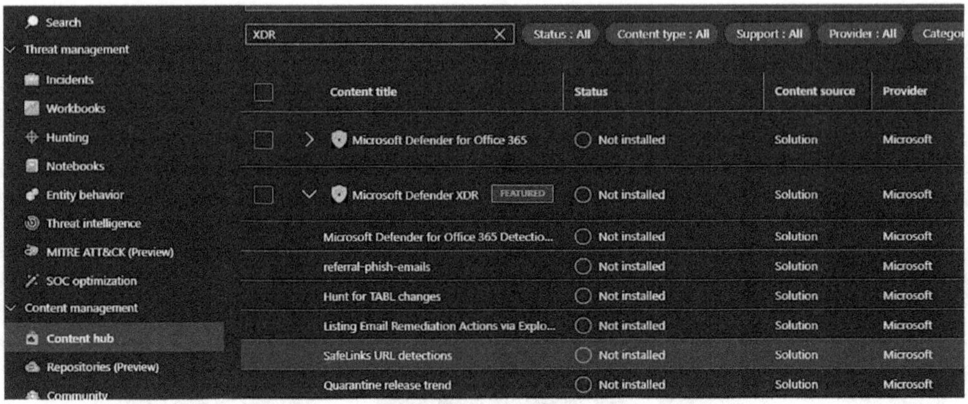

Figure 7.7: *Content Hub*

3. This brings a fly-out menu from the right-hand side that contains additional details and the **`Install`** button. Click on **`Install`**.

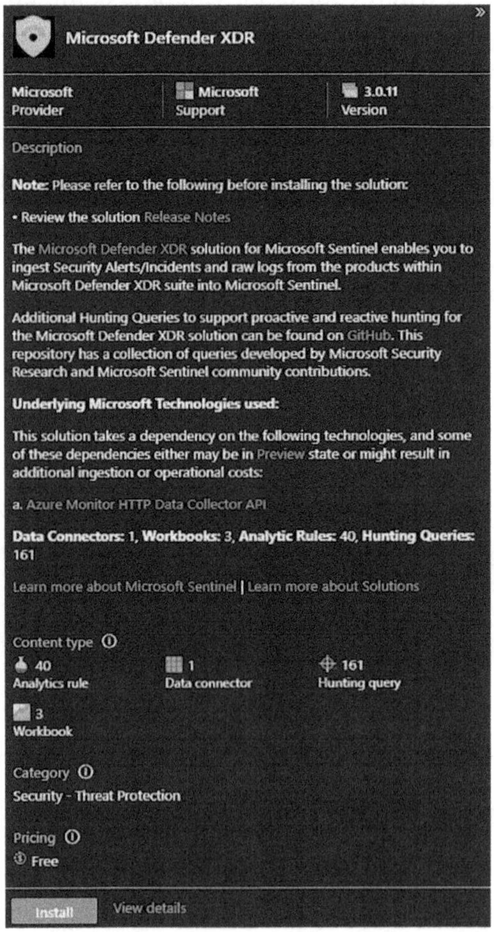

Figure 7.8: *XDR Connector in Content Hub*

4. A blue "**`In progress`**" status icon will appear to indicate the installation has started.

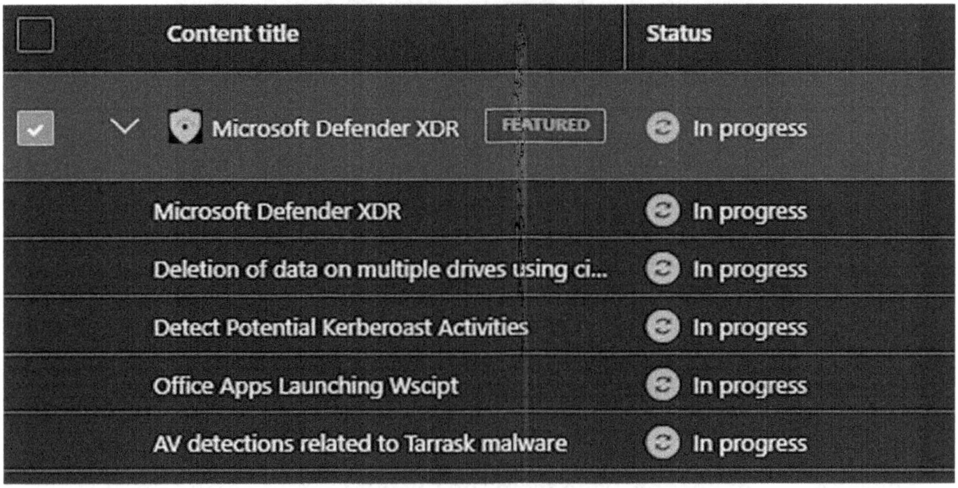

Figure 7.9: *XDR Connector Install*

5. Now, when you open the **Defender XDR** connector, you will see green check marks indicating that the connector has successfully installed. Now, let us configure and enable it.

Figure 7.10: *XDR Connector Installed*

6. Navigate to the **`Connectors`** blade in the left menu and locate the **`Defender XDR`** connector.

Figure 7.11: *XDR Connector in Data Connectors*

7. Select **`Open Connector Page`** from the fly-out menu to bring up the Connector page.

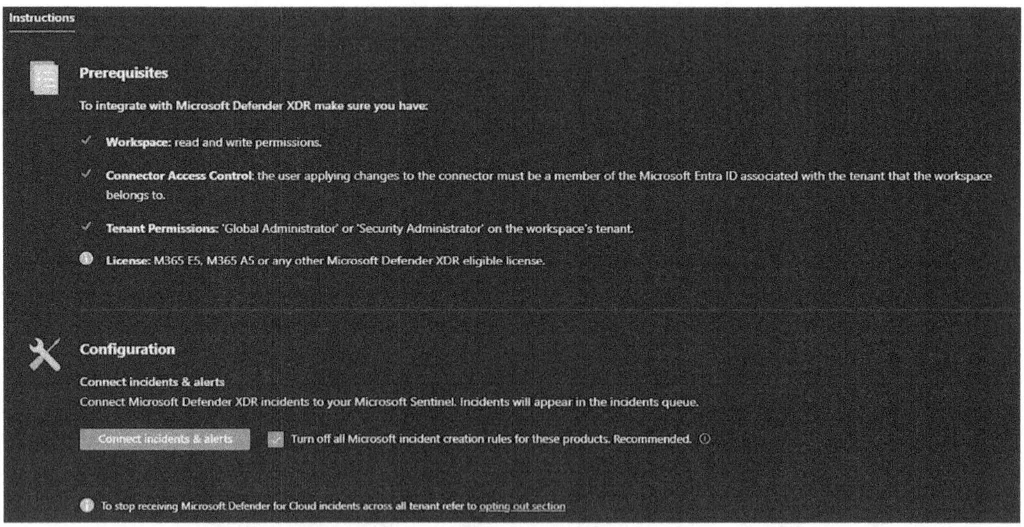

Figure 7.12: *XDR Connector Deploy*

8. Click **`Connect Incidents & Alerts`** and enable incident synchronization.
   - **Incident creation**: Turn on incident creation to synchronize Microsoft 365 Defender incidents with Sentinel.
   - **Bi-directional sync**: Enable as desired for status synchronization.
9. Next, under **`Select Tables`**, confirm telemetry types:
   - Alerts

- Incidents
- Device Events
- Identity Events
- Email Events
- App Governance

10. Click **`Apply changes`** to save the configuration.

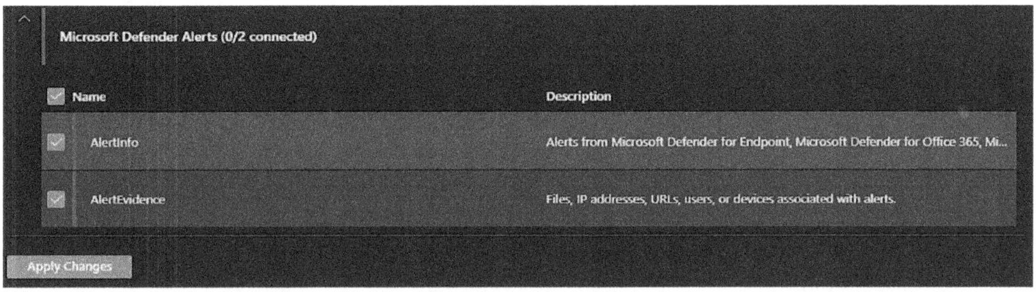

Figure 7.13: *XDR Telemetry Types*

Step 4: Validate Data Flow

1. Wait 15-30 minutes for data ingestion.
2. Navigate to **`Logs`** in your Sentinel workspace.
3. Run a query such as:

```
SecurityAlert
| where ProviderName == "MDATP"
| take 10
```

Confirm that alerts from Microsoft 365 Defender appear.

4. Repeat validation steps for **`DeviceEvents`**, **`IdentityInfo`**, **`EmailEvents`** as needed:

```
DeviceEvents
| take 10
```

Step 5: Configure Sentinel Analytics and Automation

1. Navigate to **`Analytics`** under Sentinel to configure rule templates.
2. Enable relevant rules for detection and response based on your threat model.
3. Configure automated responses through **`Playbooks`** as needed to operationalize your XDR setup.

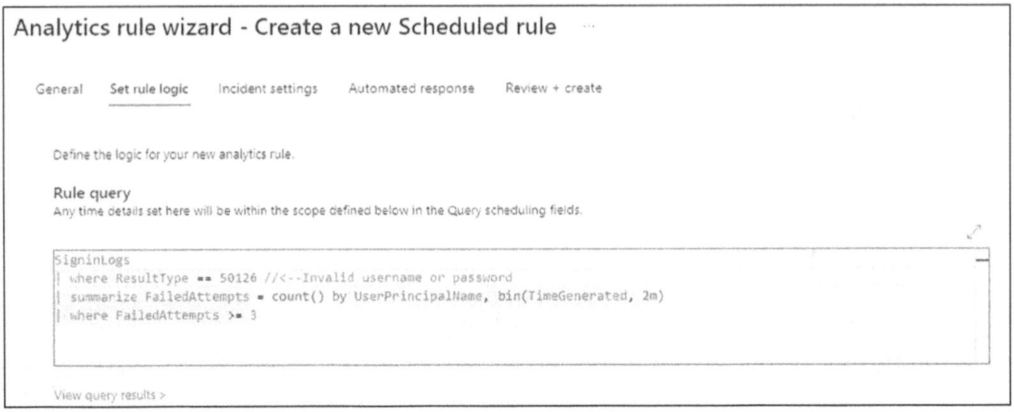

Figure 7.14: *Analytics Rule Logic*

Step 6: Continuous Monitoring and Optimization

1. Regularly review data ingestion costs and optimize ingestion by filtering unnecessary data.
2. Implement workbooks and dashboards to visualize XDR telemetry and operational KPIs.
3. Continuously refine rules and playbooks based on threat intelligence and operational feedback.

This deployment strategy ensures a secure, compliant, and optimized XDR environment, leveraging Microsoft Sentinel and Microsoft 365 Defender (**Analytics Rules**, **Workbooks**, and **Automation** will be covered in the next chapter).

Securing Your Sentinel Deployment: Credential, Access, and Network Controls

Deploying Microsoft Sentinel is only part of building a secure environment. To protect your data and operations, it is essential to secure how credentials are stored, control who can access your workspace, and limit network exposure. This section outlines key best practices to harden your Sentinel deployment.

Credential Management with Azure Key Vault

While the chapter outlines the use of data connectors and playbooks, it does not address how sensitive credentials (for example, API keys, client secrets, or agent credentials) should be securely stored. Best practice in Azure is to use **Azure Key Vault** to centrally manage and store secrets, keys, and certificates. When deploying Sentinel solutions or Logic Apps that require authentication, integrating them with Key Vault ensures:

- Secrets are not hardcoded in workflows or templates.

- Access to secrets is auditable and controlled via RBAC and managed identities.
- Secrets can be rotated without code changes.

Application: Key Vault should be explicitly referenced during connector deployment or Logic App creation for accessing APIs or third-party tools securely.

Granular Azure Role-Based Access Control (RBAC)

The chapter covers Sentinel's architecture and components, but it lacks discussion around **access control** to the Log Analytics Workspace itself. Azure RBAC allows fine-grained control over:

- Who can query, write to, or manage the workspace.
- Limiting access to specific tables (for example, only allowing security teams to view SecurityAlert and DeviceEvents).
- Enforcing **least privilege** principles across the SOC team and automation accounts.

Application: Roles such as "Log Analytics Reader," "Microsoft Sentinel Contributor," and custom roles should be strategically assigned to service principals, Logic Apps, and users based on job function and risk exposure.

Network Access Controls for Log Analytics Workspace

By default, Log Analytics Workspaces are accessible over the internet. However, you can restrict access by:

- Enabling **Private Link** to ensure that only trusted networks can connect.
- Using **IP allowlists** or **Service Endpoints** to define safe sources.
- Disabling public access where feasible.

Application: When deploying a Sentinel environment–especially in regulated industries–network access restrictions should be part of the baseline configuration to reduce exposure to potential exfiltration or unauthorized log injection.

Best Practices

To fully operationalize a secure Sentinel deployment, a supplemental section should be included that outlines:

- Storing secrets in **Azure Key Vault** with Key Vault references in Logic Apps and connectors.
- Applying **granular RBAC policies** to restrict workspace access by role and service identity.
- Configuring **network controls** on the Log Analytics Workspace to block or limit public access.

These practices align with Microsoft's Zero Trust and secure-by-design models and are critical for enterprise-grade SIEM deployments.

Microsoft Sentinel via ARM Template

An Azure Resource Manager (ARM) template is a JSON-formatted file used to define, deploy, and manage resources within Microsoft Azure. It provides a declarative way to describe infrastructure, allowing you to provision and maintain Azure resources reliably, consistently, and repeatedly.

Step 1: Prerequisites and Initial Setup

1. **Log into** your Azure Portal (https://portal.azure.com).
2. Ensure you have an active Azure subscription with appropriate permissions to create resources.
3. Verify your account has Global Administrator or Security Administrator rights within your Microsoft 365 tenant to connect data sources.

Step 2: Initiating the ARM Template Deployment

1. Navigate to the Azure Sentinel GitHub repository (https://github.com/Azure/Azure-Sentinel/tree/master/Tools/Sentinel-All-In-One).
2. Click the `Deploy to Azure` button to initiate the deployment template.
3. This action will direct you to the Azure portal's custom deployment interface.

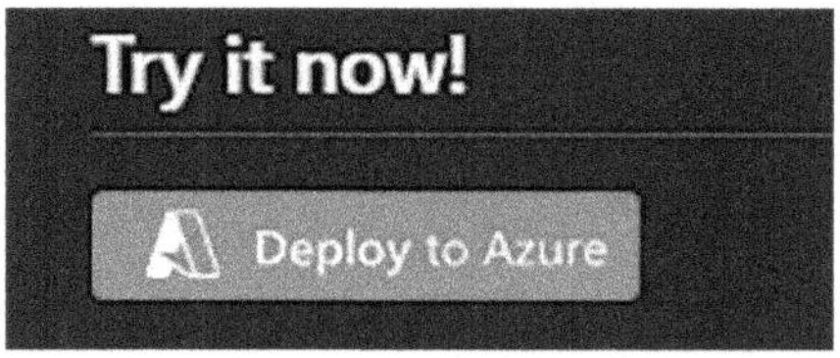

Figure 7.15: *ARM Deploy Button*

Step 3: Configuring Basic Deployment Settings

1. Provide necessary details in the Azure deployment wizard:
   a. **Subscription:** Choose the appropriate subscription.
   b. **Resource Group:** Name your resource group (for example, RG-Sentinel-ARM).
   c. **Location:** Select a region suitable for compliance and performance requirements.
   d. **Workspace Name:** Enter a unique name for your Log Analytics workspace, for example, LA-Sentinel-ARM.
   e. **Ingestion Cap:** Define daily data ingestion limits based on expected usage.
   f. **Retention Period:** Set the duration for retaining log data.

   g. **Commitment Tier:** Choose a tier aligned with your anticipated log volume and budget.

Note: *By default, Log Analytics Workspace Table Retention is 30 days, but when you deploy Sentinel on top, you can extend that to 90 days for free.*

Step 4: Advanced Options and Additional Features

1. Activate additional features such as **User and Entity Behavior Analytics (UEBA)** for enhanced threat detection.
2. From the dropdown, you can select **EntraID** and/or **Active Directory** (MDI is required for AD integration).
3. Optionally enable **Health Diagnostics** to facilitate ongoing monitoring and troubleshooting.

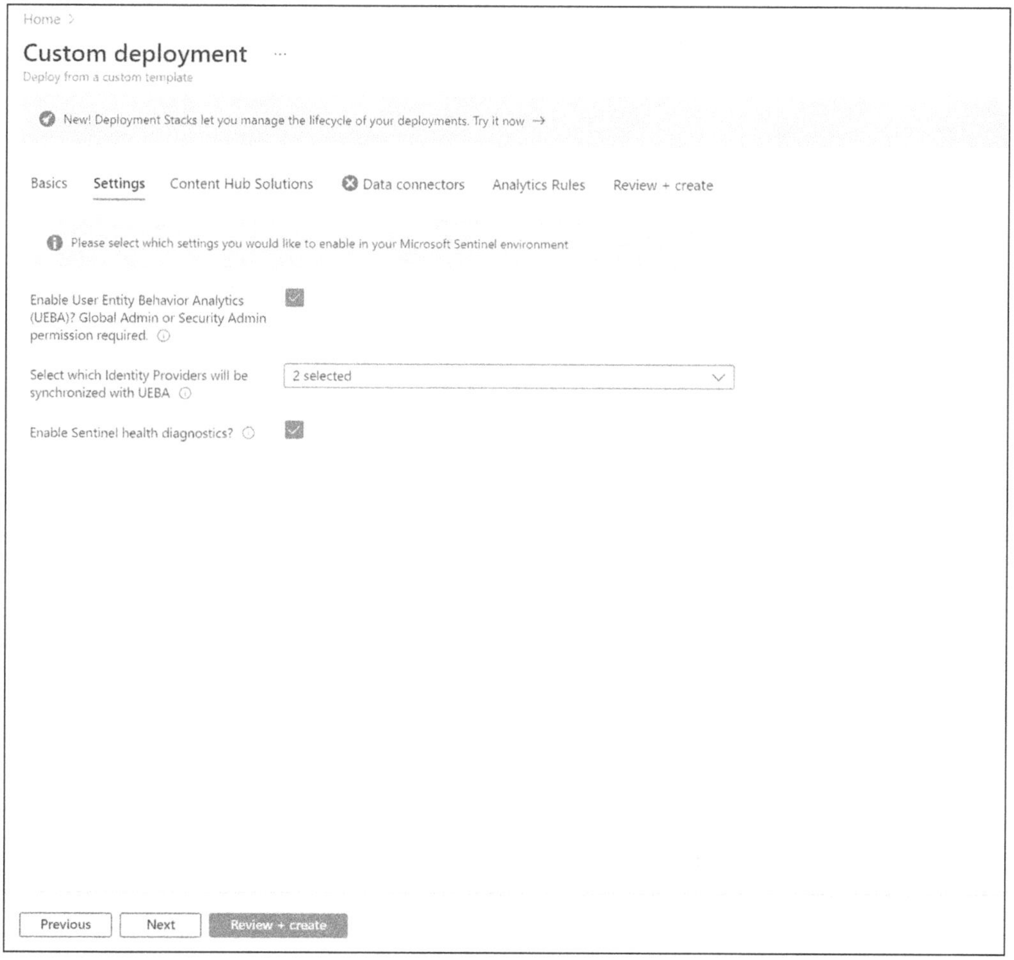

Figure 7.16: *Settings*

Step 5: Selecting and Enabling Content Solutions

1. Select desired pre-built solutions from the Sentinel Content Hub to enhance your environment immediately.
2. Enable connectors for specific log sources that align with your organization's security needs and licensing.

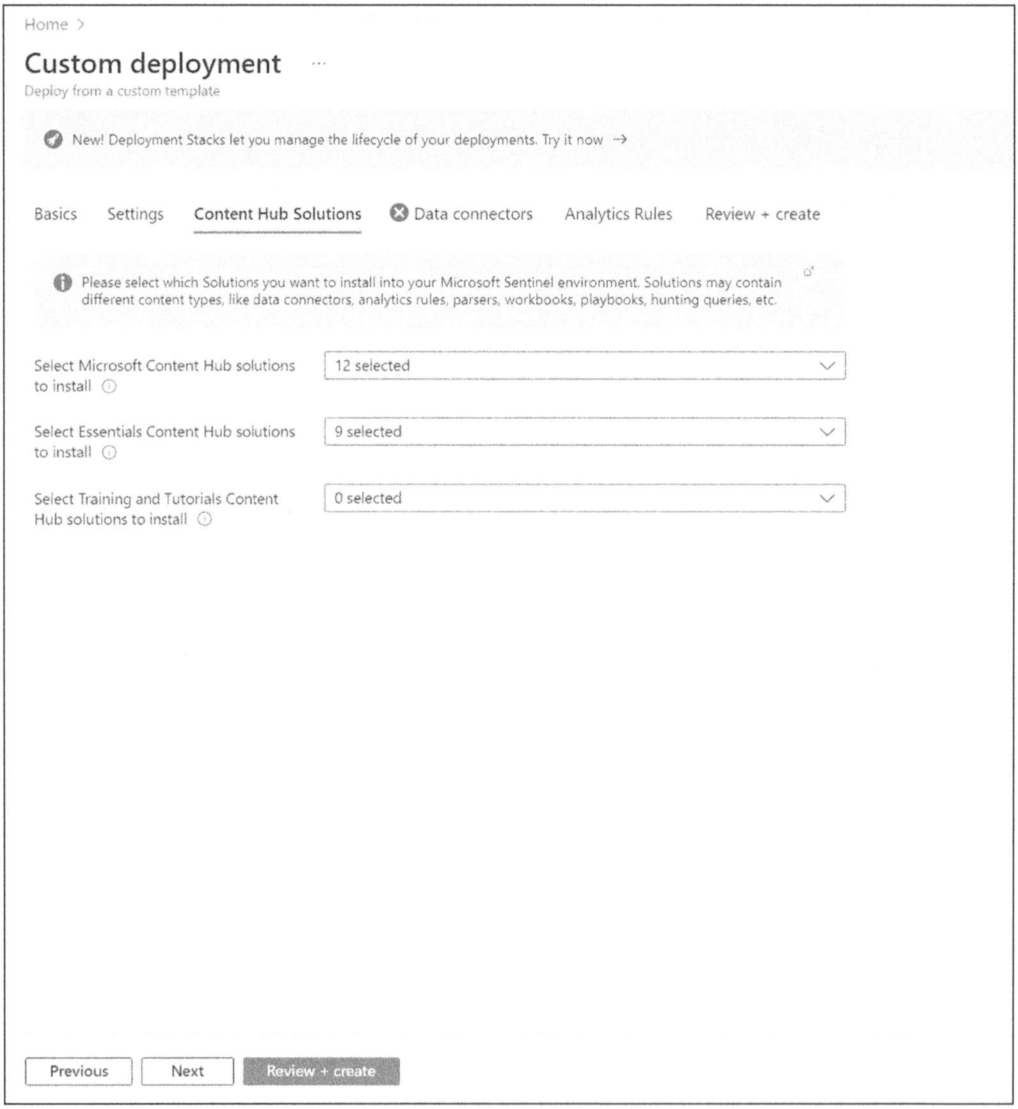

Figure 7.17: *Content Hub Solutions*

3. As this book is being written, there are 12 predefined Microsoft solutions for you to choose from.

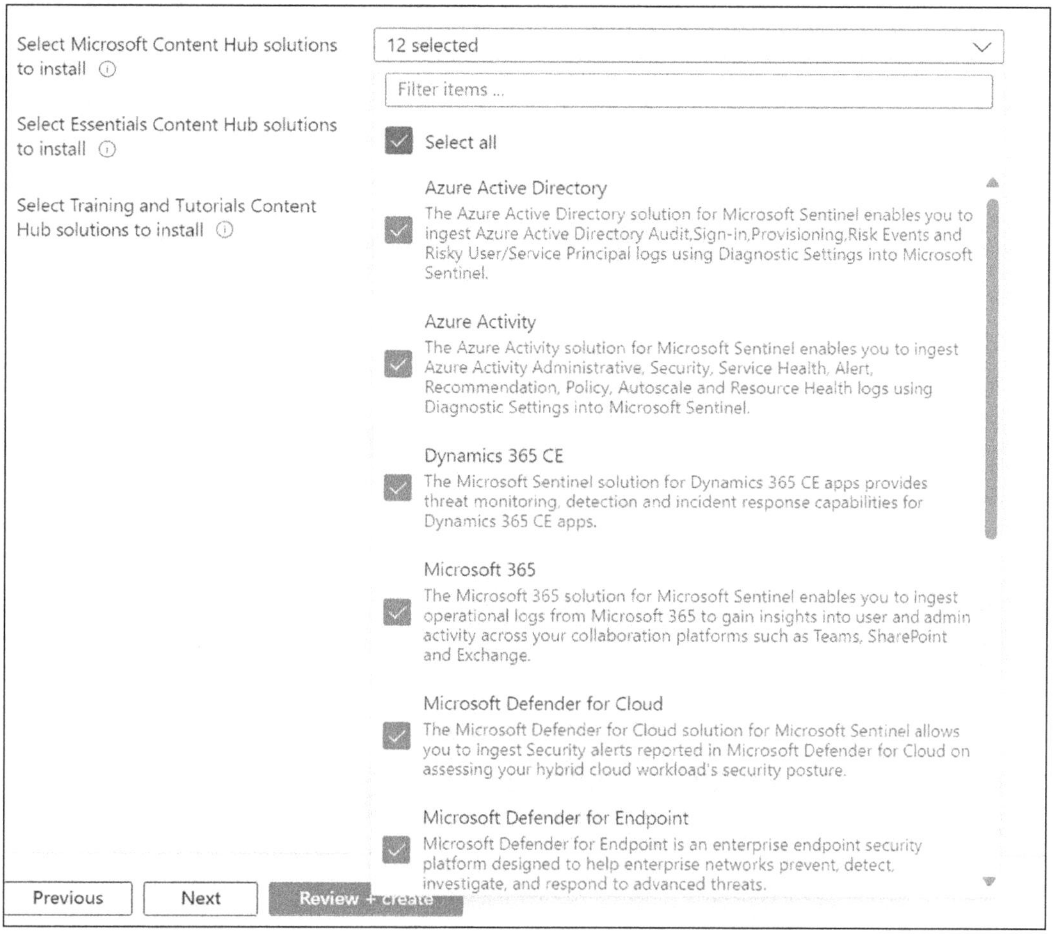

Figure 7.18: *Selected Microsoft Content Hub Solutions*

4. There are 9 available predefined Essentials from the Content Hub.

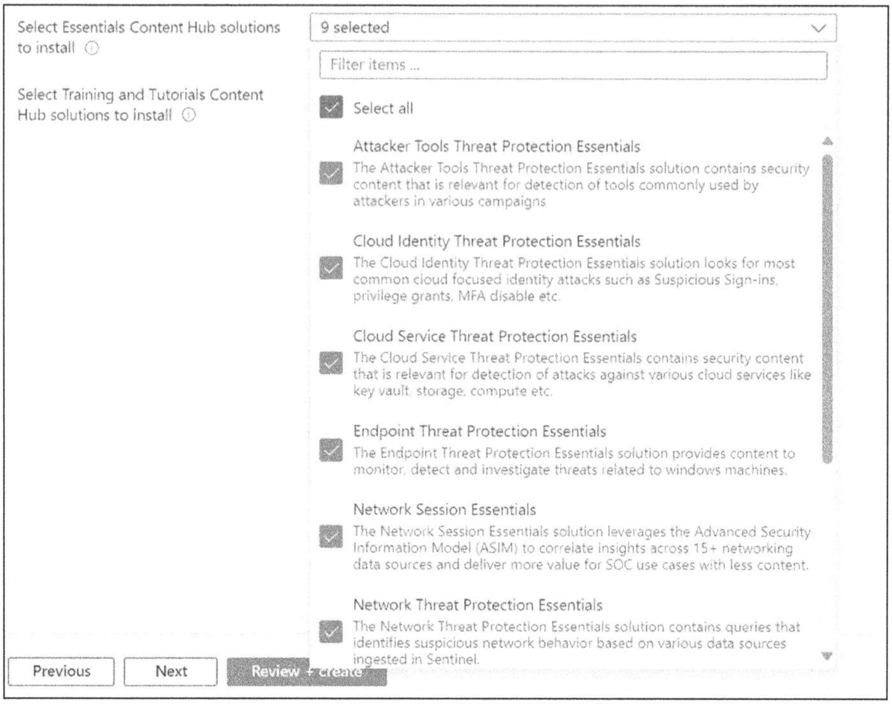

Figure 7.19: *Selected Essentials Content Hub Solutions*

5. Lastly, there are 2 **Training and Tutorial Modules** available.

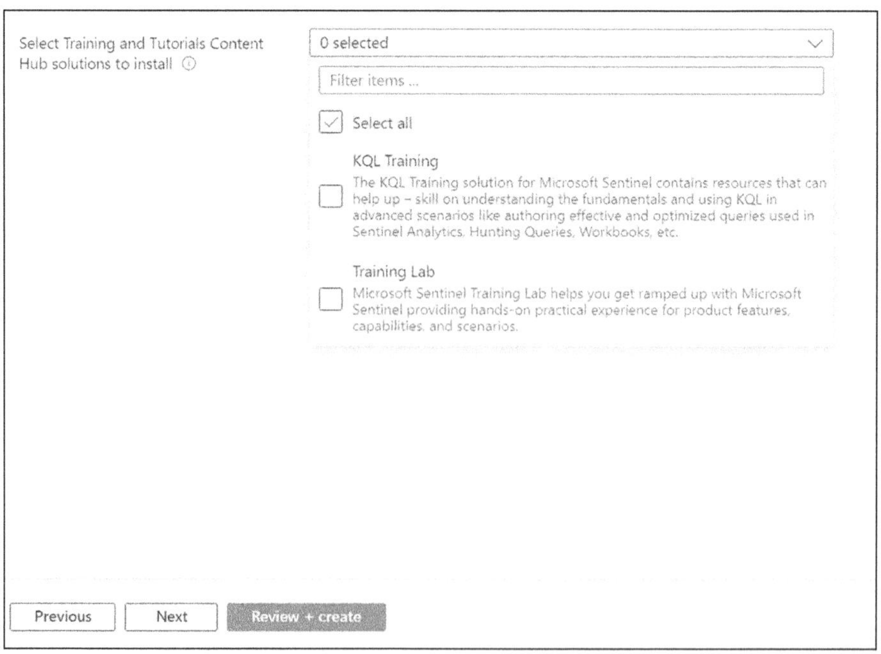

Figure 7.20: *Available Training Content*

6. Once you have selected your modules, select **`Next`** to move on to the **`Analytics Rules`**.

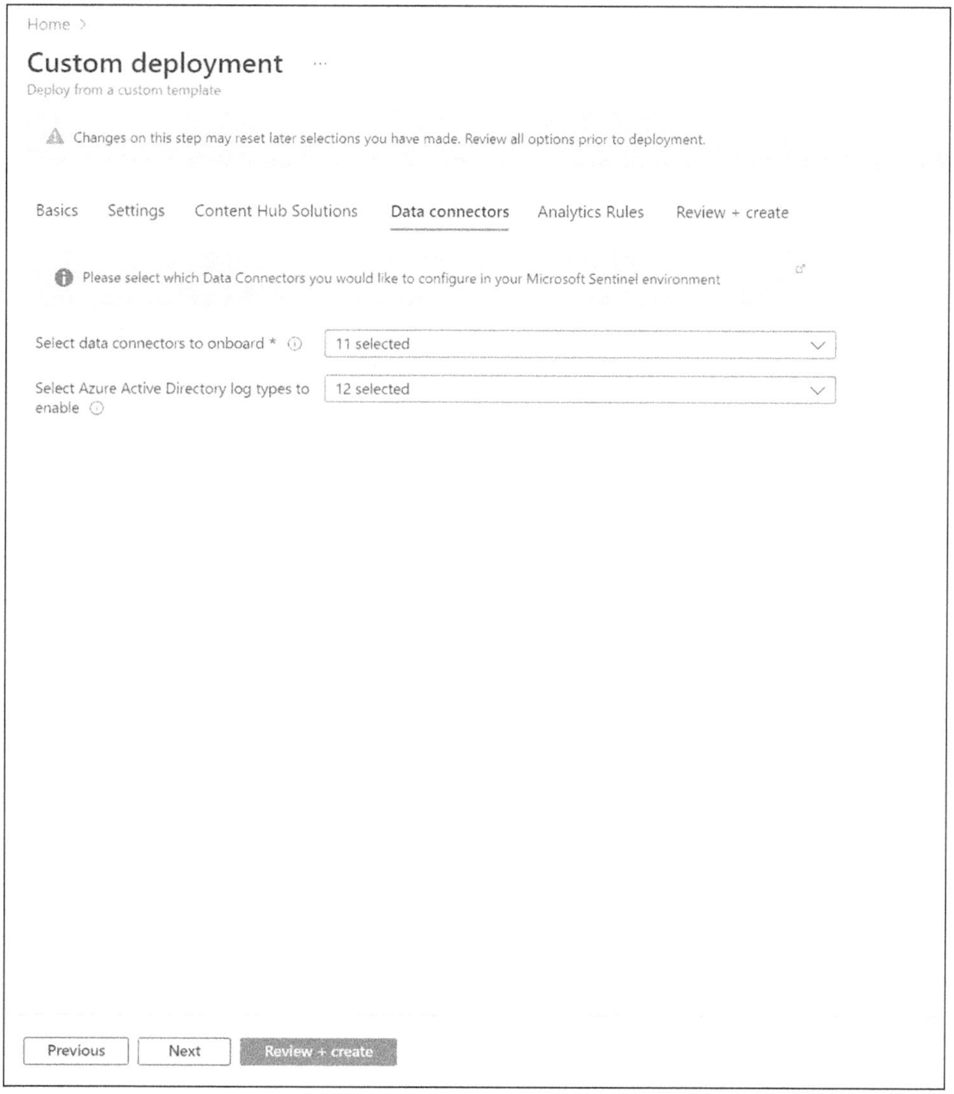

Figure 7.21: *Data Connectors*

Step 6: Configuring Analytics and Alert Rules

1. Choose and enable analytics rules designed to proactively detect threats and generate actionable alerts.
2. Configure alert severity levels to match your organization's security incident response processes.

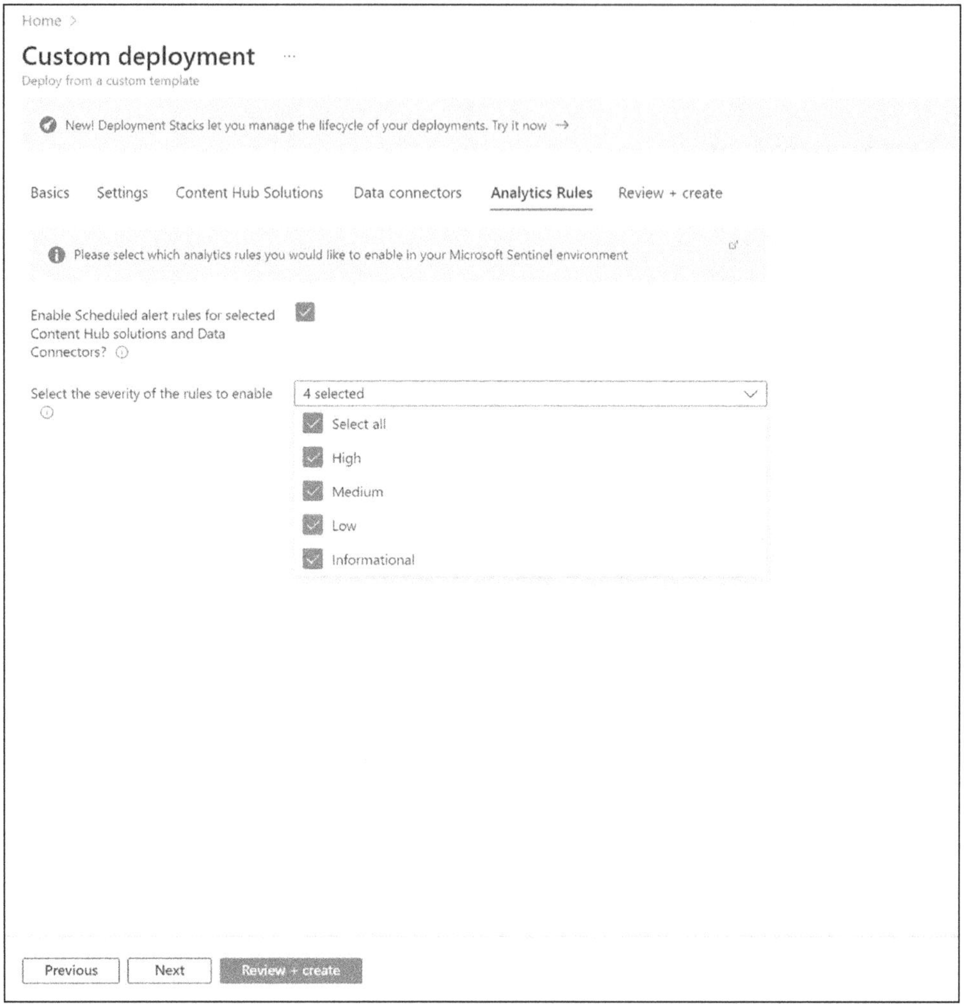

***Figure* 7.22:** *Analytics Rules*

Step 7: Deploy and Verify

1. Carefully review your configurations and click **`Create`** to start the deployment.

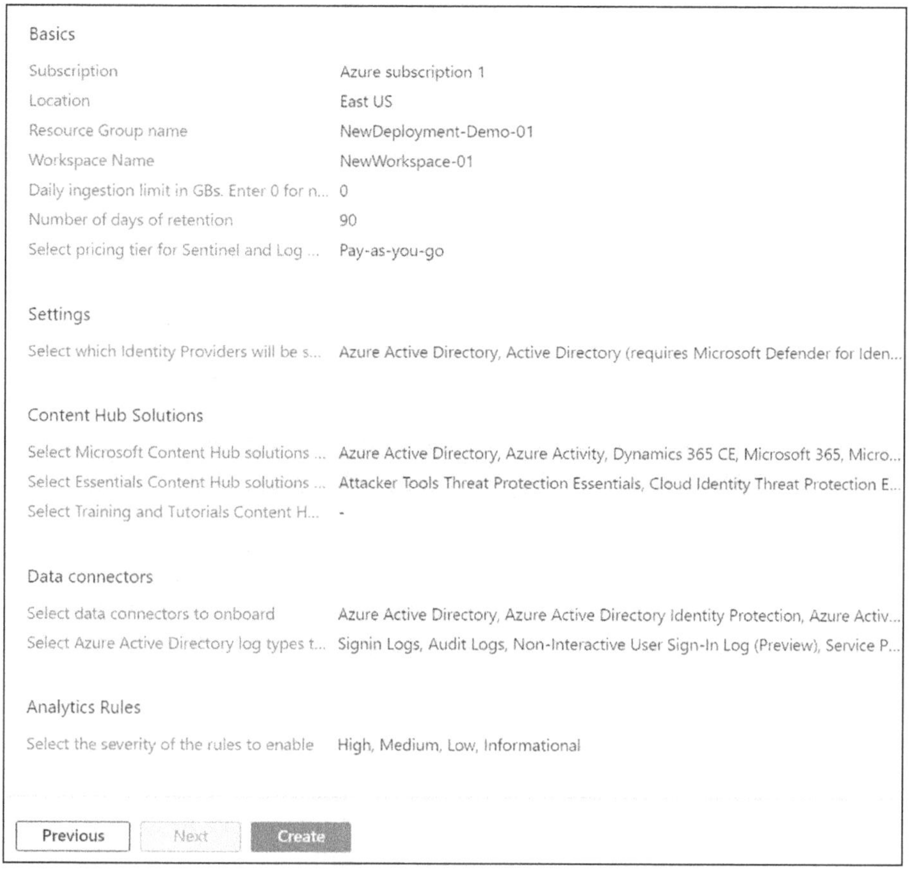

***Figure 7.23:** Create and Deploy from ARM Template*

2. Monitor deployment progress through the Azure portal notifications.

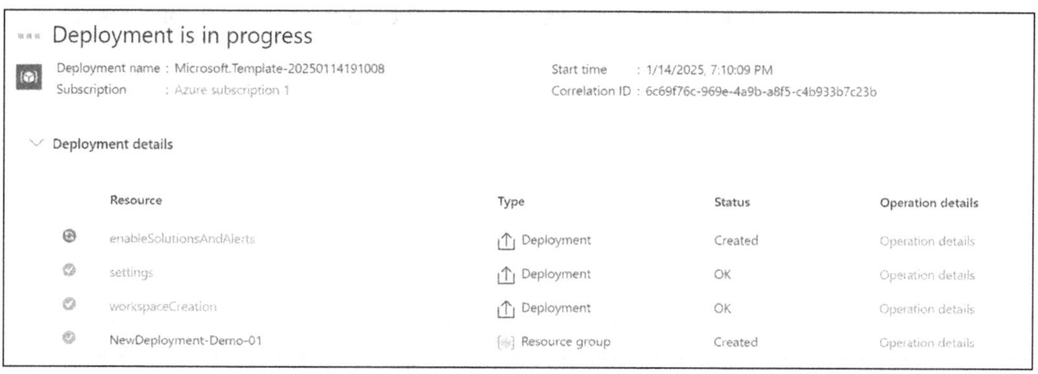

***Figure 7.24:** ARM Deployment in Progress*

3. Once deployment completes, navigate to your Sentinel workspace to confirm successful deployment and proper functionality of all selected components.

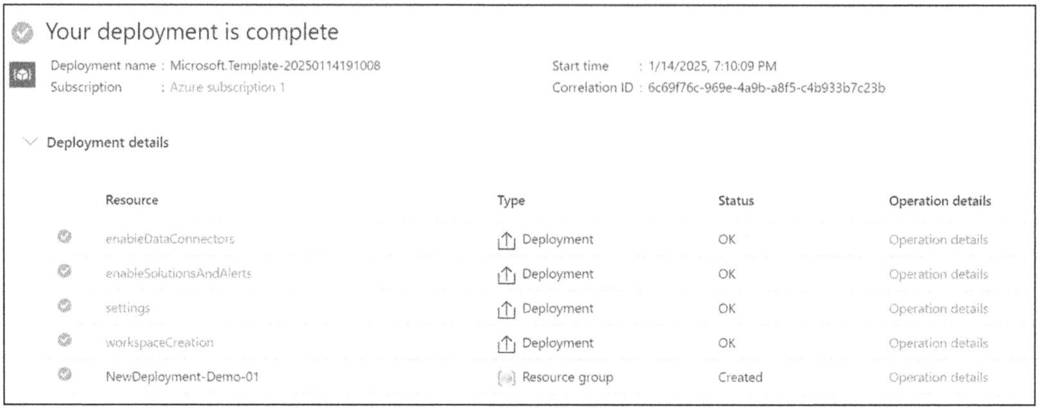

***Figure* 7.25:** *ARM Deployment Complete*

Step 8: Check out all the Deployed Rules and Connectors

1. Navigate to **`Sentinel`** from the Azure portal and select your new deployment.

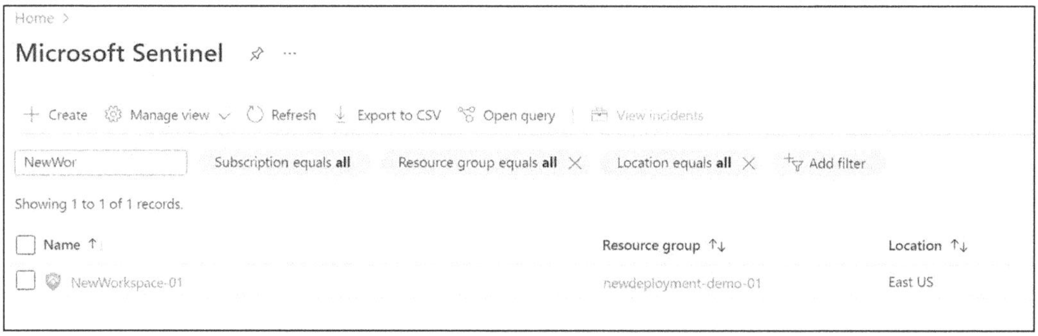

***Figure* 7.26:** *New Sentinel Workspace*

2. Navigate to the **`Data Connectors`** blade to see your installed connectors.

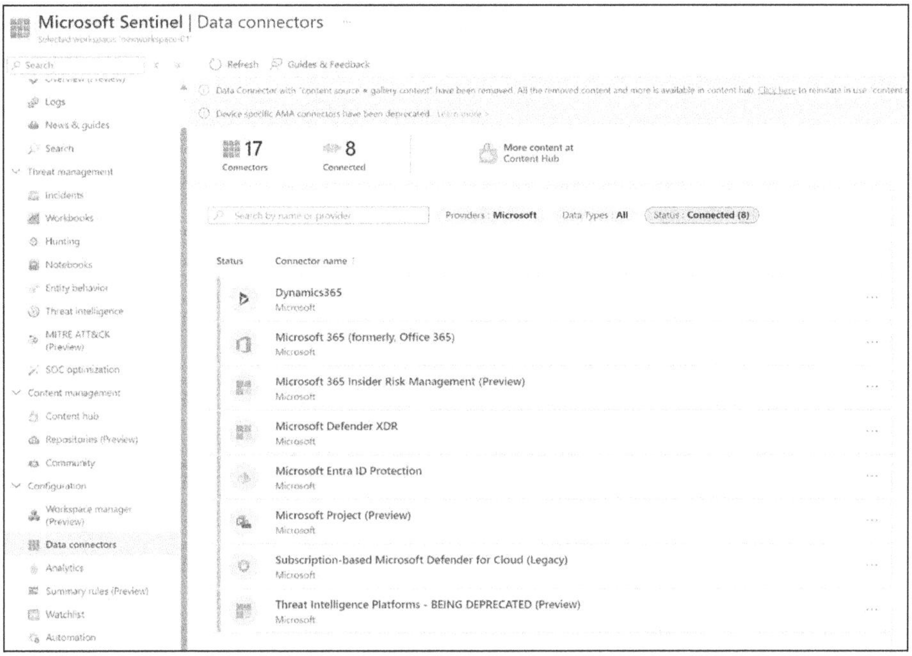

Figure 7.27: Installed Sentinel Connectors

3. Navigate to the `Content Hub` blade to see the installed Solutions selected from the dropdown during deployment.

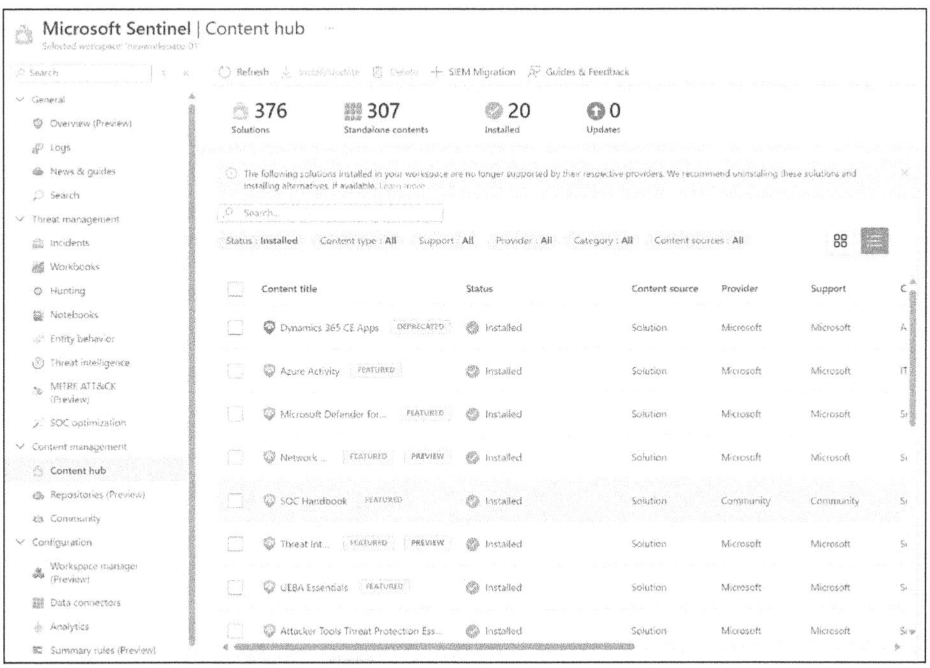

Figure 7.28: Installed Sentinel Solutions

4. Lastly, move over to the Analytics blade to see the deployed Analytics rules.

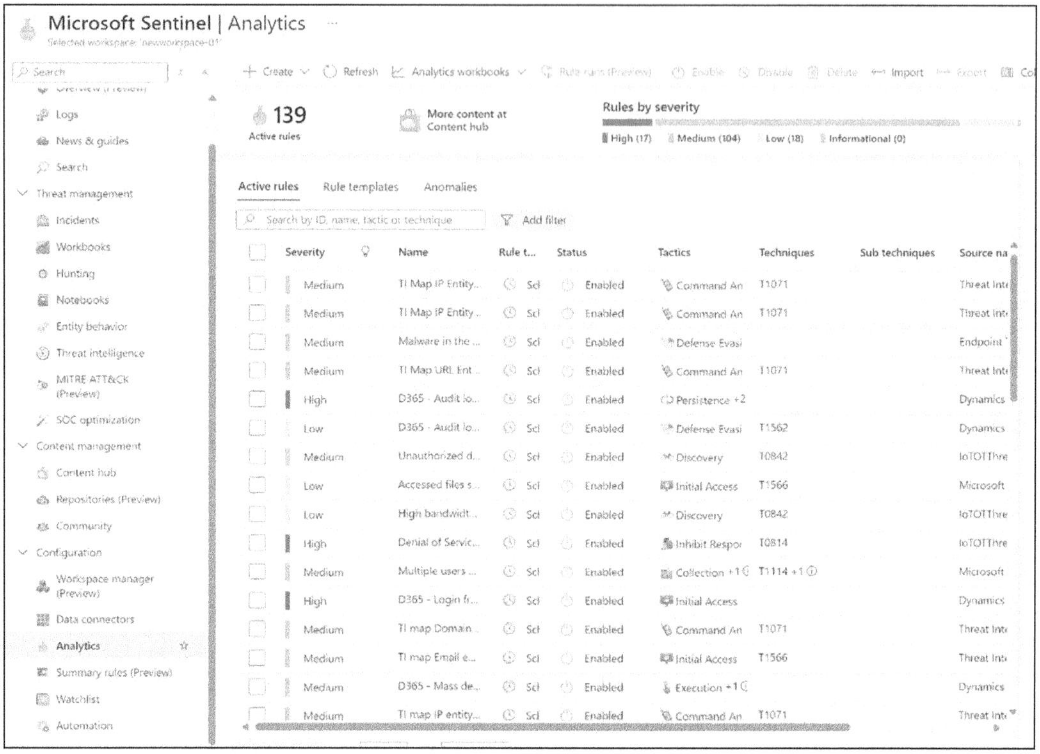

Figure 7.29: *Deployed Analytics Rules*

Step 9: Post-Deployment Optimization

1. Monitor daily ingestion closely to ensure optimal usage of your configured cap.
2. Regularly review and adjust analytics rules to maintain an effective security posture.
3. Use built-in workbooks to visualize security telemetry, cost, and operational performance.
4. Set up automation with Sentinel Playbooks to streamline threat response and remediation activities.

Following this detailed deployment guide will help establish a robust, efficient, and secure Microsoft Sentinel environment leveraging automated ARM deployment templates.

Conclusion

Microsoft Sentinel delivers a robust, cloud-native platform that fuses the analytical depth of SIEM with the operational efficiency of SOAR. Through its deep integration with Log Analytics Workspaces, Microsoft 365 Defender, and Azure Logic Apps, Sentinel enables high-fidelity telemetry ingestion, advanced rule-based detections via KQL, and automated remediation workflows. The extensibility offered by the Content Hub–ranging from data connectors and analytics rules to hunting queries and playbooks–allows for rapid deployment and iterative tuning in dynamic threat environments. Whether provisioned via ARM templates or manually through the portal, Sentinel provides a flexible deployment model that supports both greenfield and mature SOC architectures.

The next chapter will delve into configuring analytics rules, building visual dashboards, and orchestrating response logic to operationalize Sentinel at scale.

Helpful Links, References, and Resources

- Microsoft, "Microsoft Sentinel Official Documentation," accessed 2025, https://docs.microsoft.com/azure/sentinel/
- Microsoft, *Automating Incident Response with Microsoft Sentinel Playbooks*, Microsoft Official Documentation, accessed 2025, https://docs.microsoft.com/azure/sentinel/tutorial-respond-threats-playbook
- Microsoft Sentinel Documentation, *Data connectors and integrations*, Microsoft, accessed 2025, https://docs.microsoft.com/azure/sentinel/data-connectors-reference
- Gartner, "Magic Quadrant for Security Information and Event Management," Gartner Research, 2024, https://www.gartner.com/reviews/market/security-information-event-managementGartner+1Gartner+1
- Forrester, "The Total Economic Impact of Microsoft Sentinel," Forrester Research, 2024, https://tei.forrester.com/go/microsoft/microsoft_sentinel/Forrester+1Forrester+1
- SANS Institute, "Essential Capabilities of SIEM and SOAR Platforms," SANS, 2023, https://www.sans.org/webcasts/cyber-solutions-fest-2023-soc-soar/SANS Institute
- Microsoft, "Automating Incident Response with Microsoft Sentinel Playbooks," Microsoft Official Documentation, accessed 2025, https://docs.microsoft.com/azure/sentinel/tutorial-respond-threats-playbook
- Gartner, "Magic Quadrant for Security Orchestration, Automation, and Response," Gartner Research, 2024, https://www.gartner.com/reviews/market/security-orchestration-automation-and-response-solutions Gartner+2Gartner+2Gartner+2

CHAPTER 8
Microsoft Sentinel SIEM Capabilities

Introduction

Microsoft Sentinel, in its role as a Security Information and Event Management (SIEM) solution, delivers powerful capabilities for centralized log collection, data normalization, correlation, and real-time threat detection. Its SIEM functionality is built to scale with cloud-native efficiency, offering organizations a unified platform to ingest and analyze telemetry from across their environment. With an extensive library of prebuilt data connectors, flexible analytics rules, and advanced visualizations through workbooks, Sentinel enables security teams to quickly surface meaningful insights from vast datasets. These features support not only compliance and audit-readiness, but also proactive security monitoring and investigation, reinforcing Sentinel's position as a robust and modern SIEM platform.

Structure

In this chapter, we will cover the following topics:

- Core SIEM Capabilities in Microsoft Sentinel
- Workspace Transformation Rules
- Onboarding Non-Microsoft Data Sources
- Workbooks for Security Visualization
- Analytics Rules for Real-Time Threat Detection
- Proactive Threat Hunting
- Threat Intelligence Enrichment
- Flexible Log Retention

Core SIEM Capabilities in Microsoft Sentinel

- **Connector Configuration and Ingestion Transformations:** Microsoft Sentinel extends beyond simple data ingestion by offering advanced customization for connector behavior. Through workspace transformation rules–powered by Kusto Query Language (KQL)–security teams can dynamically manipulate and filter incoming data streams at ingestion time. These transformations help align log formats with organizational schemas, reduce irrelevant noise, and improve the quality of stored data. Sentinel also supports custom field mappings and schema extensions, allowing seamless integration of non-Microsoft and proprietary logs. This configurability ensures that Sentinel adapts to varied environments, optimizing data pipelines for enhanced detection and forensic investigation.
- **Workbooks for Security Visualization:** Workbooks in Sentinel function as flexible, interactive dashboards designed to help teams explore and understand their security landscape. These visual tools allow analysts to monitor key indicators such as anomalous behavior, access trends, and policy violations. Built-in templates–such as the Azure Activity workbook–offer instant visibility into cloud-based operations, while custom workbooks can be tailored to display metrics unique to the organization's infrastructure. By combining query-driven insights with intuitive visualizations, workbooks support real-time decision-making and long-term reporting.
- **Analytics Rules for Real-Time Threat Detection:** At the heart of Sentinel's detection engine are its analytics rules, which allow organizations to continuously monitor for threats across ingested data. These rules, based on scheduled KQL queries, identify suspicious patterns and trigger alerts when defined thresholds or conditions are met. Sentinel consolidates related alerts into single incidents, offering a high-fidelity, contextualized view of potential breaches. This correlation minimizes alert fatigue, helping analysts prioritize and address the most critical risks without being overwhelmed by false positives.
- **Proactive Threat Hunting:** Sentinel equips security professionals with tools for advanced threat hunting, enabling them to search proactively for malicious activity that might escape automated detection. Using custom KQL queries, analysts can dive deep into logs to uncover unusual behaviors, data exfiltration attempts, or lateral movement within the network. These capabilities support hypothesis-driven investigations and are particularly useful for detecting low-

and-slow attacks or validating threat intelligence.

- **Threat Intelligence Enrichment:** Sentinel can ingest threat intelligence feeds from both Microsoft and third-party providers, enriching security logs with contextual data such as IP reputation, known malware indicators, and attacker TTPs (Tactics, Techniques, and Procedures). This contextual layer enhances detection accuracy and supports more informed triage and investigation workflows, allowing analysts to make better decisions, faster.
- **Flexible Log Retention:** Organizations can configure Sentinel's log retention policies to meet compliance, auditing, or operational requirements. Whether the need is short-term analysis or long-term archival, the platform supports variable data lifecycles, ensuring critical information is available when needed—without incurring unnecessary storage costs.
- **Deep Integration with Azure Services:** Sentinel is designed to natively integrate with the broader Microsoft ecosystem, including Azure Active Directory, Microsoft Defender XDR, and Azure Monitor. This seamless connectivity ensures unified visibility across infrastructure, identity, and endpoint data, providing a holistic security view that aligns with zero-trust principles and enterprise cloud strategies.

With this suite of SIEM capabilities, Microsoft Sentinel empowers organizations to centralize visibility, accelerate detection, and streamline investigations—all within a scalable, cloud-first platform purpose-built for modern security operations.

Workspace Transformation Rules

Optimizing data ingestion in Azure Monitor is crucial for managing costs and enhancing efficiency. One effective strategy is implementing Workspace Transformation Rules to filter out unnecessary data. This guide outlines how to identify and exclude non-essential Event IDs from your SecurityEvent table, thereby reducing data volume and associated expenses.

Identifying High-Volume Event IDs

To pinpoint the most frequently occurring Event IDs in your SecurityEvent table over the past 30 days, execute the following Kusto Query Language (KQL) command:

```
SecurityEvent
| where TimeGenerated > ago(30d)
| summarize count() by EventID
| sort by count_ desc
```

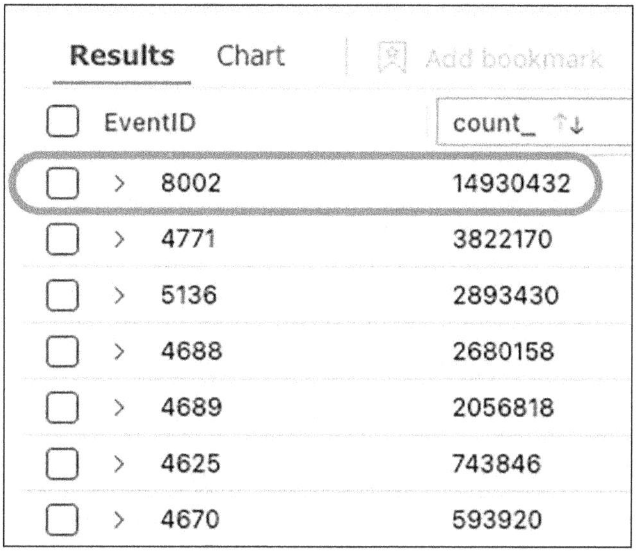

Figure 8.1: *SecurityEvent EventID 8002*

This query returns a list of Event IDs along with their occurrence counts, sorted in descending order. Suppose Event ID 8002 emerges as the most prevalent; it is prudent to assess its impact on data volume.

Evaluating Data Volume of a Specific Event ID

Event ID 8002 indicates that a **Group Policy extension was successfully applied** during a system boot or user logon. While benign in meaning, it can **generate excessive volume** in environments with:

- Frequent logons (for example, VDI, shared workstations)
- Multiple GPOs and client-side extensions
- Rapid Group Policy refresh intervals

Because each successful policy application logs a new 8002 event, **ingest volume can spike**—especially when verbose logging is enabled or applied across hundreds/thousands of endpoints. In Microsoft Sentinel or any SIEM, this can **inflate ingestion costs** without offering much security value, making it a prime candidate for **filtering or exclusion**.

To determine the data volume generated by Event ID 8002 in the past hour, use:

```
SecurityEvent
| where TimeGenerated > ago(1h)
| where EventID == 8002
| summarize VolumeInGB = sum(_BilledSize) / 1e9
```

Figure 8.2: *EventID 8002 in GB*

This calculation reveals the storage space consumed by this Event ID. For instance, if Event ID 8002 accounts for 18 GB per hour and offers minimal value for detection or investigation, filtering it out can lead to substantial cost savings.

Implementing a Workspace Transformation Rule

To exclude Event ID 8002 from ingestion:

1. **Access Log Analytics Workspace**: Navigate to your Azure portal and select **`Log Analytics Workspaces`**.

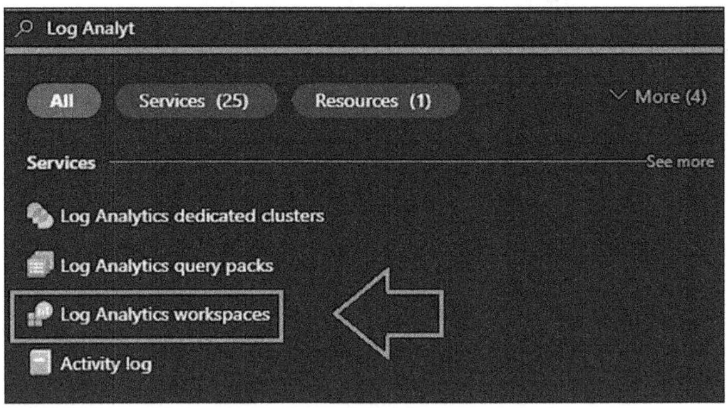

Figure 8.3: *Log Analytics Workspace*

2. **Open Tables**: In the workspace, click on the **`Tables`** section.

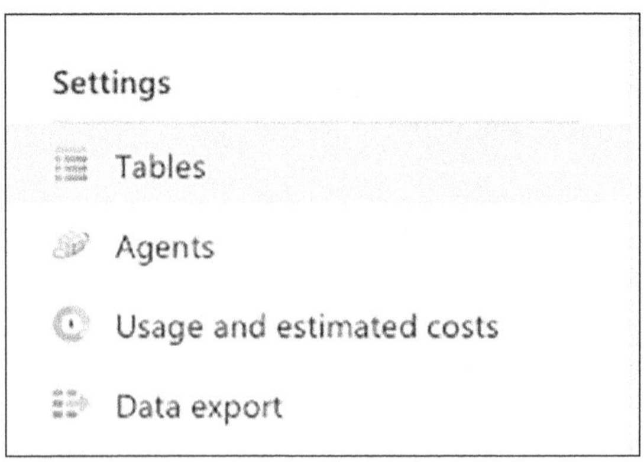

Figure 8.4: *Log Analytics Workspace Tables*

3. **Locate SecurityEvent Table**: Find and select the **`SecurityEvent`** table.

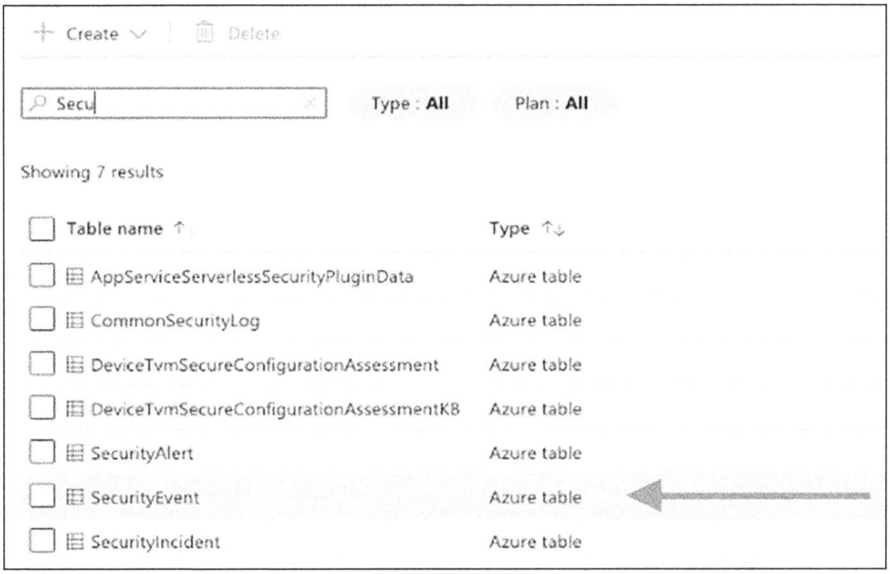

Figure 8.5: *SecurityEvent Table*

4. **Create Transformation**: Click on the "..." next to the table name and choose **`Create transformation`**.

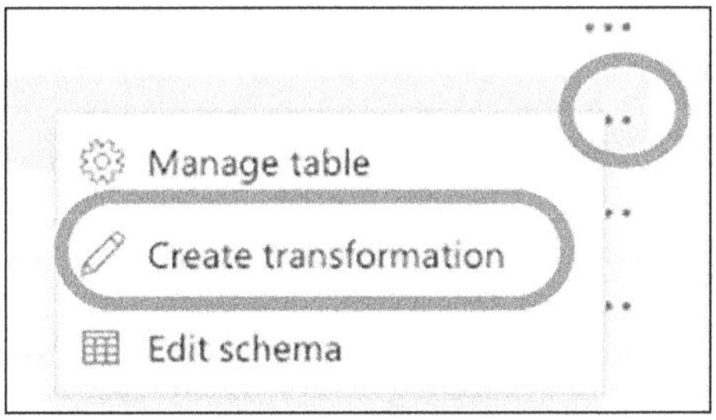

Figure 8.6: *Create Transformation*

5. **Name the Transformation:** Assign a descriptive name to your transformation rule.

Figure 8.7: *Transformation Editor Button*

6. **Edit Transformation**: Click on the **`Transformation editor`** and input the following KQL:

```
source
| where EventID != 8002
```

***Figure 8.8**: Transformation Rule KQL*

This KQL ensures that all events except those with Event ID 8002 are ingested.

7. **Review and Confirm:** Save and apply the transformation rule.

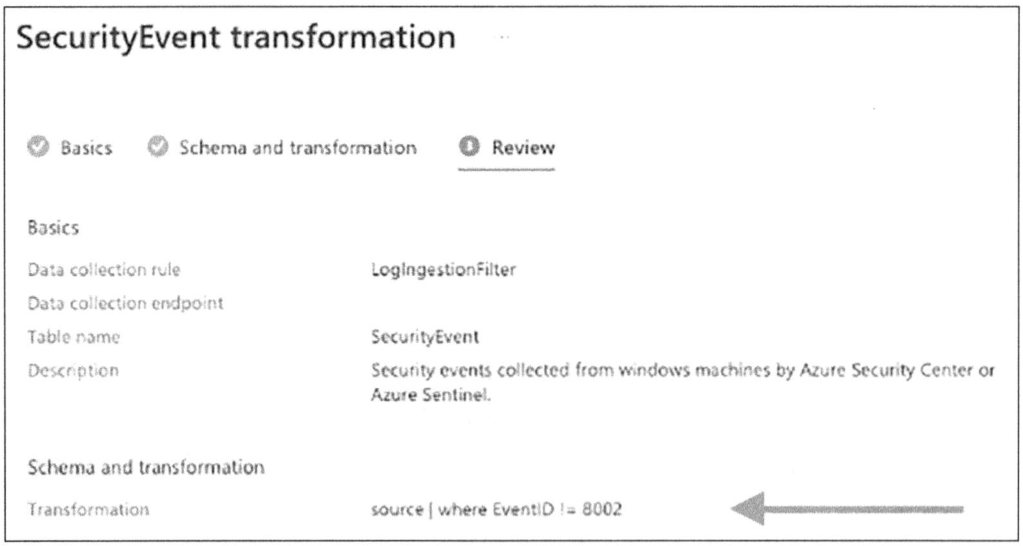

***Figure 8.9**: Confirm Transformation Rule*

Verifying the Transformation

After deployment, verify the effectiveness of the transformation by querying for Event ID 8002:

```
SecurityEvent
| where EventID == 8002
| where TimeGenerated > ago(5m)
```

If the query returns no results, the transformation is successfully filtering out the specified Event ID.

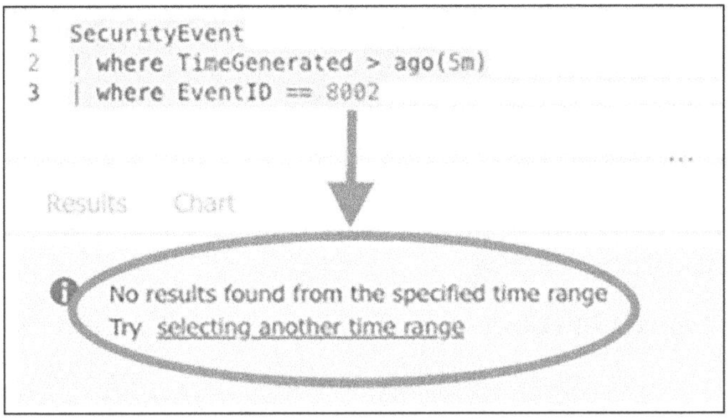

Figure 8.10: *Confirm Transformation Rule*

Important Considerations

- **Consultation**: Before implementing transformation rules, consult with your administrator or supervisor to avoid unintended consequences.
- **Cost Implications**: While transformations do not directly incur costs, be aware that:
    - Increasing data size through transformations (for example, adding calculated columns) results in charges for the additional data
    - Reducing incoming data by more than 50% without deploying Azure Sentinel may lead to charges for the filtered data exceeding the 50% threshold.

By carefully identifying and filtering out non-essential Event IDs, you can significantly reduce data ingestion volumes, leading to improved efficiency and cost savings in your Azure environment.

Onboarding Non-Microsoft Data Sources

While Microsoft Sentinel offers seamless integration with many native Microsoft services, organizations often need to onboard logs from third-party systems, network appliances, or custom applications. Fortunately, Sentinel supports several lightweight and scalable methods to bring in telemetry from non-Microsoft sources with minimal setup. The following guide outlines practical, low-overhead approaches to help you quickly ingest and operationalize external data streams.

Use Case: Quickly ingest logs from a non-Microsoft source (for example, firewall, Linux server, SaaS app) via **Syslog**, **REST API**, or **Azure Function**.

Option A: Ingesting Syslog from a Linux Collector Using Azure Monitor Agent

Prerequisites:

- A Linux VM (Ubuntu 20.04 or 22.04 recommended) to act as the log forwarder.
- Devices (for example, firewalls, Linux hosts, routers) that can forward Syslog (UDP/TCP) to the collector VM.
- A configured Microsoft Sentinel workspace (that is, a Log Analytics Workspace with Sentinel enabled).
- Contributor or higher permissions in Azure to deploy agents and DCRs.

Step 1: Provision the Collector VM

1. Deploy a Linux VM (Ubuntu preferred) that will receive Syslog from other devices.
2. Ensure the VM's NSG or firewall allows inbound traffic on UDP/514 and/or TCP/514, depending on your forwarding method.

Step 2: Install the Azure Monitor Agent (AMA)

1. On the Linux VM, install the AMA via the Azure CLI:

```
az vm extension set \
  --name AzureMonitorLinuxAgent \
  --publisher Microsoft.Azure.Monitor \
  --vm-name <vm-name> \
  --resource-group <resource-group-name>
Alternatively, install manually using the onboarding script:
wget https://aka.ms/InstallAzureMonitorAgentLinux
chmod +x InstallAzureMonitorAgentLinux
sudo ./InstallAzureMonitorAgentLinux
```

Step 3: Configure Syslog on the Collector

1. Edit the rsyslog configuration to allow remote devices to send logs:

```
sudo nano /etc/rsyslog.conf
Uncomment or add the following lines:
module(load="imudp")
input(type="imudp" port="514")

module(load="imtcp")
input(type="imtcp" port="514")
Then restart rsyslog:
sudo systemctl restart rsyslog
```

Your VM is now listening for Syslog input from network devices.

Step 4: Create a Data Collection Rule (DCR) in Azure

1. Use the Azure Portal or CLI to create a DCR that collects Syslog from the AMA.

Via Azure CLI:

```
az monitor data-collection rule create \
  --resource-group <resource-group> \
  --name "Syslog-DCR" \
  --location <region> \
  --data-sources '[{
    "syslog": {
      "facilityNames": ["auth", "authpriv", "daemon", "user"],
      "logLevels": ["All"]
    }
  }]' \
  --destinations '[{
    "logAnalytics": {
      "workspaceResourceId": "/subscriptions/<sub-id>/resource-
Groups/<rg>/providers/Microsoft.OperationalInsights/work-
spaces/<workspace-name>"
    }
  }]'
```

This sets up the collection of all log levels from select Syslog facilities.

Step 5: Associate the DCR with the Collector VM

1. Once the DCR is created, you need to bind it to your VM:

```
az monitor data-collection rule association create \
  --resource-id /subscriptions/<sub-id>/resourceGroups/<rg>/
providers/Microsoft.Compute/virtualMachines/<vm-name> \
  --rule-id /subscriptions/<sub-id>/resourceGroups/<rg>/
providers/Microsoft.Insights/dataCollectionRules/Syslog-DCR \
  --name "Syslog-DCR-Association"
```

Step 6: Verify Ingestion in Microsoft Sentinel

1. After a few minutes, go to Microsoft Sentinel > Logs and run:

```
Syslog
| where TimeGenerated > ago(30m)
```

You should start to see incoming logs from devices sending to your collector VM.

Option B: Onboard via REST API or HTTP Log Push for SaaS or custom apps with export APIs

This method is ideal for pushing structured log data from external apps or services directly into Sentinel via HTTP.

1. **Create a Custom Log Ingestion API**:
    a. Use **Azure Data Collection Rule (DCR)** with **Azure Monitor HTTP Data Collector API**.
    b. Register a **Data Collection Endpoint (DCE)**.
    c. Map incoming JSON schema using a custom **Data Collection Rule (DCR)**.
2. **Post Logs to the Endpoint**:
    a. Format logs into JSON matching your schema.
    b. POST to:

```
https://<DCE-ID>.azure.net/dataCollectionRules/<DCR-ID>/
streams/<stream-name>?api-version=2021-11-01-preview
```

3. **Verify Ingestion in Sentinel**:

   Query the custom table you specified:

```
MyCustomTable_CL
| limit 100
```

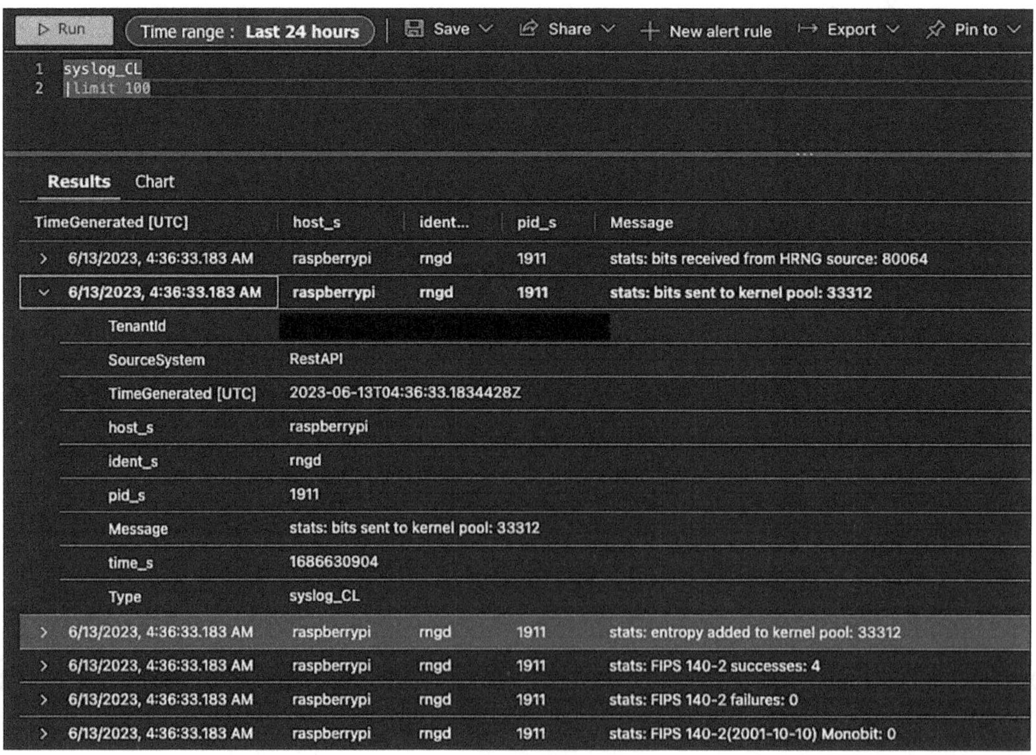

Figure 8.11: *Custom Syslog Table Query Results*

Option C: Use a Lightweight Azure Function (for Any HTTP API Source)

This approach is perfect for automating log collection from APIs that expose pull-based access.

1. **Create an Azure Function App** (Python or C#)
2. **Schedule the Function** to pull logs from a third-party API (for example, security vendor)
3. **Write logs to Log Analytics** using the Data Collector API

Sample code snippet (Python):

```
import requests, datetime, hashlib, hmac, base64, json
def send_to_sentinel(logs):
    # Send batched logs to Sentinel workspace using Data
Collector API
    pass
```

Workbooks for Security Visualization

Microsoft Sentinel Workbooks: Visual Analytics for Security Insights

Workbooks in Microsoft Sentinel serve as dynamic dashboards for visualizing and analyzing security-related data within your environment. They offer a versatile framework that allows users to combine Kusto Query Language (KQL) queries, textual commentary, and interactive controls into a single, cohesive view. These visualizations support various use cases, such as monitoring SOC operations, tracking compliance metrics, or conducting threat investigations.

Notable Capabilities of Microsoft Sentinel Workbooks:

- **Cross-Source Data Visualization:** Workbooks support the integration of datasets from multiple Azure services, enabling comprehensive, cross-domain insights.
- **Fully Customizable Layouts:** Users can tailor workbooks with custom KQL queries, parameters, markdown text, and visualizations to suit specific security or reporting objectives.
- **Interactive Elements:** Features such as time filters, dropdown menus, and slicers enhance interactivity, allowing analysts to pivot or drill into data in real time.
- **Built-in and Custom Templates:** Sentinel includes a library of preconfigured workbook templates for common monitoring scenarios, though users can also build tailored workbooks from the ground up.

Creating a Custom Workbook: A Step-by-Step Walkthrough

This guide walks through building a workbook focused on billing insights, using two key KQL queries to visualize data ingestion volume and identify top log contributors.

Prerequisites:

- Access to a Microsoft Sentinel-enabled workspace with contributor or workbook-specific permissions.
- Basic knowledge of Kusto Query Language (KQL).

Step 1: Open Microsoft Sentinel

1. Sign in to the Azure Portal (https://portal.azure.com/).
2. Navigate to your `Sentinel workspace` from the list of Azure services.

Step 2: Open the Workbooks Section

1. Within the Sentinel menu, select `Workbooks` from the navigation pane.

Step 3: Create a New Workbook

1. Click `+ New` to launch a blank workbook canvas.

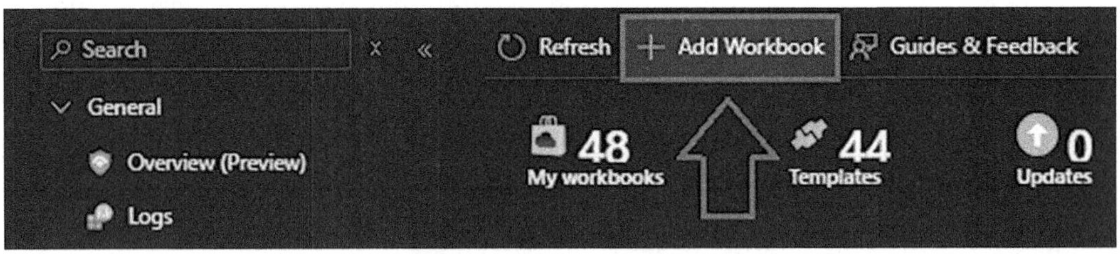

Figure 8.12: *Add Workbook*

Step 4: Add an Introductory Text Block

1. Select `Add text` to include a markdown section with a title (for example, Billing Insights) and description (for example, Visual summary of data ingestion trends and billing contributors).

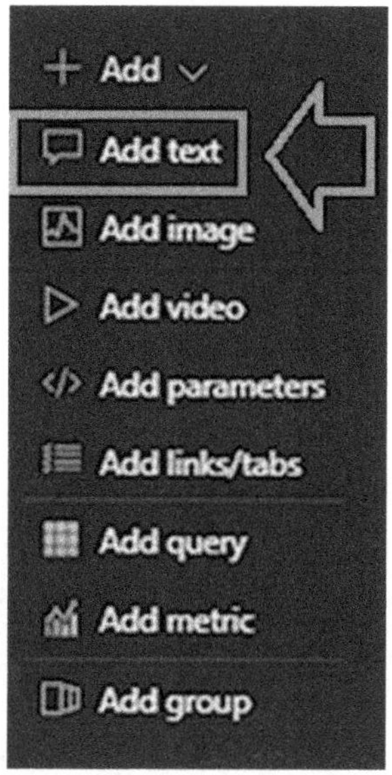

Figure 8.13: *Add Text Button*

Step 5: Visualize 90-Day Ingestion Volume

1. Choose **`Add query`** to insert your first visualization and enter the following KQL:

```
Usage
| where TimeGenerated > ago(90d)
| where IsBillable == true
| summarize TotalVolumeGB = sum(Quantity) / 1000 by bin
(StartTime, 1d), Solution
| render columnchart
```

2. Choose a time-based visualization, such as a **time chart**, to get that graphed out. Make sure to label it appropriately.

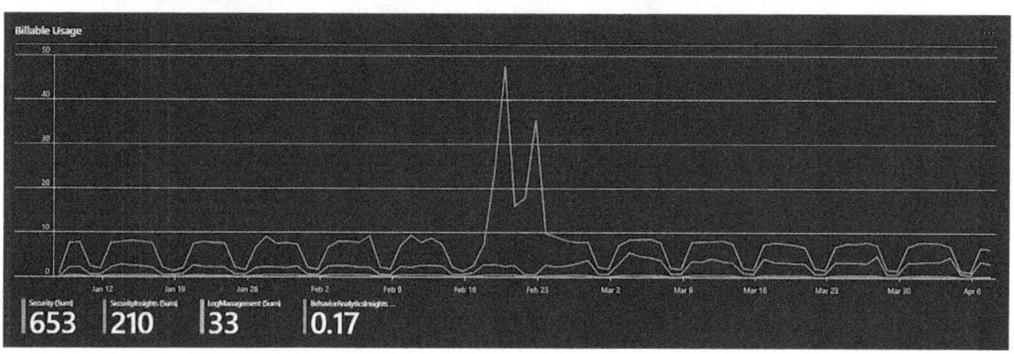

Figure 8.14: *Billable Usage Rendered as a Time Chart*

Step 6: Identify Top 10 Billable Log Sources

1. Insert another query using **`Add query`**.

```
Usage
| where IsBillable == true
| summarize GB= round(sum(Quantity) / 1000, 2) by DataType
| extend Cost=round(GB * 5.16, 2)
| sort by Cost desc
| take 10
```

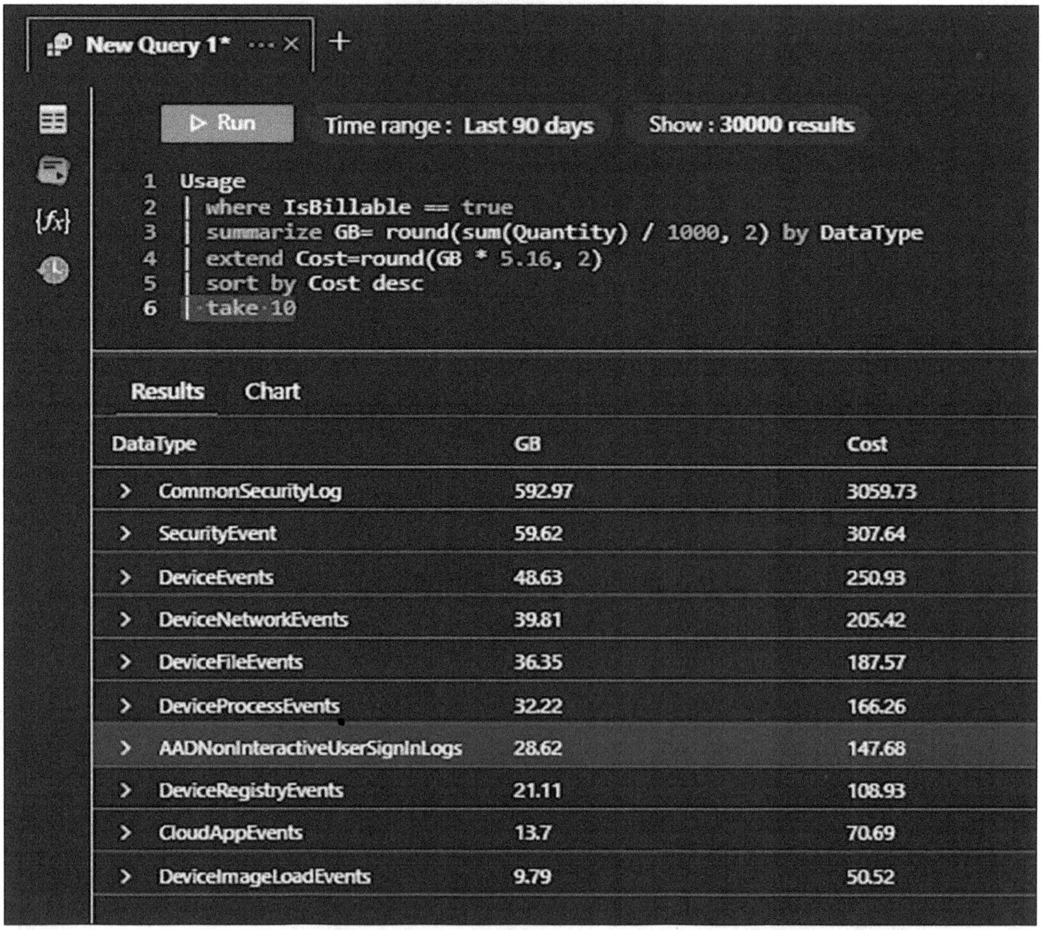

Figure 8.15: *Billable Usage Rendered as a Time Chart*

Note: *$5.16 is the rate per GB on the pay-as-you-go commitment for the Northern US. Swap this out based on your commitment tier and location from this matrix: https://azure.microsoft.com/en-us/pricing/details/microsoft-sentinel/?msockid=28aa02336b1a6db317c816bc6a836c38*

2. Add a descriptive title (for example, *Top 10 Log Sources by Billable Volume*).

Step 7: Optimize the Layout

1. Drag, resize, and reposition your visual and text elements for readability and logical flow.
2. Add filters or time pickers as needed to enhance user interactivity.

Step 8: Save Your Workbook

1. Click `Save`, assign a name such as *Billing Insights Workbook*, and store it in your preferred resource group or shared workspace.

Step 9: Share with Team Members

1. Navigate back to the `Workbooks` tab to view your saved dashboard.
2. Assign appropriate RBAC roles to allow collaborators to view or edit the workbook.

By following this process, you will have a tailored workbook in Microsoft Sentinel that highlights 90-day billable data trends and reveals your most data-intensive sources—offering actionable insights into cost drivers and usage patterns within your environment.

Analytics Rules for Real-Time Threat Detection

Build a custom Analytics Rule for Detections

1. Go to your Microsoft Sentinel workspace, open the `Analytics Rules` section, and click `+ Create` to begin setting up a new rule.

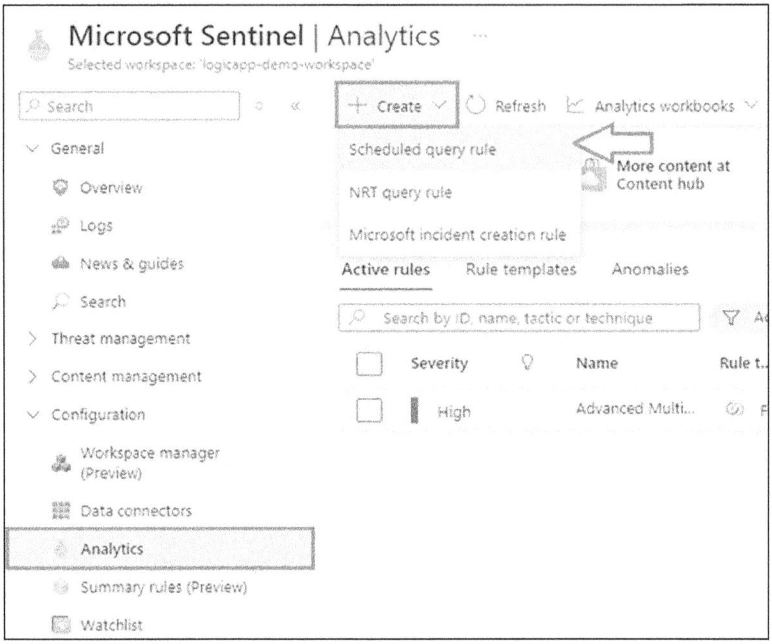

Figure 8.16: *Create Analytics Rule*

2. Give the rule a **`name`**, **`description`**, and set it to **`enabled`** as shown below:

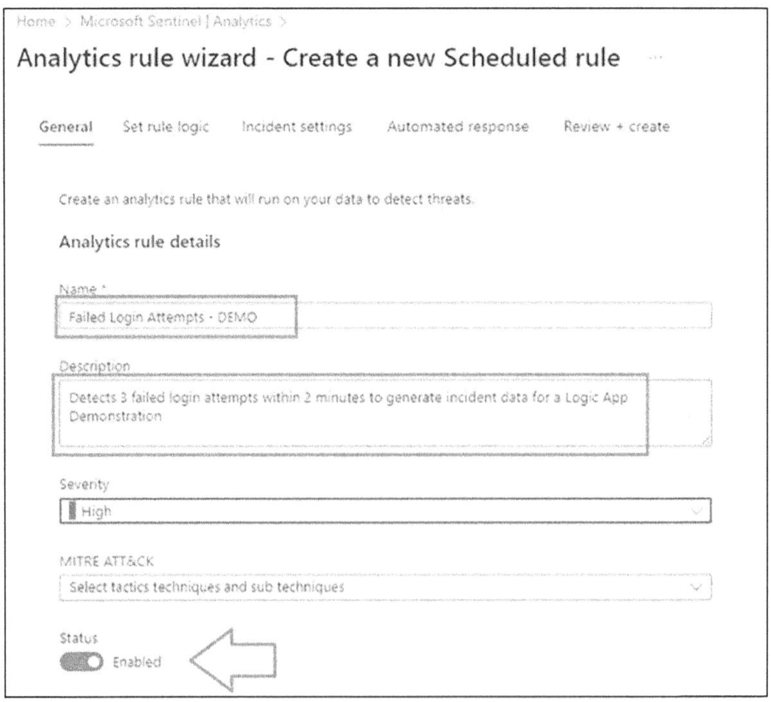

Figure 8.17: *Analytics Rule Details*

3. Enter the KQL logic to determine what activity should trigger the rule:

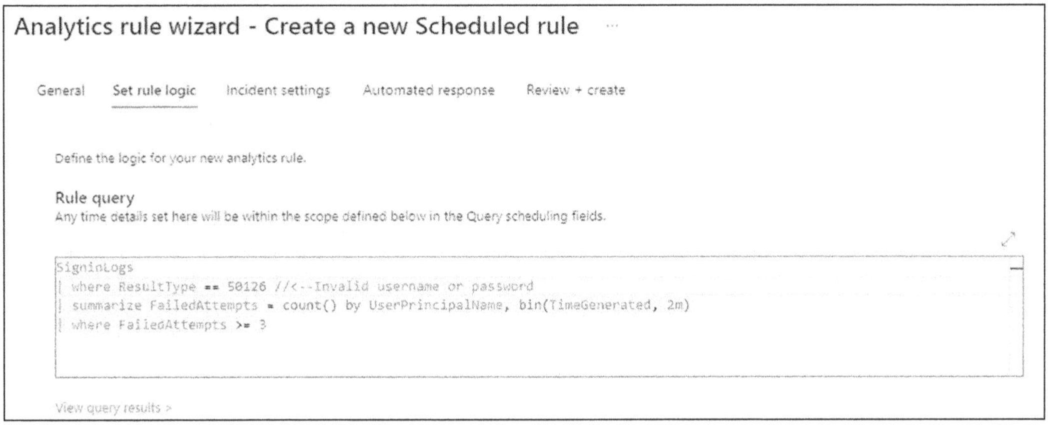

Figure 8.18: *Analytics Rule Logic*

You can find and copy this KQL here (https://github.com/EEN421/KQL-Queries/blob/Main/FailedLoginAttempts.kql) directly from my KQL repo on github (https://github.com/EEN421/KQL-Queries).

EventID 50126 (https://www.manageengine.com/products/active-directory-audit/kb/azure-error-codes/azure-ad-sign-in-error-code-50126.html) corresponds to authentication failures due to invalid credentials, which aligns with our use case.

4. Entity mapping is necessary here to carry the user's UPN suffix from the incident context into the Logic App workflow:

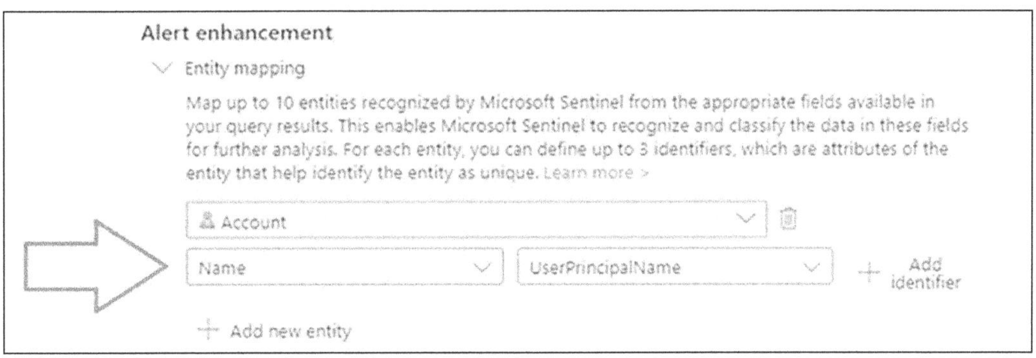

Figure 8.19: *Analytics Rule Entity Mapping*

5. For the purposes of this demonstration, schedule the rule to trigger every 15 minutes and to run against the last 15 minutes of logs, as shown here:

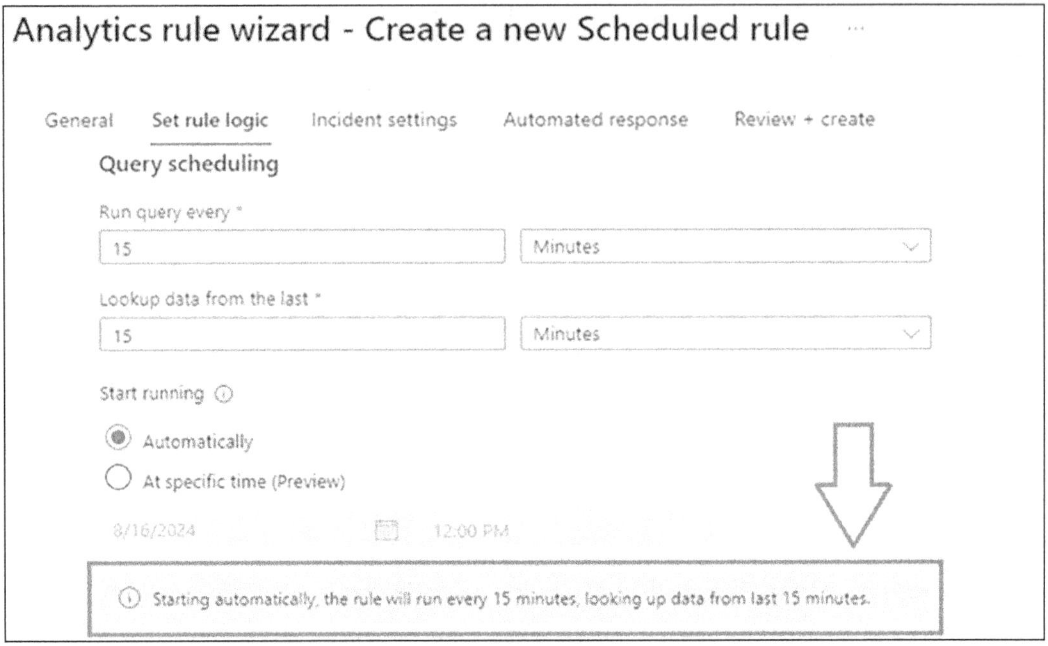

Figure 8.20: *Analytics Rule Schedule*

6. Do not forget to configure **Grouping.**
   - To meet our objective, it is important to minimize operational load on the SOC. One effective approach is consolidating similar alerts into a single incident, which helps combat alert fatigue.
   - For instance, our rule is designed to trigger an incident if a user experiences 3 or more failed logins within a 2-minute window. If someone say, Joe has 12 failed attempts in that timeframe, instead of overwhelming the SOC with multiple alerts, we can group them by user to streamline response.
   - This kind of alert grouping is key to preserving the efficiency and focus of your SOC team, especially during high-pressure situations. In the following screenshot, alerts are grouped by user and 8-hour workday to keep things manageable.

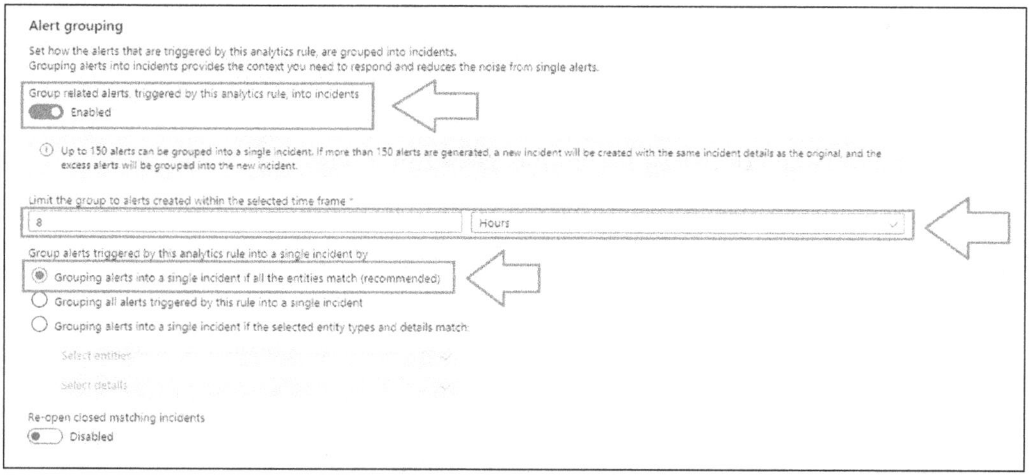

Figure 8.21: *Analytics Rule Alert Grouping*

Now that you have an Analytics Rule configured to throw alerts on 3 failed login attempts within 2 minutes, let us test it by attempting to log into the Azure portal with a bad password 3 times in under 2 minutes and watch an alert come in through Sentinel:

Figure 8.22: *Sentinel Incident*

Proactive Threat Hunting

Step 1: Define a Hypothesis

1. Start with a question like a security analyst or threat hunter would:

   "Are there any failed login attempts from unusual geolocations in the last 24 hours?"

Common areas to build hypotheses around:

- Identity compromise (for example, brute force, MFA fatigue).
- Lateral movement (for example, RDP/SMB use).
- Command and control (for example, DNS tunneling).
- Exfiltration (for example, large file transfers to unknown IPs).

Step 2: Identify Relevant Data Tables

1. Some of the most used tables:

Use Case	Table
Authentication (Azure)	SigninLogs
Authentication (Hybrid)	SecurityEvent
Endpoint Events (Defender)	DeviceEvents, DeviceNetworkEvents
Email and Collaboration	EmailEvents, TeamsMessages
DNS and Network	DnsEvents, VMConnection, Syslog

Table 8.1: *Most Used Data Table Examples*

Step 3: Build and Run Hunting Queries (KQL)

1. Start small and iterate. Example for suspicious sign-ins:

```
SigninLogs
| where ResultType != 0
| where Location !in ("United States", "Canada") //<-- adjust to
expected Location
| summarize count() by UserPrincipalName, Location, IPAddress,
bin(TimeGenerated, 1h)
| order by count_ desc
```

2. Then correlate with **GeoIP**, **MFAStatus**, or **previous behavior,** for just one example.

Another common one–MFA fatigue attempts:

```
SigninLogs
| where ResultType == 500121 // MFA denied by user
| summarize count() by UserPrincipalName, IPAddress,
bin(TimeGenerated, 1h)
| order by count_ desc
```

Step 4: Use the Hunting Blade

1. Go to **Microsoft Sentinel > Hunting**.
2. Click **+ New Query**.

3. Name your query, paste your KQL, and tag it (for example, Credential Access).
4. Add custom **Tactics and Techniques** (from MITRE ATT&CK).
5. Save and run the query.

You can also **convert a successful hunting query into an analytic rule** for automation.

Step 5: Investigate Hits and Pivot

If a hunting query returns interesting results:

1. Click into **entities** (such as User or IP).
2. Use **Entity Behavior** to visualize activity across tables.
3. Pivot into **Notebooks** or **Investigation Graph**.
4. Export or share findings for Incident response.

Step 6: Track and Iterate

Use a **threat hunting log** or a workbook to track:

- Hypothesis
- Query used
- Result
- Date/time
- Action taken

Example schema for logging hunts:

Date	Hypothesis	Query Name	Result Summary	Action Taken
2025-04-08	Unusual sign-in locations	Non-US Sign-ins	3 accounts from Russia	Escalated to IR team

Table 8.2: *Example Schema for Logging Hunts*

Bonus: Use Built-In Threat Hunting Queries

Sentinel ships with pre-built hunting queries:

1. Go to **Hunting > Templates**.
2. Filter by source (Defender, Azure AD, and so on).
3. Click "Create from template" to customize.

These are great for getting started and learning what "good hunting" looks like.

Recommended Enhancements

- **Enable UEBA** (User and Entity Behavior Analytics).
- **Add custom bookmarks** to tag data for further investigation.
- **Create custom workbooks** to visualize trends across hunts.
- **Use Notebooks** (Jupyter + KQL) for advanced correlation and documentation.

Top 10 Ready-to-Run Hunting Queries (Mapped to MITRE ATT&CK)

Each comes with a description + mapped tactic:

- **Repeated Failed Sign-ins from Single IP**

  Tactic: Credential Access

  ```
  SigninLogs
  | where ResultType == 50074 or ResultType == 50126
  | summarize count() by IPAddress, UserPrincipalName,
  bin(TimeGenerated, 1h)
  | where count_ > 10
  ```

- **Successful Sign-ins from Rare Country**

  Tactic: Initial Access

  ```
  let normalCountries = SigninLogs
  | summarize distinctLocations = make_set(Location);
  SigninLogs
  | where ResultType == 0
  | where not(Location in (normalCountries))
  | summarize count() by Location, UserPrincipalName, IPAddress
  ```

- **User with Most Administrative Actions**

  Tactic: Privilege Escalation

  ```
  AuditLogs
  | where OperationName has "Add member" or OperationName has "Role"
  | summarize count() by Identity, OperationName
  ```

- **Emails with Malware Attachments**

  Tactic: Initial Access

  ```
  EmailEvents
  | where ThreatTypes has "Malware"
  | summarize count() by SenderFromAddress, RecipientEmailAddress
  ```

- **Suspicious Command Execution (Encoded PowerShell)**

  Tactic: Execution

  ```
  DeviceProcessEvents
  | where ProcessCommandLine has "FromBase64String" or Process
  CommandLine has "IEX"
  | summarize count() by InitiatingProcessFileName, Process
  CommandLine, DeviceName
  ```

- **Unusual Lateral Movement (RDP/SMB)**

  Tactic: Lateral Movement

  ```
  DeviceProcessEvents
  | where ProcessCommandLine has "FromBase64String" or Process
  CommandLine has "IEX"
  | summarize count() by InitiatingProcessFileName, Process
  CommandLine, DeviceName
  ```

- **Large Data Transfers to External IPs**

  Tactic: Exfiltration

  ```
  DeviceNetworkEvents
  | where RemoteIPType == "Public"
  | summarize totalBytes = sum(InitiatingProcessFileSize) by
  RemoteIP, InitiatingProcessAccountName
  | where totalBytes > 100000000
  ```

- **Top 10 Users Performing Share Actions in Office**

  Tactic: Exfiltration

  ```
  OfficeActivity
  | where TimeGenerated > ago(90d)
  | where OfficeWorkload == "SharePoint" or OfficeWorkload
  == "OneDrive"
  | where Operation != ""
  | where Operation contains "shar"
  | summarize count() by UserId
  | take 10
  ```

- **Token Theft Indicator: Consent Grant by Non-Admin**

  Tactic: Persistence

  ```
  AuditLogs
  | where OperationName == "Consent to application"
  | where Identity != "Global Administrator"
  ```

- **Multiple Device Logins from a Single IP**

  Tactic: Credential Access / Lateral Movement

```
SigninLogs
| summarize UniqueUsers = dcount(UserPrincipalName) by IPAddress
| where UniqueUsers > 5
```

Turning a Hunt into a Detection Rule

Once you have validated a query, here is how to operationalize it:

Step-by-Step:

1. Go to **Microsoft Sentinel > Analytics > Create > Scheduled query rule.**
2. **Rule Details**: Name your rule after the threat pattern.
3. **Set Rule Logic**:
   a. Paste your validated KQL.
   b. Define **entity mappings** (User, IP, Hostname, and so on).
4. **Alert Threshold**:
   a. Set frequency (for example, every 1h).
   b. Set threshold (for example, count > 5).
5. **Incident Settings**: Choose whether this should auto-create incidents.
6. **Automations** (Optional): Trigger Playbooks to:
   a. Send Teams/Slack alert.
   b. Open a ticket.
   c. Enrich with threat intelligence.

Threat Intelligence Enrichment

Threat Intelligence Enrichment in **Microsoft Sentinel** refers to the process of **leveraging threat intelligence (TI) data to enrich logs, alerts, incidents, and hunting queries**, providing enhanced context for detection, investigation, and response. This typically involves **ingesting TI feeds**, **matching threat indicators against your data**, and **automating enrichment** within analytics rules and playbooks.

What is Threat Intelligence Enrichment in Sentinel?

Threat Intelligence Enrichment allows you to:

- Match IPs, URLs, file hashes, and domains in your logs against known indicators of compromise (IOCs).

- Automatically annotate incidents with TI context (for example, malware family, threat actor).
- Use **custom threat feeds**, Microsoft Defender TI, TAXII servers, and third-party integrations (MISP, AlienVault, Recorded Future, and so on).
- Enhance hunting, detection, and automation using enriched TI indicators.

Step-by-Step Guide to Deploy Threat Intelligence Enrichment in Microsoft Sentinel

Step 1: Set Up Microsoft Sentinel Workspace

Prerequisite: You must have a Log Analytics workspace connected to Sentinel.

1. Go to **Microsoft Sentinel** in the Azure portal.
2. Select your workspace or create a new one.
3. Click **"Add"** to onboard Microsoft Sentinel to your workspace.

Step 2: Enable the Threat Intelligence Data Connector

1. In the Sentinel portal, go to **Configuration** → **Data connectors**.
2. Search for **"Threat Intelligence Platforms"**.
3. Click **Open Connector** and follow the instructions:
    a. Enable the **ThreatIntelligenceIndicator** table.
    b. Optionally, configure **TAXII connector** if you have a STIX/TAXII-compatible feed.

You can manually upload or automate feed ingestion with Logic Apps, Microsoft Defender TI, or use the built-in **TI feed** from Defender.

Step 3: Ingest Threat Intelligence Data

Option A: Manually Add Threat Indicators

1. Go to **Microsoft Sentinel** → **Threat Intelligence** blade.
2. Click **"+ Add Indicator"**.
3. Choose Indicator Type: IP, domain, URL, file hash, and so on.
4. Fill out required fields (confidence, description, expiration).
5. Save the indicator.

Option B: Use Microsoft Defender Threat Intelligence

1. Configure Microsoft Defender Threat Intelligence integration.

2. Indicators are ingested automatically based on Defender for Endpoint detections and Microsoft feeds.

Option C: Configure TAXII Feed (Advanced)

1. In the **Threat Intelligence data connector**, click **TAXII settings**.
2. Add:
    a. TAXII Server URL
    b. Collection Name
    c. Username/Password
3. Configure ingestion frequency and test the connection.
4. Indicators flow into ThreatIntelligenceIndicator table.

Step 4: Use Enrichment in Analytics Rules

1. Create or edit an **Analytics Rule**.
2. In your KQL query, **join or lookup** against ThreatIntelligenceIndicator table:

```
let timeframe = 7d;
let TI = ThreatIntelligenceIndicator
| where TimeGenerated > ago(timeframe)
| where Active == true and ExpirationDateTime > now();
CommonSecurityLog
| where TimeGenerated > ago(timeframe)
| join kind=inner (
    TI
) on $left.DestinationIP == $right.NetworkIP
```

You can join on **NetworkIP, Url, DomainName**, or **FileHash** depending on your log type and IOC.

3. Use **entity mapping** to map TI fields (for example, attacker IP, malicious domain).
4. Save the rule and enable alerts.

Step 5: Automate Enrichment with Playbooks

1. Create a **Logic App playbook** from a Sentinel incident.
2. Add actions:
    a. **Get related TI indicators**
    b. **Call Defender TI API**

   c. **Post to Teams/Slack with enriched info**

3. Trigger from incident creation or alert match.

Best Practices

- Use **high-confidence indicators** to reduce false positives.
- Keep feeds up to date; stale IOCs can be misleading.
- Tag indicators with source and threat actor metadata.
- Enrich incidents for SOC analysts to improve triage speed.
- Use **Watchlists** for custom TI lists if not using TAXII or external APIs.

Flexible Log Retention

Flexible Log Retention is a powerful feature in **Microsoft Sentinel** that allows you to **customize data retention policies per table**, rather than relying on a single default retention period across the entire Log Analytics workspace.

This capability is essential for **cost management and compliance**, allowing you to retain high-value logs longer (for example, security alerts, threat indicators) while storing less critical logs for shorter periods.

What is Flexible Log Retention in Microsoft Sentinel?

- **Key Benefits:**
  - **Per-table retention**: Set retention for each table independently.
  - **Cost optimization**: Reduce storage costs by lowering retention on high-volume, low-value logs.
  - **Compliance readiness**: Retain critical audit or security data longer to meet regulatory needs.
  - **Query access**: Data in the hot tier (retention period) is instantly searchable via KQL.

Step-by-Step Guide: Adjust Retention for a Single Table

You will need **Log Analytics Contributor** or higher permissions on the workspace to make retention changes.

Step 1: Open the Log Analytics Workspace

1. Go to the **Azure portal**.
2. Navigate to **Microsoft Sentinel** > Select your **Sentinel workspace**.
3. In the workspace overview, click **"Log Analytics workspace"** (this takes you to the underlying Log Analytics blade).

Step 2: Access Table-Level Settings

1. In the left-hand menu of the Log Analytics workspace, go to **Tables** under **Workspace Data**.
2. Browse or search for the table you want to adjust (for example, SecurityAlert, Heartbeat, Syslog, or ThreatIntelligenceIndicator).

Step 3: Configure Retention Settings

1. Click on the target table (for example, Syslog).
2. In the **table settings pane**, click **"Change data retention"**.
3. In the **Retention settings dialog**:
    a. Toggle **"Use table-level retention settings"** to **On**.
    b. Set the **number of days** you want to retain data (range: 30 to 730 days for most SKUs).
4. Click **"Save"**.

    Note: *You will see estimated cost impact based on retention duration. Be strategic – keep valuable logs such as SecurityIncident or ThreatIntelligenceIndicator longer, and set short retention for noisy logs such as Heartbeat.*

Step 4: Confirm and Monitor Retention

1. Once saved, the new retention policy is applied immediately.
2. You can view retention policies under **"Tables"** again by clicking the table name and checking the current setting.

Example Scenario

- You are logging Syslog data from Linux machines via the **Syslog connector**.
- You want to **retain it for 60 days** to reduce storage costs while keeping SecurityAlert data for 365 days.

You would simply go into the Syslog table in your Log Analytics Workspace, turn on table-level retention, and set it to 60 days – done.

Tips and Best Practices

- Tables such as **SecurityAlert**, **SecurityIncident**, and **ThreatIntelligence Indicator** usually deserve longer retention.
- Tables such as **Heartbeat**, **Perf**, or **AuditLogs** often warrant shorter retention periods.
- Consider exporting old data to **Azure Data Explorer (ADX)** or **Blob Storage** for cold-tier archiving if needed beyond the retention period.
- Use **cost analysis** to monitor impact before and after applying new retention.

Conclusion

Microsoft Sentinel delivers a comprehensive suite of SIEM capabilities purpose-built for today's complex security landscapes. From ingestion optimization with workspace transformation rules to dynamic workbooks, real-time analytics, proactive threat hunting, and integrated threat intelligence enrichment, Sentinel empowers security teams to centralize visibility, accelerate detection, and respond with precision. Its deep Azure integrations and flexible retention policies offer unmatched scalability and control, enabling organizations to not only meet compliance demands but also elevate their overall security posture. As this chapter has demonstrated, mastering these features is key to deploying Sentinel as a resilient and cost-effective backbone of modern security operations.

With visibility and detection firmly in place, the next step in operational maturity is response. In the following chapter, we'll explore how Microsoft Sentinel's SOAR capabilities—driven by automation rules and Logic App-based playbooks—can empower your security team to react swiftly, reduce manual workloads, and orchestrate intelligent, automated responses across your environment.

Helpful Links, References, and Resources

- Microsoft. (n.d.). What's new in Microsoft Sentinel. Microsoft Learn. Retrieved April 8, 2025, from https://learn.microsoft.com/en-us/azure/sentinel/whats-new
- Microsoft Sentinel Team. (2025, March 27). New capabilities coming to Microsoft Sentinel this spring. Microsoft Tech Community. https://techcommunity.microsoft.com/blog/microsoftsentinelblog/new-capabilities-coming-to-microsoft-sentinel-this-spring/4390357
- Microsoft. (n.d.). Use transformations in Azure Monitor Log Analytics. Microsoft Learn. Retrieved April 8, 2025, from https://learn.microsoft.com/en-us/azure/azure-monitor/logs/tutorial-workspace-transformations-portal
- Microsoft Threat Protection Team. (2025, March 31). Monthly news - March 2025. Microsoft Tech Community. https://techcommunity.microsoft.com/blog/microsoftthreatprotectionblog/monthly-news---march-2025/4391479
- Hanley, I. (2024, August 16). Logic Apps & Automation in Sentinel. Hanley.Cloud. https://www.hanley.cloud/2024-08-16-Logic-Apps-&-Automation/
- Hanley, I. (2023, May 10). Workspace Transformation Rules Explained. Hanley.Cloud. https://www.hanley.cloud/2023-05-10-Workspace-Transformation-Rules/

CHAPTER 9
Microsoft Sentinel SOAR Capabilities

Introduction

In today's digital landscape, automating security responses is crucial for maintaining robust defense mechanisms. Microsoft Sentinel provides robust Security Orchestration, Automation, and Response (SOAR) capabilities, enabling organizations to streamline security operations, improve incident response, and minimize manual tasks. Its SOAR functionalities are primarily driven by automation rules and playbooks, underpinned by Azure Logic Apps.

Structure

In this chapter, we will cover the following topics:

- Automation Rules
- Playbooks and Azure Logic Apps
- Integration and Connectivity
- Practical Application and Benefits
- Deep Dive: Logic Apps and Automation Rules

Automation Rules

Automation rules act as the central framework within Sentinel to manage security incidents effectively. These rules enable automated actions such as assigning incidents to security analysts, modifying severity levels, adding specific incident tags, or even closing incidents automatically based on predefined conditions. For instance, an automation rule can identify high-priority incidents and immediately assign them to senior analysts, while simultaneously triggering associated playbooks to execute detailed incident response actions.

Playbooks and Azure Logic Apps

Playbooks are automated workflows within Microsoft Sentinel, built on Azure Logic Apps, which orchestrate comprehensive responses to security incidents. Azure Logic Apps facilitate integrations with various internal and external services, allowing for extensive customization of security response actions. Typical playbook scenarios include:

- **Incident Enrichment**: Automatically collecting additional data from threat intelligence feeds to augment incident context.
- **Threat Containment**: Quickly disabling compromised accounts in Microsoft Entra ID or restricting network access.
- **Notifications and Communications**: Sending immediate alerts and notifications to security teams through email or Microsoft Teams.

A real-world example could involve a playbook activated by a suspicious login attempt. The playbook might automatically investigate by querying external intelligence sources, disable the affected user account temporarily, and alert the security team with detailed information.

Integration and Connectivity

Leveraging Azure Logic Apps, Microsoft Sentinel integrates seamlessly with numerous services beyond the Microsoft ecosystem, including ServiceNow, Jira, and third-party threat intelligence tools. This connectivity allows automated workflows to perform advanced tasks, such as automatically opening and managing tickets in external incident tracking systems, enriching incident data from multiple intelligence platforms, and coordinating responses across diverse systems.

Practical Application and Benefits

Organizations leveraging Sentinel's SOAR capabilities significantly reduce their response times by automating routine tasks. For example, a phishing-related playbook could autonomously identify malicious email indicators, block malicious senders, remove threatening emails from user inboxes, and simultaneously inform the security team. Such automation not only enhances operational efficiency but also frees analysts to concentrate on high-priority investigations.

Microsoft Sentinel's SOAR capabilities, powered by automation rules and Azure Logic Apps playbooks, offer organizations extensive opportunities to automate security workflows, achieve seamless integration across security tools, and dramatically enhance their overall security responsiveness and effectiveness.

Deep Dive: Logic Apps and Automation Rules

As threats grow in complexity, automated response mechanisms play a pivotal role in modern security architecture. Microsoft Sentinel, in conjunction with Azure Logic Apps, offers a powerful solution to streamline incident detection and response. This section outlines how to set up an automated workflow that addresses multiple failed login attempts, enhances security, and reduces the workload on Security Operations Center (SOC) analysts.

Scenario Overview

Imagine a situation where a user registers three or more failed login attempts within a two-minute window. The objective is to automate the following actions:

- Disable the user's account.
- Notify the user's manager via email.
- Add a comment to the corresponding incident in Microsoft Sentinel.

This approach ensures prompt response to potential security threats, even in environments constrained by licensing limitations, such as the absence of Microsoft Enterprise E5 licenses that offer Risk-Based Conditional Access Policies.

Steps to Implement the Automated Workflow

1. **Integrating Microsoft Sentinel with Microsoft Entra ID**

   To monitor and respond to login activities, it is essential to connect Microsoft Sentinel with Microsoft Entra ID:

   a. **Access Content Hub**: In the **`Microsoft Sentinel dashboard`**, navigate to the **`Content Hub`**.

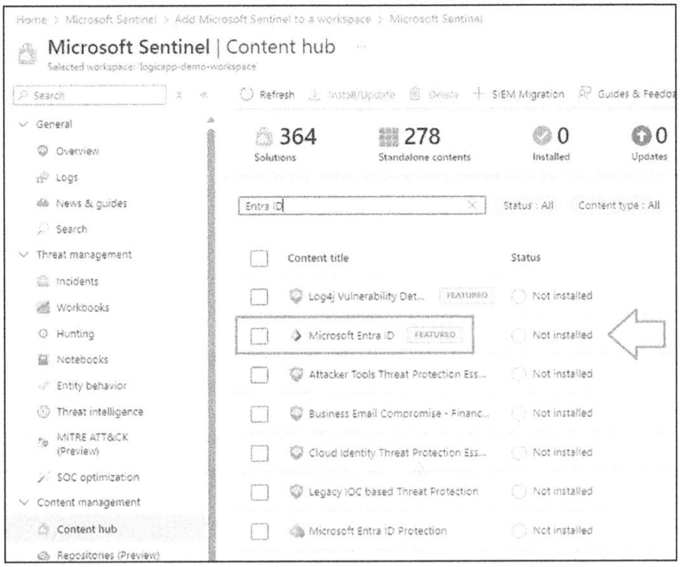

Figure 9.1: Content Hub

b. **Install Microsoft Entra ID Solution**: Search for `Microsoft Entra ID` and install the solution to enable data integration.

Figure 9.2: Install Entra ID Solution

c. **Configure Data Connector**: After installation, go to the **`Data Connectors`** section, select **`Microsoft Entra ID`**, and choose the data logs to ingest, focusing on **`sign-in logs`** for this scenario.

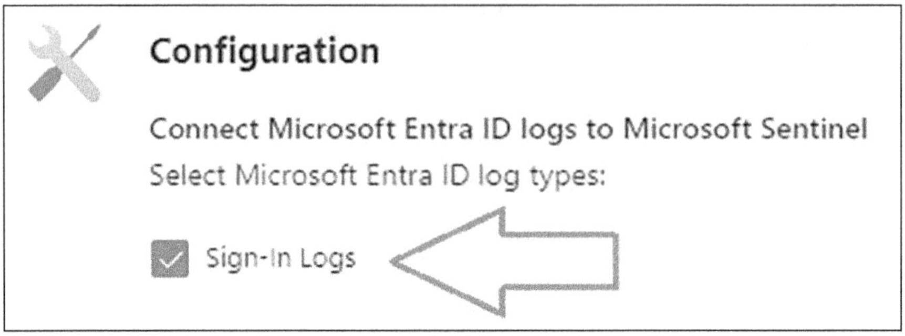

Figure 9.3: *Sign-in Logs*

This integration allows Microsoft Sentinel to receive and analyze sign-in data from Microsoft Entra ID.

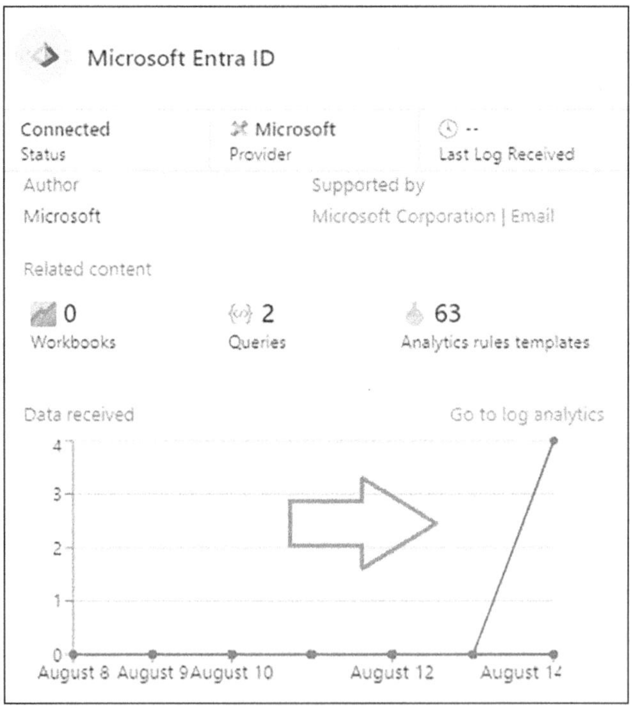

Figure 9.4: *Entra ID Log Traffic*

2. **Creating a Custom Analytics Rule**

   For this example, we can reuse the analytics rule from the previous chapter to generate an incident:

a. **Define Rule Parameters**: Set a **`name`**, **`description`**, and enable the rule (exactly the same as the example from the previous chapter).

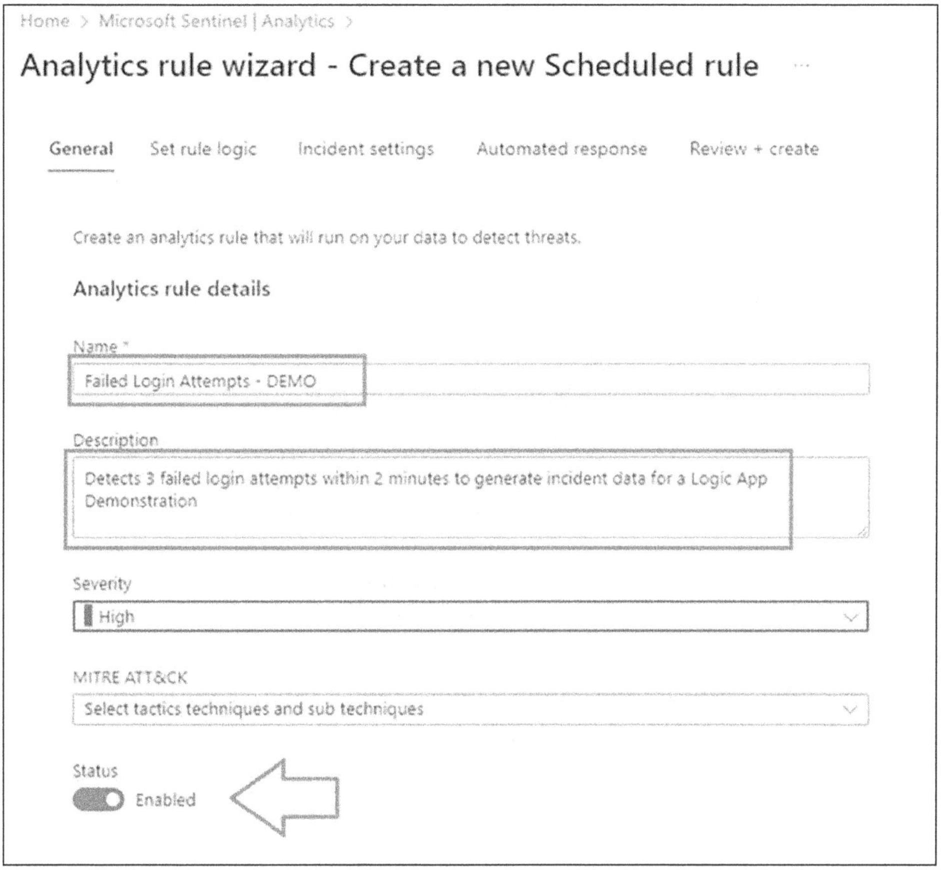

Figure 9.5: *Analytics Rule Details*

b. **Input KQL Query**: Use a Kusto Query Language (KQL) script to identify instances where a user has three or more failed login attempts within two minutes. In the following example, ResultType 50126 indicates a failed login.

```
SigninLogs
| where ResultType == 50126
| summarize FailedAttempts = count() by UserPrincipalName,
bin(TimeGenerated, 2m)
| where FailedAttempts >= 3
```

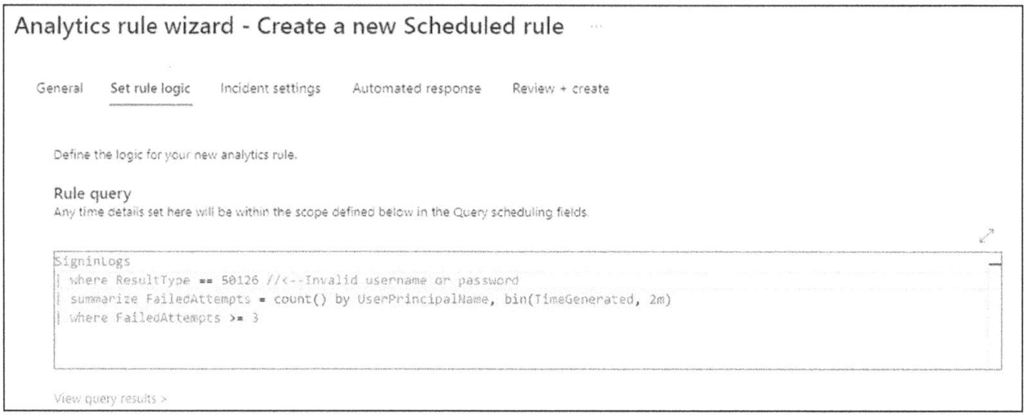

Figure 9.6: *Analytics Rule Logic*

Consider the level of customization and flexibility to adapt or create new rules to target specific behaviors. In our scenario, we are simply targeting failed logins; however, this could just as easily be adapted to foil potential exfiltration attempts by detecting unusual upload activity to an unsanctioned cloud storage provider, at which point our logic app could potentially disable the user's account before the upload completes, email the user's manager, then add a note to the Sentinel Incident for your SOC analysts. This would take a human analyst at least a few minutes to assess before taking action, in a situation where every second counts.

c. **Map Entities**: Ensure the rule maps relevant entities, such as the user's principal name, to pass data to the **Logic App**. This attaches the offending user's UPN to the alert in Sentinel so we know whose account to take action against.

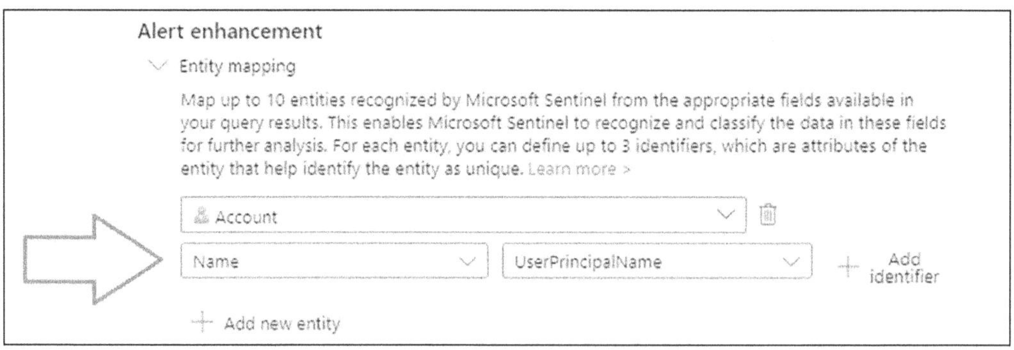

Figure 9.7: *Alert Enhancement*

d. **Set Scheduling and Grouping**: Configure the rule to run at specified intervals and group incidents based on user identifiers. This approach is essential for helping your SOC stay focused and effective, particularly during high-stress scenarios. In the following screenshot, alerts have been grouped by user over an 8-hour work shift.

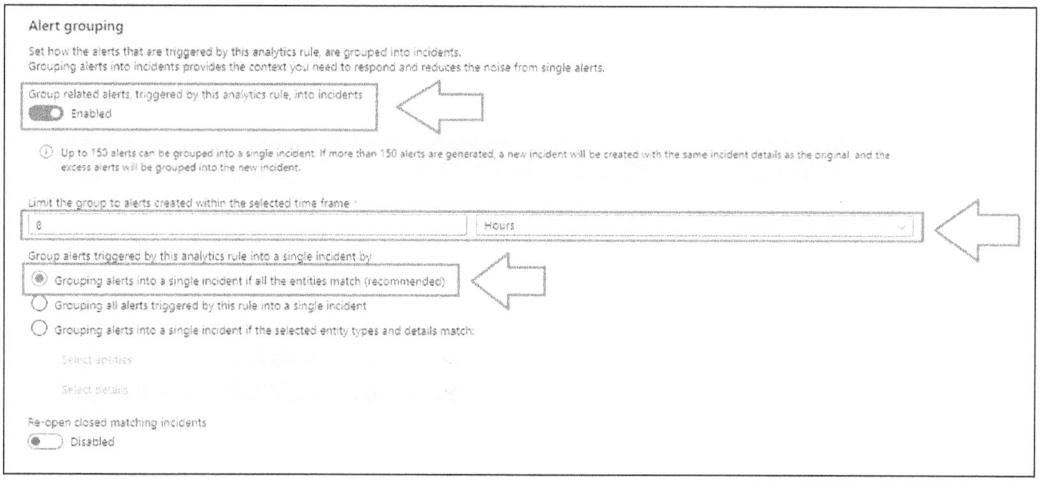

Figure 9.8: *Alert Grouping*

This rule will trigger an incident in Microsoft Sentinel later when we trigger the specified conditions.

3. **Building an Azure Logic App for Automated Responses**

   Create Logic Apps to perform the desired automated action:

   a. **Disable Account:** Set up a Logic App to disable the user's account.

   b. **Notify Manager**: Configure a Logic App to retrieve the user's manager information from Microsoft Entra ID and send an email notification.

   c. **Update Incident in Microsoft Sentinel**: Create a Logic App to append a comment to the incident, documenting the automated actions taken.

This Logic App will be triggered by the analytics rule and execute the defined actions automatically. Fortunately, there is a Logic App template built-in to the EntraID Solution we installed from the Content Hub earlier. Follow these steps to deploy it:

Browse over to the **`Content Hub`** and select the Entra ID solution, then **`Manage`**.

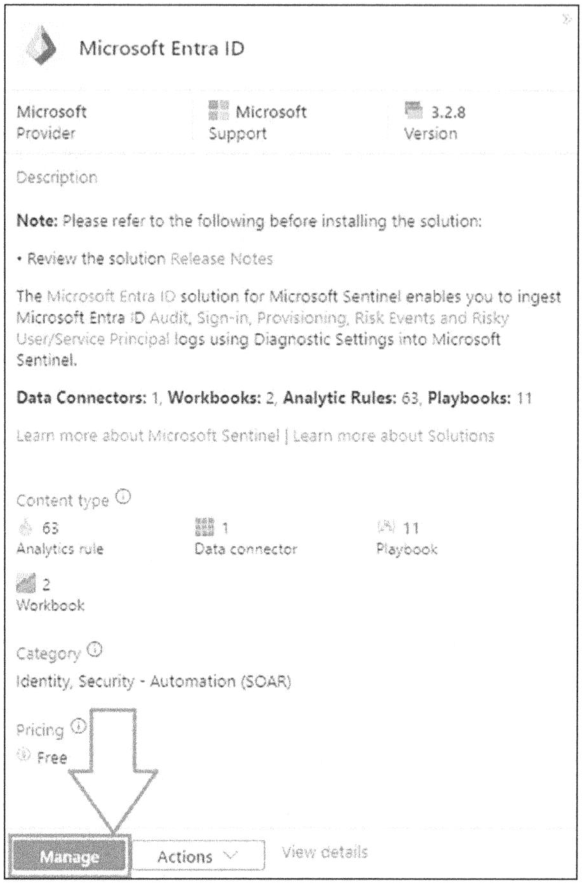

Figure 9.9: *Manage Solution Button*

The Logic App for this example can be found on the 3rd page of the **Entra ID** Solution in the **Content Hub.**

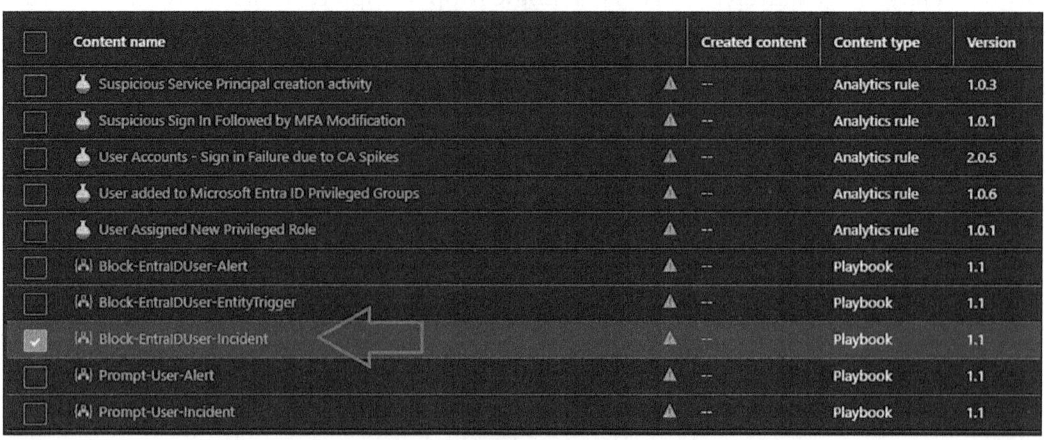

Figure 9.10: *Select Logic App*

a. Choose **Block Entra ID user - Incident** from the list, then select **Create Playbook** to proceed:

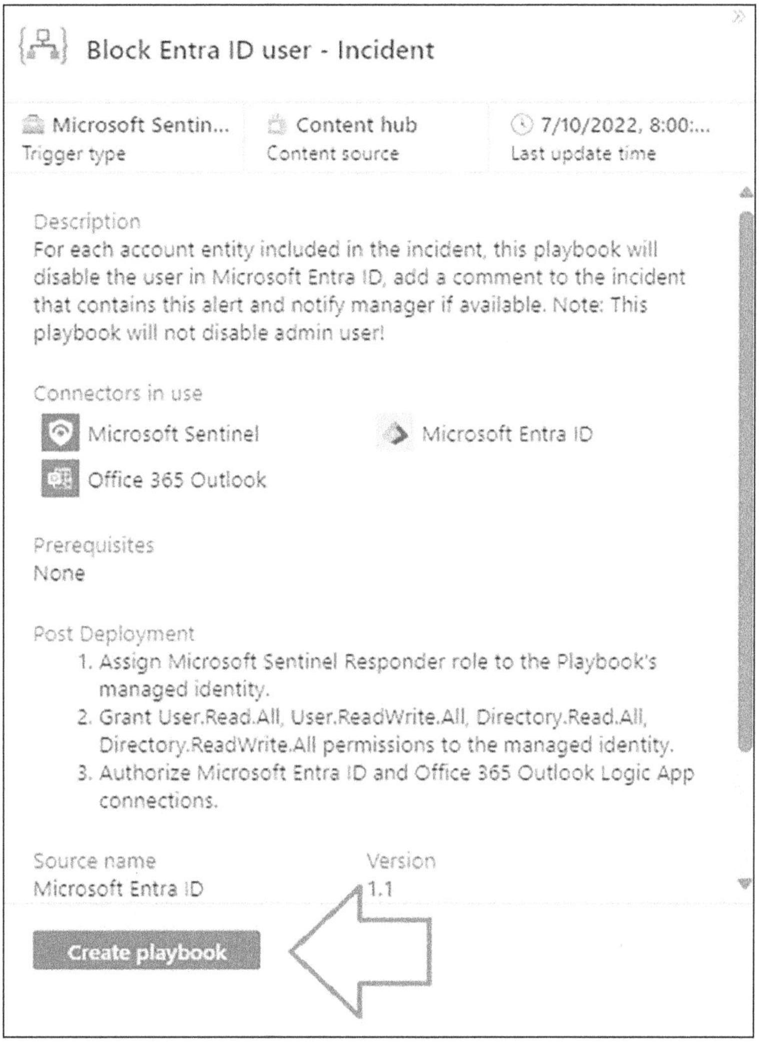

Figure 9.11: *Create Playbook Button*

b. Enter the correct subscription and resource group for your Logic App, assign a name, and proceed without modifying the Connections–leave them as default, and click **Next** through the remaining steps:

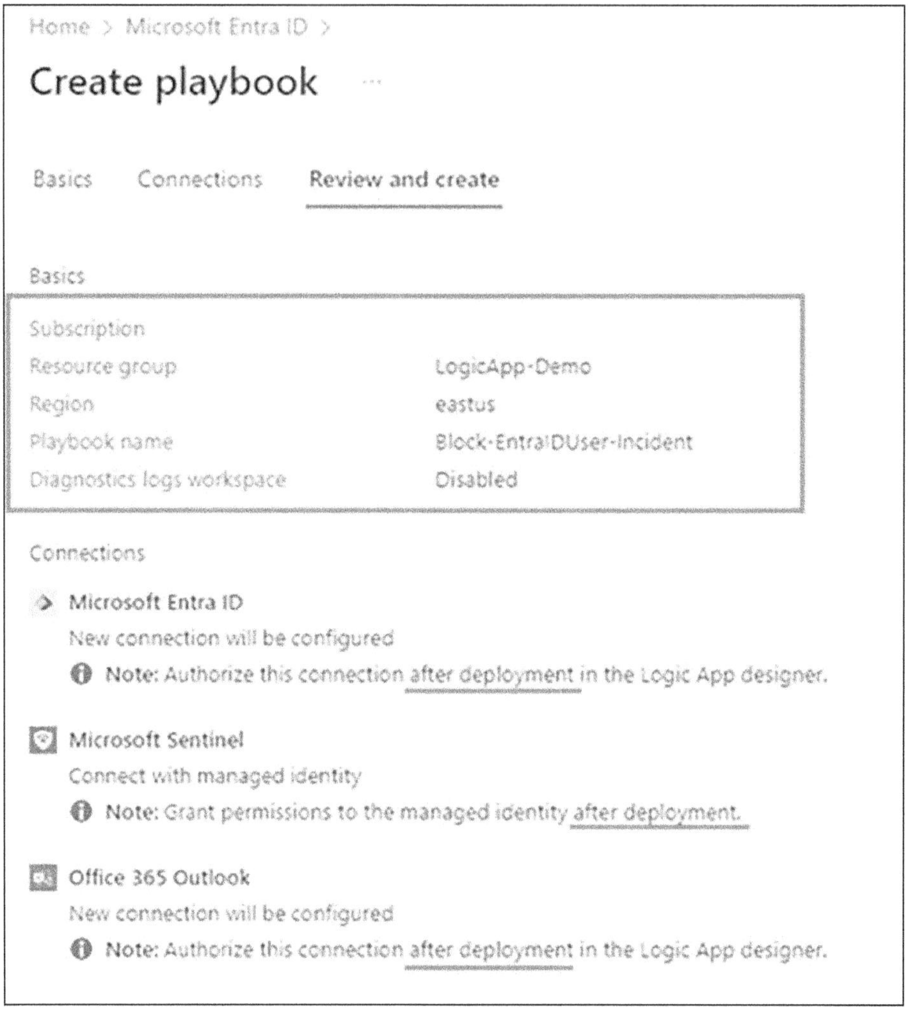

Figure 9.12: *Create Playbook*

4. **Assigning Managed Identity to Logic Apps**

   a. **Configure a Managed Identity**: In the Logic App's settings, grab the system-assigned managed identity. Go to your Logic App, open the **`Identities`** section, and locate the **`Object's Principal ID`**—make sure to save it for the next step:

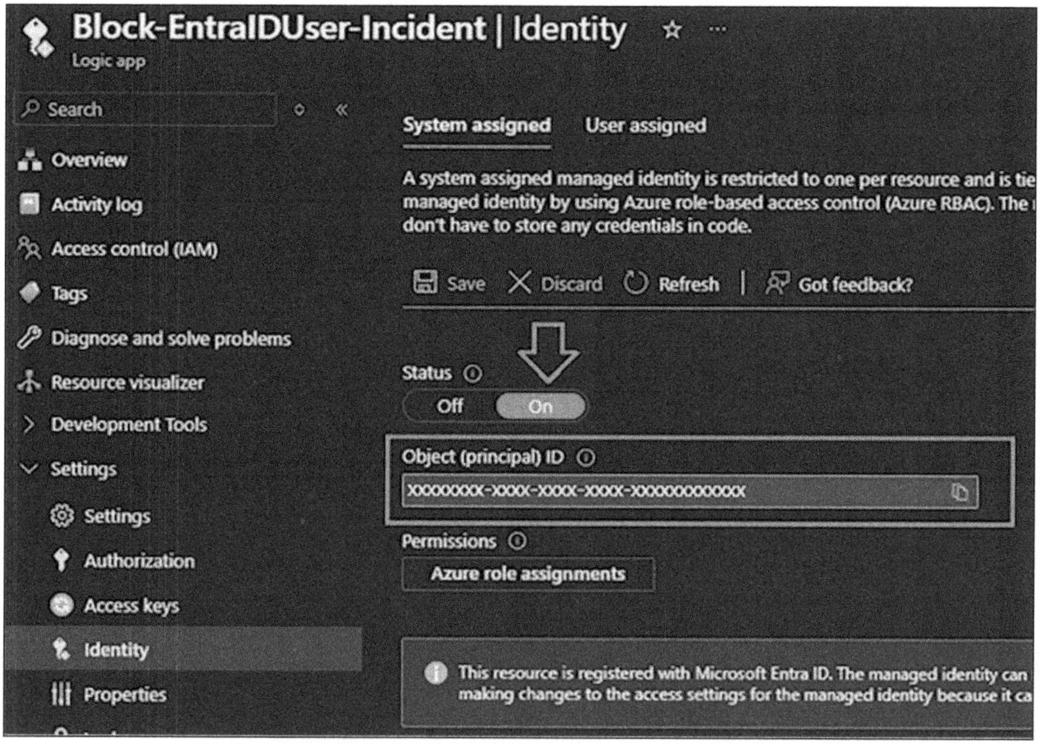

Figure 9.13: *Logic App System Assigned Object Principle ID*

b. **Assign Permissions**: Grant the managed identity appropriate roles. Click on **`Azure role assignments`** and assign the **`Microsoft Sentinel Responder`** role. Using managed identities enhances security by eliminating the need to store credentials within the Logic Apps. In this example scenario, our identity will require the following permissions:

   - **`User.Read.All`**
   - **`Directory.Read.All`**
   - **`User.EnableDisableAccount.All`**

   This can be automated via **PowerShell** as follows, just swap out the $MIGUID variable for your Object Principle ID:

```
# Run Connect-AzAccount to connect to your tenant before you
run this!

$MIGuid = "xxxxxxxx-xxxx-xxxx-xxxx-xxxxxxxxxxxx" #<-- Insert
your Principal ID
$MI = Get-AzureADServicePrincipal -ObjectId $MIGuid
```

```
$GraphAppId = "00000003-0000-0000-c000-000000000000" #<--Do
not change this
$PermissionName1 = "User.Read.All"
$PermissionName2 = "Directory.Read.All"
$PermissionName3 = "User.EnableDisableAccount.All"

$GraphServicePrincipal = Get-AzureADServicePrincipal -Filter
"appId eq '$GraphAppId'"
$AppRole1 = $GraphServicePrincipal.AppRoles | Where-Object
{$_.Value -eq $PermissionName1 -and $_.AllowedMemberTypes
-contains "Application"}
New-AzureAdServiceAppRoleAssignment -ObjectId $MI.ObjectId
-PrincipalId $MI.ObjectId `
-ResourceId $GraphServicePrincipal.ObjectId -Id $AppRole1.Id

$AppRole2 = $GraphServicePrincipal.AppRoles | Where-Object
{$_.Value -eq $PermissionName2 -and $_.AllowedMemberTypes
-contains "Application"}
New-AzureAdServiceAppRoleAssignment -ObjectId $MI.ObjectId
-PrincipalId $MI.ObjectId `
-ResourceId $GraphServicePrincipal.ObjectId -Id $AppRole2.Id

$AppRole3 = $GraphServicePrincipal.AppRoles | Where-Object
{$_.Value -eq $PermissionName3 -and $_.AllowedMemberTypes
-contains "Application"}
New-AzureAdServiceAppRoleAssignment -ObjectId $MI.ObjectId
-PrincipalId $MI.ObjectId `
-ResourceId $GraphServicePrincipal.ObjectId -Id $AppRole3.Id
```

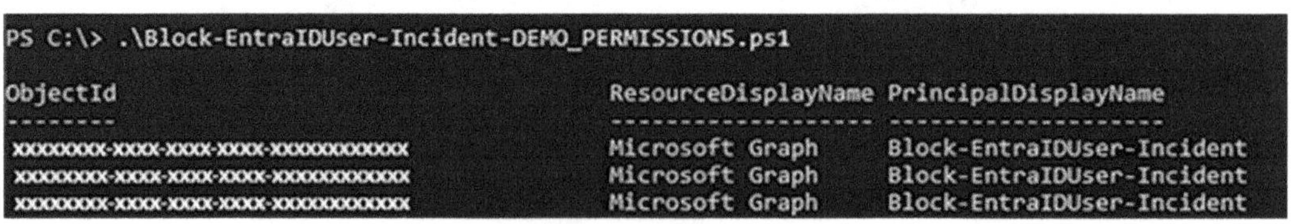

Figure 9.14: *Script Results*

The preceding PowerShell script can be found online here: https://github.com/EEN421/Powershell-Stuff/blob/Main/Logic%20App%20Demo/Block-EntraIDUser-Incident-PERMISSIONS.ps1

Other scripts for different logic apps included in the Entra ID solution (reset password, revoke sessions, and so on) can be found here: https://github.com/EEN421/Powershell-Stuff/tree/Main/Logic%20App%20Demo

To allow the Logic App to access the Sentinel workspace, open the **Settings** section in Sentinel, expand the **Playbook Permissions** dropdown, and select **Configure Permissions**:

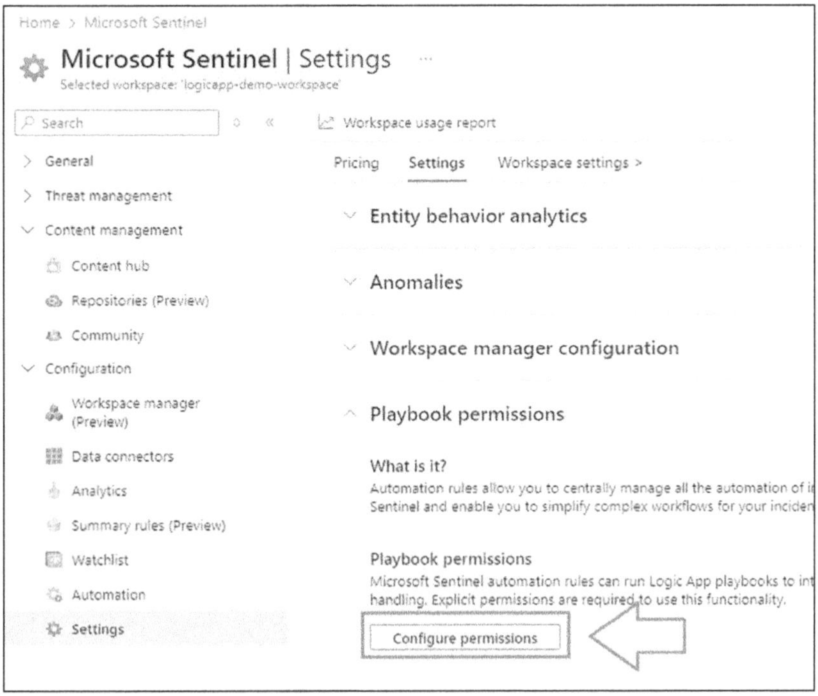

Figure 9.15: *Configure Permissions*

Select the **Resource Group** where your **Logic App resides** to allow it to interact with your Sentinel workspace.

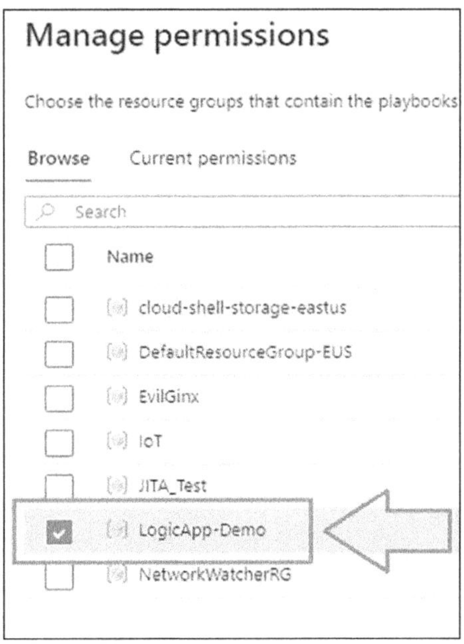

Figure 9.16: *Grant Permissions to Sentinel via Resource Group*

Note that Azure Logic Apps are separate from Sentinel and thus have their own space. This is confusing at first since we are building a logic app for security purposes in Sentinel, but keep in mind that you can build logic apps for much more than just security purposes.

Return to your Logic App and go to Development Tools > API Connections to complete the authorization of the connections we postponed during initial setup.

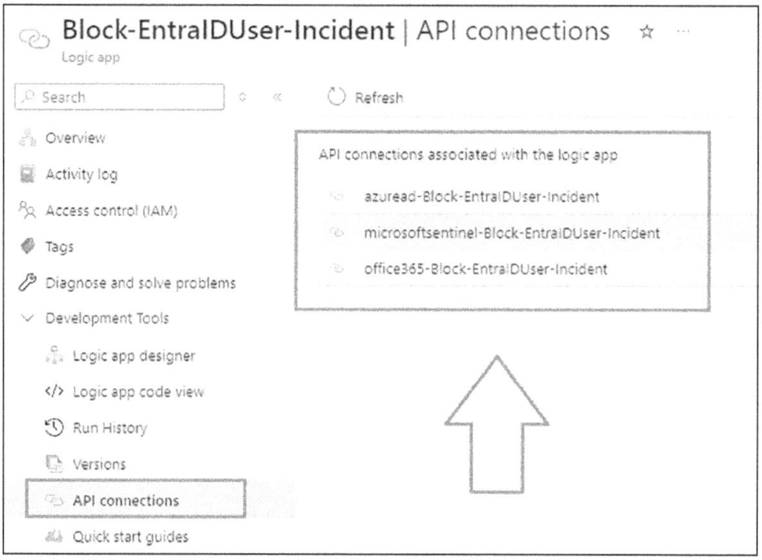

Figure 9.17: *API Connections*

In the left-hand menu, expand the **`General`** section and open the **`Edit API Connection`** blade. From there, click **`Authorize`** and then **`Save`**.

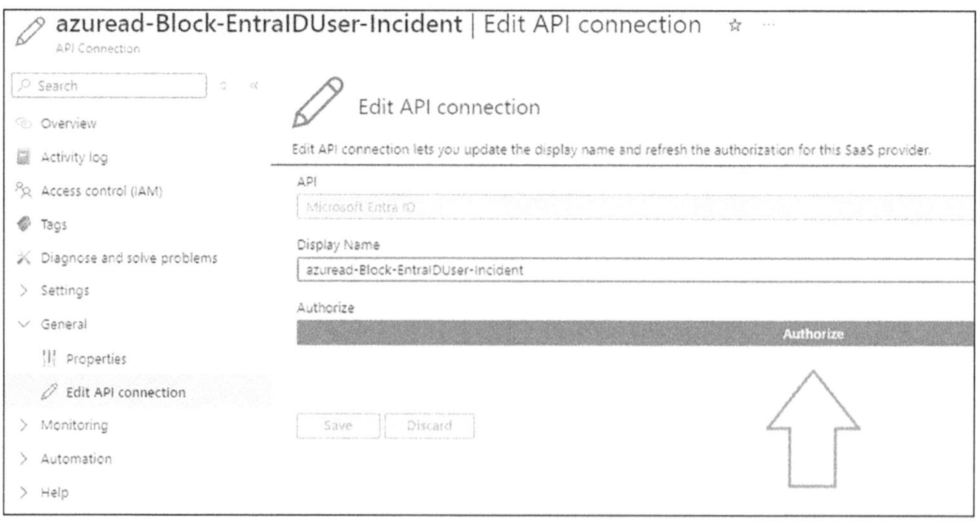

Figure 9.18: *Authorize API Connection*

Go through this step for each API connection listed. If the O365 email connector returns an authorization error, confirm that the account being used has mailbox capabilities–this requires an Exchange license. When configured correctly, the red 'invalid connector' indicators in the Logic App Designer should be resolved.

5. **Testing Your New Logic App**

   Now that we have our Entra ID telemetry connected to our Sentinel Workspace and deployed an Analytics Rule to detect 3x failed logins within 2 consecutive minutes: all that is left to do is test it. Open a browser window in Private/Incognito mode and attempt to log into the Azure portal with a non-admin test account 3 times in 2 minutes to trigger an alert in Sentinel:

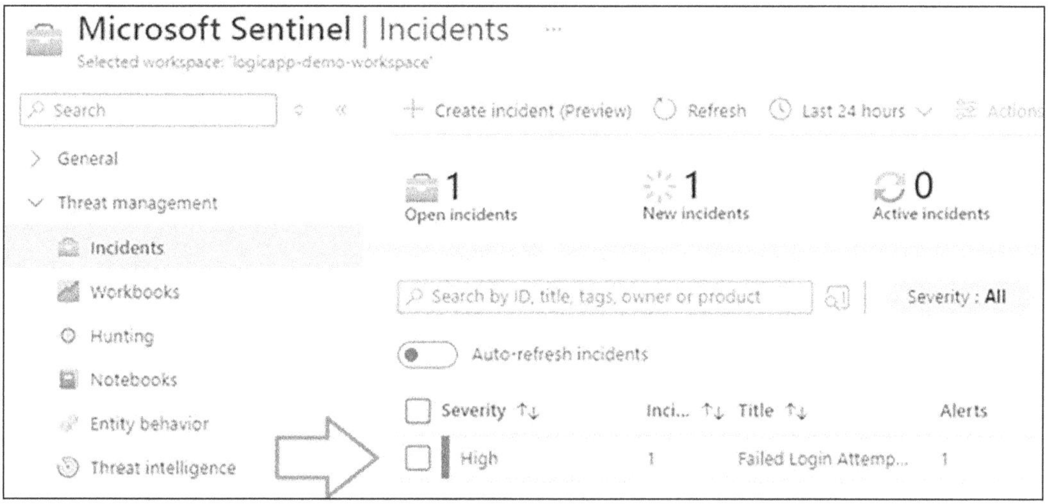

Figure 9.19: *Incidents*

If you open the incident details, you can see the entities associated with it. Because we mapped the **User Principal Name (UPN)** to the **Account Name** in the **Analytics Rule** that generated the alert, we now know which user account triggered the alert:

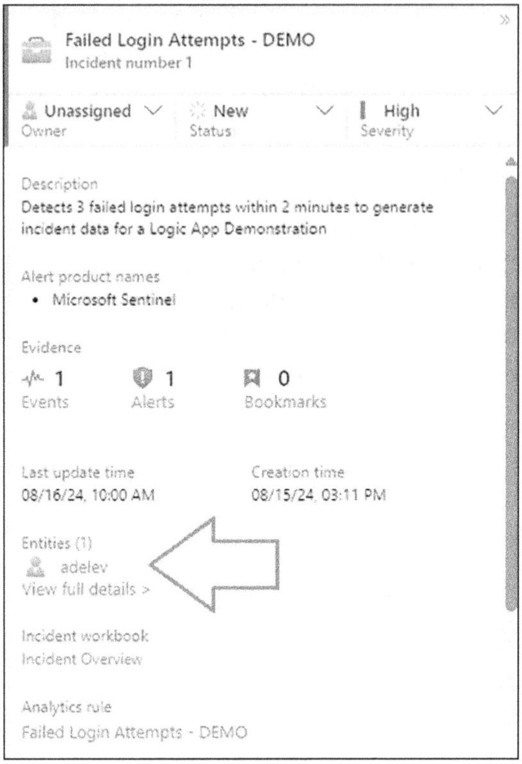

Figure 9.20: *Incident Details*

From the incident fly-out menu, expand the **`Actions`** menu and select **`Run playbook`**:

Figure 9.21: *Incident Actions Menu*

This brings up the **`Run playbook`** on the **`Incident`** menu. From here, select our workbook and click on **`Run`**:

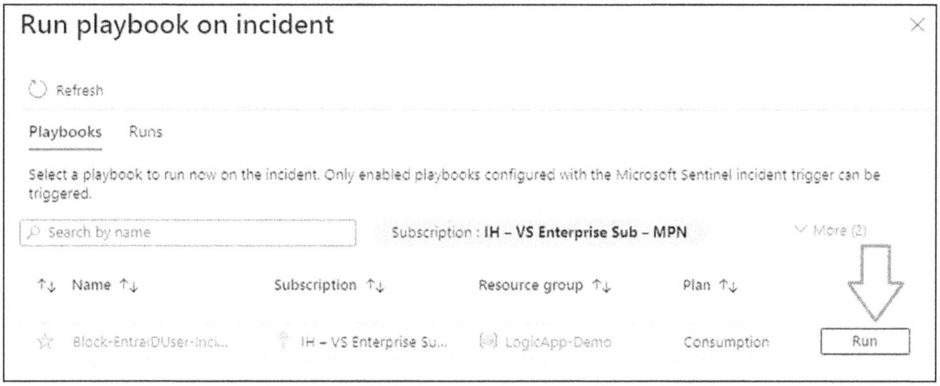

Figure 9.22: *Run Playbook Against Incident*

6. **Logic App Breakdown**

   Let us examine the logic in the app. Here is a step-by-step breakdown of what happened when we ran the **`Block-EntraIDUser-Incident`**.

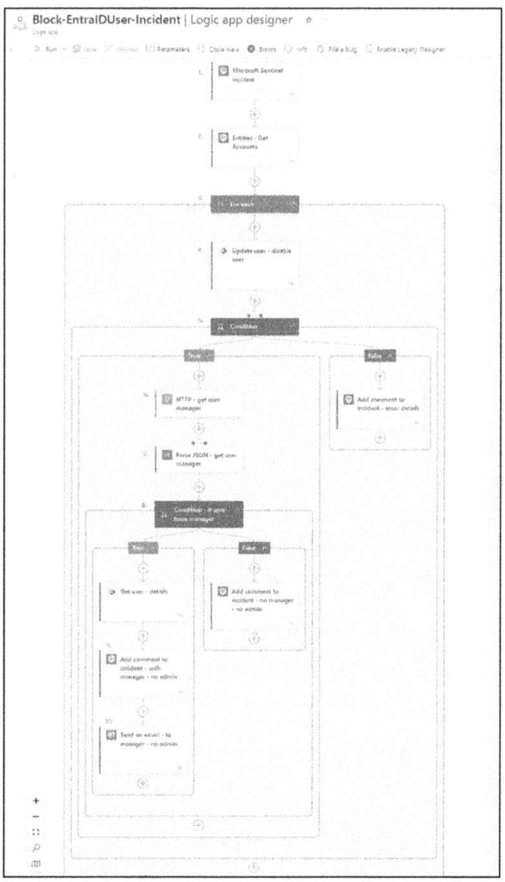

Figure 9.23: *Logic App Breakdown*

1. `Microsoft Sentinel Incident Trigger` triggers the app upon receipt of new incident data.
2. `Entities - Get Accounts` grabs the **User Name** and **UPN Suffix** from the incident data.
3. `For Each` is a loop that runs until it has iterated through all the User accounts associated with the incident.
4. `Update User - Disable User` combines the User Name and UPN Suffix from the previous step using the concatenation function, then appends the "disabled" flag.

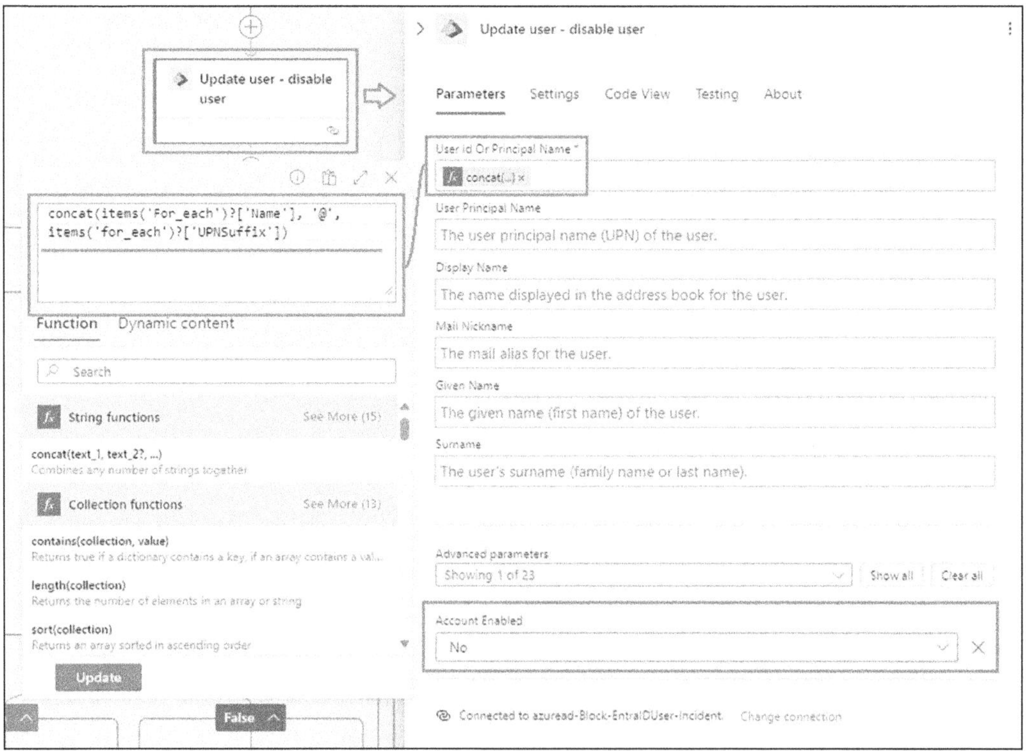

Figure 9.24: *Disable User Parameters*

In the next step, the app uses the preceding information to generate a Microsoft Graph URI to send the disable parameter to the appropriate account in Entra ID, as follows.

Figure 9.25: *Disable User via Microsoft Graph API*

5. **`Condition - Did the previous action complete successfully (Yes/No)?`**
   - **`No`**: Add a comment to the incident indicating that the account could not be disabled automatically.
   - **`Yes`**: Proceed to the next step in the workflow.
6. **HTTP - Retrieve User's Manager:** Query EntraID to find the manager of the offending user and pass the result to the following step.
7. **`Parse JSON - Extract Manager Info`:** Parse the returned manager details using the defined schema (String Object format).
8. **`Condition - Is a Manager Listed?`**: Check whether the Manager field contains a valid value or is null.

- **`No`**: Add a comment to the incident noting that the user was successfully disabled in AAD using the Block-AADUser playbook but no manager was notified because one could not be identified.
- **`Yes`**: Capture the user's name and related details to forward to the next action.

9. **`Add Comment to Incident - Manager Notified`**: Append a note to the Sentinel incident confirming that the user was disabled and the manager has been notified, so the assigned SOC analyst knows what steps have already been taken via automation.
10. **`Send Email - Notify Manager`**: Dispatch an email to the manager using the email account configured with the connector.

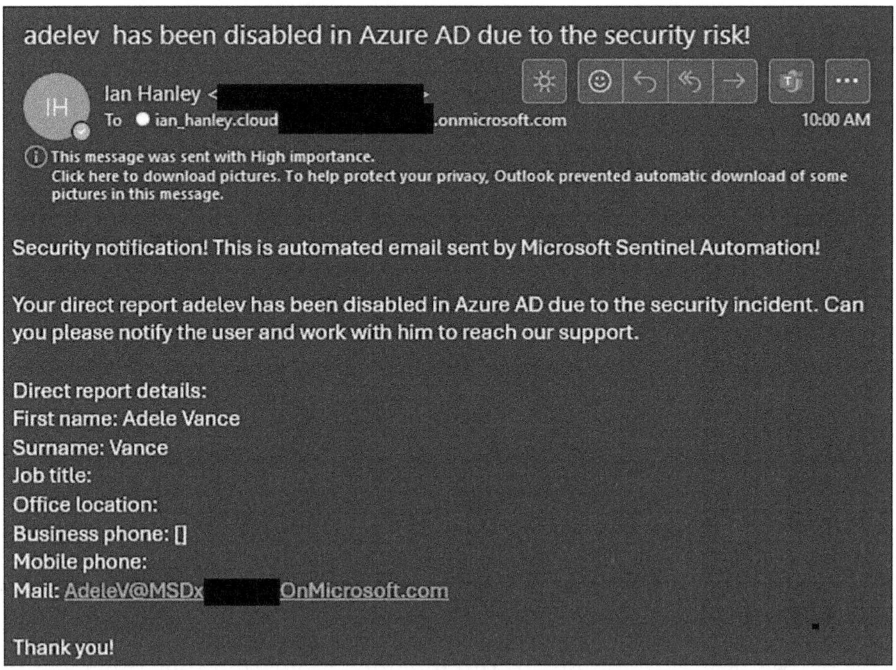

***Figure 9.26:** Email Notification to Manager*

Navigate to the test user's **account overview** page in **Entra ID** to confirm their status.

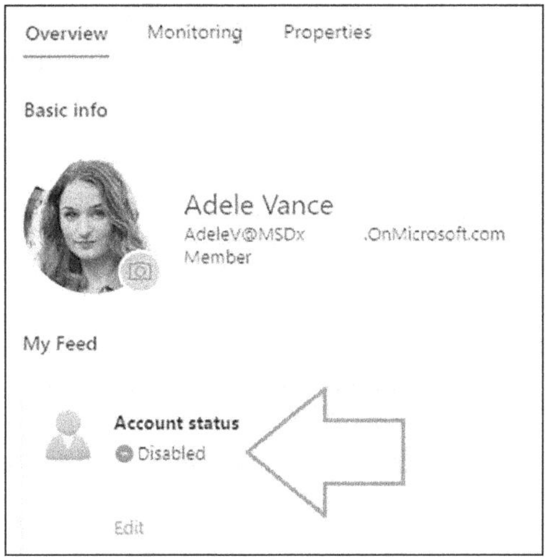

Figure 9.27: *Account Disabled*

7. **Fine-tune and Test the Automation**
   a. After setting up, fine-tune the Logic App to handle exceptions and ensure reliability. Test the entire workflow to confirm that each component functions as intended and that the automation effectively responds to multiple failed login attempts.
   b. To review a prior run or iteration through a logic app, navigate to the Azure portal and search for Logic Apps in the search bar, then open your app and expand the **`Development Tools`** blade, then select **`Run History`**.

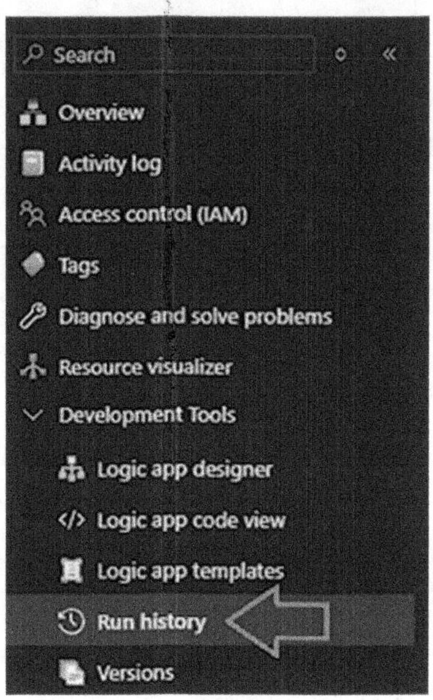

Figure 9.28: *Run History*

From here, any issues are highlighted and associated with the corresponding step where the failure occurred, helping you pinpoint what went wrong.

8. **Automation Rules: Tying it all Together**

   Now that we have an analytics rule generating incidents and a logic app/ playbook to run against them, let us configure our environment such that Sentinel automatically runs our playbook against new failed sign-in alerts from Entra ID.

   a. Navigate to your Sentinel workspace and select the **`Automation`** blade (under the **`Configuration`** drop-down).

   b. Select **`+ Create`** and choose **`Automation Rule`** from the menu.

   c. Provide a rule name, select your Analytics Rule in the **`Conditions`** menu, then choose your playbook from the **`Actions`** drop-down menu.

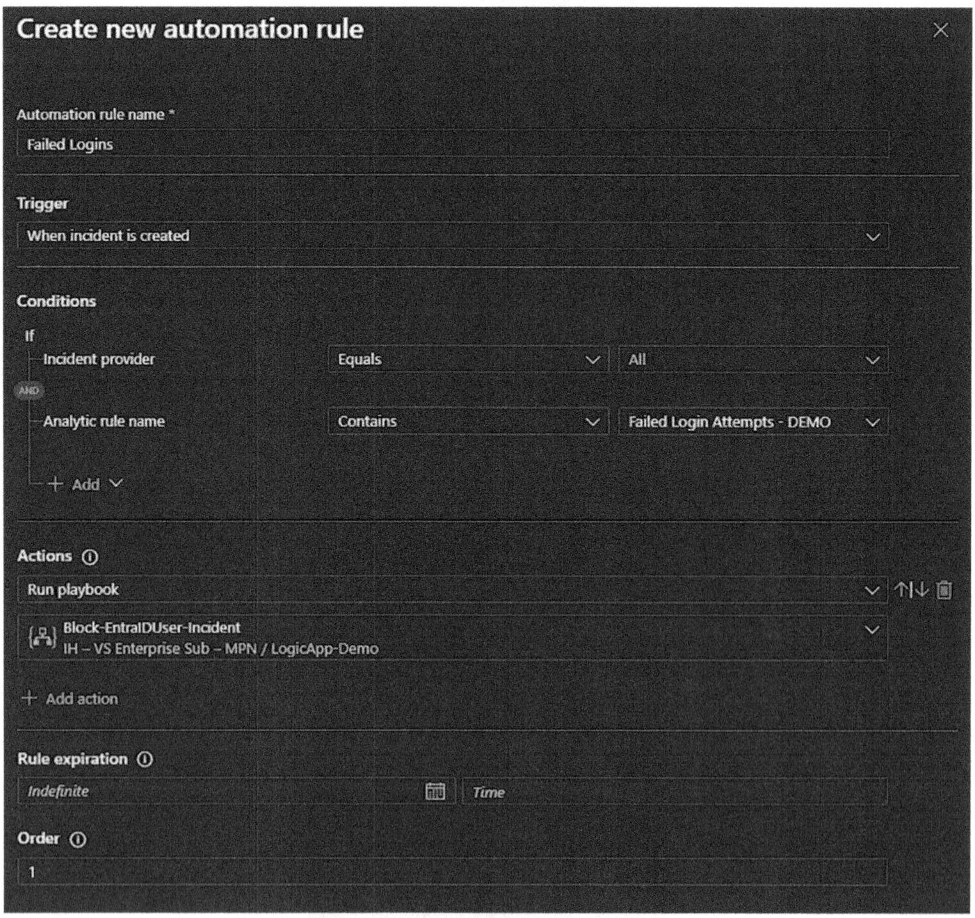

Figure 9.29: *Create a New Automation Rule*

You now have an Automation Rule deployed to Microsoft Sentinel that will automatically trigger against a user account when it fails to log in 3 times within 2 minutes, disable the account, email the account holder's manager, and then update the incident in Sentinel.

Conclusion

By integrating Microsoft Sentinel with Azure Logic Apps, organizations can automate responses to potential security threats, such as multiple failed login attempts. This automation not only enhances security posture but also reduces the manual workload on SOC analysts, leading to more efficient and effective security operations.

In the next chapter, we will take a deeper dive into Microsoft Sentinel's SOAR capabilities–focusing on automation rules, playbooks, and how these components work together to orchestrate dynamic, real-time responses. From deploying Logic Apps through the Solutions Hub to integrating with Entra ID and building custom analytics rules, you will gain hands-on insight into building powerful automated workflows that elevate your security operations center to the next level.

References

- Microsoft. (n.d.). What is Azure Logic Apps? Microsoft Learn. https://learn.microsoft.com/en-us/azure/logic-apps/logic-apps-overview/
- Microsoft. (n.d.). What is Microsoft Entra ID? Microsoft Learn. https://learn.microsoft.com/en-us/entra/id/
- Microsoft. (n.d.). Kusto Query Language (KQL) overview. Microsoft Learn. https://learn.microsoft.com/en-us/azure/data-explorer/kusto/query/
- Microsoft. (n.d.). Create and manage automation rules in Microsoft Sentinel. Microsoft Learn. https://learn.microsoft.com/en-us/azure/sentinel/automation-rules
- EEN421. (n.d.). Block-EntraIDUser-Incident-PERMISSIONS.ps1. GitHub. https://github.com/EEN421/Powershell-Stuff/blob/Main/Logic%20App%20Demo/Block-EntraIDUser-Incident-PERMISSIONS.ps1
- EEN421. (n.d.). Logic App Demo Scripts. GitHub. https://github.com/EEN421/Powershell-Stuff/tree/Main/Logic%20App%20Demo
- Hanley, I. (2024, August 16). Logic Apps & Automation in Sentinel. Hanley.Cloud. https://www.hanley.cloud/2024-08-16-Logic-Apps-&-Automation/

Chapter 10
Efficient KQL Query Design and Optimization

Introduction

Kusto Query Language (KQL) is the foundation of querying and interacting with data in Microsoft Sentinel. From visualizing security metrics in workbooks to powering detections in analytics rules, KQL enables analysts to transform raw telemetry into actionable insight. Though powerful, KQL is intuitive enough to get started with basic filters and aggregations—yet flexible enough to drive complex hunting logic, entity behavior analysis, and automated threat detection workflows.

This chapter introduces you to the core syntax of KQL, walks through practical examples, and offers a deep dive into advanced techniques and performance optimization best practices. Whether you are building your first workbook or tuning a detection query, mastering KQL is essential to unlocking the full capabilities of Sentinel.

Structure

In this chapter, we will cover the following topics:

- KQL Basics: Syntax and Operators
- Core Query Patterns for Security Use Cases
- Using KQL in Workbooks
- KQL in Analytics Rules
- Deep Dive: Advanced Querying Techniques
- Performance and Cost Tuning

KQL Basics: Syntax and Operators

KQL is a read-only, declarative language designed to analyze large datasets efficiently. Its syntax is pipe-based, meaning each stage of the query feeds into the next. It is comparable to SQL if it were read-only.

Basic Example: Return failed sign-in attempts

```
SigninLogs
| where ResultType != 0
| project TimeGenerated, UserPrincipalName, IPAddress, Location
```

Refer to the following table for key KQL operator concepts and what they do.

Key Concepts:

Concept	Description
where	Filters rows by condition
project	Selects specific columns
summarize	Aggregates values
extend	Adds calculated columns
join	Combines tables
render	Visualizes results (used in workbooks)
Let	Defines reusable variables or subqueries

***Table 10.1:** Key KQL Operator Concepts*

Core Query Patterns for Security Use Cases

Here are some common patterns analysts use daily.

Top 10 IPs with failed sign-ins:

```
SigninLogs
| where ResultType != 0
| summarize Failures = count() by IPAddress
| sort by Failures desc
| take 10
```

User sign-ins outside expected geolocations:

```
SigninLogs
| where Location !in ("United States", "Canada")
| project UserPrincipalName, Location, TimeGenerated
```

Count of distinct users accessing a system:

```
SecurityEvent
| where EventID == 4624
| summarize UniqueUsers = dcount(Account)
```

Crafting an Initial KQL Query

Crafting efficient KQL queries is essential for timely and accurate data analysis, which is crucial for effective threat detection and response. This chapter delves into optimizing KQL queries to enhance performance and result accuracy.

Consider a scenario where you need to determine the average daily data ingestion over the past 30 days. A straightforward approach might involve querying all data and then filtering it:

```
search *
| where TimeGenerated > ago(30d)
| where _IsBillable == true
| summarize TotalGB = round(sum(_BilledSize / 1e9)) by
bin(TimeGenerated, 1d)
| summarize AvgGBPerDay = avg(TotalGB)
```

Breaking Down the Query:

1. `search *                // Retrieves all data across tables.`
2. `| where TimeGenerated > ago(30d)        // Filters records from the past 30 days.`
3. `| where _IsBillable == true // Includes only billable data.`
4. `| summarize TotalGB = round(sum(_BilledSize / 1e9)) by bin(TimeGenerated, 1d)    // Calculates daily ingested data in gigabytes.`
5. `| summarize AvgGBPerDay = avg(TotalGB)    // Computes the average daily ingestion.`

While functional, this query is inefficient due to the initial **`search *`**, which scans all tables and can lead to prolonged execution times, especially in large environments.

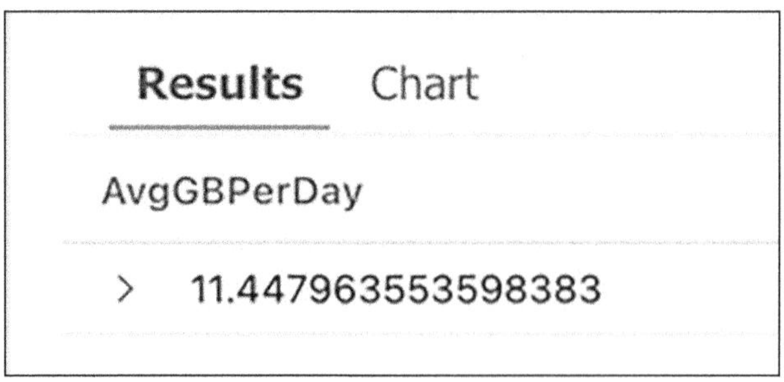

Figure 10.1: *Average GB per Day*

Enhancing Query Efficiency

To improve performance, specify the exact table containing the relevant data. For ingestion metrics, the Usage table is appropriate:

```
Usage
| where TimeGenerated > ago(30d)
| where IsBillable == true
| summarize GB = sum(Quantity) / 1000 by bin(TimeGenerated, 1d)
| summarize AvgGBPerDay = avg(GB)
```

Improvements Made:

- **Table Specification**: By querying the **Usage** table directly, the system processes only pertinent data, reducing load and execution time.
- **Efficient Filtering**: Applying filters immediately after specifying the table ensures that only necessary data is processed.

Best Practices for KQL Query Optimization:

- **Specify Tables Explicitly**: Avoid using **`search *`**. Directly reference the necessary table to minimize data scanning.
- **Apply Filters Early**: Filter data as close to the source as possible to reduce the volume of data processed in subsequent steps.
- **Use Appropriate Data Types**: Ensure calculations use consistent data types to prevent errors and inaccuracies.
- **Leverage Aggregation Functions**: Utilize functions such as summarize to group and compute data efficiently.
- **Avoid Redundant Operations**: Streamline queries by removing unnecessary steps or duplicate calculations.

Functions and Incorporating Cost Calculations

Understanding data ingestion costs is vital for budgeting and resource allocation. Assuming a cost rate (for example, $4.30 per GB, you can find yours here: https://azure.microsoft.com/en-us/pricing/details/microsoft-sentinel/?msockid=1186afebbd5a6f6a005dbb3dbc486e61), you can extend the query to calculate daily ingestion costs:

```
let rate = 4.30;
Usage
| where TimeGenerated > ago(30d)
| where IsBillable == true
| summarize GB = sum(Quantity) / 1000 by bin(TimeGenerated, 1d)
```

```
| extend Cost = GB * rate
| summarize AvgCostPerDay = avg(Cost), AvgGBPerDay = avg(GB)
```

Key Additions:

- **Variable Declaration**: `let rate = 4.30;` sets the cost per GB, making the query adaptable to different pricing.
- **Cost Calculation**: `extend Cost = GB * rate` computes the daily cost based on ingestion volume.
- **Average Computation**: `summarize AvgCostPerDay = avg(Cost), AvgGBPerDay = avg(GB)` provides average daily cost and ingestion metrics.

This next iteration includes an attempt to calculate the average cost and does so by introducing a rate variable (this variable holds your *effective cost per* GB based on your commitment tier) and leveraging the percentiles function (https://learn.microsoft.com/en-us/kusto/query/percentiles-aggregation-function?view=azure-data-explorer&preserve-view=true):

```
let rate = 4.30;
Usage //<-- Query the USAGE table (instead of "search *" to
query everything)
| where TimeGenerated > ago(30d)
| where IsBillable == true
| summarize GB= sum(Quantity)/1000 by bin(TimeGenerated,1d)
| extend Cost=GB*rate
| summarize AvgCostPerDay=percentiles(Cost,50),AvgGBPerDay
=percentiles(GB,50)
```

Figure 10.2: *Average Cost per Day*

Using the percentiles function to grab the 50th percentile does not give you the true average–it gives you the median, which is often a more realistic reflection of typical cost, but not the actual mean. In larger environments, this difference can be surprisingly significant. Lastly, the default output is not exactly easy on the eyes either. Let us clean that up in the next query example.

```
let rate = 4.30;
Usage
| where TimeGenerated > ago(30d)
| where IsBillable == true
```

```
| summarize GB= sum(Quantity)/1000 by bin(TimeGenerated,1d)
| summarize AvgGBPerDay=avg(GB)
| extend Cost=AvgGBPerDay * rate
| project AvgGBPerDay=strcat(round(AvgGBPerDay,2), ' GB/Day'),
AvgCostPerDay=strcat('$', round(Cost,2), ' /Day')
```

The **project** statement in the preceding query rounds up to the second decimal place and converts everything to a string in order to prepend '$' and append ' /Day' to make the results more presentable, with help from the **`strcat()`** function used to join multiple values into a single string, making raw numbers more readable—especially when presenting costs, data volumes, or units in dashboards or reports:

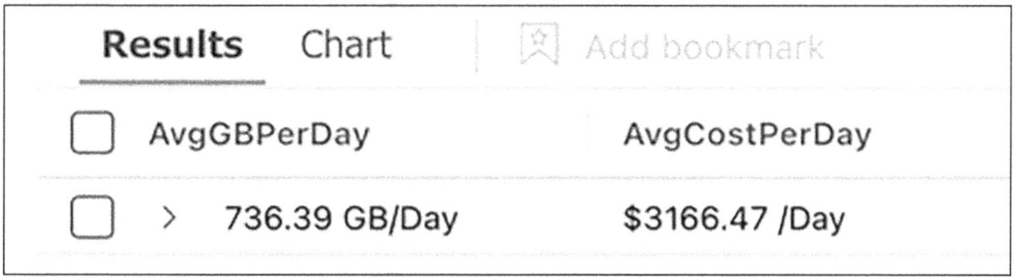

Figure 10.3: *Output Formatted with strcat()*

Using KQL in Workbooks

KQL drives all visualizations in Microsoft Sentinel workbooks. Let us say you want to graph authentication attempts over time:

```
SigninLogs
| summarize Count = count() by bin(TimeGenerated, 1h)
| render timechart
```

In the workbook editor:

- Use "**Add Query**"
- Paste the KQL
- Select "**Time chart**" visualization
- Optionally add filters (for example, time picker, IP range)

This kind of chart can be reused across dashboards to track auth trends, user behavior, or alert volume.

KQL in Analytics Rules

Analytics rules use scheduled KQL queries to detect suspicious behavior.

Example: Detect 3+ failed sign-ins from the same user within 2 minutes

```
SigninLogs
| where ResultType == 50126
| summarize Failures = count() by UserPrincipalName,
bin(TimeGenerated, 2m)
| where Failures >= 3
```

You would use this in a scheduled query rule, map the **UserPrincipalName** entity, and configure alert thresholds + automation like playbooks.

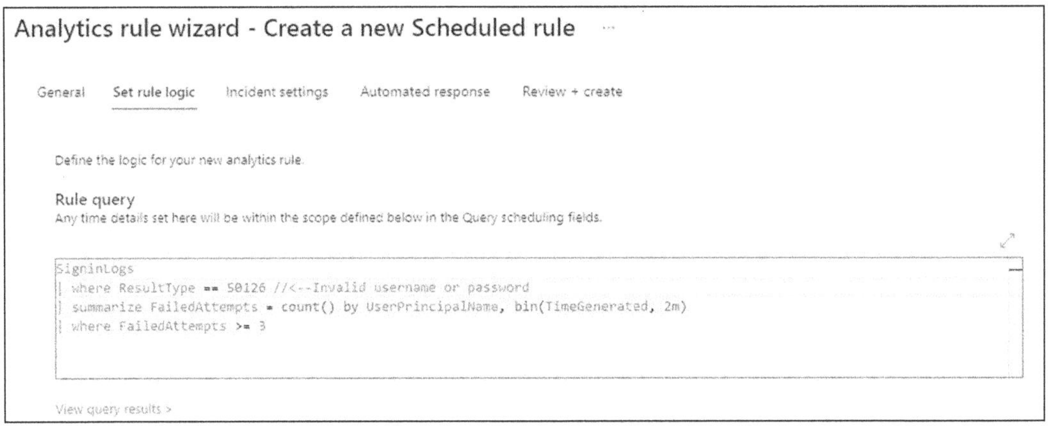

***Figure 10.4**: KQL in an Analytics Rule*

Deep Dive: Advanced Querying Techniques

Let Statements

Use let to define reusable variables or subqueries.

```
let threshold = 100;
let startTime = ago(90d);
let endTime = now();
SecurityEvent
| where TimeGenerated between (startTime .. endTime)
| where EventID == 50126
| summarize FailedLogins = count() by Account
| where FailedLogins > threshold
| project Account, FailedLogins
```

This query defines two variables, **`threshold`** and **`startTime`**, and uses them to filter and summarize security events where the number of failed logins exceeds the threshold within the last day.

Join Statements for Correlation

Join SigninLogs with **`ThreatIntelligenceIndicator`**:

```
let startTime = ago(90d);
let endTime = now();
let FailedLogins = SecurityEvent
| where TimeGenerated between (startTime .. endTime)
| where EventID == 50126   // <-- Failed Logon Attempts
| summarize FailedLogins = count() by Account;
let SuccessfulLogins = SecurityEvent
| where TimeGenerated between (startTime .. endTime)
| where EventID == 4624    // <-- Successful Logon Attempts
| summarize SuccessfulLogins = count() by Account;
FailedLogins
| join kind=inner (SuccessfulLogins) on Account
| project Account, FailedLogins, SuccessfulLogins
```

This query defines two sets of data: **`FailedLogins`** and **`SuccessfulLogins`**, summarizing the count of each by account. It then performs an **inner join** on the **Account field** to combine the data, showing accounts with both **failed** and **successful** login attempts within the last day.

Anomaly Detection with Series Analysis

```
let startTime = ago(7d);
let endTime = now();
SecurityEvent
| where TimeGenerated between (startTime .. endTime)
| where EventID == 50126
| summarize FailedLogins = count() by bin(TimeGenerated, 1h)
| render timechart
```

This can help identify unusual activity spikes that deviate from historical norms.

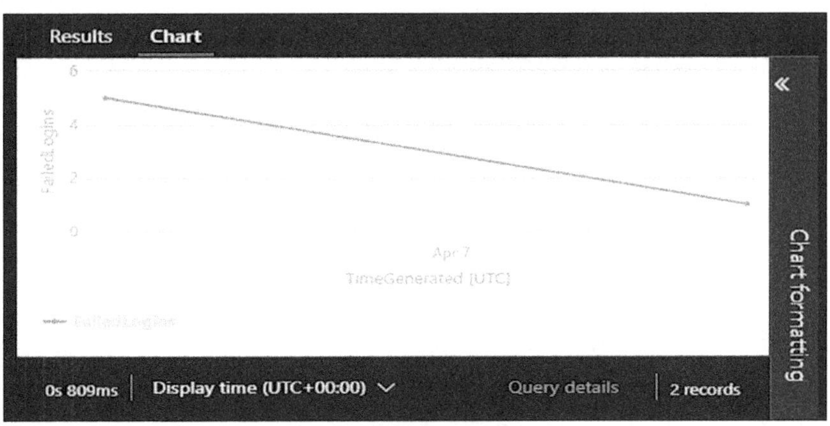

Figure 10.5: *Anomaly Detection with Series Analysis*

Conditional Statements

Use conditional statements to add logic to your queries.

```
SecurityEvent
| where TimeGenerated between (ago(7d) .. now())
| extend LoginType = case(EventID == 50126, "Failed",
EventID == 4624, "Successful", "Other")
| summarize LoginCount = count() by LoginType
| project LoginType, LoginCount
```

Figure 10.6: *Conditional Statements Output*

This query uses conditional statements to categorize login events as **`Failed`**, **`Successful`**, or Other, and then summarizes the count of each type.

Performance and Cost Tuning

To effectively manage and reduce Microsoft Sentinel's data ingestion costs, leveraging Kusto Query Language (KQL) queries is a strategic approach.

The following GitHub repository, EEN421/KQL-Queries (https://github.com/EEN421/KQL-Queries/blob/Main/QBRs/ReportQueries.kql), offers a collection of such queries designed to provide insights into data usage and costs for your reference. By integrating these queries into a Microsoft Sentinel workbook, you can monitor and optimize data ingestion, leading to cost savings.

- **Use time filters early**: Always include **`TimeGenerated > ago(x)`** to limit dataset size.
- **Minimize columns with the project**: Only return the columns you need.
- **Summarize early**: Aggregate before complex operations such as joins.
- **Avoid contains when has will work**: has is faster and more specific.

Utilizing KQL Queries to Monitor and Reduce Ingestion Costs

The following KQL queries are helpful for keeping tabs on your SOC efficiency and much more.

- **Open versus Closed Incidents over Time:**

```
SecurityIncident
| summarize IncidentsCreated = count(), IncidentsClosed
= countif(Status == "Closed") by bin(TimeGenerated, 1d)
| render timechart
```

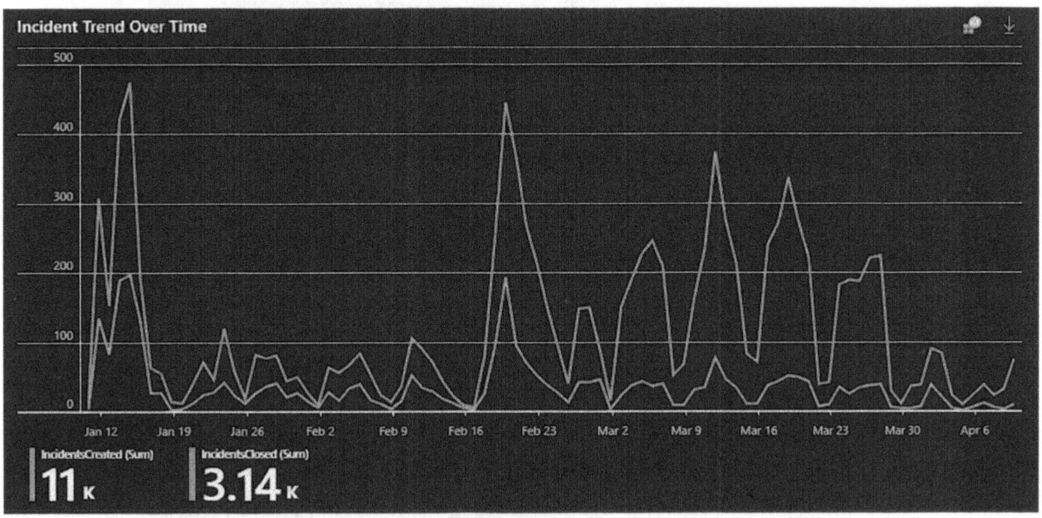

Figure 10.7: *Open versus Closed Incidents over Time*

- **Email Threat Trends**

```
EmailEvents
| where TimeGenerated > ago(90d)
| where ThreatTypes != ""
| summarize Count = count() by ThreatTypes, bin(Timestamp, 1d)
| order by Timestamp desc
| render timechart
```

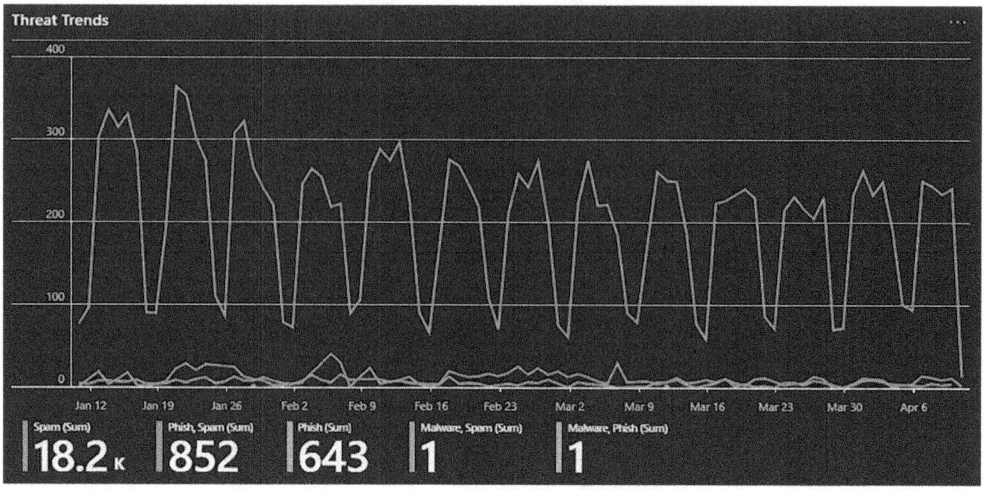

Figure 10.8: *Email Threat Trends over Time*

- **Mean Time to Respond (MTTR) Analysis**

  This query calculates the average time taken to respond to incidents:

```
SecurityIncident
| where TimeGenerated > ago(90d)
| where Status == "Closed"
| summarize MTTR = strcat(round(avg(datetime_diff('minute',
ClosedTime, CreatedTime)),2),' minutes')
```

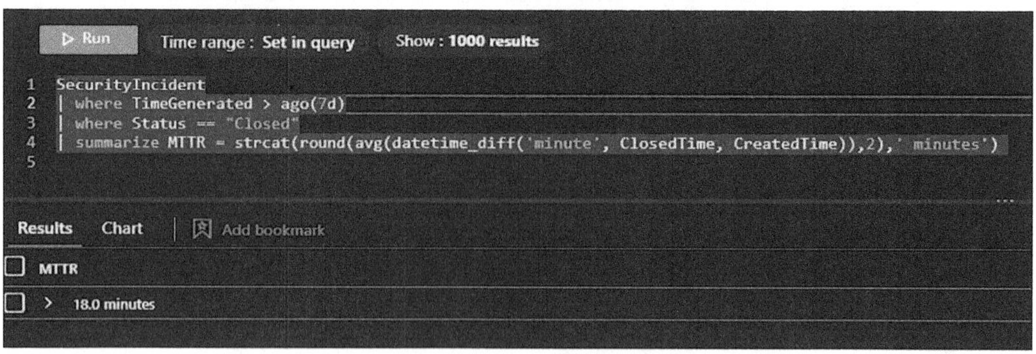

Figure 10.9: *Mean Time to Respond* (MTTR)

Understanding MTTR can help in assessing the efficiency of incident response processes and identifying areas for improvement.

- **Top 10 Frequent Alerts**

  Identifying the most frequent alerts can highlight potential noise or misconfigurations:

```
SecurityAlert
| where TimeGenerated > ago(90d)
| summarize Count = count() by AlertName
| top 10 by Count desc
```

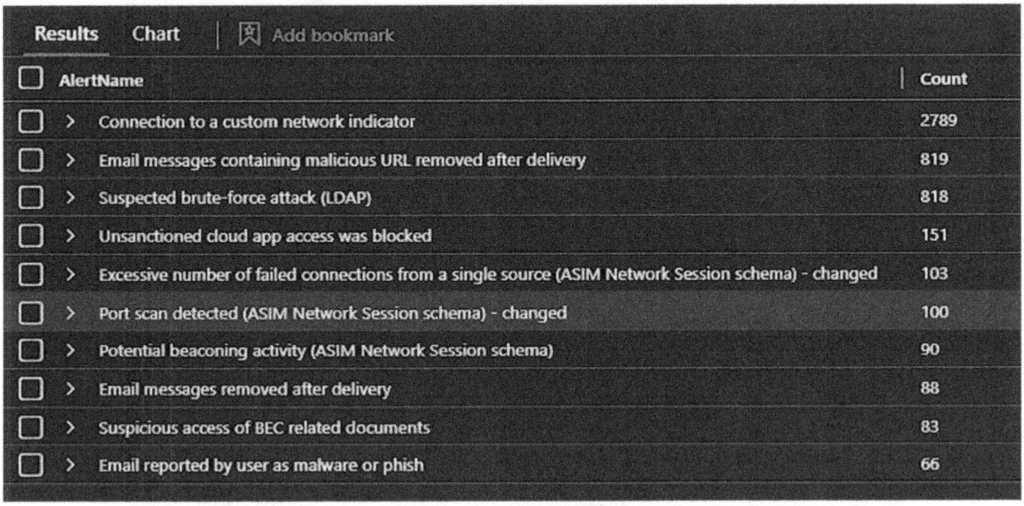

Results Chart Add bookmark

AlertName	Count
Connection to a custom network indicator	2789
Email messages containing malicious URL removed after delivery	819
Suspected brute-force attack (LDAP)	818
Unsanctioned cloud app access was blocked	151
Excessive number of failed connections from a single source (ASIM Network Session schema) - changed	103
Port scan detected (ASIM Network Session schema) - changed	100
Potential beaconing activity (ASIM Network Session schema)	90
Email messages removed after delivery	88
Suspicious access of BEC related documents	83
Email reported by user as malware or phish	66

***Figure 10.10**: Top 10 Security Alerts*

Frequent alerts may indicate redundant data ingestion. Reviewing and tuning these alerts can reduce unnecessary data flow.

- **Data Ingestion Volume by Data Type (Top 10)**

  Monitoring data ingestion by type helps in pinpointing high-volume sources:

```
Usage
| where TimeGenerated > ago(31d)
| where IsBillable == true
| summarize BillableDataGB = sum(Quantity) / 1000 by DataType
| sort by BillableDataGB desc
| project DataType = DataType, GbPerDay = strcat(round(Billable-
DataGB,2), 'GB/Day')
| take 10
```

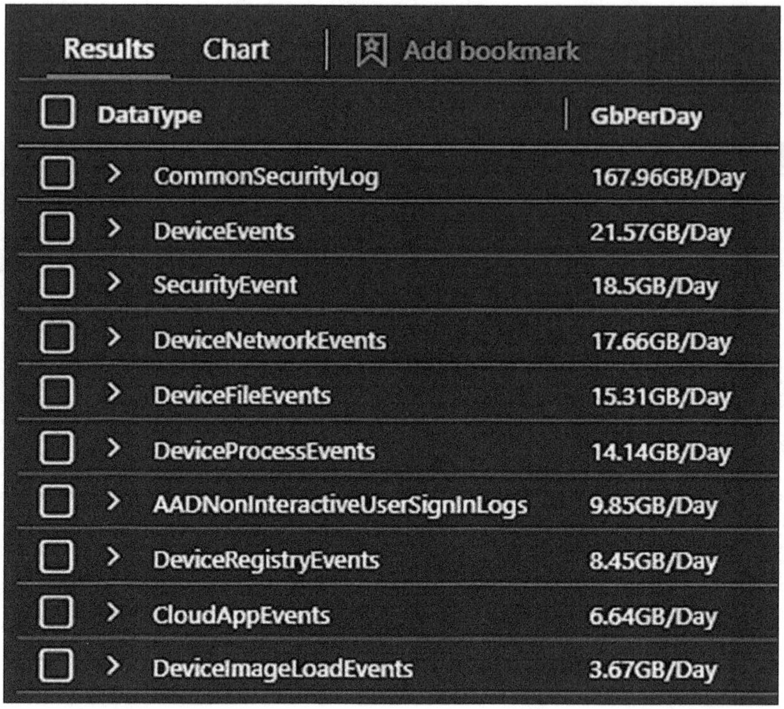

Results Chart Add bookmark

DataType	GbPerDay
CommonSecurityLog	167.96GB/Day
DeviceEvents	21.57GB/Day
SecurityEvent	18.5GB/Day
DeviceNetworkEvents	17.66GB/Day
DeviceFileEvents	15.31GB/Day
DeviceProcessEvents	14.14GB/Day
AADNonInteractiveUserSignInLogs	9.85GB/Day
DeviceRegistryEvents	8.45GB/Day
CloudAppEvents	6.64GB/Day
DeviceImageLoadEvents	3.67GB/Day

Figure 10.11: *Billable Data Ingestion Volume by Data Type*

- **Top 10 Log Sources by Cost**

```
Usage
| where IsBillable == true
//| where DataType !contains 'device'
| summarize GB = round(sum(Quantity) / 1000, 2) by DataType
| extend Cost = round(GB * 2.45, 2) // <-- swap out "2.45" for
your cost per GB*
| sort by Cost desc
| extend CostDollar = strcat('$', tostring(Cost))
| project DataType, GB, CostDollar
```

*your cost per GB can be found here: https://azure.microsoft.com/en-us/pricing/details/microsoft-sentinel/?msockid=2ae8ebcef0f5615a2c3bfed2f1326064

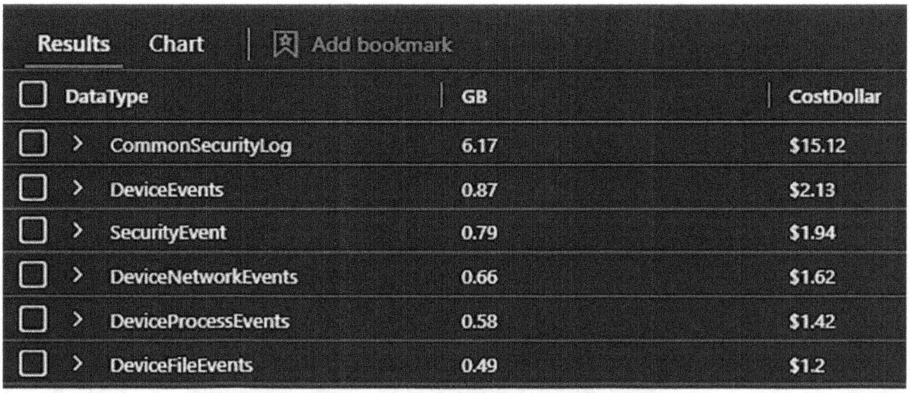

DataType	GB	CostDollar
CommonSecurityLog	6.17	$15.12
DeviceEvents	0.87	$2.13
SecurityEvent	0.79	$1.94
DeviceNetworkEvents	0.66	$1.62
DeviceProcessEvents	0.58	$1.42
DeviceFileEvents	0.49	$1.2

Figure 10.12: *Top 10 Log Sources by Cost*

- **Sources with the biggest change in ingest volume**

```
let PriorPeriod = toscalar(
    Usage
    | where TimeGenerated > ago(60d) and TimeGenerated
<= ago(30d)
    | where IsBillable == true
    | summarize min(TimeGenerated));
let CurrentPeriod = toscalar(
    Usage
    | where TimeGenerated > ago(30d)
    | where IsBillable == true
    | summarize max(TimeGenerated));
let PriorData = Usage
    | where TimeGenerated between (PriorPeriod .. ago(30d))
    | where IsBillable == true
    | summarize PriorGB = round(todouble(sum(Quantity))/1024, 2)
by DataType;
let CurrentData = Usage
    | where TimeGenerated > ago(30d)
    | where IsBillable == true
    | summarize CurrentGB = round(todouble(sum(Quantity))/1024,
2) by DataType;
PriorData
| join kind=fullouter CurrentData on DataType
| extend
    DataType = coalesce(DataType, DataType1),
    PriorGB = coalesce(PriorGB, 0.0),
    CurrentGB = coalesce(CurrentGB, 0.0)
| project
    ['Data Source'] = DataType,
    ['Previous 30 Days (GB)'] = PriorGB,
    ['Current 30 Days (GB)'] = CurrentGB,
```

```
    ['Change (GB)'] = round(CurrentGB - PriorGB, 2),
    ['Change %'] = iif(PriorGB > 0, round(((CurrentGB - PriorGB)
/ PriorGB) * 100, 1), 100.0)
| where ['Current 30 Days (GB)'] > 0 or ['Previous 30 Days (GB)']
> 0
//| where ['Data Source'] contains 'device'
| top 10 by abs(['Change (GB)']) desc
```

Results Chart Add bookmark

Data Source	Previous 30 Days (GB)	Current 30 Days (GB)	Change (GB)	Change %
CommonSecurityLog	272.79	156.6	-116.19	-42.6
SecurityEvent	22.69	17.29	-5.4	-23.8
DeviceEvents	17.21	20.14	2.93	17
DeviceNetworkEvents	13.68	16.52	2.84	20.8
DeviceProcessEvents	10.5	13.22	2.72	25.9
CloudAppEvents	3.88	6.18	2.3	59.3
DeviceFileEvents	13.19	14.42	1.23	9.3
AADNonInteractiveUserSignInLogs	9.85	9.18	-0.67	-6.8
DeviceRegistryEvents	7.39	7.96	0.57	7.7
IdentityQueryEvents	0.33	0.22	-0.11	-33.3

Figure 10.13: *Log Sources with Largest Deltas in Ingest Volume*

From a security and infrastructure perspective, it is just as important to know which log tables shrank as well as which ones grew. From a security perspective, it is just concerning when a log source drops off as when a log source doubles in ingest. Either way indicates something worth investigating.

- **Incidents by Product**

```
let TotalAlerts = SecurityAlert
    | where TimeGenerated > ago(90d)
    | summarize TotalCount = count()
    | extend Key = 1;
SecurityAlert
| where TimeGenerated > ago(90d)
| summarize Count = count() by ProductName
| extend Key = 1
| join kind=inner (TotalAlerts) on Key
| extend PercentageOfTotal = strcat(round(Count * 100.0 / Total-
Count, 2),'%')
| top 10 by Count
| project ProductName, PercentageOfTotal
```

This one is great for discerning your ROI on Defender product. In this example, MDCA has just been deployed and so has not been in use, and could be more effectively configured for added value, illustrated in the following results:

Incidents by Product	
ProductName	**PercentageOfTotal**
Microsoft Defender Advanced Threat Protection	51.23%
Office 365 Advanced Threat Protection	18.33%
Azure Advanced Threat Protection	14.86%
Azure Sentinel	14.44%
Azure Active Directory Identity Protection	0.59%
Microsoft Cloud App Security	0.56%

***Figure 10.14**: Incidents by Product*

- **Top Phishing Addresses**

```
// Identifies top recipients of phishing emails and categorizes
severity based on volume
EmailEvents
| where ThreatTypes has "Phish"
| summarize PhishCount = count() by RecipientEmailAddress
// Assign severity level indicators based on PhishCount
| extend SeverityIndicator = case(
    PhishCount >= 500, "🔥 Extreme Target",
    PhishCount >= 200, "🔴 Critical Target",
    PhishCount >= 100, "🟠 Major Target",
    PhishCount >= 50, "🟡 Moderate Target",
    "🟢 Low Target"
)
// Apply color coding to PhishCount
| extend CountColor = case(
    PhishCount >= 500, "🔥",
    PhishCount >= 200, "🔴",
    PhishCount >= 100, "🟠",
    PhishCount >= 50, "🟡",
    "🟢"
)
// Sort by the highest volume of phishing emails received
| top 10 by PhishCount desc
// Improve column naming for readability
| project ["Recipient Email"] = RecipientEmailAddress,
```

```
            ["Phishing Emails Received"] = strcat(CountColor, " ",
PhishCount),
            ["Severity"] = SeverityIndicator
```

Top Phishing Addressess

Recipient Email	Phishing Emails Received	Severity
User1@DevSecOpsDad.com	736	Extreme Target
User3@DevSecOpsDad.com	133	Major Target
User6@DevSecOpsDad.com	56	Moderate Target
User7@DevSecOpsDad.com	46	Low Target

Figure 10.15: *Top Phishing Addresses*

This query is excellent for identifying who is getting hit the hardest with phishing emails. These are the users you will want to apply stricter policies against in Defender for Office.

- **Most Commonly Observed MITRE ATT&CK Tactics:**

```
let totalCount = toscalar(
    SecurityAlert
    | where TimeGenerated > ago(90d)
    | where isnotempty(Tactics)
    | mv-expand tactic = split(Tactics, ", ")
    | summarize Total = count()
);
SecurityAlert
| where TimeGenerated > ago(90d)
| where isnotempty(Tactics)
| mv-expand tactic = split(Tactics, ", ")
| summarize Count = count() by tostring(tactic)
| extend Percentage = strcat(round(Count * 100.0 / totalCount,
2),'%')
| extend TacticEmoji = case(
    tactic == "InitialAccess", "🚪",
    tactic == "Execution", "💥",
    tactic == "Persistence", "📌",
    tactic == "PrivilegeEscalation", " ",
    tactic == "DefenseEvasion", " ",
    tactic == "CredentialAccess", " ",
    tactic == "Discovery", "🔍",
    tactic == "LateralMovement", " ",
    tactic == "Collection", " ",
    tactic == "Exfiltration", "",
    tactic == "Impact", " ",
```

```
    tactic == "CommandAndControl", "📡",
    "?"  // Default emoji for unknown tactics
)
| project Tactic = strcat(TacticEmoji, " ", tactic), Count,
Percentage
| sort by Count desc
| top 10 by Count
```

Most Common MITRE ATT&CK Tactics

Tactic	Count	Percentage
CommandAndControl	2929	49.24%
InitialAccess	1286	21.62%
CredentialAccess	856	14.39%
? Unknown	172	2.89%
Impact	132	2.22%
Collection	126	2.12%
Persistence	114	1.92%
Discovery	113	1.9%
DefenseEvasion	72	1.21%
Exfiltration	52	0.87%

Figure 10.16: *Observed MITRE ATT&CK Tactics*

This query is great for identifying the **`most common MITRE ATT&CK Tactics`** observed in your environment, so you know where to focus your efforts.

- **Alert Trends over Time**

```
let timeRange = 90d;
SecurityAlert
| where TimeGenerated > ago(timeRange)
| summarize CurrentCount = count() by AlertName
| join kind=fullouter (
    SecurityAlert
```

```
    | where TimeGenerated > ago(2 * timeRange) and TimeGenerated
<= ago(timeRange)
    | summarize PreviousCount = count() by AlertName
) on AlertName
| project AlertName,
          CurrentCount = coalesce(CurrentCount, 0),
          PreviousCount = coalesce(PreviousCount, 0),
          PercentChange = iff(PreviousCount == 0, 100.0,
(CurrentCount - PreviousCount) * 100.0 / PreviousCount)
// Apply filters to focus on meaningful trends
| where CurrentCount > 10
| where PercentChange > 50
// Assign severity level indicators
| extend SeverityIndicator = case(
    PercentChange >= 500, "● Extreme Spike",
    PercentChange >= 200, "● Critical Increase",
    PercentChange >= 100, "● Major Increase",
    PercentChange >= 50, "● Moderate Increase",
    "● Low Increase"
)
// Apply color coding to % Change
| extend ChangeColor = case(
    PercentChange > 200, "●",
    PercentChange > 100, "●",
    PercentChange > 50, "●",
    "●"
)
// Sort by absolute % change in descending order to highlight
most significant shifts
| sort by abs(PercentChange) desc
| top 10 by abs(PercentChange) desc
// Improve column naming for readability
| project ["Alert Type"] = AlertName,
          ["Current Period Alerts"] = CurrentCount,
          ["Previous Period Alerts"] = PreviousCount,
          ["% Change"] = strcat(ChangeColor, " ",
round(PercentChange, 2), "%"),
          ["Severity"] = SeverityIndicator
```

Alert Trends

Alert Type	Current Period Alerts	Previous Period Alerts	% Change	Severity
Connection to a custom network indicator	2789	2	139350.0%	Extreme Spike
Excessive number of failed connections from a single sour...	103	1	10200.0%	Extreme Spike
Unsanctioned cloud app access was blocked	151	30	403.33%	Critical Increase
Suspicious Resource deployment	24	7	242.86%	Critical Increase
Activity from an anonymous proxy	24	8	200.0%	Critical Increase
Privileged Accounts - Sign in Failure Spikes	27	13	107.69%	Major Increase
AD user enabled and password not set within 48 hours	21	12	75.0%	Moderate Increase
Email messages containing malicious file removed after d...	56	37	51.35%	Moderate Increase

Figure 10.17: *Alert Trends over Time*

The preceding query is fantastic for identifying alert trends so you can adapt your security posture accordingly.

For more KQL queries that can help identify areas where data ingestion can be optimized, visit: https://github.com/EEN421/KQL-Queries/blob/Main/QBRs/ReportQueries.kql

Common KQL Query Pitfalls

- **Using search * Instead of Specifying a Table**
    - **Why it is bad: `search *`** *scans all tables*, consuming more compute and potentially returning irrelevant or excessive data. This drastically slows performance.
    - **What to do instead:** Always specify the exact table you need (for example, **`SigninLogs`**, **`SecurityEvent`**, **`Usage`**) to minimize overhead.
- **Not using the project to Trim Columns**
    - **Why it is bad:** By default, KQL returns *all columns*, which leads to bloated output and slower query results–especially in workbooks and visualizations.
    - **What to do instead:** Use the project to return only the fields you actually need.
- **Applying Filters Late in the Query**
    - **Why it is bad:** Filtering after joins, summarize, or mv-expand forces the engine to process more data than necessary, hurting performance and accuracy.
    - **What to do instead:** Apply where filters as early as possible to reduce data volume quickly.

Correct Example:

```
SecurityEvent
| where EventID == 4624
| summarize count() by Account
```

Incorrect Example:

```
SecurityEvent
| summarize count() by Account
| where EventID == 4624
```

- **Overusing 'contains' Instead of 'has'**
    - **Why it is bad:** contains is a substring search and is less efficient than has, which performs word-boundary matches. Using contains everywhere increases CPU time and yields noisy results.
    - **What to do instead:** Use **has** or **hasprefix** when you know the structure of the value you are looking for.

Conclusion

Mastering Kusto Query Language is not only foundational to working effectively within Microsoft Sentinel—it is essential for driving meaningful security outcomes across detection, investigation, and response workflows. This chapter has explored everything from the building blocks of KQL syntax to advanced techniques for performance tuning, anomaly detection, and cost optimization. By applying the principles and patterns discussed, security professionals can develop high-performing, cost-aware queries that unlock deeper insights from their data. Whether you are building dashboards, crafting analytics rules, or proactively hunting threats, the strategic use of KQL empowers you to operate at the intersection of precision, efficiency, and impact.

In the next chapter, we will shift from query design to environment setup, walking through the steps to build a cost-effective Microsoft Security lab using Defender products and Sentinel. With a focus on leveraging Visual Studio subscription credits, you will learn how to stand up a functional, cloud-based security lab to test, simulate, and hunt threats in a safe, hands-on environment.

References

- Microsoft. (n.d.). Percentiles aggregation function (Kusto). Microsoft Learn. https://learn.microsoft.com/en-us/azure/data-explorer/kusto/query/percentiles-aggregation-function
- Microsoft. (n.d.). Microsoft Sentinel Pricing. Microsoft Azure. https://azure.microsoft.com/en-us/pricing/details/microsoft-sentinel/
- EEN421. (n.d.). KQL-Queries Repository. GitHub. https://github.com/EEN421/KQL-Queries/blob/Main/QBRs/ReportQueries.kql

CHAPTER 11

Hands-On Lab Setup

Introduction

The following chapter provides a detailed, step-by-step walkthrough for setting up a Microsoft Security lab environment using Defender products and Microsoft Sentinel. It is designed with cost-efficiency in mind, specifically focusing on how to make the most of Azure credits available through Visual Studio (MSDN) subscriptions—particularly the $150/month recurring credits offered to Partner and Enterprise subscribers. Whether you are building a personal lab or testing security solutions in a controlled environment, this chapter will help you get started quickly and effectively.

Structure

In this chapter, we will cover the following topics:

- Objective
- Setup a Microsoft 365 Dev Tenant
- Activate Visual Studio Subscription
- Connect Azure sub to Dev Tenant
- Create and Configure Azure Resources
- Deploy Windows 10/11 and Server VMs
- Onboard Devices to Defender for Endpoint
- Setup Microsoft Defender for Identity
- Configure Defender for Cloud Apps
- Connect Defender Products to Sentinel
- Simulate Threats and go Hunting!

Objective

Build a robust lab environment to test Microsoft Defender (for Endpoint, Identity, Office 365, and Cloud Apps) and Microsoft Sentinel.

- Focus on **minimizing cost** using:
  - **Microsoft 365 Developer E5** (for licensing)
  - **Visual Studio Subscription (MSDN)** credits for **Azure**
  - Optional: Free Defender trials and eval tools

Tools and Subscriptions Required

Tool	Source	Cost	Purpose
Microsoft 365 E5 Dev Tenant	Microsoft Developer Program	Free	Licenses for Defender tools
Visual Studio/MSDN Subscription	Partner/MSDN/ Enterprise	Varies	Includes **$150/month Azure credit**
Windows OS	Eval Center or Azure	Free or usage-based	Endpoint testing
Azure Portal	azure.com	Free + Credit	Sentinel, VM hosting, log ingestion
Defender Trials	Optional	Free (up to 90 days)	Additional Defender capabilities

Table 11.1: *Tools and Subscriptions Required*

Set Up a Microsoft 365 Dev Tenant

1. Go to the Microsoft 365 Developer Program (https://developer.microsoft.com/en-us/microsoft-365/dev-program).

Figure 11.1: *Microsoft 365 E5 Developer Subscription*

2. Sign in with your personal Microsoft account.
3. Join the program and choose the **Microsoft 365 E5 subscription with pre-hydrated sample data pack**.
4. This gives you 25 users and includes:
   - Microsoft Defender for Office 365 P2

- Defender for Cloud Apps
- Intune
- Entra ID P2
- Teams, Exchange, SharePoint

Pro Tip: *This environment auto-renews every 90 days if actively used.*

Activate Visual Studio Sub

This is the core step for recurring **$150/month Azure credits**.

1. Visit: https://my.visualstudio.com
2. Sign in with your MSDN/Partner/Enterprise account.
3. Under **"Benefits"**, locate **Azure Monthly Credit**.
4. Click **"Activate"**.
5. This will:
   - Create a **linked Azure subscription**
   - Apply $150/month recurring credits
   - Prevent Azure billing (beyond this limit)

   Notes:
   - Credits renew monthly (no rollover).
   - Ideal for testing **Azure Sentinel, VMs, Defender integrations**.
   - Available for Visual Studio Enterprise, MSDN, Partner benefits, and certain Action Pack subscriptions.
6. Alternatively, if your organization does not have a visual studio sub available to provision to you, you can opt for the one-time $200 Azure credit (note that this does not renew monthly).

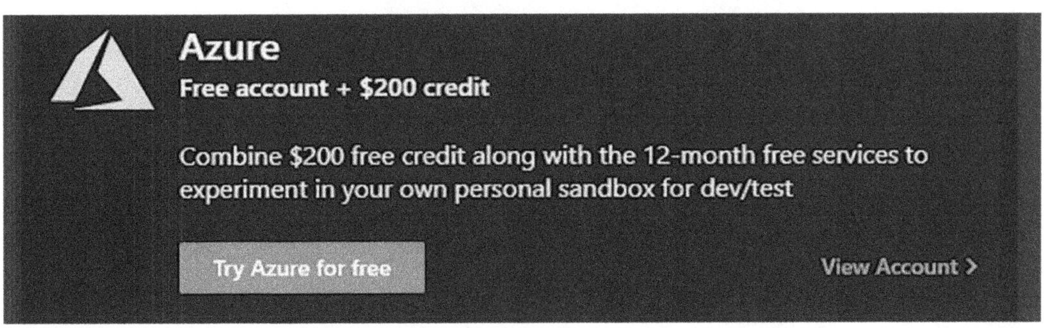

Figure 11.2: *One-Time Azure Free $200 Credit*

Important note: As of mid-2025, the **Microsoft 365 E5 Developer Subscription** is still technically available to the general public through the Microsoft 365 Developer Program, but there are some important caveats:

- **Eligibility and Activity Requirements**: Microsoft uses telemetry and activity tracking to determine whether a user is actively developing. If your subscription shows inactivity (typically no development-related activity within a 90-day window), it may not be renewed automatically.
- **Subscription Expiration Issues**: Several users have reported inconsistencies in subscription status across different Microsoft portals. Some subscriptions appear active in the Admin Center but are marked as expired in the Developer Program dashboard.
- **Renewal and Deletion**: If your subscription is flagged as inactive, it may be scheduled for deletion—even if you believe you have been using it actively. In such cases, contacting Microsoft support directly through the Admin Center is recommended.
- **Re-enrollment**: If your subscription expires or is deleted, you can usually reapply for a new one through the Developer Program site, assuming you still meet the eligibility criteria.

Connect Azure Sub to M365 E5 Tenant

1. In the Azure Portal, go to `Microsoft Entra ID`.
2. Click on `Switch Directory`:

***Figure 11.3**: Switch Directory Button*

3. Select or invite your M365 Dev tenant directory.

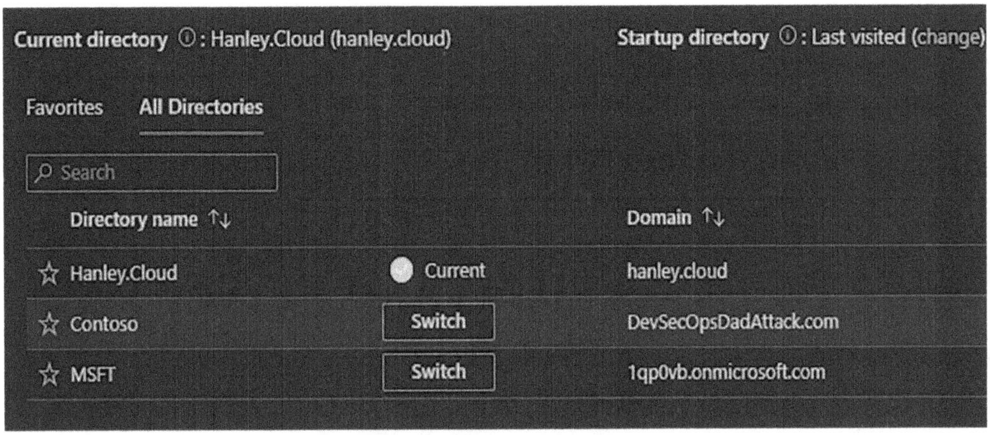

Figure 11.4: *Select Directory*

4. Grant **Global Admin** access in both directories for full control.
5. Use this cross-tenant setup to:
    a. Link Sentinel to Defender data
    b. Use Azure Lighthouse or Arc for multi-tenant security
    c. This is also important in order to move your subscription over, as it enables subscription transfer between tenants. Most of the time, your employer can provision a visual studio subscription for you; however, this will automatically apply to the tenant you are a part of (that is, your organization's production tenant). Once the cross-tenant relationship is established, you can then move the subscription to your new test/dev tenant. **Make sure to leave the billing with your original tenant.**

Create and Configure Azure Resources

Step 1: Log Analytics + Sentinel

1. In Azure, create a **Log Analytics Workspace**.
2. Enable **Microsoft Sentinel** on the workspace.
3. Name your resource group (for example, **`sec-lab-rg`**).
4. Region: Keep consistent across all resources (for example, East US).

Step 2: Connect Sentinel Data Sources

Use built-in connectors for:

- **Microsoft Defender for Endpoint**

- **Microsoft Defender for Cloud Apps**
- **Microsoft 365 Defender**
- **Office 365**
- **Azure Activity and Entra ID logs**

Tip: *Data ingestion within the first* **5 GB/month** *is free per workspace.*

Deploy Windows 10/11 and Server VMs

Option A: Azure VMs

- Use your monthly Azure credits to spin up:
    - 1–2 x **Windows 10/11 Pro** VMs
    - 1 x **Windows Server** (Domain Controller)
- Use **B2s** or **D2s_v3** for cost-effective sizes.
- Join these machines to your M365 Dev tenant.

Option B: Local Virtualization

- Use Hyper-V or VirtualBox with 90-day eval ISOs from:
    - https://www.microsoft.com/en-us/evalcenter/
- Join these machines to Entra ID or create a hybrid setup with a local domain
    - https://learn.microsoft.com/en-us/entra/identity/domain-services/join-windows-vm

Onboard Devices to Defender for Endpoint

1. Log in to Microsoft 365 Defender Portal (https://security.microsoft.com/).
2. Go to **Settings > Endpoints > Onboarding**.
3. Select OS type and method (script or Intune, refer to the previous chapter on Defender for Endpoint).
5. Run onboarding on test VMs.
6. Validate devices in the **Device Inventory**.

Set Up Microsoft Defender for Identity

1. Deploy a server to function as a domain controller manually or leverage the following JSON ARM deployment template to speed things up: https://github.com/EEN421/Defender-for-Identity/blob/Main/dc-parameters.json

2. Promote the Server VM to a Domain Controller.
3. Install the **Defender for Identity Sensor** from the M365 Defender portal.
4. Configure directory service accounts and configure the DC for Advanced Auditing and NTLM logging (refer to the previous chapter on MDI for guidance. Make sure to leverage gMSA accounts instead of the built-in system accounts).
5. Monitor alerts such as:
    - Pass-the-Hash
    - Suspicious replication requests
    - Lateral movement

Configure Defender for Cloud Apps

1. Go to: https://portal.cloudappsecurity.com
2. Configure MDCA to collect telemetry from your Endpoints (refer to the previous chapter on MDCA for further details).
3. Configure policies, for example:
    - Ransomware detection
    - Anomalous login detection
    - Data exfiltration alerts
4. Tag applications as monitored or un-sanctioned, then test access.

Connect Defender Products to Sentinel

1. In **Sentinel > Data Connectors**, enable:
    - Defender for Endpoint
    - Defender for Cloud Apps
    - Office 365
    - Azure AD Identity Protection
    - Defender XDR Connector
2. Use built-in **Workbooks** for visual dashboards.
3. Run **KQL queries** in Logs:

```
SecurityAlert
| where TimeGenerated > ago(1d)
| summarize count() by AlertName, Severity
```

Simulate Threats and Go Hunting!

Use these tools to test detections:

- **Atomic Red Team**: https://github.com/redcanaryco/atomic-red-team
- **Caldera by MITRE**: https://github.com/mitre/caldera
- **Sysinternals Suite**: For monitoring and lateral movement
- **Invoke-AtomicRedTeam** PowerShell module

Track and validate results in both **Defender** and **Sentinel**.

Monthly Credit Strategy (Visual Studio Subscription)

Category	Estimated Cost	Notes
Azure VMs (2 small)	~$60/month	Keep auto-shutdown on
Sentinel + Logs	~$20–40/month	Stay under 5 GB free ingestion
Defender integrations	Free (E5)	Sent to Log Analytics
Additional services	<$30/month	Storage, identity, Arc
Buffer	~$20	Room for automation, testing

Table 11.2: *Visual Studio Subscription Monthly Credit Strategy*

Tip: *Use Azure Cost Management + Budgets to track usage and avoid overages.*

Common Pitfalls

Letting the Microsoft 365 Dev Tenant Expire

Pitfall: The M365 E5 Developer tenant **auto-expires after 90 days** if there is no usage activity.

Avoid it by:

- Logging in at least once a week.
- Sending test emails, using Teams, or modifying tenant settings to show activity.
- Scheduling recurring tasks such as Defender tests or KQL queries to keep usage up.

Blowing Through Azure Credits

Pitfall: It is easy to unknowingly exceed your $150/month Visual Studio credit if:

- VMs are not properly sized, or auto-shutdown is not configured.
- Ingestion goes over 5GB/month (Sentinel logs).
- You are spinning up too many resources without budgeting.

Avoid it by:

- Using B2s or D2s_v3 VMs with auto-shutdown.
- Tracking usage in **Azure Cost Management**.
- Setting budgets and alerts at the subscription level.

Not Linking Azure Subscription to M365 Dev Tenant

Pitfall: If your Visual Studio Azure subscription is stuck in your **organization's tenant**, it will not connect cleanly with your M365 Dev environment.

Avoid it by:

- Creating a **cross-tenant relationship** using Microsoft Entra ID.
- Granting **Global Admin** rights across both tenants.
- Moving the Azure sub to the dev tenant before deploying key resources.

Missing Required Permissions or Misconfigured Roles

Pitfall: Defender components like **MDI or MDE** require specific roles, permissions, and configurations (such as gMSA for MDI sensors).

Avoid it by:

- Reviewing required roles for each product.
- Avoiding built-in SYSTEM accounts for security tools.
- Using Microsoft's least privilege recommendations and onboarding guides for each Defender product.

Ignoring Regional Consistency

Pitfall: Spinning up resources across **multiple regions** can cause:

- Latency issues.
- Inconsistent data routing.
- Pricing anomalies.

Avoid it by:

- Picking a single Azure region (for example, East US) for **all** resources: Sentinel workspace, VMs, storage, and so on.
- Keeping your Log Analytics Workspace and Sentinel instance in the **same** region as your data sources.

Conclusion

By following the lab setup outlined in this chapter, you now have a hands-on environment where you can safely explore Microsoft's Defender suite and Sentinel in action–without incurring unexpected costs. This foundation empowers you to simulate threats, refine detection rules, and test automated responses in a controlled setting. But building an isolated lab is only the beginning.

In the next chapter, we shift from test environments to production strategy, where the true power of Microsoft's XDR ecosystem is realized. You will learn how to unify these tools into a mature, cohesive defense framework–operationalizing Microsoft XDR at scale to drive efficiency, resilience, and measurable security outcomes.

Helpful Links, References, and Resources

- Microsoft. (n.d.). Microsoft 365 Developer Program. https://developer.microsoft.com/en-us/microsoft-365/dev-program/
- Microsoft. (n.d.). Visual Studio Subscriber Benefits. https://my.visualstudio.com
- Microsoft. (n.d.). Microsoft Evaluation Center. https://www.microsoft.com/en-us/evalcenter/
- Microsoft. (n.d.). Join a Windows VM to a managed domain. Microsoft Learn. https://learn.microsoft.com/en-us/entra/identity/domain-services/join-windows-vm
- EEN421. (n.d.). Defender for Identity Domain Controller Deployment Template. GitHub. https://github.com/EEN421/Defender-for-Identity/blob/Main/dc-parameters.json
- Microsoft. (n.d.). Microsoft Defender for Cloud Apps. https://portal.cloudappsecurity.com
- Red Canary. (n.d.). Atomic Red Team. GitHub. https://github.com/redcanaryco/atomic-red-team
- MITRE. (n.d.). CALDERA. GitHub. https://github.com/mitre/caldera
- Microsoft. (n.d.). Azure Cost Management and Budgets. https://learn.microsoft.com/en-us/azure/cost-management-billing/costs/
- Microsoft. (n.d.). Urgent: Developer subscription deletion despite active usage. https://answers.microsoft.com/en-us/msoffice/forum/all/urgent-developer-subscription-deletion-despite/cf265fbc-fc8f-4f50-8a00-996c8f0cb048

- Microsoft. (n.d.). Issue regarding inconsistent status of Microsoft 365 Developer Subscription. https://learn.microsoft.com/en-us/answers/questions/2144558/issue-regarding-inconsistent-status-of-microsoft-3
- Microsoft. (n.d.). My Microsoft 365 E5 developer subscription expired unexpectedly. https://learn.microsoft.com/en-us/answers/questions/2282016/my-microsoft-365-e5-developer-subscription-expired

CHAPTER 12
Building and Operating a Mature Unified XDR Strategy

Introduction

Having explored the capabilities and components of Microsoft's Extended Detection and Response (XDR) ecosystem in the preceding chapters, we now turn our attention to the practical reality of bringing all of these solutions together. This final chapter will serve as your blueprint for operationalizing a unified Microsoft XDR strategy. Beyond individual product deployments, the true power of Microsoft XDR is realized when these tools work in concert—automating defenses, correlating cross-domain signals, and elevating your Security Operations Center (SOC) to a new standard of efficiency.

In this chapter, we will define what a cohesive XDR strategy looks like, introduce a maturity model for evaluating progress, and offer a real-world implementation blueprint to help security teams maximize the value of their Microsoft investment.

Structure

In this chapter, we will cover the following topics:

- Why a Unified Strategy Matters
- The Microsoft XDR Maturity Model
- Operationalizing XDR
- Case Study
- Maintaining and Advancing your XDR Program
- Quick Wins and Common Pitfalls

Why a Unified Strategy Matters

Security programs often evolve reactively–purchasing tools to plug specific gaps or meet urgent compliance requirements. This ad hoc approach leads to siloed defenses, where the lack of integration slows incident response and obscures visibility across the attack surface.

Microsoft's XDR vision offers a fundamentally different approach: a converged security ecosystem where telemetry flows freely between tools, automation bridges operational gaps, and context-rich alerts empower faster decisions. Implementing this strategy demands alignment between people, processes, and technology.

Security should no longer be viewed merely as a cost center–it is increasingly becoming a **strategic differentiator**. As Ted Harrington argues in *Hackable*, organizations that prioritize security can use it to drive business growth. Customers, partners, and investors alike are demanding assurances of robust cybersecurity practices. A well-implemented XDR strategy helps communicate those assurances through measurable outcomes. When security is demonstrably proactive, transparent, and integrated across an enterprise, it builds **trust**, enhances **reputation**, and in competitive markets, can even win deals that would otherwise be lost.

The Microsoft XDR Maturity Model

To help organizations assess where they are on their XDR journey, here is a four-tiered maturity model:

Level 1: Tool Adoption

- Standalone deployment of Microsoft Defender products
- Manual incident investigation and triage
- Limited alert correlation across domains

Level 2: Signal Correlation and Automation

- Integration with Microsoft Sentinel for centralized visibility
- Use of analytics rules and playbooks for cross-product automation
- Basic KQL queries and workbook use for visibility

Level 3: Threat-Centric Operations

- Unified incidents across endpoint, identity, email, and cloud apps
- Proactive threat hunting using Sentinel and Defender workbooks
- KPI tracking (MTTD, MTTR, false positive rate) via custom dashboards

Level 4: Business-Aligned Resilience

- Security operations aligned to business risk and compliance goals
- Full automation for known threats and common playbooks
- Continuous improvement processes driven by analytics and purple teaming

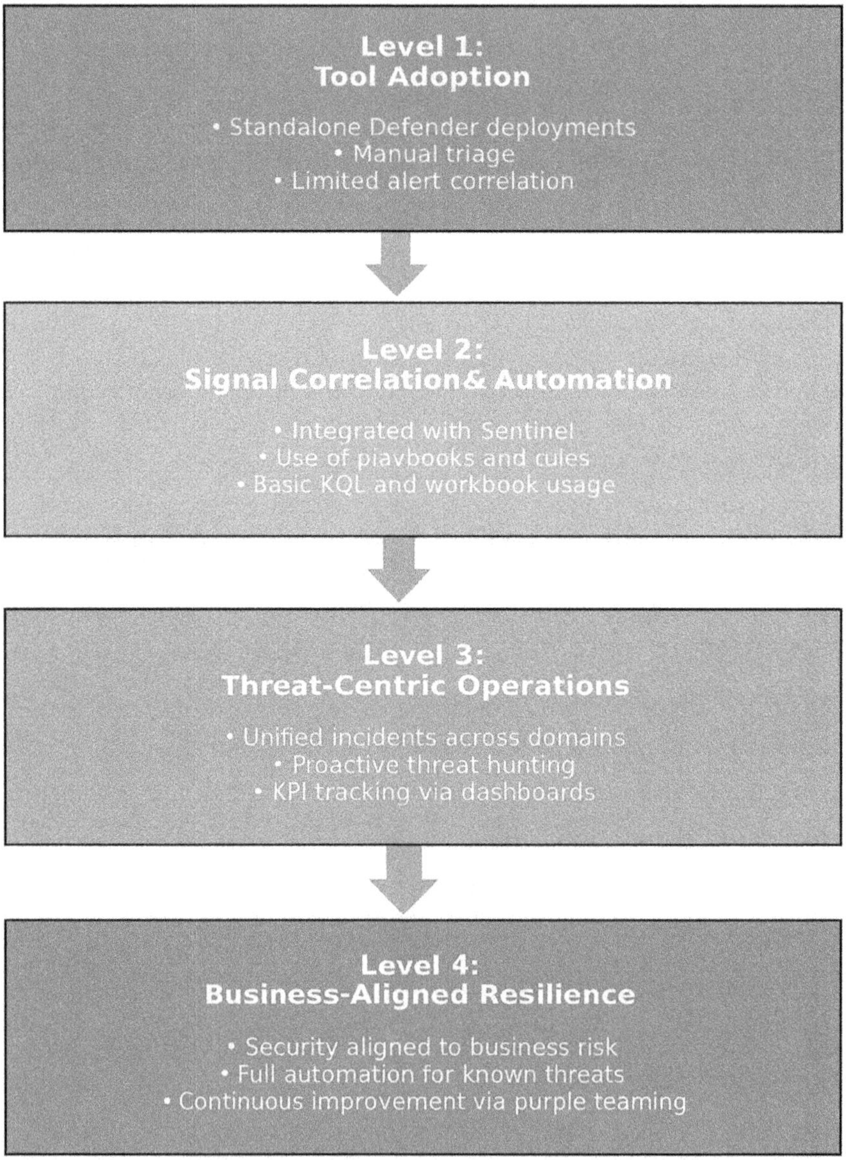

Figure 12.1: *Microsoft XDR Maturity Model*

Operationalizing Microsoft XDR

1. **Establishing Unified Telemetry**

Ensure that Defender for Endpoint, Identity, Office 365, and Cloud Apps are all connected to Microsoft Sentinel. Leverage native connectors for consistent schema alignment and correlation.

2. **Enriching Detection and Response**

In Sentinel, build custom analytics rules that supplement built-in detection logic.

3. **Automating at the Right Layer**

Use Sentinel playbooks to automate:

- User notifications
- Incident tagging and triage
- Threat containment (for example, disabling accounts, isolating devices)

Use Defender XDR's automatic response capabilities to block attacks in real-time at the endpoint or identity layer.

4. **Empowering the SOC with Context**

Configure workbooks and custom views to include:

- Entra sign-in logs
- Endpoint alerts and exposure scores
- Email delivery and click metrics
- OAuth app usage from Defender for Cloud Apps

This context allows Tier 1 analysts to resolve more alerts without escalation.

Case Study: Mid-Market Implementation Blueprint

A financial services firm with 500 employees adopted Microsoft XDR to modernize its fragmented SOC. Their phased approach included:

- **Phase 1**: Deployed Defender for Endpoint and Defender for Office; enabled email and endpoint telemetry into Sentinel
- **Phase 2**: Onboarded Entra ID Protection and Defender for Identity for credential protection and lateral movement detection

- **Phase 3**: Enabled SOAR playbooks for phishing and impossible travel alerts
- **Phase 4**: Built cost visibility and incident KPI workbooks in Sentinel

Challenges Overcome

- Early efforts revealed that alert fatigue was affecting analyst productivity. By tuning built-in analytics rules and eliminating low-fidelity alerts, they reduced noise by 40%.
- Legacy domain controllers initially failed to report signals consistently. This was resolved by deploying gMSA accounts and refining Active Directory integration practices (configuring advanced auditing for domain controllers, just like in chapter 3).
- There was internal resistance to retiring a third-party endpoint solution. Stakeholder alignment was achieved through phased A/B testing and demonstrable improvements in MTTR.

Results

- MTTR dropped by 45% within three months
- Reduced license sprawl by 60% by retiring third-party tools
- Gained visibility into OAuth abuse and insider threats via Cloud Apps

Note: *This case study is based on a composite of real-world customer engagements and best practices observed across multiple mid-market deployments. While the organization described is fictional, the implementation phases and outcomes are grounded in verified Microsoft XDR adoption patterns.*

Maintaining and Advancing Your XDR Program

- **Regular Rule and Policy Reviews:** Security policies, analytics rules, and conditional access should be reviewed quarterly.
- **Purple Teaming and Simulated Attacks:** Use Microsoft Attack Simulation Training and custom red team scenarios to test defenses.
- **KPI Metric Tracking:** Track core metrics such as:
  - Mean Time to Detect (MTTD)
  - Mean Time to Respond (MTTR)
  - False Positive/True Positive ratios
  - Alert-to-Incident Ratio

- **Training and SOC Enablement:** Invest in continuous SOC training around:
    - KQL and custom detection
    - Defender and Sentinel investigation workflows
    - Threat hunting and workbook development

Quick Wins and Common Pitfalls

Quick Wins

- **Deploy high-impact playbooks**: Start with phishing alert automation and incident tagging workflows.
- **Ingest core logs first**: Prioritize Defender for Endpoint, Office 365, Entra sign-in logs, and Defender for Identity logs as applicable, such as ADFS or CA for hybrid scenario examples.
- **Leverage built-in workbooks**: Customize existing templates for cost analysis and KPI tracking.
- **Use MITRE-aligned analytics rules**: These provide out-of-box detections that align with attacker behavior.

Common Pitfalls

- **Over-collecting logs**: Avoid ingesting unnecessary tables without a use case—this drives up costs fast. Only enable data collection for log types tied to specific detection, compliance, or threat hunting goals.
- **Failing to tune alerts**: Leaving default thresholds untouched can lead to alert fatigue.
- **Neglecting user training**: Playbooks and rules are only as effective as the analysts who use them.
- **Delayed integration**: Do not postpone connecting Entra ID or Defender for Identity—identity telemetry is foundational.

Conclusion

Microsoft's XDR platform provides an end-to-end security solution that, when fully integrated and operated strategically, enables real-time defense, cross-domain visibility, and automated resilience. The journey to unified XDR maturity is iterative and demands organizational alignment—but the payoff is a security posture that evolves as fast as the threats it counters.

Security is also no longer just about risk mitigation—it is about **brand value, buyer confidence, and long-term viability**. Organizations that invest in strong, transparent security postures signal to their stakeholders that they take trust seriously. Microsoft XDR equips you to deliver on that promise.

By unifying operations, automating intelligently, and relentlessly tuning your defenses, your organization can't only defend against modern threats–but outpace them.

Final Thoughts

This book has taken you through the full lifecycle of Microsoft's security ecosystem–from understanding the core Defender products and learning the intricacies of KQL, to operationalizing automation, threat intelligence, and incident response at scale. But the journey does not end here. The threat landscape is dynamic, and so too must be your security posture. By embracing Microsoft XDR not just as a set of tools, but as a cohesive strategy aligned to business outcomes, you are positioning your organization for proactive resilience. Stay curious, keep tuning, and do not stop challenging assumptions. Mastery is not about reaching the end–it is about building the capability to evolve with confidence.

Helpful Links, References and Resources

- Harrington, T. (2020). Hackable: How to Do Application Security Right. Lioncrest Publishing. https://www.tedharrington.com/hackable/ Used in the discussion of security as a sales differentiator.
- Microsoft. (2024). Microsoft Sentinel Documentation. Microsoft Learn. https://learn.microsoft.com/en-us/azure/sentinel/ Referenced throughout for connectors, playbooks, analytics rules, and workbooks.
- Microsoft. (2024). Microsoft Defender XDR Documentation. Microsoft Learn. https://learn.microsoft.com/en-us/security/defender-xdr/ Supports automation, unified incidents, and XDR alignment.
- Hanley, I. (2024, August 16). Logic Apps & Automation in Sentinel. Hanley.Cloud. https://www.hanley.cloud/2024-08-16-Logic-Apps-&-Automation/ Relevant to the automation and playbook design guidance.
- Microsoft. (2024). Microsoft Security Best Practices. Microsoft Learn. https://learn.microsoft.com/en-us/security/ Supports best practices for SOC operations, KPI tracking, and red teaming.
- Microsoft. (2023). Microsoft Defender for Identity Prerequisites. Microsoft Learn. https://learn.microsoft.com/en-us/defender-for-identity/prerequisites Relevant to domain controller integration issues mentioned in the case study.

Index

A

E

F

M

N

O

P

Q

R

S

T

U

V

W

X

www.ingramcontent.com/pod-product-compliance
Lightning Source LLC
Chambersburg PA
CBHW061158240926
51846CB00006B/1050
9789349888715